FAILED STATE
A Guide to Russia's Rupture

By Janusz Bugajski

Washington, DC
2022

THE JAMESTOWN FOUNDATION
Published in the United States by
The Jamestown Foundation
1310 L Street NW
Suite 810
Washington, DC 20005
http://www.jamestown.org

ISBN: 978-1-7352752-2-2

Library of Congress Cataloging-in-Publication Data

Names: Bugajski, Janusz, 1954- author.
Title: Failed state : a guide to Russia's rupture / Janusz Bugajski.
Description: Washington, DC : The Jamestown Foundation, 2022 | Includes bibliographical references.
Identifiers: LCCN 2022024400 (print) | LCCN 2022024401 (ebook) | ISBN 9781735275222 (paperback) | ISBN 9781735275222 (adobe pdf)
Subjects: LCSH: Russia (Federation)--Politics and government--1991- | Russia (Federation)--Foreign relations.
Classification: LCC JN6695 .B855 2022 (print) | LCC JN6695 (ebook) | DDC 320.947--dc23/eng/20220729
LC record available at https://lccn.loc.gov/2022024400
LC ebook record available at https://lccn.loc.gov/2022024401

Distributed worldwide by Lynne Rienner Publishers, Inc.
Tel: +1 303-444-6684; Fax: +1 303-444-0824; Email: cservice@rienner.com
www.rienner.com

Cover art provided by Peggy Archambault of Peggy Archambault Design, archdesign1.com.

Jamestown's Mission

The Jamestown Foundation's mission is to inform and educate policy makers and the broader community about events and trends in those societies which are strategically or tactically important to the United States and which frequently restrict access to such information. Utilizing indigenous and primary sources, Jamestown's material is delivered without political bias, filter or agenda. It is often the only source of information which should be, but is not always, available through official or intelligence channels, especially in regard to Eurasia and terrorism.

Origins

Founded in 1984 by William Geimer, The Jamestown Foundation made a direct contribution to the downfall of Communism through its dissemination of information about the closed totalitarian societies of Eastern Europe and the Soviet Union.

William Geimer worked with Arkady Shevchenko, the highest ranking Soviet official ever to defect when he left his position as undersecretary general of the United Nations. Shevchenko's memoir *Breaking With Moscow* revealed the details of Soviet superpower diplomacy, arms control strategy and tactics in the Third World, at the height of the Cold War. Through its work with Shevchenko, Jamestown rapidly became the leading source of information about the inner workings of the captive nations of the former Communist Bloc. In addition to Shevchenko, Jamestown assisted the former top Romanian intelligence officer Ion Pacepa in writing his memoirs. Jamestown ensured that both men published their insights and experience in what became bestselling books. Even today, several decades later, some credit Pacepa's revelations about Ceausescu's regime in his bestselling book *Red Horizons* with the fall of that government and the freeing of Romania.

The Jamestown Foundation has emerged as a leading provider of information about Eurasia. Our research and analysis on conflict and instability in Eurasia enabled Jamestown to become one of the most reliable sources of information on the post-Soviet space, the Caucasus and Central Asia as well as China. Furthermore, since 9/11, Jamestown has utilized its network of indigenous experts in more than 50 different countries to conduct research and analysis on terrorism and the growth of al-Qaeda and al-Qaeda offshoots throughout the globe.

By drawing on our ever-growing global network of experts, Jamestown has become a vital source of unfiltered, open-source information about major conflict zones around the world—from the Black Sea to Siberia, from the Persian Gulf to Latin America and the Pacific. Our core of intellectual talent includes former high-ranking government officials and military officers, political scientists, journalists, scholars and economists. Their insight contributes significantly to policymakers engaged in addressing today's newly emerging global threats in the post 9/11 world.

Table of Contents

Foreword

Since the early draft of this book was completed in January 2022, the Kremlin tried to achieve several objectives through its expanded invasion of Ukraine. It intended to replace the government in Kyiv with a pro-Moscow regime, ensure Ukraine's permanent international neutrality, and demonstrate Russia's military prowess in order to halt any further NATO enlargement. It also sought to terminate Ukraine's development as a viable model for successful statehood, pluralistic democracy, and economic growth. Domestically, President Vladimir Putin sought to cement his legacy as an "in-gatherer" of Russian lands and rebuilder of the empire, as his term in office after 2024 remained uncertain. And with economic conditions in Russia already stagnating amidst growing official fear of public unrest, a successful war against Ukraine was intended to mobilize support for the regime regardless of economic conditions. Russia's fear of state failure was a key factor that convinced the Kremlin to launch a full-scale invasion and try to replicate the "Crimea consensus." External expansion was intended to disguise growing internal decay.

At a deeper level, revealed in Putin's bogus historical diatribes on the eve of the invasion, Moscow views Ukraine as an existential threat to Russia. The invasion was not simply a question of seizing Ukraine's territory, controlling its government, and deciding on its international alliances. It became a struggle for something much more profound—identity and history. Much of Ukraine's history and identity has been distorted or appropriated by Moscow, and Ukraine's revival has exposed the fragile foundations of the Russian state. Russia's war against Ukraine became a desperate attempt to salvage its own brittle history and confused multi-ethnic and imperial identity. Paradoxically, Russia's identity has been further questioned by the war against Ukraine, which has bolstered Ukrainian solidarity and further alienated Ukrainians from Russians. This blatant act of aggression also underscored the imperative of decolonization to reverse generations of state oppression and russification of indigenous nations within the Russian Federation.

At an international level, the status of Russia itself may need to be reconsidered in any post-war settlement, including the potential renouncement of the 1991 United Nations decision to recognize the Russian Federation as the "successor state" of the Soviet Union. Extensive international sanctions and isolation are likely to be maintained until Russia's military forces evacuate Ukraine and will have severe long-term repercussions for Russia's military capabilities, economic performance, and political stability. Most notably, Europe is weaning itself away from dependence on Russian oil and natural gas and finding alternative sources of energy irrespective of its sanctions on Russia.

Moscow grievously miscalculated that Ukraine's armed forces would quickly disintegrate and that the Western response would be weak and divisive. Despite significant losses of troops and equipment, the Kremlin does not admit its weaknesses, and Putin could still use substantial military reserves in a long-term war while pulverizing towns in Donbas to drive out Ukrainian defenders. The Kremlin may declare victory after the seizure of the Donetsk and Luhansk *oblasts* and large parts of Kherson and Zaporizhzhia *oblasts*. Putin could claim that the "limited military operation" had been achieved while disguising Russia's inability to take any major cities. He may calculate that the West would support a ceasefire even if that benefits Russia because it would prevent a direct confrontation with the North Atlantic Treaty Organization (NATO). Moscow would then expect sanctions to be eased so that it could restore its own economy and rebuild its military in preparation for another military assault on Ukraine.

However, by the summer of 2022, it was evident that Kremlin will not be successful in "neutralizing" Ukraine, and a long-term war will further expose Russia's internal weaknesses. Regarding Russia's military capabilities, Western analysis has been largely formalistic, with insufficient attention paid to morale, ethics, competence, training and educational levels, systematic corruption, falsified reporting, inter-ethnic tensions, and regular mistreatment of troops. This resulted in a failure to foresee Russia's military shortcomings in Ukraine. Although the state apportioned resources to modernize the military, much of that money disappeared into Russia's corrupt networks at the cost of equipment, maintenance and logistics. Major deficiencies in military reform have been glaringly exposed, including an incompetent non-commissioned officer (NCO) corps, dismal inter-unit coordination, poor command and control (C2), munitions failures, insecure communications, logistical and resupply inefficiencies, indiscipline, coverups, and criminality.

A significant part of Russia's military resources has been deployed to the Ukrainian conflict, and the prospects for major rearmament will recede in a contracting economy. Russia's military-industrial complex has been targeted by Western sanctions and will be unable to produce key weapon systems without technology imports from the West to compensate for the heavy losses sustained in Ukraine. Moscow cannot speedily replenish the hundreds of tanks and other armored vehicles that have been destroyed or captured in Ukraine. And without new satellites to replace its aging equipment, Russia's intelligence-gathering capabilities will further decline and weaken future military operations.

Moscow's military casualties in the war demonstrate that non-Russians and rural residents are significantly overrepresented, largely because the military offers poorer populations career prospects and overcomes the stigma of not being Russian. Moscow has also sought to deflect blame for any war crimes on national minorities in the Russian military in its traditional pursuit of a "divide and conquer" approach to absolve ethnic Russians of genocide. Nonetheless, the deployment of other nations as cannon fodder in a foreign war will intensify anger against Moscow, and military losses in Ukraine will make Russian armed forces more prone to conflicts, mutinies, and abandonment by that portion of the officer corps not composed of ethnic Russians. They will increasingly question why they should sacrifice their lives for Muscovite imperialism. The return of tens of thousands of traumatized and disillusioned military veterans into Russian society will further criminalize the country and increase opportunities for violence against state institutions and more widespread armed conflicts. If the Kremlin announces a mass mobilization, it would place Russia on a war footing, exacerbate fear and anger in Russian society, increase the number of war casualties, and further deplete the economy.

On the economic front, international sanctions will have a litany of negative effects. Although before the war, Russia claimed about $640 billion in foreign currency and gold reserves, much of it was held overseas and was frozen by the sanctions. Russia was cut off from Western capital markets and unable to borrow money; and in July 2022, it technically defaulted on its foreign debt. The Russian economy is expected to shrink by up to 15 percent during 2022 and living standards for most citizens are likely to plummet to pre-1980 Soviet levels. A dramatic rise in unemployment is expected as private Russian companies close and hundreds of foreign enterprises have left the country. Growing state spending on the war will undercut production in the civilian sectors. Although unemployment has remained hidden by delayed layoffs and temporary salary deferments, millions of workers will find themselves redundant in the latter part of 2022. In addition, the mass outflow of young and educated people will continue. The shortage of foods and medicines will accelerate, inflation will increase, and many manufacturers will cease production because of a lack of components from abroad.

Western export controls will prevent Russia from importing vital inputs such as microchips for its manufacturing sectors, whether military or civilian. The country's transportation networks will also start to fray as the aviation sector contracts, road and rail systems become increasingly dilapidated and starved of investments, car plants built by Western companies close, and supply chains break down. Even non-Western states such as China are unwilling to invest in major energy and transit projects while Russia remains under international sanctions. Severing ties with Western energy companies will leave Russia without cutting-edge technologies in drilling and liquefied natural gas (LNG) compression, thus hobbling the development of new energy fields and infrastructure. Moreover, the absence of foreign funding will contribute to derailing several projects and even Chinese investors have reduced their interest in Russia's northern energy deposits.

Economic hardships will also exacerbate regional alienation, with a potential for social explosions in the smaller cities and towns, where the economic costs of war and sanctions have been more pronounced. Even physical links between Moscow and many regions will be affected as several regional airports have closed down because of fewer airplanes and decreasing consumer demand. While Moscow's subsidies decline, most regions will lack sufficient reserves to support local economies and social services. Regional budgets will suffer as increasing demands are placed on them to keep the public pacified by controlling inflation and providing essential services. As the economy contracts, the more far-sighted governors will seek to protect their positions and prevent local unrest by withholding resources and payments to Moscow. Without large-scale energy exports, the budget simply cannot sustain the spending necessary to keep the federation intact. Many of Russia's regions will seek alternative revenues to survive, whether by curtailing Moscow's exploitation of their natural resources or turning to neighboring states for direct economic ties. As the country's budget depletes and its energy revenues decline, any incentive to remain in the failing federation will rapidly diminish and the Russian state's fragility will be increasingly transparent.

On the political front, the war against Ukraine failed to restore the "Crimean consensus" in support of the regime. Political purges will accelerate in all state institutions to root out those opposed to the war and the policies of the Putin regime. As the war continued to rage with the prospect of growing domestic opposition, the regime has made preparations for imposing martial law and further restricting free speech and movement. Facing defeat in Ukraine and on the international stage more generally, Putin may seek domestic scapegoats by targeting religious and ethnic minorities. This can deepen ethnic cleavages and generate fresh conflicts.

Public opposition to the war in Ukraine has been evident in a growing underground movement of resistance that includes hacking of pro-Kremlin media sites, evasion of the military draft, telephone bomb threats, and arson attacks on military commissariats where the military draft is conducted. Moreover, an increasing number of Ukrainians in Russia, including those displaced by the 2022 war, will become more nationally conscious and oppose the Kremlin. Additionally, movements for national liberation have been animated in various parts of the federation; for instance, in May 2022, indigenous activists representing six national movements announced the creation of the League of Free Nations—a political platform for the decolonization of indigenous peoples in the Russian Federation and the gaining of each nation's sovereignty.

Moscow has a long record of deceiving Westerners and depicting its empire as invincible. In a previous imperial incarnation, Soviet Communism and socialist internationalism were supposed to ensure salvation for all humanity until they were exposed as an unworkable fraud. Today's Russia has created an image of great power status, economic strength, and military power that is unravelling in Ukraine and revealing that the state structure itself stands on rotting foundations. According to Western analysts, on the eve of the war Russia's state disinformation was sophisticated and persuasive. In reality, it failed to convince anyone outside of a narrow group of true believers that Moscow is conducting a just war of "de-Nazification" in Ukraine. Attempts to control the narrative has failed because of early exposure of Kremlin war aims by Western intelligence services and by an effective information campaign by the Ukrainian government and civil society. Similarly, Russia's much-vaunted cyberwarfare capabilities appear exaggerated, as Ukraine was evidently well-prepared for any digital disruption of its critical infrastructure. Another notable weakness has been the decline of Russian intelligence operations, as evident in failures to anticipate the scale of Ukrainian armed resistance.

Russia's military stalemate or defeat in Ukraine will reveal the inherent weakness of the Kremlin and Ukrainian resistance and success will inspire subject nations in the Russian Federation to demand autonomy and independence. Crippling economic sanctions that collapse living standards will provoke public unrest, regional revolts, and power struggles within and between various elites. In an indication of regime anxiety, Moscow may abolish any direct elections of regional governors in all federal subjects, fearful of protest voting and the prospect of disloyal candidates passing through the existing system of filters. As sanctions further weaken the economy, many governors will also be exposed to growing public discontent and local political opposition. Intensifying political battles in a collapsing economy will culminate in state fracture and the emergence of new entities that will reject Moscow's delusional imperial project.

In such an unfolding scenario, NATO should not intervene militarily unless its territory is breached; but it can encourage and develop political, economic, and security links with the fledgling states that emerge from a crumbling Russian empire. Despite its escalating failures, Moscow still possesses sufficient military tools to damage its neighbors, and state decline could encourage more desperate and risky operations against Western interests. Although the Kremlin will be unable to rebuild its conventional military capabilities to challenge a united NATO, especially if stringent international sanctions are maintained, it can still use significant power to attack smaller neighbors. Hence, the Alliance must prepare for a range of responses, from deterrence and defense to active military engagement in order to contain any destructive repercussions of Russia's impending rupture.

Janusz Bugajski
July 4, 2022

1.

Introduction: Russia's Test for the West

Russia presents a dual challenge for the West—its persistent neo-imperial ambitions and its impending state rupture. Since Vladimir Putin gained presidential powers in December 1999, the Kremlin has pursued a policy of imperial restoration by subverting or partitioning states along Russia's borders, undercutting the United States' influence in Europe, undermining the North Atlantic Treaty Organization (NATO), discrediting Europe's democratic systems, and campaigning to dismantle the West.[1] But while pursuing its imperial project, Russia's domestic failures have become starker and the centralized "federation" confronts decay, turmoil, and fracture. Both imperialization and implosion will present the US and NATO with critical policy decisions to deter and defend from Russia's attacks while concurrently managing Russia's demise. Such a process will engender both instabilities and opportunities in several regions

---

[1] Janusz Bugajski, *Cold Peace: Russia's New Imperialism*, Praeger/Greenwood, 2004; Janusz Bugajski, *Expanding Eurasia: Russia's European Ambitions*, CSIS Press, 2008; Janusz Bugajski, *Dismantling the West: Russia's Atlantic Agenda*, Potomac Books, 2009; and Janusz Bugajski and Margarita Assenova, *Eurasian Disunion: Russia's Vulnerable Flanks*, Jamestown Foundation, 2016.

bordering the Russian Federation for which Washington is not prepared.

Kremlin officials claim that Russia is destined to be a great power and the United States is the main adversary obsessed with preventing the country from maintaining its rightful global status. They have accumulated numerous grievances against the West since Moscow's defeat in the Cold War and operate on the premise that the US dismembered the Soviet Union and capitalized on Russia's weaknesses after the unravelling of the Soviet bloc. Other alleged transgressions have included forcefully expanding NATO eastward, breaking up federal Yugoslavia, placing NATO troops along Russia's European borders, and challenging Moscow's predominant influence over Eastern Europe, the South Caucasus and Central Asia.

In response to these offensives, Putin has purportedly restored Russia's national unity and reasserted its economic and military power. Moscow claims it stands at the forefront of global resistance to US hegemony through its promotion of "multipolarity" and its model of "sovereign democracy." The Kremlin has deployed a wide range of tools to undermine bordering states and Western democracies—including territorial seizures, cyberattacks, disinformation campaigns, energy blackmail, corruption offensives, political influence operations, all the way up to armed invasion and outright war. Nonetheless, all these efforts have failed to establish Russia as a global hegemon or a model for emulation on the international stage. On the contrary, they have earned Russia a pariah status, especially among Western states. Moreover, Moscow's neo-imperial ambitions and assertive foreign policies only thinly disguise Russia's internal failures; and its escalating domestic vulnerabilities will make the Kremlin more confrontational and desperate to demonstrate strength before its capacities seriously deteriorate. Russia's 2022 war of conquest in Ukraine will only quicken those preexisting trends.

According to constitutional amendments approved in July 2020 through a rigged referendum, Putin will be enabled to hold two more six-year presidential terms, in 2024 and 2030, and remain in power until 2036 or until his death, incapacitation, or ouster.[2] But despite such attempts to ensure political continuity and maintain central control, Russia's problems are accumulating. The longer that the Kremlin tries to maintain the artificial and misnamed "federation" through centralization and repression the more likely that it will rupture. Even attempted reforms are likely to unleash destabilizing and disintegrative trends. With deep structural, political, and economic reforms, the rupture may be mostly peaceful; but without reform, it could prove violent and impact on several neighboring countries. Paradoxically, while Putin's insertion into power was based on the premise that he would prevent Russia's disintegration, he may ultimately be remembered in Russian history as a failed leader who presided over the country's downfall.

Russia as Failed Empire

President Putin has bemoaned the expiration of the Union of Soviet Socialist Republics (USSR) as the demise of "historical Russia," revealing a deeply rooted conviction that the multi-national Communist construct had evolved into an elaborate disguise for another Russian or Muscovite imperium.[3] Kremlin officials continue to believe in global empires and assert that the world should be organized on a "multipolar" or "polycentric" basis. The terms were coined shortly after Putin gained the presidency to signify an

---

[2] "Putin's Constitution," Warsaw Institute, June 30, 2020, https://warsawinstitute.org/putins-constitution/.

[3] Andrew Osborn and Andrey Ostroukh, "Putin Rues Soviet Collapse as Demise of 'Historical Russia'," *Reuters*, December 12, 2021, https://news.yahoo.com/putin-rues-soviet-collapse-demise-140632311.html?fr=sycsrp_catchall.

international system in which great powers balance their interests and smaller countries orbit around them as satellites. The Kremlin views its "pole of power" as consisting of Eurasia, or the northern Eurasian landmass, and as much of Europe as it can capture, especially those regions that were part of the Russian sphere in Soviet or even Tsarist times. In this geostrategic equation, the US should be confined to the Western hemisphere and its role in Europe minimized.

Yet despite assertive rhetoric and persistent offensives, Putin has failed to transform Russia into a major "pole of power" or a genuine source of political, economic, or cultural attraction for neighboring states. Threats against neighbors and Western adversaries are not a sign of strength but of Moscow's weakness and inability to cower them into submission. Instead of successful and extensive empire building, the Putin regime has truncated and absorbed parts of neighboring countries but has failed to gain international legitimacy for its territorial acquisitions. In addition, the partition of neighboring states has raised the economic and security burdens on Moscow with only short-term benefits of patriotic mobilization and public support for the regime. The extensive invasion of Ukraine in February 2022 may have initially raised public support, but a prolonged and costly military operation will further expose Russia's imperial failure.

Russia's neo-imperial project does not always replicate the Soviet era by demanding ideological allegiance or controlling the internal political and institutional arrangements of targeted states. The primary goal is to exert predominant influence over the foreign and security policies of neighboring governments so they will either remain internationally neutral or support Russia's foreign policy agenda. In the case of Ukraine, Moscow's frustrations in failing to neutralize the country through the creation of separatist entities on its territory in 2014 led to a large-scale military intervention in February 2022. The aim was to replace the government in Kyiv, substantially weaken Ukraine's military potential, prohibit any closer ties with NATO, and ensure more direct Russian control.

The Kremlin administration has employed numerous enticements, threats, incentives, and pressures to gain and maintain the acquiescence of nearby capitals. However, Moscow is also failing in this endeavor, as targeted countries such as Ukraine and Georgia continue to aspire to NATO membership in order to uphold their independence and security, as well as closer links with the EU to help develop their economies. Putin's ambition to create a Russia-centered "pole of power" through various multi-national institutions has failed to solidify a bloc of loyal allies, as compared to successful Western structures such as NATO and the EU.

Unlike most other European nation-states that either liberated themselves from foreign empires or discarded their overseas possessions, Russia needs liberation from itself. The Russian state became an empire before Russians became a nation and before the vast country could evolve into a nation-state. As an empire, Russia focused on expanding its territorial holdings and competing with imperial adversaries, it largely neglected nation building as the foundation for a durable state. Russia expanded by incorporating numerous ethnic groups whose national identities were often more consolidated and who could not be fully assimilated and russified. Even after the disintegration of the USSR, the territory lost by Moscow was smaller than that surrendered by Western empires following their post-imperial decolonization.[4]

Russia's internal transition to a nation-state has been blocked by its imperialist approach toward federal regions and non-Russian ethnicities. Unlike the overseas West European empires, the Russian imperium developed contiguously and the distinction between center

---

[4] Alexander Etkind, *Internal Colonization: Russia's Imperial Experience*, Polity Press, Cambridge, UK, 2011, p.4.

and periphery was not fixed.[5] Even the Moscow metropolis became a colony of the Tsar and then of the Kremlin. To prevent its imperial decay from devolving into full-scale disintegration, the regime has imposed increasingly authoritarian measures under the Putin presidency, and these will paradoxically hasten the collapse of the current state.

Russia as Failed State

The multi-national Russian Federation is plagued by persistent internal anxieties about its survival and territorial integrity. This is evident in frequent assertions by political leaders and debates among academics and journalists. Allegations about Western intentions camouflage the deep-rooted paranoia about Russia's future. High officials and their advisors and propagandists recognize that the Russian Federation remains an unstable remnant empire, despite shedding many of its imperial possessions following the collapse of Tsardom and the demise of the Soviet Bloc and the Soviet Union. They also fear further state rupture by repeating Soviet Secretary General Mikhail Gorbachev's attempts at reforming the Communist system in the late 1980s. Paradoxically, such anxieties will preclude the necessary economic and political transformation to avoid a systemic collapse.

Putin and his security services, Kremlin-tied oligarchs, corrupt officials, and the privileged class of civil servants are not prepared to endanger their power and purses by pursuing reforms that would accord citizens political choices through democratic elections. On the other hand, without economic modernization and market

---

[5] "Владислав Иноземцев: «Россия не существовала вне имперского состояния»," *IFV24.ru*, August 11, 2020, https://www.if24.ru/vladislav-inozemtsev-rossiya-i-imperia/.

diversification, in combination with political democratization, decentralization and genuine federalism, Russia will not only stagnate and decline, but it will also slide toward an existential convulsion.

State officials appear to be fully cognizant of the oncoming dangers because Russia remains a weak multi-national, multi-republican and multi-regional assemblage. For instance, in August 2021, Defense Minister Sergei Shoigu compared Russia to the former Yugoslav Socialist Federation, warning about external pressures in combination with internal threats that could divide the country along nationality, class and religious lines, and result in disintegration.[6] However, he failed to point out that it is precisely Moscow's policies of hyper-centralization, regional exploitation, economic mismanagement, deepening political repression, and manipulation of Russian ethno-nationalism that can drive the country toward a chaotic implosion.

Fear of collapse is pervasive in the country and is also manipulated by officials to scare people into blindly following the regime as the alleged savior of Russian statehood. For instance, a senior Russian Sinologist has claimed that the Chinese will negotiate with the Americans on how to divide their spheres of influence inside Russia, with China taking Siberia and US influence meeting China at the Urals.[7] Meanwhile, Russia's military and intelligence leaders have warned that the West is using the internet and other means to radicalize and

---

[6] "Шойгу заявил о необходимости укрепления общества и армии на фоне внешнего давления," *Interfax-AVN*, August 10, 2021, https://www.militarynews.ru/story.asp?rid=1&nid=554699&lang=RU.

[7] "Андрей Девятов: 'Китайцы будут договариваться с американцами, как разделить сферы влияния в России,'" July 11, 2021, https://www.business-gazeta.ru/article/515396.

criminalize Russian youth and preparing them for an uprising.[8] In attempts to subdue debate and dissent about Russia's future, state officials disguise the lessons of Russia's history. In July 2021, Moscow announced the creation of an interagency Commission on Historical Education, considered to be vital for defending national interests.[9] One pro-Kremlin historian claimed that the government was trying to preserve the state within its current borders; and if history was rewritten, he asserted, then the country would cease to exist. Officials stress the need for a "unified" version of history otherwise Russia would collapse into a number of small states. The new history commission was to include representatives of the Ministry of Interior, the presidential administration, the Security Council, the Prosecutor-General's Office, and two major intelligence services—the Federal Security Service (*Federalnaya Sluzhba Bezopasnosti*—FSB) and the Foreign Intelligence Service (*Sluzhba Vneshney Razvedki*—SVR).

Russia's revised national security strategy, approved in a decree by President Putin in July 2021, primarily focuses on preventing the country's demolition. It envisages various measures in response to the actions of foreign states that allegedly threaten Russia's sovereignty and territorial integrity.[10] Officials frequently repeat government-driven conspiracy myths that Western powers seek to divide and fracture Russia. The fear of encirclement by hostile powers is

---

[8] Paul Goble, "To Combat Radicalization of Russia's Young, Kremlin Must Re-Establish Administration of State Youth Policy, Military Sociologist Says," August 14, 2021, http://windowoneurasia2.blogspot.com/2021/08/to-combat-radicalization-of-russias.html.

[9] Mikhail Sokolov, "'A Dangerous Commission': Russian Historians Alarmed as Putin Creates State Body On 'Historical Education'," August 10, 2021, https://www.rferl.org/a/russia-history-commission-putin/31403236.html.

[10] President of Russia, "The President Approved the National Security Strategy, July 2, 2021, http://en.kremlin.ru/events/president/news/66098.

reinforced by alarm over supposed internal enemies working in tandem with Western agencies. The US and its surrogates are allegedly escalating their propaganda offensive against the country by employing Russian saboteurs, propagandists, "sleeper cells," and other "fifth columnists" to weaken and destroy the country. In such uncertain conditions, driven by paranoia, guilt and imperial complexes, a key purpose of the Kremlin's "power vertical" is to prevent the country's fragmentation.

Russia's Future

The rupture of the Russian Federation can be viewed as the continuation of the process of collapse of the Soviet bloc and the Soviet Union in the 1990s. Thirty years after the dismantling of the Soviet empire in Central-Eastern Europe and the disintegration of the USSR, the Russian Federation, the inheritor of Moscow's remaining dominions, is a failed state with an incomplete national identity. It has proved unable to transform itself into a nation-state, a civic state, or even an effective imperial state. Russia's numerous weaknesses are exacerbated by a convergence of factors, including dependence on unpredictable export revenues based predominantly on fossil fuels, a contracting economy with little prospect of growth or global competitiveness, declining social trust and support for the central government, and intensifying regional and ethnic unrest. In 2020–2021, the country's failures were aggravated by the rampant COVID-19 pandemic, which further undermined the government's credibility. Moscow's full-scale invasion of Ukraine in February 2022 failed to oust the government in Kyiv and led to substantial Russian military casualties and comprehensive international economic sanctions. This has deepened Russia's internal problems and will accelerate the consequences outlined in this guide.

The Kremlin believes that preserving an autocratic government, reasserting Russian dominance over its neighbors, and restoring

Russia's great power status are mutually reinforcing elements. However, the Russian Federation is approaching the end of a regime cycle in which the political *status quo* will become increasingly precarious. Not since the fracturing of the Soviet Union have several simultaneous crises become so stark, including the government's inability to ensure sustained economic development, widening disparities between Moscow and the federal regions, deepening distrust of Moscow's governance, public resistance to unpopular decisions, increasing disbelief in state propaganda, and the regime's inability to permanently stifle resistance by imposing mass repression.

Without political pluralism, economic reform, regional autonomy and local control of resources, the federal structure will become increasingly unmanageable and public resistance will mushroom. In order to prolong its survival, Russia needs to develop into a genuine federal democracy. But instead of pursuing decentralization to accommodate the aspirations of distinct ethnic rights and regional interests, the Russian government is engaged in their wholesale restriction. Resentments proliferate over Moscow's unilateral appointment of regional governors, its appropriation of local resources, its inadequate response to the COVID-19 pandemic and other national emergencies, as well as mounting casualties in the war against Ukraine among non-Russian and rural Russian populations in the federal regions. A failure to reform the state "from above" or "at the center" places more onus and urgency on revolutionizing the country "from below" and in the regions. Deepening discontent has been evident in periodic protest actions in diverse parts of the country—from the High North to the North Caucasus, the Middle Volga and the Pacific regions. Although the regime is obsessed with quelling and preventing further outbursts, simultaneous crises in several far-flung regions may overwhelm Moscow's repressive apparatus or its ability to provide any durable economic relief and political concessions to control unrest.

Social protests have erupted over various grievances, whether against dumping Moscow's trash in Arkhangelsk *Oblast* and the Komi Republic, economic exploitation and curtailment of the national language in the Tatarstan Republic and other ethnic entities, the building of Orthodox cathedrals in Siberia's Krasnoyarsk *Krai*, the falsification of elections in the Buryat Republic, the appointment of outsiders as governors in the Kalmyk Republic and other regions, the unilateral replacement of governors in the Pacific region, the arbitrary changes of borders between the republics of Chechnya and Ingushetia, or growing ethnic tensions in the Republic of Dagestan fueled by unilateral government decisions. And since February 24, 2022, the Russian authorities have been preoccupied with squelching any anti-war protests across the country. Almost any unpopular issue can trigger unrest and demonstrations against Moscow's rule and accelerate demands for autonomy and self-determination. Regardless of official or independent opinion polling, one cannot assume that the public mood is accurately monitored or cannot rapidly radicalize given a confluence of political, social and economic conditions.

The Kremlin fears any repetition of the "color revolutions" that shook Ukraine in 2004 and 2014 and Georgia in 2003, when corrupt authoritarian governments were toppled because they could no longer suppress public protests against election fraud. Mass demonstrations in Belarus in the summer of 2020 over blatant vote rigging disproved the conventional wisdom about a predominantly passive Belarusian public that mirrors the widely held image of Russian citizens.[11] Although the protests in Belarus were ultimately extinguished, the root causes of public unrest were not addressed. As Russians and Belarusians consider themselves to be close in terms of language, culture, ethnic origin and behavior, events in Belarus could become

---

[11] "Belarus: Mass Protests after Lukashenko Secretly Sworn in," *BBC News*, September 23, 2020, https://www.bbc.com/news/world-europe-54262953.

another contributing factor for public protests and escalating demands in Russia itself.

The unexpected demonstrations and storming of government buildings in Kazakhstan in early January 2022 in response to rising fuel prices were evidently manipulated by rival factions in the ruling elite, but they served as another warning to Moscow that public anger simmers below the surface and can explode suddenly and spread rapidly.[12] The appearance of stability and public passivity, for which Kazakhstan has been renowned, cannot be taken for granted in Russia either. Moreover, a triggering event such as substantial price increases for produce or services or a blatantly forged election can unexpectedly escalate public demands for broader political changes, and it can also assume ethnic and nationalist dimensions. The results of Moscow's war against Ukraine, particularly the successful resistance of its citizens against invasion and the imposition of an autocratic regime, can also have social reverberations in Russia by inspiring protests against government policy.

Although Moscow camouflages its deepening fragility through external aggression, brewing domestic problems can precipitate a range of crises including intra-elite power struggles and open conflicts between Moscow and several Russian regions. Kremlin attempts to deflect attention from its internal troubles will also have security consequences for neighboring European countries. An accelerated decline of the Russian state and the emergence of quasi-independent entities will challenge the responses of the NATO alliance and the diplomatic versatility of Western governments. One cannot assume that Russia's fracture will be a swift process marked by a sudden governmental collapse or by a broad state-wide revolution. Much

---

[12] Margarita Assenova, "The Two Faces of Kazakhstan's Civil Unrest," *Eurasia Daily Monitor*, Vol.19, Issue 4, January 21, 2022, https://jamestown.org/program/the-two-faces-of-kazakhstans-civil-unrest/.

more likely it will be an evolving process that can accelerate at critical junctures. The triggers for rupture can include an attempted transfer of power by Putin to a successor; a power play to replace Putin that provokes intra-elite conflicts; a violent spark during massive election fraud; an explosive protest against economic impoverishment; an inter-ethnic clash that escalates into a wider conflict; a violent provocation by hard-liners or nationalists that escapes police control; and military mutinies or intra-military clashes based on ethnic allegiances.

A reactive Western defense toward a declining but antagonistic Russia is insufficient to defend transatlantic interests. Policy makers cannot operate on the assumption that Russia will transform itself into a stable and internationally constructive polity because of economic necessity, political rationality, or generational change. Western decision-makers need to acknowledge that the multi-national Russian Federation has failed to develop into a stable national state with a binding ethnic or civic identity and into a regional power without neo-imperial aspirations. In these conditions, a more informed and assertive Western strategy is needed to constrict Moscow's external aggression while working with allies and partners to manage and benefit from Russia's rupture. This Guide is intended to both analyze the failure of the Russian Federation and to provide ammunition for US and NATO policymakers in managing the consequences of that failure.

2.

State Failures

The multi-national Russian Federation has entered a new "time of troubles" (*smutnoie vremya)*, a period of political crisis and chaos that Muscovite Russia experienced in the late 16th and early 17th centuries and was replicated during the disintegration of Tsarist Russia in World War One. However, unlike in the 17th and 20th centuries, modern-day Moscow lacks the capacity and geopolitical opportunity to reconstitute Russia as a continental empire. Two core questions need to be addressed in devising an effective anticipatory strategy toward the Russian Federation: how deep and widespread are the failures of the current state structure, and how rapid and disruptive will be the country's demise? The multi-national state, held together by highly centralized decision-making and a hierarchical structure of power, is approaching a period of destabilization precipitated by several simultaneous crises. Intensifying repression and a stifling political system disguise a legion of economic and social grievances that fuel public disaffection and camouflage the government's decreasing capacity to maintain the loyalty of key elites. During this critical decade, which will include an unpredictable period of presidential succession in the wake of a costly war against Ukraine, the Russian administration will be hard pressed to pacify growing public aspirations for individual liberties, economic freedoms and political alternatives.

Russia's new national security strategy, released in July 2021, highlights the mounting domestic vulnerabilities recognized by the Kremlin.[1] The document is more inward looking than previous versions and focuses on countering instability while protecting "sovereign statehood." The main threats facing Russia avowedly stem from the crisis in economic development, rising social inequality, the intensification of interstate conflicts, the weakening influence of international organizations, and the ineffectiveness of the global security system. The Strategy admits that Russia faces a demographic calamity as a result of rapid population decline and major economic challenges, including low competitiveness, technological backwardness and growing poverty.

In an attempt to deflect attention away from its maladies, state propaganda claims that the integrity of the Russian state is under foreign attacks, together with traditional Russian morals and values. Information technology is allegedly increasingly used to violate Russia's "cultural sovereignty," foster political instability and challenge its territorial integrity. The strategy document charges Western governments with manipulating Russia's socio-economic problems in order to divide its society and dissolve its internal unity. Escalating military pressure around Russia's borders are also purportedly intended to aggravate its internal problems.

Persistent fears of state disintegration among Russian officials are grounded in two major historical precedents—the crumbling of the Tsarist empire during World War I (1914–1918) and the dissolution of the Soviet empire in 1990–1991. Paradoxically, by regularly railing about the dangers of state collapse in order to prolong the Putin regime and to discredit any political opposition, Russian officials are engaged in a self-fulfilling prophecy. Regularly focusing attention on

[1] http://static.kremlin.ru/media/events/files/ru/QZw6hSk5z9gWq0plD1ZzmR5cER0g5tZC.pdf.

state fragmentation exposes deep-rooted anxieties about another state failure and contributes to questioning the legitimacy and longevity of the current Russian Federation.

Government officials fear a repetition of Gorbachev's reforms (*perestroika)* in the 1980s, which snowballed toward the breakup of the Soviet Union. Ironically, extensive economic and political restructuring is becoming increasingly necessary to prevent an unravelling of the Russian Federation, while office holders in Putin's power pyramid are not prepared to endanger their rule by pursuing destabilizing reforms. Russia's political elites also fear any repeat of the "color revolutions" that shook Ukraine, Georgia, and Serbia in the 2000s, when corrupt authoritarian governments could no longer contain or suppress public demands for genuine democracy. The mass protests in Belarus against extensive vote rigging in the August 2020 presidential elections struck even closer to home. They were a major protest example for the Russian public and a model of crisis for the Russian regime that was forcefully pacified but not resolved. State repression has a limited life span. Without economic modernization and market diversification, in combination with political democratization and decentralization, Russia is stagnating, declining, failing, and facing a multi-dimensional crisis.

Since 2009, the Russian economy has been stagnant and its society trapped in a stalemate. The authoritarian regime has no incentive for drastic reform, because this would weaken its hold on power and spark conflicts between interest groups dependent on state corruption and clientelism.[2] At the same time, the Putinist system is not equipped to emulate the mass repressions, slaughters, imprisonment, and population expulsions conducted by the Soviet Communist Party and security apparatus, especially during Joseph Stalin's rule. It is also even

---

[2] Dmitry Travin, Vladimir Gel'man, Otar Marganiya, *The Russian Path: Ideas, Interests, Institutions, Illusions,* Stuttgart: Ibidem Verlag, 2020, p.203.

less able to isolate all citizens from outside influences. Instead, government attempts to control growing unrest in multiple cities and regions will itself provoke more extensive social revolts at a time of political volatility over Putin's succession maneuvers. The resulting conflicts will lead to federal fractures with potentially destabilizing consequences for Russia's neighbors, the United States' European allies, and for relations between Moscow and Washington.

Measuring Failure

Not since gaining power at the end of 1999 has President Vladimir Putin faced such a confluence of domestic problems compounded by his own policy missteps and imperial overreach. The "stagnation" (*zastoy*) of the 1980s, which precipitated Soviet state collapse, reflects both similarities and contrasts to the deepening decay of today's Putinist Russia. Similarly to the late Leonid Brezhnev era, economic growth is slowing, revenues are dropping, social services are shrinking, state ideology shows limited value in mobilizing citizens, the political elite is increasingly viewed as self-serving and incompetent, and foreign military escapades are widely perceived as unnecessary and damaging. However, in contrast to its late-Soviet predecessor, the Putin regime has been able to disguise its failures through an assertive foreign policy, a façade of national unity, and a comprehensive propaganda and disinformation assault on its own citizens and against Western institutions.

The Russian economy was already showing signs of shrinking before the COVID-19 pandemic struck and the global recession began.[3] International financial sanctions on Russia for its war against Ukraine and the subversion of Western democracies contributed to the

[3] The World Bank, *Russia Economic Report*, December 1, 2021, https://www.worldbank.org/en/country/russia/publication/rer.

decline, but it is Moscow's over-reliance on revenues from energy sales that provided an illusion of prosperity while ensuring an even deeper long-term downturn. Economic disparities in Russia have ballooned, official corruption has become systemic, internal security service repressions have expanded, and regional alienation from Moscow has escalated.

Nonetheless, Russia's decay does not signify that the government is weak and incapable of inflicting serious damage to its neighbors and international rivals, even aside from its nuclear and conventional military capabilities. Decline does not mean that Moscow no longer challenges the West and subverts its institutions through a range of hard power and non-military or "soft power" tools. On the contrary, the Putin regime tries to camouflage its increasing fragility and unpopularity through external aggression. In efforts to ensure internal control, it needs to project its power abroad.[4] In effect, imperialism prevents or delays implosion. Kremlin attempts to deflect attention from a multitude of internal crises can also have serious security consequences for neighboring European countries. Indeed, as illustrated by the February 24, 2022, large-scale Russian invasion of Ukraine, state failure and potential rupture apparently convinced the Kremlin that it has limited time to equalize the "playing field" by disrupting its adversaries, engineering or expanding conflicts in several regions, and dismantling Western unity. Russia's decline and ultimate state failure can be measured from several vantage points, including its incompleteness as a nation-state, its mendacious historical narratives, persistent identity disputes, ideological disarray, persecuted politics, demographic defects, economic decay, environmental dangers, social pressures, regional challenges, and international defeats.

---

[4] Kathryn E. Stoner, *Russia Resurrected: Its Power and Purpose in a New Global Order*, Oxford University Press, 2021, pp.19–20.

Incomplete Nation-State

Kremlin officials and advisors have endeavored to construct a model of nationhood and statehood that would appeal to the majority of citizens and keep the multi-national Russian Federation intact. However, despite various imperial iterations under Czarism, Communism, and Putinism, the Moscow-centered state has failed to produce a durable national consensus that would encompass its entire population.[5] The inability to create a unified national state, whether civic or ethnic, has prevented Russia from developing into a stable democratic country at peace with its neighbors. It has generated a prolonged contest over Russian identity and ethnicity, not only between differing strands of nationalists and imperialists but also with several non-Russian populations within the Russian Federation as well as with neighboring countries. Russia's size and reach, accomplished through hundreds of years of imperial conquest and colonization, is a fundamental structural weakness. It inhibits the development of an enduring nation-state by focusing government attention primarily on preserving extensive territories, diverse ethnicities, and disparate regions within its borders.

Brittle Historical Foundations

One foundational problem is that Russia's rulers have historically claimed non-Muscovite state structures as part of Moscow's heritage and lineage and as essentially "Russian" entities in a "single stream" of development. These include Kyivan Rus, the Novgorod Republic, and

---

[5] Peter Eltsov, "The Best Way to Deal With Russia: Wait for It to Implode," August 3, 2019, https://www.politico.com/magazine/story/2019/08/03/russia-separatism-vladimir-putin-227498.

the Galician-Volhynian Principality.[6] Moscow has promoted and benefited from the terminological confusion between the proto ethnonyms of *Rus* and *Russkii*. In historical records, the "Rus" were either a Scandinavian Viking tribe or an eastern Slavic tribe who founded the first eastern Slavic state of Kyivan Rus based around present-day Ukraine between the 10th and 13th centuries.[7] Moscow was merely a small trading outpost on the periphery of this Kyiv-centered tribal confederation. The Rus people were not the ancestors of Muscovites, and Kyivan Rus did not evolve into a Russian entity. Leaders of the Muscovite principality subsequently adopted the name *Russkii* from the *Rus* stem to help justify their territorial conquests and linguistic and cultural assimilation of neighboring peoples from the 15th century onward.[8]

The propaganda narrative that Russia's history began with Kyivan Rus in the 9th century was invented in the 18th century, when Catherine the Great invited German scholars to construct a history of Russia based on an allegedly ancient lineage.[9] As a result, Muscovite-Russian identity became flexible and expansive, historically and territorially. It continues to be challenged by neighboring nations possessing their own non-Russian ethnic identities, particularly Ukrainians and

---

[6] Taras Kuzio, *Crisis in Russian Studies: Nationalism (Imperialism), Racism and War*, E-International Relations Publishing, Bristol, England 2020, pp.17-24, https://www.e-ir.info/publication/crisis-in-russian-studies-nationalism-imperialism-racism-and-war/.

[7] *Encyclopedia Britannica*, "Rus," April 16, 2013, https://www.britannica.com/topic/Rus.

[8] Serhii Plokhy, *Lost Kingdom: The Quest for Empire and the Making of the Russian Nation*, Basic Books, 2017, and *The Origins of the Slavic Nations: Premodern Identities in Russia, Ukraine, and Belarus*, Cambridge University Press, 2010.

[9] Peter Eltsov, *The Long Telegram 2.0: A Neo-Kennanite Approach to Russia*, Lanham: Lexington Books, 2020, p.65.

Belarusians, and who expose and criticize Moscow's appropriation of their histories and cultures. The term "*Russkii*" is employed by pan-Slavic Russian imperialists to subsume Ukrainians and Belarusians as purportedly two additional stems of the "All-Russian" nation (*Obshcherusskiy narod*) or the "Triune Russian nation" (*Triyedinyy Russkii narod*) led by the Great Russian nation (*Velikorusskii narod*). This historical and terminological deception has been promulgated through generations of Muscovite, Tsarist, Soviet and Russian state propaganda and disinformation.

Although the Kremlin has endeavored to unify the country's nationalities by promoting a non-ethnic identity within the Russian Federation, the conflation of the ethnic "*Russkii*" with the broader statist "*Rossiiskii*" also generates tensions between mono-ethnicity and multi-ethnicity. It is problematic to build a non-ethnic civic identity around a particular ethnic stem or the distinct national marker of "Russian" appropriated by Moscow. This is especially egregious when, on the pretext of de-ethnification and construction of a uniform civic citizenship, the concept of a superior *Russkii* cultural and linguistic core is promulgated by the state and the Russian Orthodox Church and depicted as a foundation of Russian nationhood, statehood and spirituality.[10] In effect, the objective is to expand and legitimize ethno-Russian cultural, linguistic, and political dominance.

The process of russification under a civic cover serves to undermine support for a civic identity and raises demands for the recognition of ethnic distinctiveness among non-Russians. Suspicions proliferate that ambiguity between the terms "*Russkii*" and "*Rossiiskii*" is

---

[10] Yuri Teper, "Kremlin's Post-2012 National Policies: Encountering the Merits and Perils of Identity-Based Social Contract," in Pål Kolstø and Helge Blakkisrud (Eds.), *Russia Before and After Crimea: Nationalism and Identity, 2010-2017*, Edinburgh University Press, 2019, p.73

designed to appease Russian ethno-nationalists by promoting the unifying role of the *Russkii* people as the core of the Russian Federation.[11] Simultaneously, state policy is viewed as weakening the ethnic identities of non-Russians and is based on the supposition that other nations will not be permitted to compete with either the "*Russkii*" or "*Rossiiskii*" designations. In effect, the dominant ethnicity enshrines and promulgates its expansive identity in the trappings of civic nationalism, state patriotism, and loyalty to the regime.[12]

The Putin government has pursued the constitutional recognition of an "all-Russian" civic identity *(Obshcherossiyskoy grazhdanskoy identichnosti)* rather than a non-ethnic Russian nation (*Rossiiskaia natsiia*). The goal is to combine civic and ethnic components so as not to alienate Russian or non-Russian ethnics and to blend this identity with loyalty to the regime, state patriotism, and devotion to imperial assertiveness. Russian language and culture are promulgated by state organs to dominate other national groups and a policy of de-ethnification and uniformity is actively pursued that favors the Russian ethnos. However, the passage of laws that attempt to define the civic Russian nation can backfire in both directions. They can be interpreted by Russian nationalists as diluting or undermining the ethnic distinctiveness of the Russian ethnos and will be viewed by non-Russians as seeking to assimilate them into an essentially Russian-dominated state under the cover of civic citizenship. Such

---

[11] President Vladimir Putin's Address to the National Assembly of the Russian Federation, December 12, 2012, http://eng.kremlin.ru/transcripts/4739.

[12] J. Paul Goode, "Everyday Patriotism and Ethnicity in Today's Russia," in Pål Kolstø and Helge Blakkisrud (Eds.), *Russia Before and After Crimea: Nationalism and Identity, 2010–2017*, Edinburgh University Press, 2019, p.275.

moves by the government expose fears of growing ethnic cleavages and endanger social stability.[13]

Russia's history of imperial statehood has been turned into a great power cult and highlighted in opposition to other states and "civilizations," especially the disparaged "collective West." This is founded on two interwoven principles. First is a deep-rooted and officially promulgated notion of a civilizational or even messianic element in the supposed supremacy of Russian culture, language, and spirituality, particularly in contradistinction to the allegedly decadent West. And second, due to their alleged envy and spite, Western powers are depicted as seeking to fragment and dominate the Russian state, which has become a besieged fortress. As a consequence, a state-centered or empire-centered identity is promoted ahead of an ethno-national identity. A centralized regime presided over by a strong leader are viewed as the indispensable defenders of both the Russian nation and the imperial Russian state from predatory outside powers.

Confused Identities

The Russian Federation has failed to establish a civic identity to which most citizens would subscribe regardless of their ethnic background.[14] Instead, the country has witnessed constant identity battles between ethno-nationalists, imperialists and non-Russians. Under the Soviet system, Russian ethno-nationalism was suppressed or curtailed,

---

[13] Yuri Teper, "Kremlin's Post-2012 National Policies: Encountering the Merits and Perils of Identity-Based Social Contract," in Pål Kolstø and Helge Blakkisrud (Eds.), *Russia Before and After Crimea: Nationalism and Identity, 2010-2017*, Edinburgh University Press, 2019, p.85.

[14] Paul Goble, "Moscow Says Pandemic has Weakened Russian-Centric Civic Identity," February 3, 2022, http://windowoneurasia2.blogspot.com/2022/02/moscow-says-pandemic-has-weakened.html.

especially during Vladimir Lenin's rule. Bolshevik leaders warned about the dangers that "Great Russian chauvinism" thwarted "socialist internationalism." Lenin viewed ethnic revivals among minority nations as a struggle for liberation from Russian imperialism in the construction of socialism. He believed that "backward" peoples had to pass through an ethno-national identity and consciousness as they progressed toward a proletarian identity, internationalist consciousness, and full "ethnic fusion" (*sliianie*). The Bolshevik program of indigenization (*korenizatsiia*) in the 1920s, coopted native elites in state structures and Communist Party organs. It also sought to placate non-Russians and curtail local rebellions by establishing national institutions and administrative structures and promoting diverse languages and cultures. However, local elites loyal to Moscow stifled any independent manifestations of ethno-nationalism that were prohibited by the ruling party. Russian cadre also played a supervisory role in each of the ethnic republics. Bolshevik decisions to establish, adjust, or abolish ethno-territorial units were politically motivated and rarely involved close consultations with the leaders of ethno-national groups.

Stalin, who was responsible for determining Soviet policy toward the country's nationalities during Lenin's tenure, also initially denounced Russian "imperialist oppression." During his intensified "cultural revolution" in the 1930s, Stalin gave preferential treatment to members of particular ethnic groups who were deemed to be more advanced and defined as "nations" (*naciia*) rather than as "nationalities" (*narodnosti*). "National proletarian cadres" were to be trusted builders of socialism, and many were recruited into management, party, and educational positions.[15] Under Stalin, the notion of "counter-revolutionary nations" also gained prominence and justified wholesale population expulsions and mass murders.

---

[15] Yuri Slezkine, *Arctic Mirrors: Russia and the Small Peoples of the North*, Ithaca: Cornell University Press, 1994, p.221.

Stalin subsequently mobilized Russian ethno-nationalism in the service of the state, particularly during World War II (the Great Patriotic War) in a policy often termed as "National Bolshevism." Russian language, culture, history, education, and identity played the "leading role" in the USSR after World War II and became a core element of Soviet identity.[16] Nonetheless, Russian ethno-nationalists harbored a sense of grievance that the Russian ethnos was weakened by Sovietization, that it was not provided with separate political and republican institutions but a multi-ethnic federation (the Russian Soviet Federative Socialist Republic), and that the Russian federal structure included non-Russian ethno-republics that persisted even after the disintegration of the USSR.

In the post-Soviet era, divisions among Russian nationalists have been amplified and range from imperialist statists to ethno-exclusivists, with numerous actors combining elements from both main ideological magnets.[17] Imperialists are either ethnicity-neutral or seek the cultural assimilation of non-Russian ethnics into a super-national identity in which the Russian ethnos dominates as the majority population. Ethno-exclusivists or racist supremacists promote a homogenous Russian nation within an ethnic homeland that should either fully assimilate acceptable non-Russians or preclude any ethnic mixing that would dilute the Russian singularity. Ethno-nationalists also view the larger East Slavic ethno-linguistic cluster, including Ukrainians and Belarusians, as essentially "Russian," or in which the

---

[16] Emil Pain, "Contemporary Russian Nationalism in the Historical Struggle Between 'Official Nationality' and 'Popular Sovereignty,'" in Pål Kolstø and Helge Blakkisrud (Eds.), *Russia Before and After Crimea: Nationalism and Identity, 2010-2017*, Edinburgh University Press, 2019, pp.27–28.

[17] Marlen Laruelle, *Russian Nationalism: Imaginaries, Doctrines, and Politcal Battlefields*, Routledge Series on Russian and East Europeans Studies, 2019, pp.7–8.

"Great Russians" (*Velikorussy*) naturally predominate over "Little Russians" (*Malorussy*—Ukrainians) and "White Russians" (*Bielorussy*—Belarusians). Through this prism, the seizure of Crimea and the occupation of parts of eastern Ukraine in 2014 and 2022 were depicted as the rightful "ingathering of Russian lands" and uniting a single nation.[18] The attack on Ukraine can therefore be considered both as an ethno-national project and an imperial-statist agenda.

Definitions of identity have implications for the territorial contours of the aspiring state. Imperialists are revisionist and expansionist in seeking to restore a larger state along the borders of the former Soviet Union or even the Tsarist Empire. Ethno-nationalists generally seek a more compact Russian state in which nation and state are more coterminous and where culture and identity are not endangered by ethnic aliens. The broader pan–East Slavic Russian nation can therefore include Ukrainians, Belarusians, and Ruthenians and even assimilate suitable non-Slavs. Ethno-nationalists also seek a clear acknowledgement of the country as the expression of *Russkii* statehood in which the Russian nation is declared as the sole state-forming entity.[19] The more ardent ethno-nativists want to replace the Russian Federation with a distinct Russian national state.[20] In this

---

[18] Taras Kuzio, *Crisis in Russian Studies: Nationalism (Imperialism), Racism and War,* E-International Relations Publishing, Bristol, England 2020, p.104, https://www.e-ir.info/publication/crisis-in-russian-studies-nationalism-imperialism-racism-and-war/.

[19] Pål Kolstø, "The Ethnification of Russian Nationalism," in Pål Kolstø and Helge Blakkisrud (Eds.), *The New Russian Nationalism: Imperialism, Ethnicity and Authoritarianism, 2000-15,* Edinburgh University Press, 2016, p.39.

[20] Anastasia Mitrofanova, "Russian Ethnic Nationalism and Religion Today," Pål Kolstø and Helge Blakkisrud (Eds.), *The New Russian Nationalism: Imperialism, Ethnicity and Authoritarianism, 2000–15,* Edinburgh University Press, 2016, pp.106–107.

vein, some ultra-nationalists have adopted anti-migrant and white identity themes, mimicking their counterparts in Western Europe and the United States in avowedly defending the "white race."[21]

Combining the two major "Russist" positions (imperial and ethnic) are ethno-nationalist irredentists or "imperial nationalists" who seek to "reunite" the divided Russian nation by annexing territories from neighboring states containing sizeable ethnic Russian populations, including Kazakhstan, Ukraine, Belarus, Moldova, and even Estonia, Latvia and Lithuania. While some demand an ethnically hierarchical structure controlled by ethnic Russians, others seek a more "ethnically pure" state and envisage relinquishing the North Caucasus and other regions that cannot be integrated in the Russian core and where the ethnic Russian population has dwindled. They complain that the current federal structure favors the ethnic republics at the expense of the metropolitan center and the predominantly ethno-Russian regions. Differences can also be found between groups advocating for the creation of several Russian republics in the existing federation and those seeking to transform the federal structure into a more unitary state without ethno-titular republics. The latter contend that the new state must consist only of administrative-territorial units such as *oblasts* and *krais*, while non-Russians will simply be granted cultural autonomy.

Russia's "Eurasianist" ideologues, who synthesize pan–East Slavic Russian imperialism and Greater Russian messianism, advocate the unity of post-Soviet states under Moscow's hegemony. They warn that the promotion of any Russian ethno-national state would tear the

---

[21] Marlène Laruelle, "How Islam Will Change Russia," in S. Enders Wimbush and Elizabeth M. Portale (Eds), *Russia in Decline,* Jamestown Foundation, March 2017, p.245.

current Russian Federation apart.[22] Eurasianists view Russia as the center of a supra-ethnic or multi-national and multi-confessional empire, bearing a unique civilization, and with a predestined mission to guide the development of its neighbors through political, economic, and security integration. The current Russia has allegedly inherited the mantle of both the Tsarist Empire and the Soviet Union in addition to all previous state versions of Russian "civilization" since primordial times.[23] This worldview has become a core ingredient of state policy under the Putin administration, both institutionally through the creation of the Eurasian Economic Union and doctrinally through the promulgation of the "Russian World" (*Russkii Mir*) as a linguistic, cultural and historical bond between all nationalities under ethnic-Russian leadership.

In the view of Eurasianists, calls for dismantling the non-Russian republics in the current Russian Federation and the comprehensive assimilation of non-Russians, while defining them as Russians of some other "ethnic origin," would be a recipe for Russia's disintegration and a loss of its leading role in Eurasia. Civic nationalists among non-Russians could just as easily advocate that local Russians in the non-Russian republics must call themselves by the local nationality, such as Tatar or Yakut, and merely of "Russian origin." Eurasianists believe that the growth of ethno-nationalism among both Russians and non-Russians serves Western goals to fracture Russia and promote pan-Atlanticism. Instead, they believe in the necessity of a multi-ethnic continental empire controlled by

---

[22] Paul Goble, "Destroying Non-Russian Republics will Destroy Russia, Vakhitov Says," November 28, 2020, http://windowoneurasia2.blogspot.com/2020/11/destroying-non-russian-republics-will.html.

[23] Charles Clover, *Black Wind, White Snow: The Rise of Russia's New Nationalism,* New Haven: Yale University Press, 2017, p.11.

Muscovite Russia, whether this only includes lands historically dominated by Russia or a much larger part of the Eurasian landmass.[24]

Eurasianism is an ideology that largely defines itself in opposition to Westernism, feeds into the Russian besieged victim complex, and promulgates "russophobe" stereotypes cultivated by officials against critics of the Kremlin. It also bolsters contentions that the Soviet collapse was the consequence of Western machinations and that foreign powers continue to undermine Russia's territorial integrity and imperial statehood. In contrast, Russian ethno-nationalists tend to turn their ire against supposed racial, ethnic, and religious adversaries within the current state or along its borders, including Caucasians, Central Asians and Muslims, and favor a "purer" Russian state although its dimensions may be flexible and changeable.

The Kremlin has tried to harness the diverse forms of Russian nationalism in the service of Russia's neo-imperialism and statist patriotism, with alternating periods of tolerance and repression, but the balance remains precarious. Officials have endeavored to channel Russian ethno-nationalist sentiments into support for the Putin regime and against alleged Western attempts to destroy the Russian state. But the symbiosis is not always digestible. For instance, in launching the war against Ukraine and seizing Crimea in February 2014, Russian ethno-nationalists were allowed to gain some prominence alongside statist imperialists. Although they helped to legitimize the seizure of Crimea, major policy differences emerged over the Moscow-directed separatist war in eastern Ukraine. Imperial nationalists bemoaned the failure of the more ambitious *Novorossiya* (New Russia) project to seize all of southern and eastern Ukraine, while some ethno-nationalist groups opposed any seizure of

---

[24] Marlène Laruelle, *Russian Eurasianism: An Ideology of Empire*, Washington DC: Woodrow Wilson Center Press, 2008, p.217.

Ukrainian territory and the expanding war between the two "fraternal peoples."

Nonetheless, a major corpus of Russian imperial nationalists supported the forcible annexation of *Novorossiya,* as this would entail both territorial expansion and the in-gathering of pan-Russian ethnics or Russian speakers into a single state. Moscow subsequently subdued and silenced the most outspoken nationalists who criticized government policies in case they provoked inter-ethnic discords inside the Russian Federation or challenged the legitimacy of the Putin administration.[25] Moscow banned or dispersed several nationalist groups following the military intervention in Ukraine and arrested prominent nationalist figures who either criticized Moscow's policies or engaged in actions that could provoke inter-ethnic conflicts.[26] It also targeted nationalist groups seeking major structural changes in the Russian Federation and the official recognition of Russia as the national state of ethnic Russians (*Russkii*). This included the Russian Republic *Rus* organization, which called for the breakup of the existing Federation and the formation of a state uniting the predominantly ethnic-Russian regions into a single republic.[27] By cracking down on the ethno-nationalist opposition, the regime essentially reasserted its monopoly over the deployment of Russian nationalism and statist imperialism.

---

[25] Marlène Laruelle, *Russian Nationalism: Imaginaries, Doctrines, and Politcal Battlefields*, Routledge Series on Russian and East Europeans Studies, 2019, p.204.

[26] Alexander Verkhovsky, "The Russian Nationalist Movement at Low Ebb," in Pål Kolstø and Helge Blakkisrud (Eds.), *Russia Before and After Crimea: Nationalism and Identity, 2010-2017*, Edinburgh University Press, 2019, pp.144–146.

[27] Paul Goble, "Moscow Bans as Extremist Group Seeking to Unite Ethnic Russian Regions," September 4, 2020, https://windowoneurasia2.blogspot.com/2020/09/moscow-bans-as-extremist-group-seeking.html.

The national-democratic stream among Russia's political opposition rejects imperialist ideology tied to an authoritarian state, although when tested during the seizure of Crimea many supported Putin's irredentist project.[28] Leaders of the democratic opposition have also proposed the idea of a civic identity that can assimilate non-Russians or maintain their loyalty to the Russian state. Much of the liberal opposition as well as radical leftists and rightists do not support authentic federalism but view it as a dangerous prelude to disintegration rather than a shield against it. Many are likely to support the outright elimination of federal units. As a result, they may have little to offer the increasing number of people in the regions who are seeking greater control over their lives. This leaves space for new groups to emerge advocating decentralization, regionalism, federalism and confederalism.[29]

Regionalist commentators point out that most of Russia's prominent opposition figures are imperialist-minded and centrist, and their foreign policy would be similar to that of Putin. The political opposition broadly subscribes to the consensus that the question of state structure, federalism, regionalism and ethnic autonomy are secondary, and they generally hold to the conviction that genuine parliamentary democracy will by itself resolve the country's problems.[30] Such a position assumes that Russia can be democratized without significant decentralization. In contrast, regionalists and

---

[28] Emil Pain, "Contemporary Russian Nationalism in the Historical Struggle Between 'Official Nationality' and 'Popular Sovereignty,'" in Pål Kolstø and Helge Blakkisrud (Eds.), *Russia Before and After Crimea: Nationalism and Identity, 2010-2017*, Edinburgh University Press, 2019, pp.36–37.

[29] "Оппозиции бывают разные," November 5, 2020, https://www.idelreal.org/a/30927651.html.

[30] Private interview with Stephen Nix, International Republican Institute, March 2021.

federalists fear that a more benevolent centralism, as proposed by the liberal opposition, will simply replace the current autocracy without devolving any meaningful powers to the federal subjects. The Moscow-based opposition understands federalism mostly as an economic arrangement. They may seek to limit the extraction of resources and taxes from the regions but are not prepared for authentic federalism—as a voluntary and equal agreement between the republics and regions.[31]

Prominent oppositionists campaign for improving the state apparatus and combating official corruption, but for the most part they supported Crimea's annexation and other Putinist foreign policy objectives.[32] Most Russian liberals seek to create a single "civic nation" that is fully russified in language and culture. Opposition leaders such as Aleksei Navalny and Mikhail Khodorkovsky, as well as the liberal Free Russia Forum, are in essence opposed to genuine federalism.[33] They do not support the existence of larger territorial units such as *oblasts, krais* and republics, but favor a limited devolution of powers from the center to municipalities that would further undercut the position of existing federal subjects.[34] Leading opposition figures do not view Russia as "a multi-national state" and prefer a unitary structure without ethnic-based subdivisions. They evidently fear that

---

[31] Private interview with Vadim Shtepa, Editor in Chief, Region.Expert, Tallinn, March 2021.

[32] Private interview with Valery Dzutsev, Radio Free Europe/ Radio Liberty, March 2021.

[33] Marlène Laruelle, *Russian Nationalism: Imaginaries, Doctrines, and Politcal Battlefields*, Routledge Series on Russian and East Europeans Studies, 2019, p.183.

[34] Paul Goble, "Leaders of Extra-Systemic Opposition Fail to View Russia as 'Multi-National State,' Sidorov Says, January 8, 2021, http://windowoneurasia2.blogspot.com/2021/01/leaders-of-extra-systemic-opposition.html.

federal decentralization based on ethnic and regionalist identities will encourage autonomism and separatism.

Khodorkovsky has openly called for transforming Russia into a "nation-state," although he claims he wants a political rather than an ethnic nation. Such a non-ethnic Russian nation (*rossiiskaya natsiya*) would supposedly be based on the principles of citizenship regardless of ethnicity. However, Khodorkovsky's position seems to be essentially ethno-assimilationist, in which Russian political, cultural and linguistic dominance is disguised by civic identity as it was by Soviet identity during much of the Communist period. Khodorkovsky has proposed the disbanding of current federal subjects and a union of urban megalopolises serviced by surrounding territories and subordinate to Moscow. However, Khodorkovsky has also warned about Russia's impending disintegration with conflicts intensifying in the North Caucasus, the Middle Volga and Sakha.[35] His assertion that the country could either be democratic or united but not both indicated that several republics should secede.

Other opposition leaders from the national-democratic stream have proposed establishing a number of ethnic-Russian republics based on the current *krais* and *oblasts* and a new federal agreement with the existing non-Russian ethnic republics.[36] Navalny is more ambiguous on his federal plans than Khodorkovsky. At times he appears willing to recognize non-Russian nations by supporting their languages,

---

[35] Ramada Alpaut, "Ходорковский заявил, что Россия может быть либо единой, либо демократической," *IdelReal*, December 4, 2021, https://www.idelreal.org/a/31593573.html.

[36] Alexandra Kuznetsova and Sergey Sergeev, "Revolutionary Nationalism in Contemporary Russia," in Pål Kolstø and Helge Blakkisrud (Eds.), *Russia Before and After Crimea: Nationalism and Identity, 2010-2017*, Edinburgh University Press, 2019, pp.133–134.

cultures, and other distinct attributes, while also enabling Russians to identify ethnically and not just as a civic nation. However, his approval of regions as federal subjects is unclear, and critics believe he is willing to dispense with the federal structure altogether. His views on federalism have not differed significantly from that of the current regime. He also envisages enhancing the role of cities and not federal regions in order to stem what he perceives as the "threat of separatism."[37] In practice, this would undermine distinct ethnic identities and strengthen the Russian or *Russkii* ethnos as the "civic core" and anchor of assimilation.

Ironically, some pro-Kremlin propagandists, in a simmering stew of conspiracy narratives, accuse Navalny of working with Washington to destroy Russia and divide it into 32 puppet states.[38] Despite hopes among Western policymakers, Russia's urban liberals, especially in Moscow and St. Petersburg, seem unlikely to have the mass support, statewide reach, or effective strategy to democratize or transform the country. Instead, it is disaffected citizens, local activists, regionalists, autonomists, ethnic advocates, and pro-independence groups who will increasingly challenge Putin's authoritarian rule.

Ideological Disarray

Russia's state officials and their advisors have failed to develop an appealing ideology to provide the underpinnings of consensus among diverse sectors of the population or to inspire and mobilize the public. Much of what is presented as ideology has amounted to shallow propaganda and justification for Putin's dictatorship and external

---

[37] Tatiana Vintsevskaya, "Президент Навальный – новый ремейк империи?" March 1, 2017, http://region.expert/navalny/.

[38] Ilya Yablokov, *Fortress Russia: Conspiracy Theories in Post-Soviet Russia,* Cambridge, UK: Polity Press, 2018, p.62.

aggression. Domestically oriented state propaganda focuses on simplistic overarching themes—for instance, that democracy must be limited in order to preserve the state and prevent Western subversion, that "sovereign democracy" (a euphemism for central control) is essential to protect the country's independence, that democracy promotion by the West is merely a cover for US interference, and that Russians are a "state forming people" and therefore cannot exist without a strong state.

Attempts to create a message of unity through eclectic ideologies, grievance narratives, and conspiracy theories (more accurately, conspiracy myths) seemingly worked for short periods after Putin's ascent to power, particularly during times of economic growth propelled by high energy revenues and during the Crimea *Anschluss* in 2014. A sense of pride in the country was partially restored by blaming the West for the disruptive 1990s following the disintegration of the Soviet Union and praising Putin's successes in stabilizing the state.[39] However, the Kremlin has not offered any compelling or attractive vision for the future. Instead, an all-encompassing statist patriotism or loyalty to the strong state (*derzhavost* or *gosudarstvennichestvo*) has been promulgated, fixated on Russia's purportedly glorious past, its unique historical mission, and its great power status regardless of any guiding ideology or political system.

In its eclectic and flexible ideological packaging, Putinism consists of a blend of Muscovite statism, great power chauvinism (*velikaya derzhava*), neo-imperial Eurasianism, pan-Slavism, pan-Orthodoxy, Russian nationalism (with some ethnocentric ingredients), social conservatism, anti-liberalism, anti-globalism, anti-Americanism and

---

[39] Gulnaz Sharafutdinova, *The Red Mirror: Putin's Leadership and Russia's Insecure Identity*, Oxford University Press, 2020, p.9.

anti-Westernism, although not necessarily anti-European.[40] The purpose is to create an image of Russia's revived glory and global status that was avowedly subdued and denied after the collapse of the Soviet Union through Western machinations. However, this self-portrait is reliant on three constructs defining Russia—the glorious past, the collective victim, and the besieged fortress—rather than on a successful model of statehood and development. All these elements are intended to provide a sense of historical continuity ensured by the country's President and to placate fears of another comprehensive state rupture.

In reviving the image of greatness, Russia continues to live in the categories of World War II and Stalin's achievements in building a strong state and a global empire regardless of the cost to millions of human lives. The officially promoted historical narrative of the "Great Patriotic War" has been employed as a justification for imperial reconstruction, national unity and loyalty to the state. A skewed version of the war is a key element in the Kremlin's self-glorifying propaganda. Officials endeavor to erase the facts of Stalin's collaboration with Adolf Hitler to carve up eastern Europe through the Molotov-Ribbentrop Pact of August 1939 and Moscow's provisioning of raw materials such as oil, grain and iron to Germany to enable the Third Reich to expand westward. Instead, Stalinism is depicted as a necessary system that modernized the state, defeated Nazi Germany, and defended the country against the West. This imparts the message that the current authoritarian regime can similarly violate human rights, prohibit political freedoms, capsize living standards, and attack neighboring states, as long as it is successful in restoring Russia's glory. In July 2021, Putin signed a law that prohibits and punishes comparisons of the Soviet Union and Nazi

---

[40] Marlène Laruelle, "Russia as an Anti-Liberal European Civilisation," in Pål Kolstø and Helge Blakkisrud (Eds.), *The New Russian Nationalism: Imperialism, Ethnicity and Authoritarianism, 2000-15,* Edinburgh University Press, 2016, p.282.

Germany or even criticisms of Kremlin disinformation about Moscow's role during World War II.[41]

World War II myths also perpetuate two stark stereotypes beneficial for the Kremlin: people who support the Kremlin are patriots and antifascists, while those who oppose its policies are labeled as fascists, Nazis and "Russophobes" regardless of actual political persuasions.[42] In December 2021, Russia's Supreme Court ordered the closure of the Memorial Human Rights Center, which chronicles current repression, and Memorial International, the country's oldest human rights organization, which worked to preserve the memory of the millions of innocent people executed, imprisoned, exiled and persecuted during Soviet times. Tellingly, the court labeled Memorial a "public threat," in the pay of the West, for focusing attention on Soviet and current state crimes instead of highlighting Russia's "glorious past."[43]

Various elements of Soviet *chekism* (or the cult of state security) have also been revived and presented as a rebirth of national pride: "Growing reverence for the security apparatus reflects a broader trend toward reverence for strong statehood in Russia," according to

---

[41] "Kremlin Bans Historical Truth about Stalin-Hitler Pact," *Disinfowatch,* July 8, 2021, https://disinfowatch.org/disinfo/kremlin-bans-historical-truth-about-stalin-hitler-pact/.

[42] Konstantinas Ameliuškinas, "Lithuanian Historian: Moscow Does Not Have Moral Right to Host End of WWII Celebrations," Vilnius *Delfi*, February 11, 2015, http://en.delfi.lt/lithuania/society/lithuanian-historian-moscow-does-not-have-moral-right-to-host-end-of-wwii-celebrations.d?id=67143936.

[43] Sarah Rainsford, "Russian Court Orders Oldest Civil Rights Group Memorial to Shut," December 28, 2021, https://www.bbc.com/news/world-europe-59808624.

historian and Russia scholar Julie Fedor.[44] This bolsters the values of hierarchy, obedience, and punishment for dissent and political deviance. Putin has been heralded as a single-minded, vigilant, and incorruptible *chekist* patriot who is restoring Russia's internal order and international stature.

The "ideology of identity" has grown into a vital component of Putin's national populism, expressed in the concept of the "Russian World" (*Russkii mir*). This collectivist formula is both cultural and genetic and supposedly includes all Russian ethnics, Russian speakers, people that have lived in any Muscovite-controlled iteration of the state, and descendants of all these categories in any country. The term is underpinned by statist messianism, whereby the Russian government is obliged by history and divine fate to protect this broad community and defend it in particular against Western influences. The "Russian World" may be presented as multi-ethnic but it is undergirded by the leading role of the *Russkii* (ethnic Russian) people, language, and culture that unites (*sblizhenie*) and merges (*sliianie*) them.[45] Not surprisingly, claims of ethnic unity, linguistic dominance, and cultural supervision are deeply resented by non-Russians and help strengthen their national identities within the country and in neighboring states. The "Russian World" concept is a national-imperialist manifestation of "Soviet Man" (*Homo Sovieticus*). But just as distinct nations did not disappear and blend into an overarching Soviet identity, they evidently will not evaporate in the Russian equivalent.

---

[44] Julie Fedor, *Russia and the Cult of State Security: The Chekist Tradition, from Lenin to Putin,* London and New York: Routledge, 2013, p.130.

[45] Mikhail A. Alexseev, "Backing the USSR 2.0: Russia's Ethnic Minorities and Expansionist Ethnic Russian Nationalism," in Pål Kolstø and Helge Blakkisrud (Eds.), *The New Russian Nationalism: Imperialism, Ethnicity and Authoritarianism, 2000-15,* Edinburgh University Press, 2016, p.161.

Russia is depicted by state officials and Russian Orthodox Church leaders as the heart of Christian civilization or the "Third Rome," saving humanity from Western secularism, atheism, and liberalism. Justifications for the annexation of neighboring territories combine ethnic and religious constructs by coupling the notion of "Holy Russia" with that of the "Russian World" under Moscow's guidance. Claims that the Russian Orthodox Church is the direct inheritor of Byzantium after the latter fell to the Muslim Turks in the 15th century is another mendacious imperial construct. The oldest Slavic Orthodox Church is that of Bulgaria when Khan Boris I officially adopted Christianity in 865. Christianity was adopted in Kyivan Rus after the conversion of its ruler Volodymyr I in 988, following prolonged efforts of Greek and Bulgarian missionaries from the Byzantine Empire. The rulers of Moscow unilaterally claimed to be the inheritors of the Kyivan Church after the region's conquest by the Mongols in the 13th century, even though Moscow itself was a vassal of the Mongol empire and its imperial expansion as the Grand Duchy of Moscow only began in the late 15th century.

Despite the propagandistic claims of a communal Russian soul nurtured by the Church, Christian Orthodoxy is failing to provide an overarching ideology for national unity and state consolidation.[46] Church leaders do not view Russian Orthodoxy as an exclusively ethno-nationalist phenomenon but as a foundation of the "multinational Russian world" with universal values that other nations should emulate.[47] The influence of the Moscow Patriarchate

---

[46] Paul Goble, "'Orthodox Consensus' Collapsing in Russia, Uzlaner Says," November 29, 2020, http://windowoneurasia2.blogspot.com/2020/11/orthodox-consensus-collapsing-in-russia.html.

[47] Anastasia Mitrofanova, "Russian Ethnic Nationalism and Religion Today," in Pål Kolstø and Helge Blakkisrud (Eds.), *The New Russian Nationalism: Imperialism, Ethnicity and Authoritarianism, 2000-15*, Edinburgh University Press, 2016, p.111–112.

over the Kremlin has not significantly increased. On the contrary, the Orthodox Church has been transformed into a tactical and propaganda appendage of the Russian state both for domestic and foreign operations. Since the passage of the Yarovaya Law in July 2016, the state has used the Orthodox Church to expand its influence over society and to restrict the reach of other religions aside from the four classified as "traditional" (Orthodox Christianity, Islam, Judaism, and Buddhism), especially various Protestant denominations.[48] The Kremlin has mobilized the Church to justify its war against Ukraine and the seizure of Ukrainian territories and to denounce alleged "foreign agents" who are intent on undermining Russia's security and integrity. The Russian Orthodox Church itself has benefited from the curtailment of religious freedoms and denominational pluralism and the clericalization of national education.

Nonetheless, rifts are visible between the Church hierarchy and the more radical Russian ethno-nationalists who reject its alleged cosmopolitanism and collaboration with the Putin regime, which is viewed as "anti-Russian." Although "Russian" and "Orthodox" are often thought to be synonymous, the "Orthodox consensus" may be unravelling as a result of corruption and scandals within the Church and its perceived slavish obedience to the Kremlin. The alleged religious awakening among Russians has been exaggerated, as an increasing number of Russians reject the link between the nation and the official religion and in some cases the Orthodox Church has become a source of conflict among citizens, as witnessed during protests against building new churches in major cities.[49] The readiness of Russians to automatically identify as Orthodox is declining, and the

---

[48] Lincoln E. Flake, *Defending the Faith: The Russian Orthodox Church and the Demise of Religious Pluralism,* Verlag: Stuttgart, 2021, pp.5, 11, 227.

[49] "Activists Storm Yekaterinburg Russia Park in Protest Against New Church, May 15, 2019, www.bbc.com/news/world-europe-48276170.

Kremlin may no longer be able to fully count on the Church to strengthen "national unity" in the service of the state.

Ethnic-Russian xenophobia, anti-Semitism, and nationalism has been on the rise, especially during the pandemic, which intensified social tensions. In a Levada Center poll in the summer of 2020, a majority of Russians wanted to organize the country on the basis of "Russia for the Russians."[50] Anti-Caucasus racism is a major ingredient in Russian ethno-nationalism and has even been espoused by anti-Putin democrats. During the 2011 anti-government protests, one of the major nationalist slogans was "Stop Feeding the Caucasus," underscoring support either for a system of apartheid or a full separation of the North Caucasus from Russia.[51] On occasion, officials have demonstrated that they tolerate or support ethno-Russian supremacists at the expense of other nations.[52] Such an approach will generate defensive nationalism among other ethnic groups. Many Russians want to go further than the new constitutional amendment declaring Russian to be the language of the "state-forming people" by specifying that ethnic Russians are the country's "state-forming nation." This has resonance from Soviet times, and the notion was resolutely condemned by the Bolsheviks as "Greater Russian chauvinism."

---

[50] "ксенофобия и национализм," September 23, 2020, https://www.levada.ru/2020/09/23/ksenofobiya-i-natsionalizm-2/.

[51] Julie Wilhelmsen, "Russian Governance of the North Caucasus: Dilemmas of Force and Inclusion," in Derek Averre and Kevork Oskanian (Ed), *Security, Society and the State in the Caucasus*, Routledge, 2019, p.48.

[52] Paul Goble, "Kremlin has No Problem with Poll Showing Majority Favors 'Russia for the Russians'," September 30, 2020, http://windowoneurasia2.blogspot.com/2020/09/kremlin-has-no-problem-with-poll.html.

An essential component of contemporary Russian state ideology are conspiracy narratives against external and internal enemies. These have been vastly magnified by the Putin regime in order to preserve its power.[53] As Western governments and intelligence services purportedly seek to fracture Russia and create US puppet states on its territory, the Kremlin is depicted as Russia's savior that ensures state security, social cohesion, and a unified national identity by eliminating dissent and opposition and challenging the West on different fronts. In effect, conspiracy myths are ideological weapons for explaining the world and promoting the current regime.

But despite its incessant propaganda barrage, the Putin administration has forfeited its monopoly over information and shaping public opinions. Fewer people, especially among the younger generation, watch or believe government-controlled television, and many dismiss it as "fake news." The internet and digital social communications have become more significant. This does not mean that young people are necessarily more democratic or liberal, but they are more exposed to a wide range of ideologies and political programs—from anarchism, radical leftism, and Bolshevism, through conservatism and liberalism, to fascism, white racism, and Nazism—and can be attracted to movements that blend themes from differing political belief systems. This makes future ideological developments and the loyalty of citizens less predictable for the state.

Persecuted Politics

Political failure can be measured by increasing authoritarianism and centralism in an effort to eliminate public dissent and organized opposition. Russia's state institutions, including parliaments and courts, do not protect the rights of ordinary citizens. They serve the

---

[53] Ilya Yablokov, *Fortress Russia: Conspiracy Theories in Post-Soviet Russia,* Cambridge, UK: Polity Press, 2018, pp.185-195.

interests of high officials, patronage networks, and Kremlin-connected businesses. The key mechanism of the authoritarian "power vertical" is the presidential administration, with a large executive staff that duplicates functions that are formally assigned by the constitution to the cabinet.[54] The Russian Constitution, adopted in 1993, provides the Russian President with strong powers to control all other branches of the administration. The government cabinet has minimal autonomy and mostly performs technical not political functions by implementing the decisions of the presidential inner circle.[55] Additionally, the President has direct control over several government agencies and can bypass the Prime Minister, particularly in the arenas of law enforcement, foreign policy and national security. The Security Council of the Russian Federation (*Sovet Bezopasnosti Rossiyskoy Federatsii*—SBRF) plays a major role in decision making and is composed of a small group of top government officials and heads of key security agencies; it is chaired by Putin.

The national parliament rubber stamps Kremlin policy decisions, as its members are emplaced through state-sponsored political parties, financial benefits and falsified elections. The state owns the major national businesses, particularly in the energy and resource sectors, and facilitates the corruption of officials and businessmen to maintain their loyalty. The central executive controls regional and local governments through appointments, inducements, and punishments. The Kremlin established the United Russia (*Yedinaya Rossiya*) party in December 2001 to counter any credible political opposition, to control the parliament, and to maintain an extensive political patronage system for loyalists across the country. However, the party's

---

[54] William M. Reisinger and Bryon J. Moraski, *The Regional Roots of Russia's Political Regime*, Ann Arbor: University of Michigan Press, 2017, p.14.

[55] Dmitry Travin, Vladimir Gel'man, Otar Marganiya, *The Russian Path: Ideas, Interests, Institutions, Illusions*, Stuttgart: Ibidem Verlag, 2020, p.202.

name also highlighted government anxieties about national disunity and political conflicts.

The justice system is similarly beholden to Kremlin interests and follows government instructions. State actors or pro-Kremlin businessmen control all major media outlets that disallow or censor any criticisms of government policy. Elections provide a veneer of public legitimacy and the appearance of democratic choice. Even the Soviet Union held elections as performance politics to demonstrate popular support; and in some Communist states, several minor loyalist parties were also allowed to function and participate in the balloting to create the appearance of pluralism. The Russian Federation has permitted several loyalist parties to take part in national and local elections and gain seats in the State *Duma,* the lower chamber of the parliament, which exerts no control over the executive and the presidential administration.

Putinist Palliatives

On December 31, 1999, KGB Colonel Vladimir Putin was appointed as acting President of the Russian Federation. In March 2000, he narrowly won a manipulated presidential election with 53 percent of the vote. Since that time, all national elections have been closely supervised by the Kremlin and the results increasingly falsified to stifle any challenges to Putin's rule. For instance, legislation stipulates that all elections be conducted according to party lists, and so independent candidates and parties are routinely disqualified, while non-partisan oversight of elections is prohibited. Such measures indicate that officials are fearful that non-systemic opposition parties may receive significant public backing. However, by banning independent parties and candidates, the regime increases its own uncertainties and fears about the real extent of public support and opposition.[56] In the *Duma* elections of September 18, 2016, opposition parties registered little impact, with United Russia officially gaining 54 percent of the vote and 343 seats in the 450-seat chamber. At that time, Putin and United Russia were still benefiting from significant popular approval for the annexation of Crimea from Ukraine in February–March 2014, which they had depicted as the return of Russian territory.

Hundreds of citizens are barred from standing for political office on the basis of numerous exclusionary laws. Genuine opposition parties and movements are hounded by the regime. Independent civic initiatives are discouraged and repressed in case they prepare the organizational basis for future large-scale public protests. To shelter the ruling clique from concerted opposition, Russian courts have deployed the concept of "extremism" to include almost any expression or activity critical of the regime. The law "On Countering Extremist Activities," first adopted in July 2002 and amended on several occasions affirms the vague notion of "undermining" the security of the Russian Federation or violating its territorial integrity.[57] It is used to persecute independent activists, journalists, and scholars, and it bans Putin critics from appearing in the mass media.

Such repressive measures have convinced some analysts that a new totalitarianism is descending upon Russia. A 2015 law expanded criminal punishment for membership in "extremist" or "undesirable" organizations, and over 30 groups were initially banned, including Open Russia, funded by the exiled Russian oppositionist Mikhail Khodorkovsky. Another law, introduced in December 2019, required

---

[56] Regina Smyth, *Elections, Protest, and Authoritarian Regime Stability: Russia 2008-2020*, Cambridge University Press, 2021, p.32.

[57] Andrei A. Kovalev, *Russia's Dead End: An Insider's Testimony from Gorbachev to Putin*, Potomac Books/ University of Nebraska Press, 2017, pp.221–222.

all non-governmental organizations (NGO) receiving outside funding to register as "foreign agents," implying that they were "fifth columnists" operating against Russia's interests by engaging in espionage for foreign governments.[58] The regime uses "anti-extremism" measures to disguise its violation of civil liberties and punish dissent. State *Duma* deputies also introduced a bill in May 2021 to retroactively ban employees, volunteers, and donors of "extremist organizations" from running as election candidates.[59] Dozens of internet websites linked with the political opposition and with independent journalism were also blocked. Repressive measures on the eve of the September 2021 *Duma* elections, such as banning independent candidates and prohibiting public rallies, demonstrated the regime's fear of opposition and its inherent weakness, despite the fact that it controlled the majority of the media, all state resources, and the entire election process.

With Putin's popularity ratings in decline during 2019 and the ruling United Russia party widely despised, Kremlin strategists launched a sustained campaign against the anti-Putin opposition that had registered some successes in previous local elections. Independent candidates and non-systemic parties were severely hamstrung in competing with the ruling party and its surrogates in the September 2021 *Duma* elections. The official campaign against political opponents, human rights campaigners, NGO organizers, and independent journalists included obstructive legal requirements, police harassment and intimidation, imposition of fines, threats of

---

[58] "Russia's New 'Foreign Agent' Law, Explained," December 2, 2019, https://www.themoscowtimes.com/2019/12/02/russias-new-foreign-agent-law-explained-a68311.

[59] Igor Slabykh, "How the Russian Government Uses Anti-Extremism Laws to Fight Opponents," Institute of Modern Russia, June 4, 2021, https://imrussia.org/en/analysis/3291-how-the-russian-government-uses-anti-extremism-laws-to-fight-opponents.

imprisonment, punitive psychiatry, arrests, trials, maiming, and assassinations. In March 2019, Putin signed a new law that allows the punishment of individuals and online media for spreading "fake news" and information that "disrespects" the government, state symbols, the constitution, and government institutions.[60] The purpose was to protect Russian officials from corruption investigations and to demonstrate that the regime was above the law.

Another law, passed in December 2020, expanded the definition of "foreign agents" in existing legislation to cover individuals deemed to have received material or organizational support from overseas. They would henceforth be banned from holding municipal government positions and labeled as "foreign agents" in all official documents. More than 90 organizations were classified as "foreign agents" by the summer of 2021 and faced existential challenges. Several independent media outlets were closed down and their reporters hounded by the police. Thirty-four foreign organizations were listed as undesirable, half of which were American.[61] Lawyers defending independent activists were also threatened with the "foreign agent" label and could be held responsible for the views of those they defended and subjected to disbarment from practicing law.[62] Human rights groups launched

---

[60] Shannon Van Sant, "Russia Criminalizes The Spread Of Online News Which 'Disrespects' The Government," March 18, 2019, *NPR*, https://www.npr.org/2019/03/18/704600310/russia-criminalizes-the-spread-of-online-news-which-disrespects-the-government.

[61] Sabine Fischer, "Repression and Autocracy as Russia Heads into State Duma Elections," SWP Comment, No.40, June 2021, German Institute for International and Security Affairs, https://www.swp-berlin.org/publications/products/comments/2021C40_Russia_Duma_Elections.pdf?mc_cid=79336cb6eb&mc_eid=223d2dad2a.

[62] Paul Goble, "Kremlin Moves to Geld Lawyers, 'Last Line of Defense' Against Untrammeled State Rule," January 5, 2022, http://windowoneurasia2.blogspot.com/2022/01/kremlin-moves-to-geld-lawyers-last-line.html.

a campaign to abolish the "foreign agents" law and gathered hundreds of thousands of signatures on a petition declaring it as "discriminatory and unlawful."

Even according to official surveys, including the state-run pollster VCIOM, support for United Russia sank to under 30 percent on the eve of the September 2021 *Duma* elections, highlighting gross incompetence by the Kremlin in popularizing a party that is not permitted to have genuine competitors.[63] It also indicated that election rigging needed to be expanded in order for United Russia to obtain a two-thirds majority in parliament and pass major legislation. Although the permitted systemic opposition, such as the Liberal Democratic Party of Russia (LDPR) and the Communist Party of the Russian Federation (KPRF), benefited from the shortcomings of United Russia, they may experience increasing radicalization in seeking votes from citizens disillusioned with United Russia, while not all their representatives may be reliable Kremlin loyalists.

United Russia won 49.82 percent of the votes, the KPRF came second with 18.93 percent, the LDPR finished third with 7.55 percent, A Just Russia came in fourth with 7.46 percent, and New People fifth with 5.32 percent. Local observers estimate that about 15 million citizens who voted against constitutional reforms in the June–July 2020 referendum, designed to extend Putin's terms in office, and against the ruling party and its surrogates in the September 2021 *Duma* elections were left without any representatives in the legislature. This will compound political pressure on the regime, as

---

[63] "Третья волна накатилась: «Единая Россия» не видит проблемы в снижении рейтингов," July 3, 2021, https://www.kommersant.ru/doc/4887516.

dissatisfaction will accumulate and can find outlets in radicalism, xenophobia, and violence.[64]

Elections have also become an international public relations fiasco for Moscow. Even the Office for Democratic Institutions and Human Rights (ODHIR), a key agency of the Organization for Security and Cooperation in Europe (OSCE), of which Russia is a member, as well as the OSCE's Parliamentary Assembly, declined to send a mission to monitor the September 17–19, 2021 *Duma* balloting, complaining about the restrictions imposed on election observers in Russia.[65] This was the first time that ODHIR had boycotted Russia's regularly rigged elections since 1993.

Accusations of vote-rigging and other forms of fraud during all elections are pervasive in the country. If an incumbent party controlled by the Kremlin has to engage in obvious falsifications in order to win elections, then its aura of invincibility is evaporating.[66] The September 2021 elections were a hollow victory for United Russia. Even in the least democratic and competitive elections in post-Soviet history, the party lost approximately a fifth of its previous

---

[64] "Ставка на страх: Что случилось с нашей Госдумой: десять тезисов," *Novaya Gazeta*, September 21, 2021, https://novayagazeta.ru/articles/2021/09/21/stavka-na-strakh.

[65] "No OSCE Observers for Russian Parliamentary Elections Following Major Limitations, August 4, 2021, Organization for Security and Cooperation in Europe, https://www.osce.org/odihr/elections/russia/494488?utm_source=POLITICO.EU&utm_campaign=f5f3dae5a7-EMAIL_CAMPAIGN_2021_08_05_05_08&utm_medium=email&utm_term=0_10959edeb5-f5f3dae5a7-189069597.

[66] Donna Bahry, "Making Autocracy Work? Russian Regional Politics Under Putin," in William M. Reisinger (Ed.), *Russia's Regions and Comparative Subnational Politics*, London: Routledge, 2013, p.169.

support.[67] According to official results, its share of the vote decreased to 49.8 percent from 54.2 percent in the 2016 parliamentary elections, while support for the Communist Party grew from 13.3 percent to 18.9 percent. Navalny's "smart voting" strategy, for people to cast ballots for any credible candidates outside of United Russia, worked in some districts by helping to elect Communist candidates.[68] According to several independent analysts, without widespread falsifications, United Russia would have won less than 33 percent of the vote and lost numerous seats to the Communists and other permitted parties.

United Russia acquired 324 deputies in the 450-seat *Duma*, enabling it to unilaterally pass any laws or constitutional amendments requiring a two-thirds majority.[69] Four other parties obtained mandates, with the KPRF taking 57 seats. Communist Party members subsequently staged protests in Moscow, with party leaders charging that the regime engaged in mass electoral fraud. The protests were supported by some radical socialists and Navalny backers who voted for the KPRF as a protest vote against United Russia. Demonstrations against election fraud also took place in several regional capitals, including Yekaterinburg, Novosibirsk, Tyumen, Chita, Irkutsk and

---

[67] Центральная избирательная комиссия Российской Федерации, September 20, 2021, http://www.cikrf.ru/analog/ediny-den-golosovaniya-2021/p_itogi/.

[68] Paul Goble, "United Russia Won Less than a Third of the Vote and Not the Nearly Half Reported, Shpilkin Says," September 26, 2021, http://windowoneurasia2.blogspot.com/2021/09/united-russia-won-less-than-third-of.html.

[69] Pavel Felgenhauer, "Kremlin-Backed Forces Sweep Duma Elections," *Eurasia Daily Monitor*, Vol. 18, Issue 145, September 23, 2021, https://jamestown.org/program/kremlin-backed-forces-sweep-duma-elections/.

Khabarovsk.[70] The KPRF has been loyal to the Kremlin but has criticized the ruling kleptocracy in the economic arena by supporting the nationalization of banks and heavy industry. It also maintains an extensive regional presence that could prove beneficial in raising the party's profile in the event of power struggles around the Kremlin. Support for the party could also increase when living standards decline more precipitously due to the impact of international sanctions for Russia's invasion of Ukraine.

As an additional pressure valve to try and limit youth disaffection, the Kremlin allowed a new formation, the New People Party (NPP) into the State *Duma*.[71] The NPP received 5.32 percent of the vote and gained 13 seats. Officials calculated that a simple regurgitation of aging leaders would increase alienation and spur protests among young, democratic-minded voters with no parliamentary representation. However, the NPP was a camouflage for politicians that the Kremlin trusted. Its head, Alexei Nechayev, was involved in the leadership of the Putin-founded All-Russia People's Front and was the owner of the largest cosmetics company in Russia, Faberlic, which operates with state approval. The NPP was created by Putin's colleague and oligarch Yuri Kovalchuk.

Even according to some long-standing Putin sympathizers, Russia needs to deal with its numerous vulnerabilities before its adversaries are able to exploit them.[72] This would necessitate an elite overhaul that rewards merit and accountability rather than loyalty and passivity, "a

---

[70] "Протесты в регионах," September 28, 2021, sovross.ru/articles/2177/53827.

[71] Vadim Shtepa, "How New Are the 'New People' in Russia's Parliament?" *Eurasia Daily Monitor*, Vol. 18, Issue 152, October 6, 2021, https://jamestown.org/program/how-new-are-the-new-people-in-russias-parliament/.

[72] Dmitry Trenin, "Biden's Approach to US Allies and Adversaries Will Challenge Russia," November 27, 2020, https://carnegie.ru/commentary/83336.

serious audit of domestic policies," and "a foreign policy audit based on a public consensus on national interests." However, pro-Kremlin observers believe there is little prospect for Russia's vulnerabilities to be "repaired internally before they are exploited from the outside." Elite institutions such as the security services, business networks, and state bureaucracies have solidified into privileged nepotistic castes and are increasingly alienated from ordinary citizens.

Repressive Weakness

Government weakness can be assessed by the degree of repression the state needs to impose in order to keep the open opposition in check and the public quiescent. In contemporary Russia, the regime is either incapable of applying the kind of extensive and intensive repression visible in Communist times, especially during Stalin's rule, or it calculates that comprehensive mass repression will rebound against it by severely damaging economic performance, alienating ever-larger sectors of the population, further isolating Moscow on the international arena, and potentially provoking violent unrest. As a result, the Kremlin endeavors to engage in a sufficient measure of repression with the threat of escalation in order to terrorize the population, stifle large-scale opposition, and ensure regime control. The ratcheting up of repressive measures in recent years indicates that the government may be failing in its ability to comprehensively pacify the public without enforcing a more extensive crackdown and prohibiting all autonomous public activism.

Since the waves of mass protests under the slogan "For Fair Elections" in December 2011, involving tens of thousands of citizens outraged at the defrauded *Duma* elections, targeted repression has become the primary tool for preserving the Putin regime. The protests included a heterogeneous population the Kremlin tried to depict as a primarily "middle class" phenomenon alienated from the mass of ordinary citizens.[73] But despite official accounts that the rallies were simply centered in Moscow and St. Petersburg, in reality protest actions took place in at least 80 federal subjects and over 100 cities.

The Federal Security Service (*Federalnaya Sluzhba Bezopasnosti*—FSB) has played a major role in domestic repression after being resurrected from the former Communist-era KGB and steadily permeated all spheres of public life.[74] In 2004, Putin extended its powers by disabling any institutional supervision over its activities and transforming it into a self-governing structure answerable only to the presidential administration. The appointment of commanding positions in all *siloviki* (power ministry) structures, including the FSB, in each region of the country is decided by the Kremlin. [75] The main task of the FSB is to protect the regime from foreign and domestic political threats, but it also controls several state institutions, including the law enforcement apparatus, and can exert substantial pressure on the justice system. Members of Putin's inner circle manage various FSB sections, including Security Council Secretary Nikolai Patrushev, Rosneft Chief Executive Officer Igor Sechin, Gazprom Chairperson Viktor Zubkov, and former Security Council member Sergei Ivanov. They use the FSB to advance their political ambitions and economic interests based on an extensive network of cronyism and corruption.

---

[73] Mischa Gabowitsch, *Protest in Putin's Russia,* Malden, MA: Polity Press, 2017, pp.27, 32–33.

[74] Atlantic Council, Dossier Center, "Lubyanka Federation: How the FSB Determines the Politics and Economics of Russia," October 2020, https://www.atlanticcouncil.org/in-depth-research-reports/report/lubyanka-federation/.

[75] The Russian term "*siloviki*" also refers to the personnel who work at the power ministries.

The Kremlin has organized the murders of several prominent opposition organizers and investigative journalists, including Boris Nemtsov and Anna Politkovskaya, as well as defectors from the intelligence services such as Alexander Litvinenko.[76] It uses an assortment of security agencies to silence and eliminate opposition. Nonetheless, political murders, attempted assassinations, and other forms of state repression betray the Kremlin's weakness. To remove any viable alternatives to Putin's rule though outright murder indicates that officials in the presidential administration calculate that his authority may be fragile because his political survival is constantly under threat.[77] According to the Memorial human rights center in Moscow, the number of known political prisoners continues to grow and reached 420 by October 2021, though the real figure could be several times higher, and increased again after the February 2022 invasion of Ukraine.[78]

Under former President Boris Yeltsin, Russia had a competitive and vibrant media, although key outlets were owned by powerful oligarchs, such as Boris Berezovsky and Vladimir Gusinsky. After claiming the presidency in 1999, one of Putin's first priorities was to seize control of the major media, including TV channels and leading newspapers. Some of the most effective journalists exposing corruption and other abuses of office at the highest political levels were harassed, beaten, or murdered. Government anxieties about

---

[76] "The Putin Critics Who Have Been Assassinated," March 3, 2015, https://news.sky.com/story/the-putin-critics-who-have-been-assassinated-10369350.

[77] Private interview with Valery Dzutsev, Radio Free Europe/ Radio Liberty, March 2021.

[78] "в преддверии дня памяти жертв политических репрессий «мемориал» публикует новые списки политзаключённых," October 27, 2021, https://memohrc.org/ru/news_old/v-preddverii-dnya-pamyati-zhertv-politicheskih-repressiy-memorial-publikuet-novye-spiski.

maintaining public trust and its fear of independent opinion is evident in efforts to dominate the media space. It controls all national television networks and the majority of radio and print outlets, whether directly or through pro-government oligarchs. Only a handful of independent outlets still operate, mostly online or headquartered abroad, and the remnants are hounded and face imminent closure. State-managed media are expected to glorify Putin, demonize the opposition, and attack the West.

As all media outlets are perceived as a potential threat to the stability of the state, the goal of the regime is to restrict public access to independent information and to feed citizens with propaganda, half-truths, and outright disinformation to deflect attention from government incompetence and failure. During 2021, the authorities intensified their attacks on independent investigative media outfits, which were labeled as "undesirable" or as "foreign agents."[79] The aim was to suppress any revelations about official corruption ahead of the September 2021 *Duma* elections. The regime has also restricted the share of foreign ownership of the media, pressured journalists into exile, forced anonymous bloggers to register with the authorities, and published a list of topics mostly related to the military that are prohibited to journalists.[80] The remaining independent outlets were pressured to close in the wake of the February 2022 military invasion of Ukraine, which the government tried to present as a limited operation and not a full-scale war and sought to censor all accurate reporting on the conflict.

---

[79] "How Do Russia's 'Undesirable Organizations' and 'Foreign Agents' Laws Work?" https://www.themoscowtimes.com/2021/07/16/how-do-russias-undesirable-organizations-and-foreign-agents-laws-work-a74547.

[80] Veera Laine and Jussi Lassila, "Internet and Media Repression in Russia: Avoiding the Complicity of Western Actors," Finnish Institute of International Affairs, *Briefing Paper* 320, November 2021, https://www.fiia.fi/en/publication/internet-and-media-repression-in-russia.

Officials have also increased pressure on Russian internet operators. In March 2019, thousands of activists rallied across the country against a new censorship law, the "sovereign internet" bill, designed to increase state control over the internet, and several dozen people were arrested.[81] One of the organizers of the protests was the *Roskomsvoboda* movement or the Russian Freedom Committee. The Sovereign Internet Law came into force in November 2019, and it obliges internet operators to connect to the National Domain Name System, which in turn makes it easier for the authorities to close banned sites. Although television remains the main source of information for a majority of citizens, young people increasingly rely on web and social media platforms, indicating that the regime is losing its propaganda and information monopoly.

Moscow has passed legislation giving the government greater control over the internet infrastructure, including a law permitting officials to monitor all internet traffic and establish an alternative internet system, enabling the Kremlin to disconnect Russia from the global internet.[82] The authorities have ratcheted up pressure and imposed fines on social media platforms, including Google, Facebook and Twitter, and accused them of failing to remove content that undermines the Russian state. They also demand that foreign tech companies store the personal data of Russian citizens on servers in Russia, threatening them with bans if they fail to comply. In preparation for a potential domestic crisis and mounting public turmoil, the Kremlin is prepared to disconnect the country from the

---

[81] "Russians Rally For Internet Freedom," *Radio Free Europe/ Radio Liberty,* March 10, 2019, https://www.rferl.org/a/russians-rally-against-moves-to-tighten-the-screws-on-internet-freedom/29813172.html.

[82] "Putin Signs 'Sovereign Internet Law, Expanding Government Control of Internet," Radio Free Europe/Radio Liberty, May 1, 2019. https://www.rferl.org/a/putin-signs-sovereign-internet-law- expanding-government-control-of-internet/29915008.html.

global internet or to implement a partial or complete shutdown to limit communications between protestors. After enforcing the "sovereign internet law" in November 2019, officials stated that they planned to establish a domestic internet that does not rely on any infrastructure or resources located outside the state. In July 2021, Moscow announced that it had successfully tested severing Russia from the internet and routing online traffic within the country through chokepoints for purposes of better surveillance of internet users. However, Russia cannot both disconnect from the global internet and still be able to use all of the online services and access websites hosted in other countries.[83] Such a move to undercut domestic unrest would further isolate the state.

The authorities have essentially banned all public protests, fearing that Russian citizens would be willing to participate in response to economic stagnation, glaring material inequalities, growing social stratification, elite nepotism, and systematic corruption. Nonetheless, mass protests continue to erupt, as during the July–August 2019 rallies of some 60,000 people in support of fair elections that were violently dispersed by the police.[84] During demonstrations against the arrest of anti-corruption campaigner Alexei Navalny in January and February 2021, tens of thousands of protestors rallied in dozens of cities and some 17,600 were arrested. The protests were coordinated online and featured several political demands including an end to corruption, competitive elections, and the termination of the Putin regime. Several anti-war rallies were staged in opposition to the war

---

[83] Josephine Wolff, "Russia's Nonsensical, Impossible Quest to Create Its Own Domestic Internet," July 27, 2021, https://slate.com/technology/2021/07/russia-sovereign-internet-disconnection-test.html.

[84] Regina Smyth, *Elections, Protest, and Authoritarian Regime Stability: Russia 2008-2020*, Cambridge University Press, 2021, pp.208–209.

in Ukraine in February 2022 but the government undertook a major clampdown on any public protests.

Even with a limited initial agenda, protest movements can quickly develop far-reaching political demands. However, without consistently large numbers of protestors and a broader multi-class base, particularly blue-collar workers, public support for such actions may periodically decline, at least until new triggers materialize.[85] Russian society may not have psychologically matured as yet to the Ukrainian level, with a willingness to stage a prolonged popular revolution.[86] This is due to the much greater and more constant pressure on protestors, including beatings, arrests, criminal cases, dismissals, and expulsions from work or universities. The authorities also prohibit peaceful civil assemblies to devise alternative political programs, such as the Novgorod meeting of the Zemtsvo Congress in May 2021. But this can drive opposition underground and even radicalize some activists. Public gatherings are severely restricted in order to deter street demonstrations against the regime that could gain broader traction.

Transient Personality Cult

The Kremlin has cultivated a Putin personality cult, in which he is depicted as the savior of the Russian state and the paramount leader of the Russian nation. In many respects, regime legitimacy is less important under Putinism than the personalization of national unity under the indispensable leader. According to the Kremlin narrative, democracy and decentralization leads to chaos and state

---

[85] Private interview with Maria Snegovaya, George Washington University, March 2021.

[86] Private interview with Vadim Shtepa, Editor in Chief, Region.Expert, Tallinn, March 2021.

disintegration, while only dictatorship, masked as "managed democracy," can save the country. Putin is praised as the embodiment of order and discipline who is rebuilding a powerful Russian state, thus acknowledging a persistent obsession with regime collapse and state fracture.

High officials depend on Putin to provide policy direction, with input restricted to a narrow circle of advisors while the role of formal institutions remains limited.[87] The personalization of leadership is also intended to disguise any potential policy differences and factional cleavages in the administration that could precipitate open power struggles, embolden public protests, or provide inroads for Western governments. Moreover, Putin's cult deflects any blame for policy failures or economic difficulties on to state or local officials, bureaucrats, or business owners, thus elevating the President to the position of a benevolent Tsar surrounded by incompetent *boyars* (nobles) whose mistakes Putin has to correct.

Russia has failed to develop a stable method of presidential succession that would enable a predictable transition of power. Personalistic authoritarian regimes are especially ill-equipped to avoid a succession crisis and are prone to intra-elite rivalries. And the longer an autocrat remains in power, the more problematic is the transition to a new leader. Russia will increasingly experience competition among members of the President's inner circle as economic and social problems accumulate. All this can culminate in purges and showdowns.

The drive to prolong Putin's rule has included constitutional amendments that will enable him to remain as President until 2036 by serving two additional six-year terms after his current mandate

---

[87] William M. Reisinger and Bryon J. Moraski, *The Regional Roots of Russia's Political Regime,* Ann Arbor: University of Michigan Press, 2017, p.48.

expires in 2024. Officials claimed that changing the constitution to prolong the incumbent's term will prevent factions within the Kremlin from vying for power and potentially destabilizing the state. The constitutional alterations were approved in a rigged national referendum in June–July 2020. The Central Election Commission reported that almost 78 percent voted in favor of the amendments, with a turnout of over 65 percent.[88] As with all Russian ballots, numerous charges of fraud were recorded. Over a third of Muscovites and over a quarter of the residents of 41 federal regions cast ballots against the amendments, while the electorate of the Nenets Autonomous *Okrug* rejected it outright by over 55 percent of the vote. Regardless of the weak extent of support for the measures, the constitutional changes were signed into law in April 2021.

Some analysts detect a correlation between a decline in Putin's approval ratings and intensified repression.[89] To protect the incumbent in office, the Federal Service of the Troops of National Guard of the Russian Federation (*Federalnaya Sluzhba Voysk Natsionalnoy Gvardii Rossiyskoy Federatsii)* or *Rosgvardiya* was established in 2016 as an internal military force that reports directly to the Russian President and is separate from the military and other security units. Its stated mission is to secure Russia's borders, control gun ownership, combat terrorism and organized crime, protect public order, and guard important state facilities. In essence, *Rosgvardiya* was designed to protect the Putin regime from mass protests and civic

---

[88] Central Election Commission of the Russian Federation, http://cikrf.ru/eng/.

[89] Kathryn E. Stoner, *Russia Resurrected: Its Power and Purpose in a New Global Order*, Oxford University Press, 2021, p.249.

unrest. By early 2021, it numbered 430,000 members, more than the country's land forces or any internal security agency.[90]

Officially managed public poll ratings are closely monitored by the political elites.[91] After the Crimean *Anschluss* in 2014, support for Putin increased because he was viewed as restoring lost territories to the Russian state. Since those euphoric days, such approval has precipitously declined even according to officially endorsed data-gathering agencies, including the Russian Public Opinion Research Center (VTsIOM). Putin has steadily lost popularity as the political system itself has shed public legitimacy. According to some independent polls conducted in 2019, 60 percent of citizens wanted drastic change in the country.[92] In an opinion poll released by the reputable Levada Center in February 2021, more Russian citizens voiced opposition to Putin's re-election than at any other point since the 2014 annexation of Crimea. Forty-one percent of respondents said they would not favor Putin remaining as President beyond 2024, while 48 percent claimed they would.[93] By October 2021, the anti-Putin

---

[90] "Опричники Путина. Андрей Мальгин - о парнях с дубинками," February 1, 2021, https://www.svoboda.org/a/31078963.html.

[91] John Tefft, "Understanding the Factors That Will Impact the Succession to Vladimir Putin as Russian President," July 2020, https://www.rand.org/pubs/perspectives/PE349.html.

[92] "Левада» и Московский центр Карнеги: 59% россиян хотят «решительных перемен» в стране," November 6, 2019, https://meduza.io/news/2019/11/06/levada-i-moskovskiy-tsentr-karnegi-59-rossiyan-hotyat-reshitelnyh-peremen-v-strane.

[93] "отношение к новому сроку владимира путина," February 26, 2021, https://www.levada.ru/2021/02/26/otnoshenie-k-novomu-sroku-vladimira-putina/.

figure grew to 42 percent—the highest since 2013.[94] A Levada poll issued in December 2021 showed that the number of Russians willing to vote for Putin had sunk to a record low of 32 percent.[95]

Putin's favorability ratings significantly declined in the fall of 2021 during weeks of record COVID-19 infections and deaths. Approval for his job performance dropped to 63 percent in November 2021, from 67 percent in October 2021.[96] Although official polls indicated that support for Putin surged following the large-scale military intervention in Ukraine in February 2022, the validity of polling in a climate of growing fear, tighter repression, and bellicose propaganda remained highly suspect.[97] The results served regime interests to present a united front against the West. Public support for regional leaders had also fallen to 57 percent in November 2021 in surveys conducted in 50 regions. Only 46 percent of respondents believed that Russia was moving in the "right direction," while 44 percent expressed the opposite opinion. The Kremlin remained cognizant that much of the public support claimed for Putin's regime was shallow and unreliable and could rapidly disappear. Citizens may increasingly challenge the notion that authoritarianism is more effective in

---

[94] Levada Center, October 11, 2021, https://www.levada.ru/2021/10/11/vladimir-putin-10/.

[95] "электоральные рейтинги партий и президента," December 9, 2021, https://www.levada.ru/2021/12/09/elektoralnye-rejtingi-partij-i-prezidenta/.

[96] "Putin's Approval Drops Amid Covid Surge, Partial Lockdown – Poll," *The Moscow Times*, December 2, 2021, https://www.themoscowtimes.com/2021/12/02/putins-approval-drops-amid-covid-surge-partial-lockdown-poll-a75720.

[97] Mike Eckel, "Polls Show Russians Support Putin And The War On Ukraine. Really?" April 4, 2022,

https://www.rferl.org/a/russia-support-ukraine-war-polls-putin/31791423.html

developing the economy compared to pluralism and local democracy or that Russia is destined to have an autocratic leader.

Demographic Defects

Although the Russian Federation does not face outright "demographic collapse," population trends will shorten the country's longevity in its current state form. These negative trends include a steadily shrinking ethnic-Russian population; a growing non-Russian and Muslim population; a substantial decline of ethnic Russians in the majority of ethnic republics; growing population and economic disparities between inner Russia and Moscow's Siberian, Arctic and Far Eastern possessions; a decreasing level of in-migration by Russians from neighboring states; stark population differences between large metropolises and smaller cities, towns and villages; the reduction in the working labor pool; a steadily aging population; consistently high mortality rates and low birth rates; the high outflow of well-educated and productive citizens; and declining health care and other social services that shorten lifespans and undermine growth. In addition to rural depopulation, medium-sized cities are also experiencing major outflows, as factories close and social services decline. Migrants tend to gravitate to Moscow, St. Petersburg, and other larger cities, leaving huge disparities between Inner Russia and much of the rest of the country.

Russia's population has stagnated and steadily declined from the 147.4 million recorded in the last Soviet census of 1989. The 2002 census showed a resident population of 145.1 million, and this total fell to 142.9 million, according to the 2010 census.[98] The numbers subsequently increased primarily because of the in-migration of

[98] https://eng.rosstat.gov.ru/storage/document_news/2020/02-11/2n4LMtDM/sensus%20(1).pdf.

ethnic Russians from neighboring states, but the pool of newcomers dwindled within a few years. In addition, low birthrates in the 1990s ensured a smaller number of women of childbearing age in the current decade, and this negative loop will continue into the foreseeable future.

Regularly published data indicates that the population continues to fall. According to the State Statistical Service (*Rosstat*), Russia's population stood at 146.24 million in January 2021, down from 146.75 million the previous year—a 15-year record of decline.[99] This constituted the highest natural population downturn in 11 years. In October 2021, *Rosstat* reported that the population decline, measured by the number of deaths over the number of births, increased by 71.6 percent year-on-year for the period from January to August 2021. The fall in population amounted to 595,300 people, after reaching 346,900 the previous year. *Rosstat* estimated that the country's population in August 2021 stood at 145.8 million.[100] *Rosstat* also predicted that deaths will continue to outnumber live births over the next 15 years and in one worst-case scenario, the population would fall to 134.2 million during that time and immigration will plummet. Some international agencies even estimate that the total population of the Russian Federation will fall to around 128 million by 2050.[101] The 2020

---

[99] Kester Ken Klomegah, "Moment of Truth: Russia Faces Demography Crisis," *Modern Diplomacy*, February 3, 2021, https://moderndiplomacy.eu/2021/02/03/moment-of-truth-russia-faces-demography-crisis/ and https://rosstat.gov.ru/folder/12781 and "Russia's Population Decline Hits 15-Year High – Preliminary Data," *The Moscow Times*, January 28, 2021, https://www.themoscowtimes.com/2021/01/28/russias-population-decline-hits-15-year-high-preliminary-data-a72768.

[100] "Естественная убыль населения РФ за январь-август выросла на 72%," October 8, 2021, https://www.interfax.ru/russia/796151.

[101] World Population Review, "Russia Population 2022," July 1, 2022, https://worldpopulationreview.com/countries/russia-population.

Russian census was held in October–November 2021, with final results expected in the fourth quarter of 2022. However, the census could prove less illuminating than previous ones because many citizens reportedly did not participate as they remain deeply distrustful of state representatives and official questionnaires.

According to detailed World Health Organization (WHO) data from 2018, life expectancy among Russian males stood at 66.4 years, placing Russia 125th in world global rankings and about 10 years less than the norm in industrialized states such as the US.[102] The main causes of premature deaths are inadequate health services, especially in smaller cities and rural areas, that could detect preventable illnesses. The HIV/AIDS pandemic remains rampant in Russia, with rates of infection matching those in the poorest countries of sub-Saharan Africa amidst inadequate treatment and social stigma. During the COVID-19 pandemic, Russia was expected to experience its biggest population drop since 2006, accelerated by a high number of deaths attributed to coronavirus infections. The government projected a net decrease of 1.2 million people between 2020 and 2024.[103] The Public health crisis will be exacerbated by the war in Ukraine if Russian military casualties continue to mount and Western sanctions intensify. They will be reflected in lessened availability of medications, growing abuse of alcohol and illicit drugs by veterans, and an increase in criminality and gun possession.

The number of pensioners has been growing rapidly over the past decade, and by 2030 they will form almost 29 percent of the population. Between 2018 and 2024, the figure will increase from 37.6

---

[102] World Health Rankings, "Health Profile: Russia," July 14, 2022, https://www.worldlifeexpectancy.com/country-health-profile/russia.

[103] "Правительство резко ухудшило прогноз по убыли населения России," October 15, 2020, https://www.rbc.ru/economics/15/10/2020/5f8846b39a7947323dcb06c5.

million to 40.8 million, even as the total population of Russia declines.[104] This will place additional strain on the government budget. Such depopulation, in which deaths consistently exceed births, creates a vicious circle of economic decline because an aging population intensifies the burdens on a shrinking labor pool, while the birth rate will not rise significantly because people do not want children in a stagnant economy. With extremely low birth rates in the 1990s, the labor market already faced a shortage of young workers. The number of working-age Russians declined from 85.4 million in 2015 to 81.3 million in 2019, while the inflow of migrant workers has been slowing down.[105] The growing labor shortages have also highlighted the bloated size of the unproductive internal security forces, which employ over 5 million men of working age, or between 15 and 20 percent of Russia's total, and are a major drain on economic productivity.[106]

Between 2018 and 2020, only 4 federal subjects (Chechnya, Ingushetia, Dagestan and Tuva) recorded more births than deaths, and in 44 regions the populations declined despite in-migration.[107] Predominantly Russian *krais* and *oblasts* witnessed the sharpest population drop, and the process was reinforced by outmigration

---

[104] Paul Goble, "Almost a Third of Russians Will Be Elderly by 2030, Forcing Moscow to Change Course," April 11, 2021, http://windowoneurasia2.blogspot.com/2021/04/almost-third-of-russians-will-be.html.

[105] http://www.gks.ru/free_doc/new_site/population/demo/progn3.xls.

[106] "Павел Пряников. Главная проблема России, которая мало кого пока волнует," November 23, 3021, publizist.ru/blogs/117734/41387/-.

[107] "Только в Чечне, Ингушетии, Дагестане и Тыве население увеличилось за счет рождаемости," April 5, 2021, https://capost.media/views/tolko-v-chechne-ingushetii-dagestane-i-tyve-naselenie-uvelichilos-za-schet-rozhdaemosti/.

often to European regions together with the abandonment of over 300 neglected "company towns" (*monogorody*), many of them in the Urals, based on a single and often declining industry.[108] Although the government has provided aid and encouraged private companies to operate in single-industry towns, this has not stemmed the outflow of residents. Former workers frequently move to the larger cities, where they further strain the decaying social services. Russian government projections indicate that ethnic Russians are decreasing in numbers faster than the population as a whole.[109] Federal subjects with clear ethnic Russian majorities demonstrate a more consistent decline than Muslim-majority areas such as the North Caucasus and the Middle Volga or the Buddhist republics and indigenous Siberian regions.

The population gap between European Russia and its northern and eastern possessions continues to widen. In the starkest example of depopulation, the Far Eastern Federal District, inhabited mostly by ethnic Russians, has faced a demographic crisis by losing almost 23 percent of its population between 1990 and 2014 as a result of high

---

108 Paul Goble, "Russia's One-Industry Towns Continue on the Road to Collapse," May 18, 2016, https://windowoneurasia2.blogspot.com/2016/05/russias-one-industry-towns-continue-on.html

and "Moscow's Billion-Dollar Program to Save Company Towns has Failed Completely," June 27, 2019,

https://windowoneurasia2.blogspot.com/2019/06/moscows-billion-dollar-program-to-save.html.

109 Paul Goble, "Ethnic Russians Declining in Size Faster than Russian Federation Population as a Whole," October 21, 2020, http://windowoneurasia2.blogspot.com/2020/10/ethnic-russians-declining-in-size.html.

death rates, low birth rates and increasing out-migration.[110] According to the 2010 census, the population stood at 8.3 million people but was estimated at only 6.2 million by 2020.[111] Even more seriously for Russia's territorial cohesion is the dramatic decline of Russian ethnics in the majority of non-Russian republics. This has been most stark in the North Caucasus, where the major cities are predominantly non-Russian and the region's links with the rest of the Russian Federation continue to loosen.

In Russia as a whole, official statistics show about 15 million people to be of Muslim background, accounting for 11 percent of the population, and their proportion will reach between a third and a half of the country's total by 2050.[112] Moscow has the largest Muslim population of all European cities, estimated at 1 million residents and 1.5 million migrant workers. The migrant population from Central Asia whose members decide to stay permanently in Russia will also contribute to a proportionate decline of Russian ethnics and could become a more prominent economic and political factor in the country's division and disruption.

During Putin's presidency, since 2000, more than two million Russian citizens have emigrated, mostly to the West.[113] The majority are young

---

110 Rensselaer Lee and Artyom Lukin, *Russia's Far East: New Dynamics in Asia Pacific and Beyond*, Boulder, London: Lynne Rienner Publishers, p.8.

111 https://rusmania.com/far-eastern.

112 Marlène Laruelle, "How Islam Will Change Russia," in S. Enders Wimbush and Elizabeth M. Portale (Eds), *Russia in Decline*, Jamestown Foundation, March 2017, p.225.

113 "The Putin Exodus: The New Russian Brain Drain," Atlantic Council Eurasia Center, February 19, 2019, https://www.atlanticcouncil.org/in-depth-research-reports/report/the- putin-exodus-the-new-russian-brain-drain-3.

and highly educated and qualified professionals, with more people likely to leave when pandemic restrictions are fully lifted. Since the start of Russia's war against Ukraine in February 2022, tens of thousands of IT professionals and small business owners have fled the country. Population decline in key social sectors has a deleterious impact on the labor market and on the pool of military recruits. In an independent poll conducted across 50 regions of Russia in May 2021, the percentage of citizens wanting to emigrate reached its highest level since 2013.[114] One out of five respondents asserted they would "absolutely" or "most likely" seek to emigrate. Younger citizens were twice as willing to emigrate than older people. Nearly half of those aged 18–24 and one-third of those aged 25–39 wanted to leave Russia, compared with one in five of those aged 40–54 and less than 10 percent of those 55 and older.

Economic Decay

Following significant growth in the 2000s, propelled mostly by high energy revenues, Russia has displayed prolonged economic decay with short-term cycles of recovery. The country's Gross Domestic Product (GDP) of $1.5 trillion is comparable to that of Italy if calculated by market exchange rates; this rises to over $4 trillion if purchasing power parity is included. Russia can thereby claim to be the world's sixth-largest economy but certainly not a superpower, as it is increasingly dwarfed by the US, China and the EU. The country generates just over 3 percent of global GDP, compared to about 18 percent by the US and 16 percent by China.[115] Economic performance

---

[114] "эмиграция," June 9, 2021, Levada Center, Moscow, Russia, https://www.levada.ru/2021/06/09/emigratsiya-2/.

[115] Kathryn E. Stoner, *Russia Resurrected: Its Power and Purpose in a New Global Order,* Oxford University Press, 2021, p.130.

itself does not determine strategic ambitions or short-term capabilities, but it will impact on domestic conditions if the regime overstretches and miscalculates its potential. As a major exporter of crude oil and natural gas, together with assorted minerals and metals, its performance remains highly sensitive to significant swings in world commodity prices.[116]

During 2020, Russia's economy shrank by about 3 percent in the midst of the global COVID-19 pandemic. Although growth was restored during the second half of 2021, future projections highlight deep-rooted structural weaknesses. According to state statistics, Russia's economy rebounded in the summer of 2021, with a projected GDP growth of 3.8 percent for 2021 fueled by higher consumer demand and a rise in oil prices.[117] Prior to Russia's large-scale invasion of Ukraine, the World Bank forecasted a lower GDP growth of 3.2 percent in 2021, 3.2 percent in 2022, and only 2.3 percent in 2023.[118] In the wake of extensive Western economic sanctions imposed after Russia's invasion of Ukraine in February 2022, Russia's GDP was projected to fall by at least 15 percent by the end of the year amidst a prolonged recession.[119]

---

[116] The World Bank, World Development Indicators, 2012-2020, https://databank.worldbank.org/reports.aspx?source=2&series=NY.GDP.MKTP.CD&country=# and "The Top 25 Economies in the World," December 24, 2020, https://www.investopedia.com/insights/worlds-top-economies/#citation-92.

[117] Ben Aris, "Moscow Blog: Russia in July," *Johnson's Russia List 2021*-#145, July 20, 2021, https://intellinews.com/moscow-blog-russia-in-july-215896/?source=blogs.

[118] World Bank: 45th Issue of the Russia Economic Report, May 26, 2021, https://www.worldbank.org/en/country/russia/publication/rer.

[119] Reuters, "Four Weeks of War Scar Russia's Economy, March 25, 2022, https://www.reuters.com/world/europe/four-weeks-war-scar-russias-economy-2022-03-24/

Indicating the degree of volatility in Russia's macro-economic future, pre-war estimates underscored that Russia's economy was undergoing long-term stagnation with GDP growth expected to average close to 1.5 percent over the coming years.[120] The country will gradually fall behind the rest of the economically developed world. According to World Bank statistics from 2019, Russia's GDP per capita ranked 60th in the world.[121] In International Monetary Fund (IMF) projections, by 2025 the GDP per capita of the Russian population will fall significantly and the growth of Russia's economy until 2025 will be only half of the world average of 5.2 percent.[122] According to some economists, Western economic sanctions applied since the 2014 invasion of Ukraine have contributed to economic decay by slashing foreign credits and foreign direct investment, so that the economy has only grown by an average of 0.3 percent per year, while the global average was 2.3 percent.[123] The much more onerous financial and economic sanctions imposed after February 2022 will damage the Russian economy even more severely and precipitate a long-term recession.

---

[120] International Monetary Fund, World Economic Outlook, https://www.imf.org/en/Publications/WEO/Issues/2019/03/28/world-economic-outlook-april-2019; World Bank Russia Economic Report, June 2019, https://openknowledge.worldbank.org/handle/10986/31933.

[121] The World Bank, "GDP per Capita, PPP," https://data.worldbank.org/indicator/NY.GDP.PCAP.PP.CD?most_recent_value_desc=true.

[122] "МВФ: Через 5 лет уровень жизни в России будет как в Туркмении," October 28, 2020, https://ehorussia.com/new/node/22011.

[123] Anders Åslund and Maria Snegovaya, "The Impact of Western Sanctions on Russia and how they can be made Even More Effective," *Atlantic Council Report*, May 3, 2021, https://www.atlanticcouncil.org/in-depth-research-reports/report/the-impact-of-western-sanctions-on-russia/.

Energy Trap

Russia has been highly dependent on revenues from the sale of fossil fuels (oil and natural gas) since the early 2000s, constituting up to half of the state's annual budget. Although Moscow has tried to diversify its export structure through an increase in the sale of metals, chemicals, machinery and agricultural products, about 60 percent of its export earnings remain reliant on fossil fuels.[124] Until the financial crisis of 2008, the government was able to deliver reasonable economic growth, primarily because oil and gas prices were consistently high and exports steadily grew. Since that time, the Russian budget has had to cope with periodic shocks of falling energy prices that have contributed to relatively flat economic growth.

Russia's economic stagnation could have been even more acute without sensible fiscal planning, low debt-to-GDP ratios, and an accumulation of financial reserves during the "boom" years. [125] The funds devoted to economic stabilization consisted of a National Wealth Fund and a Sovereign Reserve Fund that were merged by the close of 2017. Moscow gathered significant financial reserves, estimated at about $600 billion, during periods of high oil and gas prices in order to balance the state budget during protracted stagnation, when energy prices fell precipitously, and in order to bail out large state corporations and banks. At the close of 2021, the total National Wealth Fund reportedly stood at $185 billion.[126]

---

[124] Kathryn E. Stoner, ***Russia Resurrected: Its Power and Purpose in a New Global Order,*** Oxford University Press, 2021, pp.144–145.

[125] Kadri Liik, "Russia's Relative Resilience: Why Putin Feels Vindicated by the Pandemic," *Policy Brief,* December 17, 2020, European Council on Foreign Relations, https://ecfr.eu/publication/russias-relative-resilience-why-putin-feels-vindicated-by-the-pandemic/?mc_cid=de53610d16&mc_eid=223d2dad2a.

[126] https://minfin.gov.ru/en/key/nationalwealthfund/statistics/?id_65=104686-volume_of_the_national_wealth_fund.

Moscow refills its monetary buffers through periodic rises in energy prices, but this is not an effective long-term strategy given the uncertainties of global demand, competition with other producers, the renewable energy transition in Europe and North America, and the forthcoming imposition of a high carbon tax on oil and gas exports to the EU. In its de-carbonization strategy, the EU is planning to introduce in 2025 a carbon tax on businesses based on the emissions produced in imported fuel. This will have a major impact on Russia's budget. Taxes on Moscow are projected at between $2 billion and $5 billion annually and will affect more than 40 percent of Russia's exports, costing Russian companies more than $50 billion over the coming decade.[127] Following the invasion of Ukraine in 2022, EU countries have sought to limit and eventually sever their dependence on Russian energy imports. This will have a major impact on the Russian budget if Moscow cannot find alternative long-term customers willing to pay comparable prices for its current oil and gas exports to Europe.

Russia's energy future remains precarious, as infrastructure is decaying, older oil and gas fields are becoming exhausted, and Moscow finds it difficult to develop new reserves without importing Western technology that came under more intense sanctions during 2022. Even parts of Russia will experience energy shortages because of dilapidated infrastructure. In addition, opposition in Europe and elsewhere to dependence on Russian energy supplies in the wake of the Ukraine war will increase demands for energy diversification.

---

[127] Ksenia Potaeva, "Углеродный налог ЕС обойдется российским экспортерам в $2,2 млрд ежегодно," May 27, 2021, https://www.vedomosti.ru/economics/articles/2021/05/26/871521-uglerodnii-nalog?mc_cid=0404bd2ef8&mc_eid=4655fb8220 and "IMF Warns Russia Not to Underestimate Green Energy Transition, *The Moscow Times*, June 3, 2021, https://www.themoscowtimes.com/2021/06/03/imf-warns-russia-not-to-underestimate-green-energy-transition-a74097.

Price fluctuations can lull Russia's government into a false sense of security that the development of alternative energies is not an imperative. The world is witnessing a new post-industrial revolution based on adapting economies to new energy sources. This will lead to falling demand for oil and gas and further retard Russia's development. In July 2021, Finance Minister Anton Siluanov warned that Russia must prepare for major revenue losses due to the global push toward renewable energy that will precipitate a further decline in demand for fossil fuels.[128] The EU in particular is pursuing a shift toward renewable energy, including wind, solar, biomass, and hydropower, as part of its decarbonization plans. In 2021, alternative energies comprised less than 1 percent of Russia's power supply. The "decarbonization" drive to reduce global fossil fuels consumption will have a devastating effect on the Russian economy if it cannot transition to the production of new forms of energy, such as hydrogen, and secure alternative export earnings.

The Kremlin has failed to systematically pursue alternatives sources of economic development, as this would necessitate easing its tight grip on political power, undercutting the wealth of loyal tycoons, and allowing for innovation and competition. Putin's counterreformation nationalized over 70 percent of all privatized assets by 2017 in a systematic policy of "business capture."[129] State control of major industries has stifled competition, reduced incentives, fostered crony capitalism among Putin's allies, and maintained a high level of official corruption. The dominance of the hydrocarbon industry stifles other

---

[128] "Russia Faces Huge Revenue Losses From Renewables Push, Finance Minister Warns," *The Moscow Times*, July 8, 2021, https://www.themoscowtimes.com/2021/07/08/russia-faces-huge-revenue-losses-from-renewables-push-finance-minister-warns-a74463.

[129] Dmitry Travin, Vladimir Gel'man, Otar Marganiya, *The Russian Path: Ideas, Interests, Institutions, Illusions,* Stuttgart: Ibidem Verlag, 2020, p.200.

economic sectors, as it consumes state investment and attracts the most qualified labor. As the economy is dominated by a few dozen large state-linked conglomerates, Russia suffers from a lack of economic diversification and has been unable to develop an industrial base that can make products (other than nuclear reactors and weapons) that are competitive in international markets, including any significant high-tech goods.[130]

Russia's business climate also remains precarious, with ambiguous property rights, uncertain legal protection for investments, a corrupted and politically penetrated justice system, and a constant threat of expropriation of entrepreneurs by state agencies. Such an environment in combination with technological backwardness and Russia's distancing from world markets is not conducive to foreign investments, which fell by 95 percent between 2019 and 2020.[131] Several large global corporations have withdrawn from Russia over the past decade, as the country is not attractive in sectors other than resource extraction. Dozens more major Western businesses left Russia following its February 2022 invasion of Ukraine.

The Russian Federation is falling behind in technological development, education, research, and innovation.[132] Labor productivity is low and measures less than half of the average in G-7

---

[130] Kathryn E. Stoner, *Russia Resurrected: Its Power and Purpose in a New Global Order*, Oxford University Press, 2021, pp.147–148.

[131] "Иностранные инвестиции в Россию рухнули в 20 раз," January 19, 2021, https://www.finanz.ru/novosti/aktsii/inostrannye-investicii-v-rossiyu-rukhnuli-v-20-raz-1029982582.

[132] Andrew S. Weiss, *New Tools, Old Tricks: Emerging Technologies and Russia's Global Tool Kit*, 2021, Carnegie Endowment for International Peace, https://carnegieendowment.org/2021/04/29/new-tools-old-tricks-emerging-technologies-and-russia-s-global-tool-kit-pub-84437.

countries.[133] Since the late 1990s, a growing number of citizens with advanced technical skills have left the country in search of professional opportunities abroad. The total number of scientific and technology researchers working in Russia has declined by nearly 65 percent in the past two decades. Additionally, the reputation of the tech sector has been damaged by government policies and foreign cyber operations, which have limited collaboration with Western companies. In 2020, spending on R&D totaled a paltry 1.16 percent of GDP. At the same, capital continues to flow out of the country, with estimates of private assets abroad reaching over $1.3 trillion by 2019 and much of this wealth linked to Putin's inner circle.[134]

Military Struggles

On the security front, Russia drastically increased its defense spending between 2008 and 2016 to over 5 percent of GDP.[135] It partially restructured and modernized its military so that the country's conventional forces ostensibly remained second only to that of NATO in terms of stated capabilities. This expensive program has included upgrading weaponry in all military branches, ensuring more efficient command structures, and steps to replace the conscript system with professional troops. Nonetheless, Moscow's actual achievements rarely match its grandiose plans. In 2002, Putin approved the

---

[133] Kathryn E. Stoner, *Russia Resurrected: Its Power and Purpose in a New Global Order*, Oxford University Press, 2021, p.14.

[134] Vladimir Kara-Murza, "A Congressional Proposal Reveals the Kremlin's Achilles' Heel," The Washington Post, November 24, 2021, https://www.washingtonpost.com/opinions/2021/11/24/congressional-proposal-reveals-kremlins-achilles-heel/.

[135] Stockholm International Peace Research Institute, *SIPRI Military Expenditure Database*, 2019, https://www.sipri.org/databases/milex.

transition to a fully contract-based army by 2010, but progress has proved slow. By 2019, the ratio of draftees to contracted soldiers was roughly 7:10 (about 260,000 draftees and 370,000 contracted soldiers). A one-year draft is still mandatory for all Russian males aged 18 to 27 and full professionalization will prove financially costly.[136]

In 2008, Russian leaders announced the "New Look" program to restructure the military into a mobile rapid reaction formation. Nonetheless, in comparison to the US, Russia has struggled to equip its military with 21st century technology. It lacks proficiency in much modern weaponry, including drones, electronic components, and satellite reconnaissance. Although the military possesses long-range missiles, targeting is less precise than among NATO forces because of inadequate reconnaissance capabilities. Military modernization faces obstacles such as a decline in funding for research and development, structural deficiencies in the defense industry, low labor productivity, inadequate training, weak quality control systems, poor safety standards, and a general lack of professionalism. In addition, the military, similarly to all state institutions, is riddled with corruption, and the brutal treatment of younger officers by senior commanders damages morale and dents their patriotism.[137] Rampant fraud and theft in Russia's military sector and state-controlled arms industry

---

[136] Rossella Cerulli, "The Russian Military's Professionalization Problem," July 8, 2019, American Security Project, https://www.americansecurityproject.org/the-russian-militarys-professionalization-problem/#:~:text=Professionalizing%20the%20Russian%20military%20has%20been%20a%20topical,was%20needed%20for%20this%20switch%20to%20take%20place.

[137] Paul Goble, "Hundreds of Junior Officers in Russian Military Seeking to Leave Service, One of Their Number Says," January 26, 2022, http://windowoneurasia2.blogspot.com/2022/01/hundreds-of-junior-officers-in-russian.html.

impairs military modernization, damages capabilities, and imposes major costs on the operations of the defense ministry.[138]
Russia's nuclear arsenal has been prioritized over the last ten years, with substantial funding channeled into modernization programs in order to maintain parity with the US and even exceed Washington in some strategic and tactical weapons systems.[139] However, the nuclear "superweapons" loudly hyped by Putin, were mostly developed during the Cold War but never deployed, and it is uncertain how effective they would be in practice.[140]

Moscow has increased the number of military snap exercises in order to improve battle-readiness, maneuverability, and multi-service interoperability in all five military districts—Northern, Western, Eastern, Central and Southern. However, ambitious plans for military modernization are slowing down, as the defense budget has been steadily reduced; over the coming decade, Russia's Armed Forces will fall further behind that of the US and China. According to data from 2019, Russia's military spending was almost one quarter that of China's and less than 9 percent of the US military budget.[141] Russia's military structures are only partially reformed and modernized, and many of the loudly trumpeted programs for constructing

---

[138] Polina Beliakova and Sam Perlo-Freeman, *Corruption in the Russian Defense Sector*, World Peace Foundation, May 18, 2018, https://sites.tufts.edu/wpf/files/2018/05/Russian-Defense-Corruption-Report-Beliakova-Perlo-Freeman-20180502-final.pdf.

[139] Kathryn E. Stoner, *Russia Resurrected: Its Power and Purpose in a New Global Order*, Oxford University Press, 2021, pp.211–214.

[140] Pavel Felgenhauer, "Putin's Ultimatum to America," *Eurasia Daily Monitor*, Vol. 18, Issue 180, December 2, 2021, https://jamestown.org/program/putins-ultimatum-to-america/.

[141] Stockholm International Peace Research Institute, *SIPRI Military Expenditure Database*, https://www.sipri.org/databases/milex.

sophisticated new weaponry are incomplete. Ultimately, unless social programs are drastically cut, rising defense spending is not sustainable in a stagnant economy let alone one severely constrained by sanctions.[142]

Moscow's recent military gains are a waning asset. Since Russia's invasion of Ukraine in 2014, the US has refocused its military attention in Europe by building up its advanced military capabilities on the continent.[143] US Army modernization programs, including its missile defenses, will create a NATO Anti-Access/Area Denial (A2/AD) bubble to offset the one developed by Russia and deploy an array of hypersonic weapons. NATO allies are also increasing their military spending and modernizing their defense systems. Significantly, Poland, the key NATO state facing Russia, is acquiring F-35 stealth fighter aircraft, HIMARS rocket artillery system, Patriot missile defense systems, and M1 Abrams tanks. Above all, Moscow's military spending on an extensive array of weapons systems, bases, deployments, and exercises both inside and outside Russia, as well as the cost of its prolonged military campaign against Ukraine, will deplete the state budget, sacrifice even more social programs, and fuel social unrest.

Corruption, Inequality, Pauperization

Official corruption is one of the pillars of Kremlin control over the elites, in which it dispenses financial and other incentives to clients and cronies in order to ensure political loyalty. In times of growing economic distress among large sectors of the population, disclosures

---

[142] Stephen J. Blank, "Can Russia Sustain Its Military Capability?" in S. Enders Wimbush and Elizabeth M. Portale (Eds), *Russia in Decline*, Jamestown Foundation, March 2017, p.196.

[143] Dan Goure, "Russia Has a Clear Reason To Invade Ukraine Now if Talks Fail," *1945*, January 12, 2022, https://www.19fortyfive.com/2022/01/russia-has-a-clear-reason-to-invade-ukraine-now-if-talks-fail/.

about high-level corruption are more likely to mobilize citizens against the regime. Aleksei Navalny has tried to capitalize on public outrage and resentment of elite corruption and the fact that living standards are falling for the majority of citizens. In an effort to cover up extensive institutional corruption, in June 2021 Russian authorities banned several prominent oppositionist networks as "extremist," including the Navalny Headquarters, the Anti-Corruption Foundation, and the Foundation for the Protection of Citizens Rights.[144] They were charged with plotting an uprising and conspiring with Western intelligence services. Moscow also blacklisted activists ahead of parliamentary elections in September 2021 and disabled their participation. The retroactive law banned leaders, rank-and-file members, and the financial donors of "extremist" groups from seeking office for a period of three to five years.

State spending on social benefits such as health care and education has stagnated under the Putin regime. At the same time, Russia's aging infrastructure, especially in the transportation sector, has a negative economic and social impact, while the implementation of contracts is riddled with corruption. In a vivid example of how crumbling infrastructure can generate economic disruption and even a national security threat, the collapse of one small bridge along the Trans-Siberian Railroad in July 2021 led to Putin convening a national Security Council meeting.[145] When flooding washed away a short bridge in the Trans-Baikal region, all rail movements were terminated for several days. As a result, Russian trains were unable to meet either

---

[144] "Russia Bans Navalny's Organizations as 'Extremist' Ahead of Election," *Radio Free Europe/Radio Liberty*, June 9, 2021, https://www.rferl.org/a/navalny-political-organizations-extremist/31299415.html.

[145] Paul Goble, "Putin's Response to Bridge Collapse Highlights Infrastructure and Political Problems," *Eurasia Daily Monitor,* Vol. 18, Issue 123, August 3, 2021, https://jamestown.org/program/putins-response-to-bridge-collapse-highlights-infrastructure-and-political-problems/.

local demand or fulfill contracts for trade with China, South Korea, and other states in East Asia. Such incidents increased concerns about Russia's economic reliability and bolstered proposals for developing alternative trading routes through Central Asia or by sea. They also highlight that infrastructural dilapidation, unfulfilled investments, and widespread official corruption can create serious shortages of necessary supplies in several regions. This will add to local frustrations with the hyper-centralized administration in which the regions do not have the resources or authority to repair decaying infrastructure.

Economic reports indicate that living standards continue to fall in Russia, with fast-rising inflation, decline in real incomes, soaring food prices, and low levels of investment.[146] A fundamental problem is the government's inability to provide consistent economic benefits to the population through steadily rising living standards. Such an implicit bargain was struck by Putin in the early 2000s, whereby guaranteed income growth and a level of consumer satisfaction ensured regime legitimacy regardless of widespread official corruption and expanding socio-economic inequalities.[147] This arrangement was reminiscent of the unwritten and informal "social contract" in Soviet times, whereby the government provided steady material welfare to the masses "from cradle to grave" in return for their political passivity or non-resistance to Communist rule. However, because contractual relations carry little weight in the country, the arrangement is ultimately upheld by the threat of repression. In contemporary Russia, material welfare is not the only measure of state-society relations, as protests have erupted over a host of grievances and frustrations at the local level.

---

[146] "Russia's Inflation Hits New 5-Year High Ahead of Parliamentary Polls," *The Moscow Times*, September 9, 2021, https://www.themoscowtimes.com/2021/09/09/russias-inflation-hits-new-5-year-high-ahead-of-parliamentary-polls-a75003.

[147] Kathryn E. Stoner, *Russia Resurrected: Its Power and Purpose in a New Global Order*, Oxford University Press, 2021, p.23.

Nonetheless, the economy is one of the most significant factors that can ignite mass protests across the country and fuel other causes.

In general, unrest is more likely in a society whose rising expectations of material well-being over a prolonged period have been thwarted by failures in government policy. Russia's government does not have a long-term strategy for economic development but calculates that slow or even stagnant economic growth can be tolerated if it does not provoke broad public unrest.[148] Indeed, some analysts contend that Russia's institutions and its economic system are designed to serve the dominant interest groups within the pyramid of "state paternalism" with little concern for the public good.[149] Property rights are not protected, the threat of state pressure or expropriation of businesses is ever present, and state resources are brazenly embezzled at all levels of government. Maintaining the "power vertical" is beneficial for its insiders, as it enables them to gain resources and seek higher office with more lucrative benefits.

The government also appears determined not to repeat the Gorbachev reforms of the late 1980s, when the Soviet economy was consistently stagnant. The apprehension is that structural reforms will require economic diversification, modernization, and political restructuring that will unseat the administration. Such reforms would create a more independent middle class not reliant on fossil fuel revenues and state-managed wealth distribution and one more supportive of democracy

---

[148] Vladislav Inozemtsev, "Putin Doesn't Care about Economic Growth," *Project Syndicate*, June 2019, https://www.project-syndicate.org/commentary/russia-economic-stagnation- prospects-by-vladislav-inozemtsev-2019-06.

[149] Dmitry Travin, Vladimir Gel'man, Otar Marganiya, *The Russian Path: Ideas, Interests, Institutions, Illusions*, Stuttgart: Ibidem Verlag, 2020, pp.125–127, 135.

and the rule of law.[150] In particular, an expanding urban middle class would demand more effective city and regional governments elected on merit and not selected for political subservience to the center. Paradoxically, though higher global prices for oil and gas may bring short-term benefits for Russia's budget, they also calcify the economic structure and discourage diversification, modernization, and entrepreneurship. Russia's economy has been largely static for several years, and the recurring crises ensure a comparative decline with other major economies.

Even before the 2022 war, living standards have been steadily falling, income inequalities and wealth differentials rising, social program diminishing, poverty levels sharply rising, and a growing number of citizens facing destitution. The population's annual real income in 2020 was some 10 percent lower than in 2013, indicating a decade of stagnation. A 2018 report by the Russian Presidential Academy of the National Economy and Public Administration revealed that 22 percent of the population were in the "poverty zone," with incomes that only enabled them to buy food and basic staples. Consumers have endured falling quality in food as a consequence of Moscow's countersanctions against EU imports and inadequate "import substitution" by Russian producers.[151] The erosion of the middle class into poverty is an additional negative trend, as it damages an important constituency for economic modernization and entrepreneurship.

---

[150] Vladislav Inozemtsev, "Russia's Decline: Predictions and Recommendations," in S. Enders Wimbush and Elizabeth M. Portale (Eds), *Russia in Decline,* Jamestown Foundation, March 2017, p.23.

[151] "Санкционка» оказалась незаменимой: Россия не смогла достичь целей импортозамещения продуктов," December 7, 2020, https://www.kommersant.ru/doc/4603211.

The economic crisis accelerated by the COVID-19 pandemic reduced the income of Russia's middle class and pushed more families to the brink of poverty. By June 2020, 19.9 million people, or 13.5 percent of the population, lived below the subsistence minimum (11,468 rubles or about 128 euros per month).[152] The number had increased by 1.3 million since June 2019. About 500 super-rich Russians controlled more wealth than the poorest 99.8 percent of citizens.[153] This figure represents three times the global average. The pandemic exacerbated Russia's inequalities and wealth disparities, as household disposable incomes shrank and real estate prices surged. Rural poverty has become particularly severe, as rural residents constitute 25 percent of the population, or about 37 million people, but form half of all the poor in the country.[154] A large exodus of predominantly Russian ethnics from rural areas to the large cities is accelerating and seriously depopulating numerous regions. Since 2015, the population in 46 federal subjects has fallen by more than 2 percent.[155]

---

[152] International Security and Estonia, 2021, Estonian Foreign Intelligence Service, p.43, https://www.valisluureamet.ee/pdf/raport/2021-ENG.pdf?mc_cid=980db5c327&mc_eid=223d2dad2a.

[153] "Russia's 500 Super Rich Wealthier Than Poorest 99.8% – Pandemic Boosted Fortunes of Country's Wealthiest, While Knocking Living Standards of the Poorest," *The Moscow Times*, June 10, 2021, https://www.themoscowtimes.com/2021/06/10/russias-500-super-rich-wealthier-than-poorest-998-report-a74180.

[154] Paul Goble, "Moscow's Much-Ballyhooed Programs to Save Russian Villages aren't Working, Audit Chamber Says," March 27, 2021, http://windowoneurasia2.blogspot.com/2021/03/moscows-much-ballyhooed-programs-to.html.

[155] Paul Goble, "Russians Fleeing 'God Forgotten' Rural Areas Where Life has Become Impossible, Experts Say," November 19, 2020, http://windowoneurasia2.blogspot.com/2020/11/russians-fleeing-god-forgotten-rural.html.

There is a widening gap between stagnant incomes and rising consumer prices. The agricultural lobby largely accepted the limitations and bans on exports as a core component of encouraging "import substitution." As compensation, farmers demanded guarantees of profits on the domestic market. However, this policy undermined official instructions to ensure price stability and it propelled inflation. Growing poverty, falling incomes, price inflation, and spiraling unemployment can stimulate new waves of protests, especially where living standards fall suddenly, as during a pandemic or in the wake of war, rather than over a prolonged period that allows for some measure of public adjustment. While food prices have been steadily rising and surpassing any income increases, there are also fears of longer-term shortages.[156] As a result of climate change, Russian farmers have faced flooding in some food-growing regions and drought in others, reducing the production of staples such as bread and potatoes. Authorities face difficulties in restraining price increases or purchasing supplies abroad because of declining production in many countries and the weakness of the ruble. Russian experts warn that public discontent can spread if domestic consumers begin to face prolonged shortfalls in traditional staples.

Income inequalities and economic divisions are widening between bureaucrats working for the government or state enterprises, who have generally maintained their living standards, and people in the private sector or on pensions, who have suffered a major decline in incomes in recent years. A steep decimation of disposal incomes among non-state workers is pushing them into poverty. Unemployment has also been steadily rising during the economic downturn, especially in the first year of the pandemic in 2020. Among

---

[156] Paul Goble, "Crop Failures in Russia Point to Serious Shortages of Bread and Potatoes Ahead," *Eurasia Daily Monitor,* Vol. 18, Issue 149, September 30, 2021, https://jamestown.org/program/crop-failures-in-russia-point-to-serious-shortages-of-bread-and-potatoes-ahead/.

young people aged between 15 and 30, about a million lost their jobs, thus fueling grievances against the government.[157] Some regions have descended into poverty faster than others during the multiple crises. In parts of the North Caucasus, the unemployment rate far exceeds official figures and stands at nearly 40 percent, and much more of it may be hidden.[158] This provides fertile ground for radicalization among unemployed and impoverished youths without any prospects for economic improvement.

Pandemic Inflammation

The COVID-19 pandemic contributed to further undermining Russia's economy before it could recover from the decline following the 2014 invasion of Ukraine.[159] Ballooning budget deficits and bankruptcies in numerous regions were delayed by large subsidies from Moscow but will hit hard in the coming years. The pandemic drove down purchases of Russian goods, and industry will be hard pressed to recover given lower demand and scarcer investment. On March 1, 2021, government subsidies ended to companies that were shielded from losses caused by the pandemic. An estimated ten million Russians faced unemployment, as numerous businesses needed to scale down or close. Studies by the Higher School of

---

157 "Численность занятых россиян от 15 до 30 лет сократилась на 1 млн человек," https://www.trtrussian.com/novosti-rossiya/chislennost-zanyatyh-rossiyan-ot-15-do-30-let-sokratilas-na-1-mln-chelovek-5377113.

158 "Аналитики оценили реальную безработицу в два раза выше официальной," October 2, 2020, https://finexpertiza.ru/press-service/researches/2020/real-bezrabotitsa/.

159 Paul Goble, "2021 Will be a Year of Dashed Hopes in Russia, Zubarevich Says", December 18, 2020, http://windowoneurasia2.blogspot.com/2020/12/2021-will-be-year-of-dashed-hopes-in.html.

Economics indicated that during the pandemic, 6.1 percent of middle-class people fell into the category of "poor" largely because they lost employment when thousands of small companies folded.[160] Due to the pandemic and deepening economic crisis, the number of homeless in Russia rose to almost eight million in 2021, or about one in twenty citizens, with many turning to begging for survival.[161]

The weaknesses and poor leadership abilities of the political elite became stark during the pandemic emergency in 2020–2021. In particular, President Putin proved reluctant to take responsibility and act decisively, underscoring a failure of leadership despite two decades of incessant propaganda painting him as an effective head of state.[162] In the wake of the pandemic, with Moscow making the federal units responsible for its management, all regions found themselves in greater debt and even more dependent on Moscow for financial subsidies.[163] Few regions possessed any budgetary reserves to bail out local businesses and assist citizens but were expected to keep the public pacified and manage local problems. The debt of federal subjects, mostly to the central government, rose 18 percent in 2020

---

160 Paul Goble, "Pandemic has Increased Income Inequality in Russia, Rosstat Figures Show," October 22, 2020, http://windowoneurasia2.blogspot.com/2020/10/pandemic-has-increased-income.html.

161 Igor Pushkarev and Nikita Telizhenko, "Поставленный на поток криминальный бизнес со своими нормами и KPI," June 22, 2021, znak.com/2021-06 22/kak_ustroen_mir_poproshaek_v_rossii_territorii_kommunikacii_dohody_ierarhiya_reportazh.

162 International Security and Estonia, 2021, Estonian Foreign Intelligence Service, pp.35–38, https://www.valisluureamet.ee/pdf/raport/2021-ENG.pdf?mc_cid=980db5c327&mc_eid=223d2dad2a.

163 "Ковидный кризис бьет по продвинутым и сильным," November 25, 2020, https://www.znak.com/2020-11-25/kak_izmenilis_otnosheniya_federalnyh_vlastey_s_regionami_iz_za_koronavirusa.

and intensified their dependence on Moscow.[164] Some regions have been aided by Moscow more than others. The poorer ones in particular cannot plan for the future, and analysts expect numerous bankruptcies for small and mid-sized businesses.

The failure to effectively counter the pandemic or to distribute significant relief funds to citizens was widely viewed as a demonstration of government incompetence and neglect that increased poverty and wealth inequalities. At the same time, people distrusted official assertions that the economy had declined primarily because of the pandemic rather than government policies. Public resistance to vaccinations contributed to maintaining a high infection rate. However, the regime was also hesitant in making inoculations mandatory in case this sparked protests. An increasing number of people blamed the government for mismanagement when it sought to reimpose anti-pandemic restrictions.

Government responses to the pandemic increased tensions between Moscow and people in outlying regions. While citizens in the capital had easier access to vaccines, this proved much more difficult for those outside Moscow.[165] In the majority of federal subjects, rising COVID-19 infections, hospitalizations, and deaths were recorded throughout the fall of 2021. Putin's popularity nosedived because of poor handling of the crisis by the central government even while he tried to devolve responsibility to the regional authorities. Distrust in regional officials also intensified, whether because of insufficient medical help, cutbacks in government spending on health care, chaotic instructions, inequalities in access to the healthcare system,

---

164 "Госдолг регионов РФ в 2020 году вырос на 18%," January 31, 2021, https://krizis-kopilka.ru/archives/83381.

165 "Москвичи в эпоху пандемии стали особым сословием," January 12, 2021, https://echo.msk.ru/blog/kirillmartyn/2772678-echo/.

lockdowns that were seen as violating human rights, or the prolonged economic distress.[166]

Protest actions against lockdowns were registered in several parts of the country, including by businesspeople in Buryatia claiming that they were suffering irreversible economic hardship.[167] The pandemic also changed the nature of protests during 2020, at least temporarily.[168] It both lowered the number of open protests and moved many of them from the street to online. Additionally, professional associations and labor unions became more important as the basis for resistance by focusing on workplace grievances such as unemployment, unsafe working conditions, or non-payment of wages. Other disputes also emerged during the pandemic, especially between those supporting or opposing vaccinations, and these can further inflame pre-existing divisions in Russian society and raise opposition to the government.

The Moscow Bureau for Human Rights reported that the pandemic may have reduced the number of conflicts based on ethnicity or religion, but it also boosted hostility toward outsiders. Much of this reflected the consequences of lessened human contact, but it also

---

166 "Риски и угрозы некоторых антиковидных мер в аспекте национальной безопасности," December 1, 2020, https://zavtra.ru/blogs/riski_i_ugrozi_nekotorih_antikovidnih_mer_v_aspekte_natcional_noj_bezopasnosti.

167 "Предприниматели Бурятии пикетируют у здания правительства против локдауна," November 20, 2020, https://www.sibreal.org/a/30959940.html.

168 "Как протестуют россияне: Результаты мониторинга протестной активности во втором квартале 2020 года, подготовленного Центром социально-трудовых прав," http://trudprava.ru/images/2020_2_Quart_Monitoring.pdf.

indicated brewing anger and resentments within Russian society.[169] Vaccine skepticism was widespread, and prolonged restrictions on movement and human contacts can spark new protests. This arouses antagonism against the central and regional governments for their inadequate response to the crisis and simultaneously emboldens those who believe the pandemic scare was artificial.[170]

At least 473,000 more deaths were recorded during the pandemic until the summer of 2021 than in equivalent pre-pandemic periods. During 2020, Russia sustained 340,000 more deaths than in 2019, with another 133,000 excess deaths in the first five months of 2021.[171] Pandemic conditions deteriorated rapidly during the summer and fall of 2021 in the largest cities with a danger that the infection rate was spiraling out of control. Infections and deaths spiked even as officials tried to disguise the numbers. By proportion of the population, Russia registered the highest pandemic death toll of any major country.[172] By October 2021, even official statistics showed 221,000 pandemic-

---

[169] Paul Goble, Pandemic Reduces Ethnic and Religious Conflicts But Increases Xenophobia And Aggression, Study Finds," November 12, 2020, http://windowoneurasia2.blogspot.com/2020/11/pandemic-reduces-ethnic-and-religious.html.

[170] "В Америке расовый раскол, на нашем Дальнем Востоке — недовольство Москвой…," *Znak*, August 5, 2020, https://www.znak.com/2020-08-05/politolog_gleb_kuznecov_kak_pandemiya_vyzvala_protestnuyu_volnu_v_mire_i_kuda_eta_volna_vyneset_ross.

[171] Patrick Reevell," Data Suggests Russia's COVID-19 Death Toll Is Far Higher Than Reported," *ABC News*, July 30, 2021, https://abcnews.go.com/International/data-suggests-russias-covid-19-death-toll-higher/story?id=79145618&cid=clicksource_4380645_1_heads_hero_live_headlines_hed.

[172] Robyn Dixon, "In Russia, Experts Are Challenging Official Pandemic Figures as Too Low. They Refuse to be Silenced," *Washington Post*, October 17, 2021, https://www.washingtonpost.com/world/europe/russia-covid-count-fake-statistics/2021/10/16/b9d47058-277f-11ec-8739-5cb6aba30a30_story.html.

related deaths. However, independent sources believe that officials doctored the numbers and calculate that the real figure was closer to 750,000.

Russia's vaccination rate was one of the world's lowest. By October 2021, only 43 million citizens were fully vaccinated, according to the health ministry, or about 30 percent of the population. The number reached 47 percent by the end of 2021, but significantly lower than the 62 percent in the United States and 70 percent across the European Union.[173] The government also gave mixed signals on inoculations and refused to import more effective vaccines from abroad. The Russian population became even more distrustful of government claims, whether about the pandemic or about immunization. For many citizens, the Sputnik V vaccine developed by government laboratories was viewed with suspicion as another instrument of state propaganda. A policy of mandatory vaccinations or one that lifts all quarantine restrictions could witness a major upsurge in public protests with people expressing their repressed frustrations with glaring government failures. Above all, the impact of international economic sanctions in the aftermath of Russia's attack on Ukraine in February 2022 will prove devastating for the living standards of ordinary citizens and will affect all aspects of people's lives, including health care, nutrition, employment, and availability of basic goods and utilities.

Environmental Hazards

Russia's authorities have neglected ecological protection and actively despoiled the environment in order to ensure essential revenues from the extraction and export of fossil fuels, minerals, and other natural resources. Such policies are compounded by the customary veil of

---

[173] "Russia Steels Itself For Omicron 'Tidal Wave' As Vaccination Rates Remain Stubbornly Low," *Radio Free Europe/ Radio Liberty*, January 13, 2022, https://www.rferl.org/a/russia-omicron-tidal-wave-vaccination/31652979.html.

state secrecy that descends over any oil spill or other ecological disasters impacting on Russia's rivers, lakes, and coastlines. Environmental activists regularly complain about negligence and corruption by energy companies and that Moscow and republican authorities invariably conceal information from the public about the scale and consequences of the damage, while performing the bare minimum during clean-up efforts.[174] Only a small number of man-made environmental disasters become public knowledge. Oil giants have close ties with the government and are virtually untouchable so that the reporting of oil spills and infrastructure decay is tightly censored. Parts of Siberia and the Pacific region also regularly face widespread wildfires that incur huge ecological costs and are exacerbated by inadequate state resources, inept policies to combat them, and a collapse of reforestation efforts.

Climate change and global warming will have an immense impact on Russia's economy and environment in the vast permafrost zone. More than 60 percent of Russian territory is underlain by permafrost—the upper layer of soil that remains frozen year-round but is rapidly melting due to rising temperatures. The accelerating thaw will result in landslides, severely damage Russia's economic development, and further pollute its environment with harmful gases and forest fires. Environmentalists fear that the annual summer fires fueled by hot weather will thaw the permafrost and peatlands, releasing even more climate-warming carbon dioxide and methane stored in the frozen tundra.

Russia is warming 2.5 times faster than the rest of the planet due to its extensive Arctic territories. According to Environmental Minister

---

174 Sergey Sukhankin, "Russia's 'Green' Agenda in the Arctic and the Far East: Words vs. Deeds," *Eurasia Daily Monitor*, Vol. 18, Issue 84, May 26, 2021, https://jamestown.org/program/russias-green-agenda-in-the-arctic-and-the-far-east-words-vs-deeds/.

Alexander Kozlov, the Russian economy could lose more than 5 trillion rubles ($67 billion) by 2050 due to melting permafrost damage to infrastructure.[175] Given Moscow's customary denial of domestic disasters, the real figure is likely to be several magnitudes higher. Over 90 percent of natural gas and 75 percent of oil extraction is conducted in permafrost regions, but structures and pipelines were not designed to withstand seasonal or permanent thawing; the government will need to spend vast sums to secure it.[176] Already by 2021, about 23 percent of the technical failures and 29 percent of loss in fossil fuel extraction were caused by permafrost degradation. It is also problematic to build new railway lines and roads in thawing permafrost, where more than 40 percent of buildings and infrastructure facilities have already been damaged.

Most of Russia's oil pipelines and other facilities were built during Soviet times and require costly replacements and new technologies. Frequent leaks of aged or improperly managed pipelines pump hundreds of metric tons of potent methane gas into the atmosphere. Russia is the world's fourth-largest emitter of greenhouse gases, but only ranks ninth in population and eleventh in economic size. The government has proved incapable of addressing problems in energy efficiency, carbon-intensive manufacturing, and the widespread pollution of rivers, lakes and oceans. It is also failing to create a new domestic industry to replace the country's hydrocarbon sector. Moscow has not taken seriously the transition to a greener economy, unlike other advanced economies, who view renewable energy as a core component of post-pandemic recovery.

---

175 "Melting Permafrost Could Cost Russian Economy $67Bln by 2050," *The Moscow Times*, May 28, 2021, https://www.themoscowtimes.com/2021/05/28/melting-permafrost-could-cost-russian-economy-67bln-by-2050-a74043.

176 Marlene Laruelle, *Russia's Arctic Strategies and the Future of the Far North*, London: Routledge, 2014, p.81.

Across northern Russia, climate change and global warming present major ecological, infrastructural, economic, and social problems for Moscow and will further exacerbate regional discontent.[177] Surface air temperatures in the Siberian Arctic are warming at twice the rate of the global average, thus increasing the amount of permafrost thaw during the summer months.[178] This is transforming the landscape and resulting in subsidence and landslides while the methane leaking out of permafrost accelerates global warming and ice melting. Thawing of the permafrost will also release dangerous microbes that could spread new pandemics. Russia is losing increasing stretches of its Arctic coast as climate change accelerates natural erosion and foreshadows new ecological disasters. The loss of coastal lands will damage human infrastructure, increase hazards of fuel and chemicals spills, endanger several new oil and gas projects, pollute ecosystems, and result in major financial losses.[179] Collapsing infrastructure and transportation links will also propel out-migration and lead to the shrinking or disappearance of numerous towns. This will undermine prospects for developing the Russian-controlled Northern Sea Route and damage the livelihoods of indigenous peoples.

---

[177] Paul Goble, "Global Warming Undermining Russia's Position in the North," January 19, 2021, http://windowoneurasia2.blogspot.com/2021/01/global-warming-undermining-russias.html.

[178] Richard Gray, "The Mystery of Siberia's Exploding Craters," November 30, 2020, https://www.bbc.com/future/article/20201130-climate-change-the-mystery-of-siberias-explosive-craters.

[179] "Russia Losing 1-3 Meters of Arctic Shoreline to Climate Change Annually – Scientists," *The Moscow Times*, November 22, 2021, https://www.themoscowtimes.com/2021/11/22/russia-losing-1-3-meters-of-arctic-shoreline-to-climate-change-annually-scientists-a75625.

Another cause for environmental protest is Moscow's plans to sell freshwater to China.[180] Russia possesses the world's largest reserves of potable water, and many of these reservoirs are concentrated in sparsely populated areas lying close to the borders of China and Mongolia, particularly Lake Baikal. Many Russians view Lake Baikal as a national treasure that must be protected and not sold off as a commodity. Siberians also oppose reversing the flow of rivers to bring water to Central Asia or China and are outraged that Moscow engages in profitable deals in their territories without any local consultations. Parts of southern Russia, including the Kalmyk Republic, also face prolonged droughts as a result of long-term climate change.

A significant ecological problem is the dumping of industrial and household waste by the Russian authorities. Russia produces over seven billion tons of trash annually, and most of it is industrial waste from oil, gas, coal and mineral extraction.[181] Russia additionally generates more than 60 million tons of solid waste each year; unlike in the West, about 90 percent of this refuse ends up in landfills, many of which are illegal, with less than 8 percent recycled, as compared to 35 percent in the US. Although waste processing facilities exist, only 10 percent of their capacity is used. Overflowing landfills have generated public discontent, especially around Moscow, which generates about 20 percent of Russia's waste. Since 2017, residents of Moscow *Oblast* have been protesting against landfills close to their homes, including a major demonstration in Volokolamsk in April

---

[180] Paul Goble, "Moscow's Hopes to Use Water as 'New Oil' Outraging Siberians," *Eurasia Daily Monitor*, Vol. 18, Issue 30, February 23, 2021, https://jamestown.org/program/moscows-hopes-to-use-water-as-new-oil-outraging-siberians/.

[181] András Tóth-Czifra, "Something is Rotten in the State of Russia: How Waste Management Became a Problem for the Government," July14, 2020, Institute of Modern Russia, https://imrussia.org/en/analysis/3136-something-is-rotten-in-the-state-of-russia.

2018, sparked by toxic gases from a local dump. When dozens of landfills were closed to prevent further protests, the government decided to unload Moscow's waste in other regions. Although officials tried to keep this policy secret, it provoked outrage and protest movements in Arkhangelsk *Oblast* and the Komi Republic. The problems have been compounded by the fact that most regions do not possess garbage sorting facilities.

In March 2021, Siberian scientists blocked the publication of a major pollution report, evidently fearful of angering voters against the government ahead of the September 2021 legislative elections. According to the report, the Siberian Branch of the Russian Academy of Sciences determined that 78 percent of Russia's two dozen most polluted cities are located in Siberia and linked the findings to increased rates of birth defects, childhood disease, and cancers in the region.[182] Analysts believed that classifying the report would simply give it even more publicity and impact among the Siberian population.

Because most environmental problems are local or regional and, therefore, visible and life-threatening, citizens are more likely to engage in protests than over wider national questions that may have no immediate or noticeable impact. Moscow is evidently worried about such a prospect and even sponsored and registered a Green Alternative party in February 2020 to try and divert attention away from authentic environmental movements. The party was allowed to stand in both regional and national elections. The authorities have also claimed that "ecological extremists" who protest against environmental degradation are sponsored and funded by the US and

---

[182] "Siberian Scientists Block 'Bombshell' Pollution Report Ahead of Elections – Reports," *The Moscow Times*, March 29, 2021, https://www.themoscowtimes.com/2021/03/29/siberian-scientists-block-bombshell-pollution-report-ahead-of-elections-reports-a73403.

other Western states to undermine Russia's extractive industries, particularly its energy sector, and destroy its economy.

Social Pressures

The Russian state, centered around an elite caste of officials, officers and oligarchs, has already separated itself from the majority of the population. Divisions between state and society are deepening, and domestic pressures are mounting. By itself, Russia's economic performance is insufficient to measure susceptibility to open unrest. Numerous underlying factors must be examined, including growing public awareness of failed government policies and resentments over glaring social injustices and widening economic inequalities. All of these disorders were illuminated and magnified during the pandemic. The Kremlin can no longer rely on propaganda, political manipulation, economic stability, and imperial mobilization to keep the lid on social expectations and pressures, so it has increasingly resorted to repression.[183] However, the government has to balance its repressive policies with the assurance of sufficient public consent and passivity to ensure institutional credibility. Moscow faces a double danger—an inability to impose effective mass repression to subdue public unrest and a propensity to overreact and provoke the very scenario of turmoil that it fears.

Any rally larger than one person must obtain prior authorization from the authorities, but most opposition rallies are prohibited. During the nationwide protests in January and February 2021, triggered by the arrest of Alexei Navalny, tens of thousands of people took to the streets in more than 120 cities—the largest demonstrations since the

---

[183] Sabine Fischer, "Repression and Autocracy as Russia Heads into State Duma Elections," *SWP Comment*, No.40, June 2021, German Institute for International and Security Affairs, https://www.swp-berlin.org/publications/products/comments/2021C40_Russia_Duma_Elections.pdf?mc_cid=79336cb6eb&mc_eid=223d2dad2a.

election fraud of 2011–2012. Protestors were subjected to police violence, over 11,500 were detained, 130 criminal investigations were initiated, and several people received long prison sentences. The security forces also cracked down on journalists and independent lawyers. Following the protests, hundreds of citizens across the country were visited in their homes or workplaces by the security forces and either warned, fined, or detained. At least one-third of Navalny's regional coordinators fled Russia and resettled in the Baltic States and Georgia when the authorities banned his activist networks.

Moscow's public CCTV systems was used for the first time during the 2021 protests for large-scale facial recognition surveillance. Numerous job dismissals were apparently associated with participation in the protests. According to the Ministry for Emergency Situations, Russia is developing special artificial intelligence (AI)–powered software that will enable the detection of mass unrest.[184] The technology will conduct a "multi-factor, comprehensive analysis of the likelihood of riots and unauthorized public events." The software will also analyze news reports, social media, smart video surveillance, and public transport data to foresee upcoming riots and discern between political and religious rallies.

Moscow has largely been able to contain open political opposition and social unrest by providing substantial financial resources to local leaders in order to maintain their loyalty and dampen any movement toward popularizing regional sovereignty. However, such a policy has corrupted the heads of several republics and regions and increased resentments against providing economic assistance to the most impoverished regions, such as the North Caucasus. In the midst of the maladies, including growing poverty, expanding income

---

[184] "Russia Developing AI 'Minority Report' Protest Detector – Kommersant," *The Moscow Times*, November 30, 2021, https://www.themoscowtimes.com/2021/11/30/russia-developing-ai-minority-report-protest-detector-kommersant-a75702.

differentiation, demographic decline, and lack of access to state services, people remain largely sullen; pollsters do not really know what the subdued majority or the "deep people" believes or what would trigger an active response. Social alienation deepens distrust between elites and the populace and can lead to unpredictable explosions.[185]

Below the pacified surface, Russia is experiencing the alienation of the younger generations. Growing numbers of youths who have only known one state President during their lifetimes have become disillusioned and estranged from the regime and are more impatient than their elders. Approval ratings for government institutions are dropping dramatically, pessimism about the future has increased, and willingness to participate in protests has grown.[186] Those aged between 20 and 30 are one of the social groups that are most critical of the regime, and their level of support for protests is relatively high. Young Russians form a diverse generation, and some may be attracted to different forms of nationalism, communism, and fascism, as well as liberalism and democracy. While the Kremlin has endeavored to create a loyal youth on the basis of statism, patriotism and imperialism, this only attracts a small segment of the younger generation.

Patriotic education and militaristic propaganda have become a key ingredient of state policy. The myth of a besieged Russia that needs to rearm and defend itself against the West has been cultivated through

---

185 Paul Goble, "Impoverished Russians Won't Protest Openly but Undermine the State, Baymukhametov Says," October 25, 2020, http://windowoneurasia2.blogspot.com/2020/10/impoverished-russians-wont-protest.html.

186 Andrei Kolesnikov and Denis Volkov, "Will a New Generation of Russians Modernize Their Country?" Carnegie Moscow Center, February 4, 2022, https://carnegiemoscow.org/commentary/86355.

the educational system, mass media, the Orthodox Church, and national institutions such as the military. In October 2015, the All-Russian Military-Patriotic Public Movement "Youth Army" (*Vserossiyskoye Voyenno-Patrioticheskoye Obshchestvennoye Dvizheniye "Yunarmiya")* was established under the direction of the Ministry of Defense as an instrument of mass youth indoctrination, to train future soldiers, and inculcate their loyalty to the regime.[187] Children between the ages of eight and eighteen have been encouraged to join its ranks, and the movement boasted over 270,000 members by 2019.

Youth estrangement from the regime is a major reason why the authorities are focused on a patriotic and militaristic upbringing to depict Putin as the defender of the nation. Youth voting also provides further momentum for falsifying election results, as young people increasingly do not want to vote for Putin or his loyalists.[188] Opinion polls indicate that the younger generation opposes Russia's growing isolation from the West and welcomes open communication and an exchange of ideas. Youth alienation, whether among middle-class students or working-class youth, is compounded by shrinking job opportunities, poor economic conditions, favoritism for children of the *siloviki* and state bureaucrats in admissions to higher education and to lucrative jobs, and the increasing age of the ruling stratum. In January 2021, Putin sent a draft bill to the *Duma* that no longer obliges senior officials to retire at the age of 70.[189] This will limit the

---

[187] https://stat.mil.ru/youtharmy/info.htm.

[188] "Новое поколение," January 22, 2021, https://el-murid.livejournal.com/4653500.html.

[189] Paul Goble, "As Young Russians Protest, Putin Wants Aging Elite to Remain in Office Beyond Normal Retirement Age," January 25, 2021, http://windowoneurasia2.blogspot.com/2021/01/as-young-russians-protest-putin-wants.html.

promotion of younger people and accentuate the parallels with the stagnant Brezhnev regime in the 1970s.

Although the authorities have created various pro-Kremlin youth organizations, including *Nashi* (Ours) and the *Molodaya Gvardiya Yedinoi Rossii* (Young Guard of United Russia), they are fighting a losing battle to control and mold the majority of Russia's youth. The Kremlin establishment was jolted by the large-scale participation of youth groups in the "colored" revolutions in Georgia (2003) and Ukraine (2004 and 2014), worried that their effective street actions could be repeated in Russia.[190] The popularity of social media platforms exceeds that of state television, and there are signs of greater youth participation in opposition politics.[191] Attempts to cut off Russia from the world have angered many young people who feel globally interconnected through the internet and consider the government outdated and out-of-touch with reality. Police violence against protesters, as during the Navalny imprisonment, are less effective at intimidating young people than the middle aged, who are more likely to have steady jobs, incomes and children. When an individual has less to lose, she or he may become more prone toward defensive or even aggressive violence against the police.

To keep young people in check, a law on education that came into effect in June 2021 monitors the teaching of political issues and international research collaboration and seeks to inculcate "patriotic" themes. Kremlin attempts to control the internet or block certain social networks are ultimately counterproductive. While people will

---

[190] Ilya Yablokov, *Fortress Russia: Conspiracy Theories in Post-Soviet Russia,* Cambridge, UK: Polity Press, 2018, p.93.

[191] Anastasiia Starchenko, "Life Under One Leader: Kremlin's Relationship With the Russian Youth," *New Eastern Europe*, February 24, 2021, https://neweasterneurope.eu/2021/02/24/life-under-one-leader-kremlins-relationship-with-the-russian-youth/.

find other platforms and circumvent the restrictions, government censorship will increase anger among young people, particularly those who depend on the web for social interactions, news and entertainment. Shutting down the internet altogether could dramatically increase public antagonism toward the regime.

Russia's civil society, especially in the regions, faces an uphill struggle to develop and exert any influence. Most organizations are largely dependent on state funding and official approval, restricted from receiving foreign funds, and subjected to administrative suppression through non-registration, burdensome taxation, auditing inspections, and various legal procedures. Ethnic minorities suffer in particular, as there is an absence of effective state or regional programs to promote and protect minority rights. Paradoxically, an active and organized civil society could prevent revolutionary upheaval and potential bloodshed, as witnessed throughout Central-Eastern Europe when Communism collapsed in the late 1980s and agreements were negotiated between the government and opposition in the transformation to democratic political systems. Without a layer of counter-elites that can help steer a political transition, the country becomes much more vulnerable to violent convulsions.

The regime cannot take public support or even acquiescence for granted. During protests against the arrest of Alexei Navalny in January 2021, analysts believed there was a visible shift of opinion toward sympathy for the protesters. This presented an even more serious long-term threat for the government than the growing number of active opponents and street demonstrators. It could spell an even larger potential pool of recruits for future rebellions.[192] The protests were much larger than those against the falsification of

---

[192] Paul Goble, "Kremlin Should Be More Worried by Attitudes of Russians toward Protests than by Protests Themselves, Pastukhov Says," January 26, 2021, http://windowoneurasia2.blogspot.com/2021/01/kremlin-should-be-more-worried-by.html.

elections in the regional elections in the summer of 2019. Citizens in numerous regions were involved in the protests, thus precluding a concerted and effective regime response. Russia can also witness increasing social polarization between supporters and opponents of the *status quo* that could engender conflict or be manipulated by state actors during periods of turmoil. In non-democratic systems, abstention from public protests does not necessarily mean apathy or alienation; it may simply signal fear of retribution and calculations about the efficacy of current demonstrations.[193]

Russia is developing an aggrieved "silent majority" whose reticence will be severely tested as the multi-faceted political and economic crisis grips the country. Public opinion polls may not accurately measure the breadth of public opposition to the regime, as respondents play down their criticisms for fear of repercussions, while the Kremlin coopts, harasses, or outlaws independent polling organizations.[194] Polls also cannot measure or predict sudden jolts in public opinion or circumstances that can precipitate large-scale unrest. A lack of information and understanding of popular attitudes was evident in 2011–2012, when the Kremlin was surprised by the size of protests against election fraud and in opposition to Putin's return for a third term as President following a four-year absence.[195]

Surveys have found that during worsening economic conditions, many Russians are increasingly unwilling to bear the economic

---

[193] Regina Smyth, *Elections, Protest, and Authoritarian Regime Stability: Russia 2008-2020*, Cambridge University Press, 2021, p.147.

[194] Regina Smyth, *Elections, Protest, and Authoritarian Regime Stability: Russia 2008-2020*, Cambridge University Press, 2021, p.33.

[195] Ilya Yablokov, *Fortress Russia: Conspiracy Theories in Post-Soviet Russia,* Cambridge, UK: Polity Press, 2018, pp.145-146.

burden of an escalating confrontation with the West and oppose Russia's involvement in foreign wars.[196] It is worth remembering that large military investments and foreign campaigns, such as in Afghanistan between 1979 and 1989, conducted in the midst of an economic slowdown, contributed to the collapse of the Soviet Union. Putin's assertive foreign policy with a growing military budget is widely viewed as being conducted at the expense of domestic needs, including health care, education, and pensions. After the annexation of Crimea in 2014, Russia experienced a short-lived patriotic mobilization, and support for the authorities skyrocketed. However, as the economy sunk into prolonged stagnation, the majority of citizens expected the government to focus on declining living standards and the degradation of social welfare, instead of on further wars in Ukraine or Syria and more intensive confrontations with the West.

State propaganda promulgates submissive stereotypes. The primary goal of each Russian ruler since Tsarist times has been domestic centralization and foreign expansion. By underscoring that Russia has always been a major global empire, the regime intends to convince citizens that this is an unchangeable law of nature and the ruling stratum is ensuring Russia's continuing glory. Russian citizens are told from cradle to grave that they are not prepared for democracy and need a strong hand to rule them, otherwise the state will collapse and Russia's identity and history will disappear.[197] Hence, Russians are portrayed by their own government as essentially infantile and incapable of self-government. Such stereotypes are repeated by some Western commentators to portray Russian authoritarianism and

---

196 Maria Snegovaya, "Guns to Butter: Sociotropic Concerns and Foreign Policy Preferences in Russia," *Post-Soviet Affairs*, Vol. 36, Issue 3, 2020, https://www.tandfonline.com/doi/full/10.1080/1060586X.2020.1750912.

197 "Лжеконсерваторы: охранители против русской нации," October 26, 2020, https://www.apn.ru/index.php?newsid=38777.

statism as inevitable because of alleged genetic, historic, cultural, or "civilizational" predispositions to submissiveness and subservience in the face of dictatorship. Such perceptions assume almost instinctive popular support for Russia's state imperialism and anti-Westernism. However, if these stereotypes were fully grounded in reality, then the regime would have little need to falsify elections, control all public institutions, promulgate pro-Kremlin propaganda, disable an independent media, restrict or prohibit political opposition, and engage in extensive repression.

Regional Challenges

Russia is an economically, socially, and regionally fragmented country, consisting of a few developed cities and micro-regions and a vast impoverished and disconnected hinterland.[198] Collapsing transportation links, including air and rail connections, between regional capitals and smaller towns are isolating many regions from the rest of the country. With the closure of dozens of regional airports and railway lines, an increasing number of people are becoming confined to their home districts, where poverty grows and social services deteriorate, or they permanently out-migrate and depopulate the countryside. Despite government incentives, the population of Siberia, the High North, and the Pacific region continues to decline. Workers previously attracted to these zones because of higher pay, earlier retirement, and other benefits can no longer be certain of such prospects and are less likely to migrate there from inner Russia.

The 2010 Russian census showed that Russian villages are fast disappearing, with a growing number having fewer than ten

---

[198] Marlene Laruelle (Ed.), *New Mobilities and Social Changes in Russia's Arctic Regions*, London: Routledge, 2017, pp.2–3.

permanent inhabitants.[199] Out of approximately 153,000 rural settlements and villages, at least 20,000 have been abandoned over the past fifty years and a growing number are turning into ghost towns. An estimated 40 million people in smaller cities and towns are especially neglected by the government and face acute poverty.[200] After the Soviet collapse, the basis for the existence of many small cities vanished because of economic policies that concentrated production in selected locations and left the rest to decay. Almost 60 percent of the population of smaller cities has fallen below the poverty line, and about 10 percent of small cities are on the brink of collapse, while the remainder continue to degrade. Underfunding is an ever-larger problem, with local governments only receiving a tiny share of the state budget. Economic decline will drive many of Russia's regions into depression and detachment from Moscow.

Regional restlessness in the Russian Federation is based on an accumulation of grievances, including economic stagnation, official corruption, state exploitation of regional resources, inadequate social services, and the absence of authentic federalism, local democracy, regionalist parties, or governmental accountability. The Kremlin views the country's regions as exploitable resources and also as liabilities that need to be suppressed to prevent fragmentation. Throughout its imperial history, Russia's rulers have harbored a neurotic fear not only of enemies outside the empire's borders but also of the subject peoples within them.[201] Because economic modernization would not only require democratization but far-

---

[199] Tatiana Nefedova, "сжатие и поляризация сельского пространства россии," *Demoscop*, No. 507–508, 2012.

[200] "Скрепы или изгои?" November 25, 2020, http://www.sovross.ru/articles/2054/50301.

[201] Alexander Etkind, *Internal Colonization: Russia's Imperial Experience*, Cambridge, UK: Polity Press, 2011, pp.4–5.

reaching decentralization, regional autonomy is viewed as a threat to the autocratic center and the continuity of the state. There are no independent regionalist institutions in Russia that report on developments in Russia's diverse ethnic republics and federal regions. Independent research is discouraged and stifled as the Kremlin fears that accurate reports will encourage regional self-assertion and challenge the foundation of autocratic centralism. Any regional assertiveness, such as promoting the distinctiveness of the Pomor sub-ethnos in northern Russia, a distinctive Cossack national identity in southern Russia, or the histories of national and regional independence movements, can result in charges of separatism.

Vast disparities exist between Russia's regions in terms of wealth, investment, per capita income, educational levels, and professional opportunities. For instance, while Sakhalin *Oblast* has a Gross Regional Product (GRP) comparable to Singapore, the Ingush Republic is closer to Honduras.[202] During prolonged economic hardship, rich resource-producing regions feel increasingly aggrieved by Moscow's tax collecting regime. Tyumen *Oblast*, for example, has administrative jurisdiction over two autonomous *okrugs* (Khanty-Mansi and Yamalo-Nenets) that produce 48 percent of Russia's oil and about 80 percent of its natural gas. In 2020, these two *okrugs* supplied more than 17 percent of the federal budget's tax income and had to transfer most of their tax receipts to the federal center, receiving only a fragment in return.[203] Russia's federal budget leaves personal income tax receipts and a segment of corporate income tax

---

[202] Kathryn E. Stoner, *Russia Resurrected: Its Power and Purpose in a New Global Order*, Oxford University Press, 2021, p.174.

[203] András Tóth-Czifra, "Moscow vs Regions: Who "Feeds" Whom?" February 4, 2021, Institute of Modern Russia, https://imrussia.org/en/analysis/3230-moscow-vs-regions-who-"feeds"-whom.

receipts in regional hands, but it collects all tax receipts from mineral extraction.

Even in periods when the federal budget was booming little was accomplished to promote regional economic modernization, and there is minimal prospect that this will change.[204] Notably, Moscow's periodic pledges to economically develop Russia's Far East have not been fulfilled. It has failed to supply resources and investments, and in 2020 it only increased the budgets of the 11 federal subjects in the Far Eastern Federal District by a miniscule amount.[205] Moscow's economic policy has also failed to attract significant Asian investment or to develop the economy by boosting infrastructural linkages.[206] The central government simply pours money into existing factories and shuttles workers to distant production sites rather than linking them together and building roads, airports, hospitals, and schools. As a result, the economy is declining and people will continue to leave for European Russia. This provides more inroads for Chinese economic penetration: as Moscow gradually loses control, Beijing will seek to protect its growing investments and strategic interests in the Pacific and Siberian regions.

---

[204] William M. Reisinger and Bryon J. Moraski, *The Regional Roots of Russia's Political Regime,* Ann Arbor: University of Michigan Press, 2017, pp.213–214.

[205] Paul Goble, "Moscow's Promise to Develop Russia's East has Not Been Fulfilled, Leading Vladivostok Economist Says," August 12, 2021, http://windowoneurasia2.blogspot.com/2021/08/moscows-promise-to-develop-russias-east.html.

[206] Paul Goble, "Moscow's Failure to Develop Infrastructure in Russia's Far East Means Region Won't Develop and People will Continue to Leave, Shelest Says," January 20, 2021, http://windowoneurasia2.blogspot.com/2021/01/moscows-failure-to-develop.html.

The economic impact of the COVID-19 pandemic has also cut into federal spending, while declining oil prices in 2020 decimated the budgets of many of Russia's regional governments, which acquired record deficits.[207] The combined deficit of regional governments reached 677 billion rubles ($10 billion), the largest figure since 2006. Fifty-seven federal subjects ended the year with deficits, up from 35 in 2018 and 15 in 2019. Their combined incomes rose only 0.1 percent and incomes fell in 32 regions. Federal subjects substantially dependent on oil and gas revenues, including Tyumen *Oblast*, Yamalo-Nenets Autonomous *Okrug*, the Komi Republic, the Republic of Tatarstan and the Republic of Bashkortostan, were hit hardest. Some regional governments would have collapsed without massive transfer payments from Moscow and bank loans. Moscow planned to cut these transfers by some 25 percent after 2021. This will have a disastrous impact on social services and living standards and may force local authorities to impose taxes on the population and risk widespread disaffection and protests.

Numerous regional governments face financial disaster because Moscow imposes unfunded liabilities and confiscates most of the taxes they collect.[208] In Russia's federal budgeting system, the regions collect taxes but send almost all their revenues to Moscow and receive a small portion in return. This system was established in the 1990s to ensure greater central control. When Moscow is short of money, the regions are deprived of essential resources. Given the financial crunch, the majority of regions do not have the resources for economic development or even to meet basic social services, and

---

[207] Paul Goble, "2020 was a Hard Year for Russia's Regions; 2021 will Be Even Worse, Experts Say," March 1, 2021, http://windowoneurasia2.blogspot.com/2021/03/2020-was-hard-year-for-russias-regions.html.

[208] Paul Goble, "Moscow to Blame for Looming Financial Disaster in Russian Regions, Nechayev Says," April 9, 2021, http://windowoneurasia2.blogspot.com/2021/04/moscow-to-blame-for-looming-financial.html.

many are falling deeply into debt. Fifteen federal subjects have deficits exceeding 10 percent of their incomes and another seven exceed by more than 20 percent.

Moreover, during 2020, investments and industrial production fell in 51 federal subjects and real incomes among the population fell in 75. Regional governments do not have the authority to tax for their own needs and are dependent on Moscow's benevolence. Debt conditions in the regions worsened during the pandemic, with budget deficits reported in 57 regions during 2020 compared to 34 in 2019.[209] By the fall of 2021, sixty federal subjects were running significant deficits with shrinking options for borrowing, as banks were unwilling to bail them out.[210] Cuts in spending will intensify economic hardships, further reduce social services, and increase social frustrations. They can also increase calls for the regions to retain more taxes and other locally generated incomes.

Poorer federal regions are highly dependent on Moscow for their budgets to avoid bankruptcies. This is especially evident in the North Caucasus republics, where federal transfers account for up to 80 percent of their revenues.[211] This arrangement has several negative consequences by fostering dependence that can be damaged by budgetary shortfalls and shrinking allocations. Any subsidies or loans are strictly monitored to give Moscow a larger role in local investment

---

[209] The World Bank, "Russia Economic Report," December 1, 2021, https://www.worldbank.org/en/country/russia/publication/rer.

[210] Paul Goble, "Sixty Federal Subjects Running Deficits and Lack the Ability to Borrow to Cover Them, Economists Say," October 10, 2021, http://windowoneurasia2.blogspot.com/2021/10/sixty-federal-subjects-running-deficits.html.

[211] Emil Aslan Souleimanov, *The North Caucasus Insurgency: Dead or Alive?* US Army War College, Strategic Studies Institute, February 2017, p.15.

projects. Massive federal subsidies also encourage corruption among regional elites, which is tolerated by the Center in order to secure the loyalty of regional authorities, but it further estranges the population.[212] Subsidization also generates resentment among Russian ethno-nationalists, who view Russia as being exploited by Caucasian "foreigners."

Moscow's decision to declare Ingushetia bankrupt in November 2020 and take direct financial control over the republic is likely to be followed by similar moves elsewhere.[213] In June 2021, Russian Prime Minister Mikhail Mishustin admitted that Moscow's development programs for the North Caucasus failed to boost per capita GDP, real incomes or outside investment.[214] Although federal spending in the region in 2020 was evidently 40 percent higher than the year before, most of the funds were not allocated for economic development but for placating the regional elites and ensuring their loyalty to Moscow. A majority of Russia's federal subjects are on the brink of bankruptcy, and conditions continue to deteriorate. Under Russian law, Moscow can declare a region bankrupt and assume direct financial administration when its income makes up only 85 percent of expenditures. About 20 federal subjects faced such conditions by the close of 2021.

---

[212] Julie Wilhelmsen, "Russian Governance of the North Caucasus: Dilemmas of Force and Inclusion," in Derek Averre and Kevork Oskanian (Ed), *Security, Society and the State in the Caucasus*, Routledge, 2019, p.43.

[213] Paul Goble, "Majority of Russian Regions on Brink of Bankruptcy and More are Headed in That Direction," November 11, 2020, http://windowoneurasia2.blogspot.com/2020/11/majority-of-russian-regions-on-brink-of.html.

[214] Paul Goble, "Moscow's Development Programs in North Caucasus have Failed, Mishustin Says," June 17, 2021, http://windowoneurasia2.blogspot.com/2021/06/moscows-development-programs-in-north.html.

International Defeats

An integral part of Russia's state propaganda is to create an aura of invincibility and inevitability in its international stature. This is reminiscent of claims about the irresistible success of world Communism in a previous era. But reality is less sanguine, as the Kremlin's covert war to undermine Western governments and alliances have experienced a legion of defeats that weaken its expansionist ambitions. The most notable Kremlin failures have included the enlargement of NATO to include all former Soviet satellites and Warsaw Pact members in Central-Eastern Europe; Moscow's inability to prevent NATO membership for Montenegro and North Macedonia in the western Balkans despite its intensive anti-Alliance campaigns; ineffectual intimidation of the Baltic States and Poland from reinforcing NATO's military capabilities through its Enhanced Forward Presence (EFP) deployments; impotence in preventing Ukraine from petitioning for NATO membership; and botched efforts to cower Georgia from seeking NATO accession despite Russia's seizure of 20 percent of Georgian territory. During the past decade, NATO's refocusing on its core mission of defending Europe has been a consequence of Kremlin belligerence and strategic failure.

Russia has failed in its attempt to become a major "pole of power," a source of political, economic, or cultural attraction, or even the sole power in "Eurasia." The constant use of bellicose and threatening language against neighbors and Western powers is not a sign of strength but of Moscow's weakness and frustration in its inability to successfully intimidate neighbors and adversaries. Russian citizens will also interpret constant threats by Moscow and endless international disputes as a sign of waning power and influence. Despite Putin's promotion of a reinvigorated "Russian World," the regime has failed in achieving extensive empire building. Instead, it has truncated and absorbed parts of neighboring states but failed to gain international legitimacy for any of its actions and precipitated various Western sanctions for its irredentist and expansionist policies.

Persistent military threats against Ukraine through the concentration of significant Russian forces along its borders leading up to the massive re-invasion of the country on February 24, 2022, also demonstrated that Moscow had failed to derail Kyiv's moves toward Western institutions. The attacks on Ukraine served to strengthen Ukrainian identity and statehood, and Kyiv is regaining its history and institutions from its imperial neighbor. The most monumental Putin debacle prior to 2022 war was the official restoration of the autocephaly of the Ukrainian Orthodox Church (UOC).[215] Patriarch Bartholomew of Constantinople, the Universal Patriarch of Orthodox Christianity, ruled in favor of the UOC gaining independence from the Russian Orthodox Church (ROC). This ensured that Moscow not only lost an important tool of influence in Ukraine, but it also forfeited another fraudulent claim to dominate the Eastern Slavic world by claiming its neighbors as part of Moscow's canonical territory. Following the Moscow Patriarchate's support for the war against Ukraine, the Ukrainian Orthodox Church – Moscow Patriarchate looked set to lose most of its parishes to the autocephalous Ukrainian Orthodox Church and lose the allegiance of its own Ukrainian clergy.

The independence of its Orthodox Church signified universal recognition that Ukraine's history and identity predate that of Russia. The UOC is older than the ROC, tracing its origins back to 9th century Kyivan Rus, but its heritage has been appropriated by Moscow through generations of disinformation. The UOC is acknowledged as the sole descendant in Ukraine of the metropolis of Kyivan Rus within the jurisdiction of the Ecumenical Patriarchate of Constantinople

---

[215] "Ecumenical Patriarchate Agrees To Recognize Independence Of Ukrainian Church," October 12, 2018, https://www.rferl.org/a/constantinople-patriarchate-agrees-to-recognize-independence-of-ukrainian-orthodox-church/29538590.html.

established in Kyiv in the 10th century. At that time, there was no "Russian" nation, state, or church, and Moscow was merely a peripheral town in the Kyivan confederation. Although the ROC professed ecclesiastical jurisdiction over Ukraine, this claim was imposed by force through the imperial expansion of the Grand Duchy of Moscow since the 15th century and its subjugation of neighbors. Other Orthodox Churches are likely to follow Ukraine in claiming their independence from the ROC, including that of Belarus.

Russia has failed to offer a viable and productive alternative to constitutional pluralistic democracies, despite officials claiming that Putinism is the global vanguard of "sovereign democracy." In reality, Moscow is increasingly fearful of foreign influence, especially from Western states. The "Fortress Russia" syndrome that advocates Russia's political and cultural protection and even isolation is designed to prevent threatening Western influences that would undermine the autocratic administration. Incessant pro-Putin propaganda is intended to forge national unity, not so much as a defense against NATO's security challenges but against the political and cultural threats from the US and EU that can undermine the stranglehold of the current regime in the Kremlin.[216]

Moscow has engaged in a concerted campaign to alienate itself from Europe and the US and has depicted both the EU and the NATO alliance as grave dangers to Russia's independence and territorial unity. In promoting anti-EU-ism, Kremlin propaganda outlets claim that the Union is degenerate, hyper-liberal, militantly anti-religious, and chaotically multi-cultural, while its officials are intent on destroying the sovereignty and traditions of individual states. These themes help Moscow to influence a "fifth column" of movements and parties in several European countries, where it tries to exploit an

---

216 Regina Smyth, *Elections, Protest, and Authoritarian Regime Stability: Russia 2008-2020*, Cambridge University Press, 2021, p.199.

assortment of radical right and ultra-conservative parties to reinforce its message of Western decadence and Russia's morality.

Moscow's intelligence services also capitalize on far left and anti-globalist movements in the West, as well as regionalists and ethno-separatists. Moscow seeks to drive wedges between the "Anglo-Saxon" states of the US, UK, and Canada and continental Europe, with the latter viewed as more malleable, corruptible, and exploitable. Messages are regularly conveyed that US political hegemony, military dominance, and cultural imperialism limits the sovereignty of all EU member states. The Kremlin's objective is to divide the West and preclude any lasting transatlantic solidarity. The exit of the United Kingdom from the EU (Brexit) and other centrifugal developments such as separatist movements in Spain (Catalonia) and the UK (Scotland) are welcomed in Moscow as they divide the EU, weaken individual states, encourage beneficial bilateral deals with Russia, and limit further Euro-Atlantic enlargement.

However, vehement official attacks on the EU disguise a deep-rooted fear of European interests, values and attractions. EU standards of legality, transparency, and competition challenge Russia's business model of corruption, opaqueness, monopolization, and politicization. And the EU's political and human rights stipulations, underpinned by the rule of law, undermine the premises of Moscow's autocratic model of governance. It is such features of the European heritage that Kremlin rulers, presiding over an increasingly repressive authoritarian system, cannot digest. They are fearful that younger generations in Russia will adopt "European values" and challenge the country's governing elites.[217] According to regime propagandists, because Russia's openness to the world will ultimately result in its

[217] Igor Torbakov, "Away From Europe!" February 25, 2021, *Utrikes Magazinet*, Utrikespolitiska Institutet, Stockholm, Sweden, https://www.ui.se/utrikesmagasinet/in-english/2021/away-from-europe/.

destruction, a policy of isolation and resistance is necessary.[218] Such views have become an integral part of the official media narrative and repressive state legislation designed to marshal the populace in support of the Kremlin.

Moscow's efforts to establish an alternative fulcrum of global leadership through the BRICS (Brazil, Russia, India, China and South Africa) arrangement has largely failed. Russia's influences continue to erode in Europe's east, and its political system is not a model for emulation.[219] It has registered multiple failures in replicating a post-Soviet multi-national format that would include all former Soviet republics under its predominant control. The Commonwealth of Independent States (CIS), the Eurasian Customs Union (ECU), the Eurasian Economic Union (EEU), the Collective Security Treaty Organization (CSTO), and the Russia-Belarus Union State have all misfired in establishing a bloc of loyal Russian allies to confront successful Western structures such as NATO and the EU. The EEU is stagnating and has not resulted in closer political integration, while the CSTO has failed to develop into a coherent security alliance and is basically a cover for Moscow's unilateral military actions.

In their foreign policy, governments bordering Russia pursue hedging or balancing strategies and often search for security guarantees elsewhere to avoid becoming Moscow's vassals. This is illustrated in the refusal of all post-Soviet states to formally recognize Russia's annexation of Crimea. Moreover, Moldova, Georgia, and Ukraine have rejected any economic and political integration with Russia, and

---

[218] Ilya Yablokov, *Fortress Russia: Conspiracy Theories in Post-Soviet Russia,* Cambridge, UK: Polity Press, 2018, p.3.

[219] Arkady Moshes and Ryhor Nizhnikau, *Three Decades of Russian Policy in the European Part of the Post-Soviet Space: Swimming Against the Current*, Finnish Institute of International Studies, Briefing Paper 221, November 2021, https://transatlanticrelations.us2.list-manage.com/track/click?u=ecd50dd626cf374511464e688&id=b037467243&e=223d2dad2a.

the latter two aspire to EU and NATO membership with significant public support. Their economic and trading ties with Russia have steadily decreased, thus making each state more resilient to Moscow's economic pressure. Nonetheless, Moscow continues to manipulate energy supplies, financial incentives, political pressures, and media campaigns as weapons to undermine the independence of its neighbors and their sovereign choice of international alliances.

Unlike the United States, Russia has few genuine allies. The handful of countries that enter Moscow-led organizations or engage in joint military exercises are either intimidated or enticed to participate, or their authoritarian governments are guaranteed Moscow's support in case of domestic rebellions. Presently, Moscow projects its regional power through two main organizations—the Eurasian Economic Union and the Collective Security Treaty Organization. The EEU includes five states (Russia, Armenia, Belarus, Kazakhstan, Kyrgyzstan) and is depicted as an alternative to the EU. Its real purpose is to prevent neighbors from qualifying for the EU while intensifying Russia's economic dominance. The CSTO consists of six members (Russia, Armenia, Belarus, Kazakhstan, Kyrgyzstan, Tajikistan) and is portrayed by the Kremlin as an equivalent to NATO. Azerbaijan and Georgia withdrew from this body, as its actual goals are to bolster Russia's military presence and prevent members from moving closer to the North Atlantic Alliance. Even current CSTO members remain wary of being trapped in collective defense arrangement that would permit Moscow to station troops on their soil.

After witnessing Russia's "brotherly assistance" to Ukraine and Georgia, three European countries—Belarus, Armenia, Azerbaijan—are now on the front line in defending their sovereignty. In the economic realm, they have tried to reorient toward China and other markets as Russia's economy steadily deteriorates. In the diplomatic arena, they have refused to recognize the occupied Georgian territories of South Ossetia and Abkhazia as independent states despite Moscow's coaxing. They also adopted an ambiguous stance toward Russia's forcible annexation of Crimea, torn between appeasing Moscow and not legitimizing a precedent that could potentially threaten their own territorial integrity. Moscow uses the carrot of economic assistance and the stick of replacing the government to keep Belarus in line, and it has intensified the country's dependence on Moscow in the wake of President Alyaksandr Lukashenka's growing isolation from the West after the August 2020 crackdown on mass protests. The *Zapad* exercises in September 2021 and the joint Russian-Belarusian (Allied Resolve) exercises on Belarusian territory in February 2022 highlighted Minsk's predicament, as they entangle Belarus in the Kremlin deception that NATO is a security threat to both countries.

In the South Caucasus, Armenia and Azerbaijan remain in an exposed position. Armenia has no diplomatic relations with its neighbors Azerbaijan and Turkey, while Azerbaijan is squeezed between Russia and Iran and needs Georgia to maintain access to Europe. If Russia's influence in the region is reduced diplomatic and infrastructural connections between former rivals are likely to intensify. The South Caucasus states have endeavored to intensify cooperation with NATO and the EU and emerge from their relative isolation. Armenia hosts Russian bases and is pressured by Moscow to incorporate its armed forces into Russia's military structures. Following the September 2020 war, in which Azerbaijan regained most of its occupied territories from Armenia, Moscow emplaced its "peace-keepers" in the disputed region of Karabakh, effectively gaining a territorial foothold in all three South Caucasus states. The Kremlin has deliberately sustained the Armenian-Azerbaijani conflict to keep both governments dependent on Russia's diplomatic decisions and military involvement.

But despite Russia's presence and pressure, Armenia and Azerbaijan have continued to assert their sovereignty by expanding links with NATO, even though neither country, unlike Georgia, has petitioned for membership. Both states have participated in NATO-led operations, including in Afghanistan. Yerevan has obtained a NATO Individual Partnership Action Plan (IPAP) to enhance its interoperability with the Alliance, and Azerbaijan has been successfully fulfilling its own, bi-annual IPAPs with NATO. While diplomatic and military interactions with Russia perpetuate the state of conflict between Baku and Yerevan, closer links with the West are likely to reduce tensions and enhance Armenia's connectivity with Europe. In stark contrast to Russia's threatening military posture in the South Caucasus, NATO's multi-national involvement can strengthen regional security by improving bilateral relations among member states and partners. Ultimately, Russia's alliances forged through political coercion, economic threat, and military dominance are a sign of international failure and do not generate trust, loyalty, unity, commitment, or durability. On the contrary, resentments among vassal status will propel the process of emancipation once the Russian Federation begins to rupture.

3.

Regional Unrest

If the former Soviet republics are considered by the Kremlin as Russia's "near abroad," then the republics and regions within the multi-national Russian Federation can be designated as Russia's "inner abroad." Russia's federal structure increasingly resembles the sunset of the Soviet Union, when regional and ethno-national disquiet triggered and propelled dismemberment.[1] Widening economic and political rifts between Moscow and its federal subjects are driven by escalating resentments against the central administration.[2] The elements of state decay are far advanced, so that Moscow's reactions, whether by increasing repression or attempting some measure of liberalization, will both accelerate the process. Local grievances are more likely to mobilize the public than state-wide demands, and they encompass numerous economic, political, ethnic, regional, social, environmental, demographic, resource, and public health issues. They are driven by two core resentments—the inability of the government to ensure basic state services for the public and the ubiquitous corruption of officials in exploiting local resources and economies at the cost of citizens.

---

[1] Private interview with Enders Wimbush, Jamestown Foundation, March 2021.

[2] Ben Judah, *Fragile Empire: How Russia Fell In And Out Of Love With Vladimir Putin,* Yale University Press, 2013, pp. 251, 278.

Federalism is a political arrangement based on a contract enshrined in a constitution among the constituent units of an administrative structure that are willing to relinquish some of their powers and prerogatives to a central government. It thereby presupposes a voluntary compact formulated through democratic principles, supported by a popular mandate within each federal unit. In a genuine federation, territorial entities combine in one state structure and seek consensus in pursuit of common goals. They also maintain significant self-government to protect their distinct regional identities and uphold symmetrical equality between each federal unit within the central state institutions.

A highly centralized unitary system for a large country like Russia is an ineffective form of government. Although Russia's 1993 Constitution defines the country as a federation, in reality it is a centralized neo-imperial construct integrated on the basis of administrative proclamation and not by voluntary agreement.[3] Unlike the United Kingdom, France, or other former colonial powers, Russia has failed to fully dismantle its empire and develop either into a predominantly Russian ethno-national state, a decentralized multi-regional federation, or a multi-national democratic civic state. Officials in Moscow contend that the devolution of federal powers will lead to the dissolution of the state, as was increasingly evident during the 1990s under the presidency of Boris Yeltsin. However, hyper-centralization, as witnessed during the Putin period, will also provoke separatism and result in federal fracture.

[3] Constitute, "Russian Federation 1993," 2014, https://www.constituteproject.org/constitution/Russia_2014.

Anti-Federal Offensives

Under Vladimir Putin's presidency, the central government has pursued a policy of ethnic, cultural, and linguistic homogenization and the concentration of power over the country's regions and republics.[4] Successive government documents and pronouncements have also given more prominence to the Russian ethnic people (*Russkii narod*) as the creator, unifier, and leader of the multi-ethnic Russian state (*Rossiiskoie gosudarstvo)* and the Russian nation (*Rossiiskaia natsiia*). Government policies have deliberately blurred the differences between the civic or statist *Rossiiskii* and the ethnic *Russkii* identities and made the pre-eminence of the *Russkii* core more explicit than during the Soviet or Yeltsin periods.[5]

Assertions of *Russkii* dominance have steadily undermined the principles of federalism and raised fears of assimilation and russification among the country's numerous nations. The Cyrillic alphabet was imposed on many indigenous languages during Tsarist and Soviet rule to standardize educational and cultural policies and accelerate the russification process. Concerns over ethnic and cultural absorption are particularly pronounced among ethnic groups residing outside their titular republics, as they have fewer opportunities for education in their native languages. Government policy has alienated several nations and even estranged regions where ethnic Russians predominate but where a growing number of residents feel

---

[4] Federica Prina, *National Minorities in Putin's Russia: Diversity and Assimilation*, Routledge Contemporary Russia and Eastern Europe Series, Routledge: London and New York, 2016.

[5] Helge Blakkisrud, "Blurring the Boundary Between Civic and Ethnic: The Kremlin's New Approach to National Identity Under Putin's Third Term," in Pål Kolstø and Helge Blakkisrud (Eds.), *The New Russian Nationalism: Imperialism, Ethnicity and Authoritarianism, 2000-15*, Edinburgh University Press, 2016, pp.267, 270.

abandoned or exploited by Moscow and seek to consolidate their local and regional identities. Empirical evidence reveals that conflicts between the federal center and Russia's federal subjects includes ethnically distinct republics, ethnic Russian majority regions, economically advanced entities, and economically underdeveloped regions.[6]

Population Dynamics

According to the 2010 all-Russian census, the population of the country stood at 142.9 million, a decrease of 2.3 million (1.6 percent) since the 2002 census, with ethnic Russians accounting for 80.9 percent.[7] About one fifth of citizens officially belong to other nationalities, and that proportion has been steadily rising. The census lists 193 ethnic groups and sub-groups, with Tatars, Ukrainians, Bashkirs, Chuvash and Chechens among the largest, as well as the presence of 169 distinct languages. After Christian Orthodoxy, Islam is the main religion, with over 16.4 million adherents, and is growing faster than other major faiths.

The Russian Federation currently consists of 85 "federal subjects" (*subjekty*), including Crimea and Sevastopol, which were forcibly captured from Ukraine in 2014. Initially, 32 of the federal subjects were ethnic autonomies named after a particular nation. During a period of amalgamation in the 2000s, six ethnic *okrugs* (districts) were merged with neighboring Russian-majority *oblasts* (regions) or *krais* (territories). Currently, 22 of the federal subjects are republics (*respubliki*), including Ukraine's Crimea, occupied illegally by

---

[6] Matthew Crosston, *Shadow Separatism: Implications for Democratic Consolidation*, London: Routledge, 2004, p.10.

[7] "Всероссийская перепись населения 2010 года," http://www.gks.ru/free_doc/new_site/perepis2010/croc/perepis_itogi1612.htm.

Russian forces in February 2014. Each republic is named after the major non-Russian ethnicity resident on its territory, except for Crimea and multi-ethnic Dagestan. Four subjects are "autonomous *okrugs*" (districts) named after the predominant indigenous ethnic group. The Russian Federation also has 46 *oblasts* (regions), one autonomous Jewish *oblast*, 9 *krais* (territories), and 3 cities of "federal importance" *(goroda federalnogo znacheniya)*, including Ukraine's Sevastopol, seized illegally by Russia in February 2014.

The central government has categorized 26 ethnic groups as "indigenous small-numbered peoples of the North, Siberia and the Far East (*korennyye malochislennyye narody Severa, Sibiri i Dalnego Vostoka*), the majority of which do not possess distinct administrative territories. If southern Siberia is included, there are at least 45 distinct "small-numbered" ethnicities, each of which are comprised of fewer than 50,000 people but maintain their ancestral cultures and languages and often engage in traditional economic activities.[8] The Komi, Sakha and Karels who have their own titular federal units are not included in the "small peoples" category but are recognized as indigenous peoples (*korennye narody).*

Through a process of linguistic russification and political, economic, and cultural assimilation under the Tsarist and Soviet empires, the authorities weakened group identities so that a substantial portion of indigenous peoples identified themselves as Russian ethnics or simply as Russian citizens. After the establishment of the Russian Federation in December 1991, new legislation allowed ethnic minorities to form

---

[8] "Who are the Indigenous Peoples of Russia?" *Cultural Survival*, February 19, 2014, https://www.culturalsurvival.org/news/who-are-indigenous-peoples-russia and Arctic Network for the Support of the Indigenous Peoples of the Russian Arctic, https://ansipra.npolar.no/english/.

independent organizations to promote their languages and cultures.[9] However, most of these legal stipulations have not been implemented, and the revival of national identities has faced intense attrition during the Putin era. Moscow neither grants its indigenous people genuine political autonomy nor does it consult them over land use and resource exploitation in native areas.[10]

In the former Union of Soviet Socialist Republics (USSR), the 15 Union Republics (*Soyuznye Respubliki*—UR), also known as Soviet Socialist Republics (*Sovetskiye Sotsialisticheskiye Respubliki*—SSR), possessed the legal right to secede, while the Autonomous Republics (*Avtonomnyye Respubliki*—AR) within the URs did not have this right. But the status designations were adjustable. For instance, the status of Moldova (1940) and Kazakhstan (1936) was changed from an AR to a UR, while Karelia was downgraded from a UR to an AR in 1956.[11] When the Russian Federation gained independence from the Soviet Union in December 1991, there was an administrative hierarchy between the constituent federal subjects, with the republics possessing more attributes of statehood than other entities (*krais*, *oblasts*, and *okrugs*), including their own executives, legislatures, judiciaries and constitutions. Nonetheless, both the republics and many of the regions have developed distinct identities and interests and are becoming increasingly estranged from Moscow.

---

[9] Artem Rabogoshvili, "Ethnicity on the Move: National-Cultural Organizations in Siberia," in Joachim Otto Habeck (Ed.), *Lifestyle in Siberia and the Russian North*, Cambridge, UK: Open Book Publishers, 2019, p.297.

[10] Marlene Laruelle, *Russia's Arctic Strategies and the Future of the Far North*, London: Routledge, 2014, p.38.

[11] Andrei Illarionov and Boris Lvin, "Should Russia Recognize Chechnya's Independence?" in Tony Wood, *Chechnya: The Case for Independence*, London, New York: Verso, 2007, p.187.

Anti-Federal Propaganda

The Kremlin generates streams of anti-democratic and anti-federal propaganda. In a display of imperial insecurity, the Putin administration propagates the notion that much like the Soviet collapse in 1991, systemic democratization will lead to the disintegration of the Russian Federation.[12] Indeed, former Prime Minister and chief of the foreign intelligence service Yevgenni Primakov warned as early as 1998 that the federation was in danger of splitting into several parts and called for liquidating separatist trends and restoring the "vertical state power structure."[13] Officials manipulate fears of separatism and fragmentation to discourage demands for greater autonomy and to squash protests and other acts of opposition.

In order to justify tighter centralism and legislative repression, Moscow focuses on the danger of disintegration to frighten citizens with the prospect of anarchy, state collapse, economic disaster, mass violence, terrorism, foreign takeovers, a population exodus, and the emergence of criminal entities oppressing and exploiting citizens. In a worst-case scenario, Kremlin apologists and Russian integralists contend that any success of national and regional separatism would endanger the safety of nuclear stockpiles and nuclear power stations, which would have a devastating effect on the environment and the

---

[12] "Почему Россия не Белоруссия и кому угрожает распад страны," September 1, 2020, https://newizv.ru/comment/dmitriy-luchihin/01-09-2020/pochemu-rossiya-ne-belorussiya-i-komu-ugrozhaet-raspad-strany.

[13] Cameron Ross, *Federalism and Democratization in Russia*, Manchester University Press, 2002, p.139.

population over a wide swath of Russia.[14] Generating anxiety about the survival of the state is intended to revive memories of the Soviet collapse and justify strict central control.

Kremlin officials are fearful that if all federal subjects with majority-ethnic-Russian populations also become republics, this would cultivate more distinct regional identities in places such as Siberia, the Pacific region and the Urals. More coherent territorial and administrative identities would acquire national dimensions that could rupture the Russian state. As a result, Moscow has steadfastly opposed the creation of ethnic-Russian republics and has tried to cultivate a uniform Russian imperial history based around an avowedly singular ethnic-Russian nation. In some cases, it has co-opted distinct regional symbols and histories as representations of "real Russianness" to try and dilute their separatist potential.[15] The Kremlin's obsession with regional separatism and state rupture has been evident during the COVID-19 pandemic, viewing governors who took more independent decisions during the emergency and were responsive to the public as having secessionist tendencies.[16] Such political paranoia indicates that the federal state does not rest on solid foundations.

---

[14] Paul Goble, "After Putin, Russia May Yet Become 'a Yugoslavia with Nukes' Many Feared in 1991, Boytsov Says, January 28, 2021, http://windowoneurasia2.blogspot.com/2021/01/after-putin-russia-may-yet-become.html.

[15] Victoria Donovan, "Militarized Memory: Patriotic Rebranding in post-Soviet Pskov," in Edith W. Clowes, Gisela Ersblöh and Ani Kokobobo, *Russia's Regional Identities: The Power of the Provinces,* 2020, pp.73–95.

[16] "Эксперты: поддержка губернаторов будет напрямую зависеть от эффективности их действий в условиях пандемии," October 14, 2020, http://club-rf.ru/detail/4616.

Federal Experiments

Russia's March 1992 Federation Treaty did not establish genuine federalism through a symmetrical agreement between constituent units.[17] It was an unstable and asymmetrical system based largely on bilateral agreements between the federal center and individual federal subjects, some of whom were able to extract more concessions from Moscow than others. Between 1994 and 1998, the central government signed bilateral treaties with 46 regions in order to undercut local dissatisfaction and contain any moves toward separatism.[18] Seven republics, some with strongly separatist tendencies, also signed treaties with Russia that strengthened their autonomous political structures, promoted the creation of republican budgets, and enabled them to develop international contacts.

The Federation Treaty was viewed by some officials as a necessary compromise to salvage the precarious Russian state.[19] However, the treaty fundamentally weakened the principles of federalism and ultimately satisfied neither the centralists nor the regionalists. The arrangement generated numerous regional and republican grievances and disputes with the center, as the Kremlin focused on appeasing the wealthier entities. For instance, many federal *oblasts* and *krais*

---

17 Encyclopedia.com, "Federation Treaties," https://www.encyclopedia.com/history/encyclopedias-almanacs-transcripts-and-maps/federation-treaties.

18 Mizuki Chuman, "The Rise and Fall of Power-Sharing Treaties Between Center and Regions in Post-Soviet Russia," *Demokratizatsiya*, 2011, https://demokratizatsiya.pub/archives/19_2_L7H017206G216817.pdf.

19 Cameron Ross, *Federalism and Democratization in Russia*, Manchester University Press, 2002, p.23.

resented the enhanced claims of the republics to economic assets on their territory and their greater degree of financial autonomy.[20]

The republics also retained a higher status than *oblasts* and *krais* because they were empowered to pass their own constitutions, elect their own executive heads, and declare sovereignty before the federal constitution came into force in December 1993. Persistent disputes broke out on whether the republics had the right to secede from the Russian Federation, with 19 republics (except Ingushetia and Kalmykia) declaring their state sovereignty and right of secession. Oftentimes, the sovereignty declarations contradicted the sovereignty of the Russian state, and the republics structured themselves institutionally as quasi-independent states that did not acknowledge membership of the Russian Federation.[21] The Russian Constitution nominally afforded republics the title of states (*gosudarstava*) with their own constitutions, flags and state languages. They also obtained leeway in signing bilateral treaties with foreign governments and engaged in external economic transactions without consulting with Moscow.

The *oblasts* and *krais* were not afforded the same rights as republics, and their regional leaders continued to be appointed by the center. Demands for an equal rank with the republics led to local protests in several regions, including the withholding of tax revenues to Moscow. As a result of political pressures, several *krais* and *oblasts* signed bilateral treaties with the federal government. The treaty with Sverdlovsk *Oblast* in the Urals proved to be the most far-reaching in bestowing regional sovereignty, including local executive, legislative,

---

[20] Martin Nicholson, *Toward a Russia of Regions*, Adelphi Paper No.330, International Institute for Strategic Studies, Oxford University Press, 1999, p.16.

[21] Matthew Crosston, *Shadow Separatism: Implications for Democratic Consolidation*, London: Routledge, 2004, pp.25, 29.

and judicial branches, the management of all state property on its territory, tax collection, and the pursuit of international economic ties.[22] The region's leaders also established a short-lived Urals Republic with five other *oblasts*, and even though the initiative was thwarted by Moscow, Sverdlovsk retained much of its sovereignty during the Yeltsin years in the 1990s.

Following the dissolution of the Communist Party in the early 1990s, the country's main integrative institution rapidly evaporated and competitive elections were held for the first time. They provided regional leaders with a more legitimate social base and enabled nationalist groups to emerge in a number of republics and seize the policy initiative.[23] Regional elites were consolidated during the 1990s from local political, financial, and industrial leaders and benefited from greater autonomy and access to resources than during Soviet times.[24] They were able to use the period of a weak and divided central government to claim a greater measure of regional autonomy. The new legislatures became embryonic representative bodies rather than rubber-stamping councils (*soviets*), while some regional governors managed to carve out personal fiefdoms and quasi-state entities. In May 1993, the heads of several republics, including Tatarstan, demanded that the new Russian constitution acknowledge their "state sovereignty," their right to "self-determination," and their prerogative

---

[22] Matthew Crosston, *Shadow Separatism: Implications for Democratic Consolidation*, London: Routledge, 2004, pp.27, 81.

[23] Elise Giuliano, *Constructing Grievance: Ethnic Nationalism in Russia's Republics*, Cornell University Press, 2011, p.192.

[24] Martin Nicholson, *Toward a Russia of Regions*, Adelphi Paper No.330, International Institute for Strategic Studies, Oxford University Press, 1999, p.27.

to secede from the Federation.[25] Turmoil was also evident in several predominantly Russian regions and cities. For instance, the governor of Vladivostok, Evgenii Nazdratenko, threatened outright secession from Russia if the crisis between President Yeltsin and the parliament was not resolved.[26]

The Federation Treaty was not concluded horizontally among the regions but between the regions and Moscow. Several republics proclaimed their sovereignty on the basis of their right of national self-determination after Yeltsin announced they should take as much sovereignty as they could "swallow." In effect, Yeltsin was using the republics in order to unseat Soviet President Mikhail Gorbachev but had no intention of allowing them to pursue their independence and secede from Russia. Fourteen of the sixteen autonomous republics in the Russian Federation declared themselves as sovereign after Russia's own sovereignty declaration in August 1990.[27] Although these declarations were recognized in the 1992 Federation Treaty and in the 1993 Russian Constitution, they were not respected in practice.

Chechnya refused to sign the Federation Treaty and declared independence, leading to an outright war with Russia's military forces. Tatarstan also refused to sign the federative agreement, and on August 30, 1990, the Republic's Supreme Soviet issued a Declaration of State Sovereignty.[28] In a referendum on sovereignty on March 22, 1992,

---

[25] Vladimir Shlapentokh, Roman Levita, and Mikhail Loiberg, *From Submission to Rebellion: The Provinces Versus the Center in Russia*, Westview Press, 1997, p.106.

[26] Vladimir Shlapentokh, Roman Levita, and Mikhail Loiberg, *From Submission to Rebellion: The Provinces Versus the Center in Russia*, Westview Press, 1997, p.115.

[27] Katherine E. Graney, *Of Khans and Kremlins: Tatarstan and the Future of Ethno-Federalism in Russia*, Rowman & Littlefield: Lexington Books, 2009, p.18.

[28] Helen Faller, *Nation, Language, Islam: Tatarstan's Sovereignty Movement*, Central European University Press, 2011.

more than 80 percent of Tatarstan residents voted in favor. The republican government adopted a new constitution which declared Tatarstan a subject of international law "associated with the Russian Federation on the basis of a Treaty on the Mutual Delegation of Authority." A new power-sharing treaty was signed with Moscow in February 1994, and a treaty was initialed in July 2007 that kept alive Tatarstan's pursuit of authentic sovereignty.

Federal Evisceration

The process of regional self-determination and sovereignty went into reverse after Yeltsin attacked and dissolved the Russian parliament in October 1993 and adopted a new Russian Constitution in December 1993. It asserted the integrity and inviolability of the Federation, the equality of all federal subjects, the authority of a single unified system of executive power, the existence of a single economic space, the absence of any right of secession, and the superiority of the Constitution over the Federal Treaty.[29] Seven republics in addition to Chechnya and Tatarstan, did not endorse the December 1993 constitution, claiming that it undermined their sovereignty—Adygea, Bashkiria, Dagestan, Karachaevo-Cherkessia, Mordovia, Tuva and Chuvashia—together with ten *oblasts* in European Russia.[30]

Fearing both genuine federalism and creeping separatism, Yeltsin began to abolish any distinct rights acquired by the ethnic republics, limited the powers of regional and republican authorities, and reversed initial decisions on the democratic election of governors

---

[29] Cameron Ross, *Federalism and Democratization in Russia*, Manchester University Press, 2002, p.30.

[30] Vladimir Shlapentokh, Roman Levita, and Mikhail Loiberg, *From Submission to Rebellion: The Provinces Versus the Center in Russia*, Westview Press, 1997, p.121.

(*gubernatory*). In October 1994, he reasserted his right to appoint and dismiss the governors of all federal subjects and sought to recentralize Moscow's control by shifting authority from republican parliaments to the executives. However, such instructions were largely disregarded because the State *Duma* (the lower house of parliament) did not want the Federation Council (the upper house) to be staffed predominantly with Yeltsin appointees.[31] By 1997, 46 regions had held their first-ever popular elections for governor, and many others conducted democratic elections for regional legislatures. In addition, mayors in the larger municipalities and regional capitals gained increasing powers. Even though demands for sovereignty abated during this period, a great deal of uncertainty remained about the survival of the Russian Federation in the event of another nationwide economic and political crisis.

Russia's progress toward rupture had precedents in the 1990s, when several republics pushed toward greater sovereignty or even outright independence in the case of Chechnya. Putin was selected as President in December 1999 by Yeltsin's advisors in order to prevent the disintegration of the Russian Federation, which was perceived in Moscow as a palpable possibility. Since his appointment, Putin has taken a hardline position to curtail any meaningful sharing of sovereignty between the center and the regions and has tried to limit self-government for all federal subjects.[32] The Kremlin undercut ethnic federalism by reducing the powers of national republics to the level of *krais* and *oblasts* even if their administrative designations remained unchanged. Even the power-sharing agreements signed by

---

[31] Martin Nicholson, *Toward a Russia of Regions*, Adelphi Paper No.330, International Institute for Strategic Studies, Oxford University Press, 1999, pp.38–39.

[32] Katherine E. Graney, *Of Khans and Kremlins: Tatarstan and the Future of Ethno-Federalism in Russia*, Rowman & Littlefield: Lexington Books, 2009, p.49.

some of the *krais*, including Krasnodar *Krai* in January 1996, with the federal government that included guarantees of autonomy were subsequently abolished.[33] The declarations of state sovereignty issued in the 1990s by a number of federal units have been gradually rescinded through enforced constitutional changes or simply ignored in practice. In June 2002, Russia's Constitutional Court ruled that all declarations of sovereignty by republics and other subjects were incompatible with the sovereignty of the Russian Federation.[34]

After Putin's appointment in December 1999 and subsequent election as Russia's President in March 2000, the Kremlin condemned the "legal anarchy" of center-regional relations. Anxious that demands for sovereignty could again escalate, Putin's overriding objective was to recentralize the state and eliminate regional autonomy.[35] A Presidential Commission was established to restore central oversight in relations between the federal center and the regions. One of Putin's major anti-federal moves was to prohibit the establishment of distinct regional and ethnic parties. The June 2001 Federal Law on Political Parties specified that all parties needed to have "an all-federation character" with regional branches in more than half of the subjects of the Russian Federation.[36] In effect, citizens were prohibited from

---

[33] Mizuki Chuman, "The Rise and Fall of Power Sharing Treaties Between Center and Regions in Post-Soviet Russia," *Demokratizatsiya*, https://demokratizatsiya.pub/archives/19_2_L7H017206G216817.pdf.

[34] Cameron Ross, *Federalism and Democratization in Russia*, Manchester University Press, 2002, p.148.

[35] Elena A. Chebankova, *Russia's Federal Relations: Putin's Reforms and Management of the Regions*, Routledge Series on Russian and East Europe Studies, Routledge: London and New York, 2010, p.13.

[36] Council of Europe and Venice Commission, *Federal Law on Political Parties of the Russian Federation*, February 22, 2012,

expressing their regional and local rights and interests, as the major federal-level parties were controlled from Moscow.

Federalism has been eviscerated under Putin's rule: federal subjects today lack genuine direct elections, budgetary powers, taxation authority or distinct regional laws.[37] In reversing the decentralization that was evident during the 1990s, Putin's "power vertical" also became a "federal vertical." In May 2000, the Kremlin divided Russia into seven super regions or "Federal Districts" (*Federalnyye Okruga*)—Central, Southern, Northwestern, Ural, Volga, Siberian, and Far Eastern—as a novel administrative structure. The North Caucasus Federal District was added as the eighth federal district in January 2010, as Moscow realized that the region had not been pacified despite inserting a loyalist leader to govern Chechnya. Each district was placed under the supervision of a presidential envoy, the "plenipotentiary representative of the President" (*Polnomochnyi Predstavitel Prezidenta* or *Polpreda*), responsible for guaranteeing that regional laws and policies did not violate federal laws and that all regional departments of federal ministries and agencies abided by Moscow's decisions.[38]

All the Federal Districts contained a dozen or more federal subjects and incorporated a mixture of ethnic republics and territorially defined regions but with no capitals located in the ethnic republics in order to diminish the latter's authority. The districts were not

---

https://www.venice.coe.int/webforms/documents/default.aspx?pdffile=CDL-REF(2012)001-e.

[37] Paul Goble, "Putin's Treatment of Governors Shows that Federalism in Russia is 'Fake,' Mikhaylov Says," August 19, 2020, https://windowoneurasia2.blogspot.com/2020/08/putins-treatment-of-governors-shows.html.

[38] William M. Reisinger (Ed.), *Russia's Regions and Comparative Subnational Politics*, London: Routledge, 2013, p.xxi.

established as new levels of government but helped to streamline Kremlin supervision and guarantee that all regions implemented Moscow's domestic and foreign policies and repealed any laws that conflicted with federal legislation.[39] When Moscow decided to appoint deputy prime ministers as presidential plenipotentiaries over each mega federal district, the regional governors and local governments in each federal subject were more effectively subordinated to the Kremlin.

Under Putin, the federal Constitution became the binding document for all federal units. The Federation Council, the upper house of the Russian parliament, was restructured to increase central control and disable it from blocking legislation. The presidential administration henceforth appointed senators who became dependent on the Kremlin and no longer represented regional interests. A State Council (*Gosudarstvennyy Sovet*) of the Russian Federation was created in September 2000 to further strengthen central control over the regions. It assembled the heads of all federal subjects and was chaired by the Russian President to better supervise the policies of regional governors.[40] It evolved into a rubber stamp for regime policy and has not rejected any candidates for various federal bodies that the Kremlin has proposed.

Since Putin's appointment, the country swerved from a complex asymmetrical structure to a centralized system that only mimicked genuine federalism. Moscow also enhanced its control over socio-economic activities in the regions and turned regional authorities into

---

[39] William M. Reisinger and Bryon J. Moraski, *The Regional Roots of Russia's Political Regime*, Ann Arbor: University of Michigan Press, 2017, p.44.

[40] *The Territories of the Russian Federation 2020*, London: Routledge, 2020, p.45.

political clients of the federal executive.[41] Instead of pursuing balanced decentralization to accommodate regional aspirations, the Russian government abolished all the bilateral treaties signed in the 1990s, steadily downgraded the sovereignty of federal subjects, and increased control over financial resources. Putin guaranteed that the federal structure primarily benefited a narrow elite of security personnel, state bureaucrats, Kremlin-sponsored oligarchs, and regional authorities appointed or approved by the presidential administration.

Federal units have been transformed into nominal formations and deprived of any attributes of sovereignty that were gained during the early 1990s. The Kremlin also calculated that all the non-Russian republics, viewed as the primary threat to territorial integrity, should either be abolished or given a lower status equal to that of the predominantly ethnic Russian *oblasts* and *krais.*[42] Nonetheless, the Kremlin remains aware that attempts to eliminate the republics or their distinct status can lead to protests, opposition, and even calls for separation.

One authority on Russian regionalism, Vadim Shtepa, has posited a viable alternative solution if the country is to survive. This would entail transforming all federal subjects into republics, in which they would feel equal and better represented in a decentralized but symmetrical federation.[43] In current debates over the future structure of Russia's federalism, some analysts believe that the disparate size and

---

[41] Elena A. Chebankova, *Russia's Federal Relations: Putin's Reforms and Management of the Regions*, Routledge Series on Russian and East Europe Studies, Routledge: London and New York, 2010, p.185.

[42] Paul Goble, "'If All Federal Subjects Aren't Republics, None of Them will Be,' Shtepa Says," November 4, 2020, http://windowoneurasia2.blogspot.com/2020/11/if-all-federal-subjects-arent-republics.html.

[43] "Либо республики – все, либо не будет ни одной," November 2, 2020, http://region.expert/all_republics/

economic clout of diverse federal units indicates that the federation needs to be asymmetrical. However, if some regions obtain more powers than others this could itself generate conflicts between them and with the federal center and may lead to calls for secession. During the 1990s, Yeltsin calculated that asymmetry and mutual distrust prevented the emergence of a unified front between the regions against Moscow. However, such a policy can backfire if several republics and regions calculate that the center is simply disguising its weakness by fostering a "divide and rule" strategy while its resources are dwindling.

After December 2004, Moscow unconstitutionally nominated regional governors who were then routinely confirmed by local legislatures. The premise behind this move was that popularly elected governors would have genuine local legitimacy and this empowered them to challenge Kremlin policies. In June 2012, a new law on governors reintroduced direct gubernatorial elections to provide an appearance of choice but with a "municipal filter" so that "undesirable candidates" could be barred and only those approved by the presidential administration were included.[44] Individuals standing in elections needed to collect the signatures of between 5 percent and 10 percent of municipal deputies vetted by the Kremlin. Seventy-five regions held direct elections to choose their heads; in the others, governors were elected by the legislative assembly.

The authority of each regional governor is subordinated to Kremlin requirements. This has been evident in Moscow's use of regional heads to ensure election victories for Putin's United Russia party, whether through effective public mobilization or election

---

[44] András Tóth-Czifra, "How to Win Votes and Mobilize People in Russia: A Closer Look at the September Regional Elections," September 10, 2020, Institute of Modern Russia, https://imrussia.org/en/analysis/3167-how-to-win-votes-and-mobilize-people-in-russia.

engineering. Those who resisted or proved unable to deliver votes for Putin and United Russia have either been sidelined or sanctioned. Governors and mayors were also expected to prevent mass protests, maintain social stability, and join the party in power.[45] Moscow also drastically reduced the number of elected mayors in Russia's 109 largest cities—from 73 percent in 2008 to only 12 percent in 2020—fearing competition for loyal Moscow appointees.[45] However, public support for direct elections and the accountability of local officials is reportedly rising.

The Kremlin has also been afforded the right to disband local legislatures without any consultations or regional inputs. The Federation Council has been de-ethnified and de-regionalized and staffed with loyalists often devoid of direct links with the federal subjects they supposedly represent.[47] The power hierarchy is maintained by replacing regional leaders who demonstrate insufficient fealty to Moscow or become too popular at city or regional levels, as this directly challenges central control. They are invariably accused of corruption or some other crime to justify their removal from office. The threat of sanctions or criminal prosecution is an effective method for maintaining loyalty or acquiescence, especially

---

[45] Vladimir Gel'man, "Politics, Governance, and the Zigzags of the Power Vertical: Toward a Framework for Analyzing Russia's Local Regimes," in William M. Reisinger (Ed.), *Russia's Regions and Comparative Subnational Politics*, London: Routledge, 2013, p.29.

[46] Paul Goble, "Russian People Want Elected Mayors but Power Vertical Doesn't," November 30, 2020, http://windowoneurasia2.blogspot.com/2020/11/russian-people-want-elected-mayors-but.html.

[47] Federica Prina, *National Minorities in Putin's Russia: Diversity and Assimilation*, Routledge Contemporary Russia and Eastern Europe Series, Routledge: London and New York, 2016, p.111.

among officials who are ensnared in the web of state-controlled corruption.

In December 2021, Putin signed a new bill to bolster central control over regional governments. The legislation specifies that heads of regions nominated by the Kremlin for elections in all federal subjects can serve more than two consecutive terms, while the President will be given power to dismiss them at any time.[48] It stipulates a five-year term for both governors and regional parliaments, while previously this was decided by the regional authorities. The law also significantly increases Moscow's meddling in virtually all internal affairs of republics and regions by enshrining the right of federal officials to participate in the formation of regional ministries of education, finance, health care, housing, and construction.[49] Additionally, every regional leader is to be henceforth simply called a "head of a constituent part of Russia" with no more republican "Presidents." The State Council of Tatarstan rejected the new legislation, and authorities in other ethnic republics reacted negatively to several of its proposals. Such enhanced supervision underscores Moscow's growing anxiety about any initiatives toward regional autonomy.

Regressive Centralism

Between 2012 and 2020, 63 heads of federal subjects were replaced by the Kremlin, and regional parliaments no longer played a role in their nomination or removal.[50] Numerous officials were deemed to be

---

[48] Nadezhda Isayeva, "Губернаторам позволят обнулиться," September 27, 2021, https://novayagazeta.ru/articles/2021/09/27/gubernatoram-pozvoliat-obnulitsia.

[49] Ruslan Gabbasov, "Закат даже формальной федерации?" October 31, 2021, https://www.idelreal.org/a/31533355.html.

[50] *The Territories of the Russian Federation 2020,* London: Routledge, 2020, p.5.

disloyal to Putin or to United Russia, including Governor Dmitry Furgal in Khabarovsk *Krai* and Sardana Avksentyeva, the mayor of Yakutsk, the capital of the Sakha Republic. The Kremlin wanted to guarantee the loyalty of governors and preferred that they be members of United Russia and capable of rooting out any political opposition. Such a policy will further estrange regional elites and can create new vectors of resistance to Moscow, especially in republics such as Dagestan, where local elites have traditionally played a major role in inter-ethnic balancing in the regional government. The mass street protests in Khabarovsk in 2020–2021 over the arbitrary replacement by Moscow of the *krai's* governor, Sergey Furgal, defended the basic principles of federalism, including the division of powers between the federal center and the federal subjects and the right of residents to choose their own governors.

Constitutional changes enacted during 2020 deepened centralization and reduced the role of local governments by replacing mayoral elections with appointed city managers.[51] In the larger urban areas in particular, city managers are answerable to Moscow rather than their constituents.[52] The regional parliaments with only 30 to 40 deputies lack the means to pass any significant laws that differ from those in other regions, since the legislative system in Russia is unified.[53]

---

[51] Paul Goble, "Putin's Liquidation of Local Self-Administration Reinforces Centralization of Russian System, Kazantsev and Rumyantseva Say," December 30, 2020, http://windowoneurasia2.blogspot.com/2020/12/putins-liquidation-of-local-self.html.

[52] Federica Prina, *National Minorities in Putin's Russia: Diversity and Assimilation*, Routledge Contemporary Russia and Eastern Europe Series, Routledge: London and New York, 2016, p.113.

[53] Vadim Shtepa, "The Russian Elections and Hidden Regionalist Politics," *Eurasia Daily Monitor*, Vol. 18, Issue 138, September 13, 2021,

Moscow's appointment or close control over governors, mayors, and local councils has not only undercut regional decision-making but also reduced federal spending for local needs and thwarted the effectiveness of local governments.[54] Unelected officials have less incentive to deliver essential services to citizens who cannot vote them out, and they are more likely to pander to the central administration, which presses them to reduce spending. Moscow also employs a loyalty test whereby regions that cannot deliver expected election quotas for Putin or for United Russia or prove less capable of pacifying social unrest will suffer a reduction in their federal allocations.

The Kremlin favors appointing ethnic Russians or fully Russified officials to top positions in the federal subjects. This has been particularly evident in the North Caucasus amidst fears that regional governors could side with their constituents. Dagestan is a case in point, where a member of one of the republic's indigenous nationalities, the Avar Ramazan Abdulatipov, was replaced in 2017 by an ethnic Russian.[55] The situation was further aggravated by the appointment in October 2020 of the Russian National Guard General Sergei Melikov as the new governor, sparking concerns that Moscow was planning to impose military rule in the republic.[56] Such moves are

---

https://jamestown.org/program/the-russian-elections-and-hidden-regionalist-politics/.

[54] Paul Goble, "Ending Mayoral Elections has Reduced Effectiveness of Municipal Governance in Russia, New Study Says," December 9, 2020, http://windowoneurasia2.blogspot.com/2020/12/ending-mayoral-elections-has-reduced.html.

[55] "Прокуратор Дагестана," October 10, 2020, http://region.expert/procurator/.

[56] Paul Goble, "Is Moscow Moving toward De Facto Military Rule in Increasingly Unstable Dagestan?" February 23, 2021, http://windowoneurasia2.blogspot.com/2021/02/is-moscow-moving-toward-de-facto.html.

likely to backfire and provoke resistance by officials in a traditionally ethnically structured society.

Moscow is intent on abolishing constitutional courts, analogous to the Russian Constitutional Court, in the 13 federal subjects that still maintain them. This will further diminish human rights protections, republican sovereignty, minority rights and local democracy.[57] Russian law has few concrete guarantees for the protection of non-Russian cultures, and there is little tradition of using litigation to resolve grievances against government organs.[58] The closing of constitutional courts also raised concerns that the Kremlin would seek to disband other regional governing bodies, including local legislatures.

Moscow controls the bulk of lucrative revenue sources in each federal unit and engages in minimal investment in decaying local infrastructure. Budgetary instruments are an important tool for controlling the federal subjects by generating dependence, developing clientelist structures, and undermining potential economic self-sufficiency. The center blocks unwanted political newcomers from gaining executive powers in the regions and challenging the local clientelist network tied closely with Moscow. Budgetary adjustments

---

[57] Paul Goble, "Having Gelded Russian Constitutional Court, Putin Now Moves to Abolish Them in Federal Subjects," November 18, 2020, http://windowoneurasia2.blogspot.com/2020/11/having-gelded-russian-constitutional.html; Paul Goble, "Moscow May Move Against Regional Parliaments after It Disbands Regional Constitutional Courts, Bashkir Experts Say," November 20, 2020, https://windowoneurasia2.blogspot.com/2020/11/moscow-may-move-against-regional.html.

[58] Federica Prina, *National Minorities in Putin's Russia: Diversity and Assimilation*, Routledge Contemporary Russia and Eastern Europe Series, Routledge: London and New York, 2016, p.87.

have bolstered central controls over regional finances.[59] Since the mid-2000s, Moscow has increased revenue collection from each unit and apportioned funds in line with political rather than economic needs. This has generated anger, particularly in several wealthier republics, such as Tatarstan, that have to surrender the bulk of their revenues to Moscow and resent subsidizing poorer federal regions. Between 2012 and 2018, the revenues of regional budgets grew on average by only 5 percent, while the federal budget's revenues increased by 77 percent.[60]

During most of the 2000s, the Kremlin benefited from substantial economic growth fueled by high earnings from the export of oil and natural gas. This provided opportunities for regional oligarchs and elites to benefit from crony capitalism and networks of state corruption. Such incentives for enrichment kept local authorities in line. Since the 2008 global financial crisis, the increasing volatility in fossil fuel prices, combined with the lack of economic diversification and modernization, have significantly trimmed Russia's budgets. Budgetary shortfalls in the regions have been compounded by official corruption, bureaucratization, and mismanagement, with widening disparities evident between most of the country and the metropolitan conglomerates, the "black earth" regions of European Russia, and the fossil fuel–producing regions of Western Siberia. In other areas, industrial towns are in crisis, agriculture is imperiled, unemployment has soared, and GDP per capita is in decline.[61]

---

[59] Donna Bahry, "Making Autocracy Work? Russian Regional Politics Under Putin," in William M. Reisinger (Ed.), *Russia's Regions and Comparative Subnational Politics*, London: Routledge, 2013, p.164.

[60] András Tóth-Czifra, "Governors Redux: How Regional and Local Governments Became a Problem for Putin," February 28 2020, Institute of Modern Russia, https://imrussia.org/en/analysis/3084-governors-redux.

[61] Marlene Laruelle, *Russia's Arctic Strategies and the Future of the Far North*, London: Routledge, 2014, p.50.

Fiscal problems in numerous federal subjects have been used to impose direct financial control, as has already occurred in the Republic of Ingushetia. Other republics are likely to suffer the same fate, including Dagestan, Chechnya, Karachaevo-Cherkessia, Kabardino-Balkaria, Mordovia, Altai and Tuva.[62] This could also lead to the emplacement of new regional heads appointed by Moscow. Russia's leaders evidently understand that if they drastically reduce subsidies to the poorest republics, such as those in the North Caucasus, they will face ethnic unrest. On the other hand, state subsidies are not a long-term solution for economic development, social peace, or political stability, as they disincentivize the development of local business and productive investment and fuel corruption and clientelism among the local elites. Russia's failures in effective and flexible economic planning are evident in the fact that federal subjects do not even possess their own institutes for regional development that could represent the interests of local businesses and residents. All regional programs are determined by the federal center.

Anti-Republic Campaigns

The Kremlin has employed or threatened various administrative methods to curtail the sovereignty and autonomy of federal subjects and restrict ethno-territorial identities. Some officials have even proposed creating new administrative units based on the Tsarist model. On July 19, 2021, Russia's Prime Minister Mikhail Mishustin announced that the deputy ministers in his cabinet will each oversee

---

[62] Paul Goble, "'De Facto, All North Caucasus Republics Have Long Been Under Direct External Rule,' Markelov Says," November 6, 2020, http://windowoneurasia2.blogspot.com/2020/11/de-facto-all-north-caucasus-republics.html.

one of the country's eight Federal Districts.[63] Moscow's appointees were to supervise investment strategies, state programs, and the provision of financial assistance to the regions. For instance, Deputy Prime Minister Aleksandr Novak was appointed to oversee the North Caucasian Federal District despite having little knowledge of the region, while another deputy prime minister, Yuri Trutnev, was already supervising development programs in this Federal District. Such overlapping competencies are likely to generate conflicts, as Prime Minister Mishustin planned to supersede the presidential plenipotentiaries in each Federal District with deputy ministers, who will control the major financial flows. This will also further reduce the power and authority of regional governors, who will now have to report to deputy prime ministers instead of directly to the Prime Minister or President.

In tightening central controls, the Kremlin propagates the notion that differing statuses among federal subjects and their self-assertion based on economic performance will undermine the integrity of the state. It evidently fears that in a genuine federation, resource-rich regions will demand more revenue from the federal budget and resent subsidizing poorer regions, potentially leading to increasing calls for a looser federation or complete independence. In July 2020, Russia's lower house of parliament adopted a package of "territorial integrity" bills.[64] The laws label those who repeatedly "violate Russia's territorial integrity, including alienating part of its territory" as "extremists" with prison terms of between six to ten years.

---

[63] Valery Dzutsati, "Russian Government Builds Novel Framework for Controlling Regions," July 28, 2021, Vol. 18, Issue 120, https://jamestown.org/program/russian-government-builds-novel-framework-for-controlling-regions/.

[64] "Russian Lawmakers Propose Expanded 'Extremism' Law Aimed At Crimea," Radio Free Europe/ Radio Liberty, July 9, 2020, https://www.rferl.org/a/russian-lawmakers-propose-expanded-extremism-law-aimed-at-crimea/30716700.html.

Under constitutional amendments passed in the manipulated nationwide referendum on July 1, 2020, it became unconstitutional to "give away" any part of Russian territory to a foreign power. This new law against any calls for partition or secession was clearly designed to thwart demands for genuine federalism.[65] It strengthens the July 2014 law, whereby anyone calling for separatism on the internet or objecting to the annexation of Crimea could be prosecuted for separatism. It also reinforces article 280.1 of the Criminal Code, which prohibits any "calls to violate territorial integrity."[66] In August 2020, a military court in Samara sentenced Ayrat Dilmukhametov, a Bashkir politician, to nine years in a strict regime camp. His alleged "crime" was to point out that only authentic federalism can preserve the Russian state.

Putin has engineered the reduction of the prerogatives and status of all national republics to equalize them with those of *oblasts*, *krais* and other federal subjects.[67] After the 2020 changes in the 1993 Russian Constitution, the basic laws of the 22 republics were required to be rewritten to synchronize them with the center. However, the process has not been transparent, provoking fears that republican powers will be further diminished, while the central authorities consistently avoid

---

[65] "Пора вернуть эту землю себе," September 23, 2020, https://www.sibreal.org/a/30854174.html.

[66] https://wilmap.stanford.edu/entries/federal-law-no-433-fz-december-20-2013-and-federal-law-no-274-fz-july-21-2014.

[67] "Либо республики – все, либо не будет ни одной," November 2, 2020, http://region.expert/all_republics/.

addressing any local demands for decentralization and authentic federalism.[68]

The anti-republic campaign was encapsulated in the federal language law introduced in June 2018, designed to promote russification, as well as by plans to intensify the process of merging and eliminating autonomous republics and districts (*okrugs*).[69] The study of all non-Russian languages in schools was made voluntary, while the study of Russian remained compulsory. The bill makes education in 34 of Russia's 35 official languages optional and restricts instruction in ethnic-minority languages to two hours per week. Decisions on native-language education were previously determined by regional governments and not by the federal center.

The termination of requirements that Russian speakers in non-Russian republics learn the languages of titular nationalities can also increase ethnic tensions. Russians will feel less integrated, and indigenous nations may grow more resentful of outsiders who are not required to learn their language. Critics view the new language policy as the thin edge of a wedge that will eliminate the distinctive legal status of ethnic republics and eventually eliminate the existence of separate nations. For instance, Circassians (Adygs) consider the eradication of indigenous languages as a continuation of the Moscow-directed extermination and expulsion of the Circassian population

---

[68] Paul Goble, "Now that Russian Constitution has Been Amended, Republic Basic Laws Being Rewritten," October 27, 2020, http://windowoneurasia2.blogspot.com/2020/10/now-that-russian-constitution-has-been.html.

[69] Paul Goble, "Putin's Language Law Radicalizing Russians and Non-Russians," August 1, 2018, http://windowoneurasia2.blogspot.com/2018/08/putins-language-law-radicalizing.html.

from the North Caucasus in 1864 that some historians have designated as a genocide.[70]

The Kremlin is imposing more direct rule over national republics, where its fears of protests and separatist demands are most pronounced. Power has been fully transferred from the local legislative branch and concentrated in the closely supervised executive. In a further display of anxiety over manifestations of regional opposition, Moscow has established "centers for administration of the regions," in each of the federal subjects to monitor social attitudes and reactions.[71] The move also indicates growing suspicion about the trustworthiness of regional governors who do not control the new centers, as the Kremlin is aware that they may seek to withhold unfavorable news from Moscow. Security force supervision over regional governments has also been intensified, providing an additional layer of control and coercion to make sure that they do not step out of line.[72] For instance, officials close to the governors in Sverdlovsk, Chelyabinsk and Orenburg *oblasts* have been subject to police raids and arrests during 2021. Such measures indicate growing anxiety about regional resistance and the assertion of independence by some governors even outside the national republics.

---

[70] Private interview with Walter Richmond, Professor of Russian, Emeritus, Occidental College, March 2021.

[71] Nikolay Petrov, "Ухо государево. Как Кремль создает новую структуру внешнего контроля за регионами," March 11, 2021, https://theins.ru/opinions/nikolai-petrov/240028.

[72] Paul Goble, "'The Siloviki have Seized Power in Russian Regions,' Minchenko Says," June 21, 2021, http://windowoneurasia2.blogspot.com/2021/06/the-siloviki-have-seized-power-in.html.

Regional Amalgamation

Moscow has amalgamated several federal subjects to form super regions, federal districts, or electoral districts in order to save on budgets, undermine ethnic and regional identities, and ensure central control.[73] During Soviet rule, an ethnic hierarchy was imposed in the country, whereby ethnic groups considered as "nations" (*natsiya)* obtained autonomous republics (simply "republics" since 1991), while smaller and less "developed" ethnicities or nationalities (*narodnosti*) were given autonomous *oblasts*, all of which became republics in the Russian Federation, except for the Jewish Autonomous *Oblast*.[74] Some ethnicities, including several indigenous peoples in the High North, were entitled to national *okrugs* (districts) that were part of the surrounding *krais* (territories) or *oblasts* (regions). In the 1993 Constitution, the autonomous *okrugs* became fully-fledged federation entities, although still remaining parts of bigger *oblasts* or *krais*, except Chukotka Autonomous *Okrug*.

Between 2003 and 2008, the federal center carried out a series of administrative reforms to curtail the ethnic factor in the country's structure. The number of federal subjects was reduced from 89 to 83, thus eliminating six autonomous *okrugs* that had a substantial proportion of non-Russians. As a result of local opposition, four out of the ten autonomous *okrugs* were left intact and considered as distinct federal subjects: the Nenets Autonomous *Okrug*, which was

---

[73] Paul Goble, "Kurgan Oblast Reportedly to Be Combined with Tyumen into Single Duma Constituency But Some Kurgan Officials Said Seeking an Alternative," December 25, 2020, http://windowoneurasia2.blogspot.com/2020/12/kurgan-oblast-reportedly-to-be-combined.html.

[74] Petr Oskolkov, "Merging Russia's Autonomous Entities: Ethnic Aspect," June 15, 2020, International Center for Ethnic and Linguistic Diversity Studies, Prague, Czech Republic, https://www.icelds.org/2020/06/15/merging-russias-autonomous-entities-ethnic-aspect/.

administratively subordinate to Arkhangelsk *Oblast,* the Yamalo-Nenets Autonomous *Okrug* and the Khanty-Mansi Autonomous *Okrug*–Yugra within Tyumen *Oblast*, and the Chukotka Autonomous *Okrug*, which remained outside of any *oblast.*

Full-scale mergers were intended to subsume ethnically designated regions within predominantly ethnic-Russian ones. They included the creation of Perm *Krai,* with the merger of Perm *Oblast* and the Komi-Permyak Autonomous *Okrug*; Krasnoyarsk *Krai* absorbing the Evenk Autonomous *Okrug* and the Taimyr Dolgano-Nenets Autonomous *Okrug*; the establishment of Kamchatka *Krai*, combining Kamchatka *Oblast* and the Koryak Autonomous *Okrug*; Irkutsk *Oblast* merging with the Ust-Orda Buryat Autonomous *Okrug*; and the formation of Zabaikalskii *Krai*, combining Chita *Oblast* and the Agin Buryat Autonomous *Okrug*.[75] In addition, the Kurgan *Oblast* was combined with Tyumen *Oblast* and the Khanty-Mansi Autonomous *Okrug*-Yugra with the Yamalo-Nenets Autonomous *Okrug* as single constituencies in the 2021 *Duma* elections.

The proclaimed benefits of the federal mergers, such as boosted investments, economic development, or higher living standards, have not materialized but unfulfilled promises aggravated resentment in several regions.[76] Among the other rationales for the mergers were improvements in local administration and the amelioration of the population's access to public services. The autonomous *okrugs* were

---

[75] Federica Prina, *National Minorities in Putin's Russia: Diversity and Assimilation*, Routledge Contemporary Russia and Eastern Europe Series, Routledge: London and New York, 2016, p.122

[76] András Tóth-Czifra, "Lessons in Division: Is It a Good Idea to Merge Russian Regions?" June 3, 2020, Institute of Modern Russia, https://imrussia.org/en/analysis/3120-lessons-in-division-is-it-a-good-idea-to-merge-russian-regions.

transformed into municipal districts or administrative units within larger federal entities and received special legislative guarantees and pledges of increased funding, developmental programs, and infrastructural projects. However, the affirmations about special status proved to be mostly ornamental and not buttressed by either administrative efficiency or financial resources.[77]

Residents of the former autonomous *okrugs* have repeatedly complained about cuts in funding, neglect, and poor management by the new regional capitals that are located far from their territories. Local leaders in the Khanty-Mansi Autonomous *Okrug*–Yugra and the Yamalo-Nenets Autonomous *Okrug* have sought to keep a larger share of their substantial hydrocarbon revenues and have pressed for separation from Tyumen *Oblast*. Having failed in this quest, both *okrugs* have endeavored to take over the Tyumen economy and gain greater control of the *oblast* administration.[78] Activists in the Evenk and Taimyr Dolgano-Nenets Autonomous *okrugs* contested the results of the April 2005 referendum that merged both territories into Krasnoyarsk *Krai*, demoting them to an internal district status. In contrast, Buryat activists have continued to call for the merger of the Ust-Orda Buryat Autonomous *Okrug* and the Agin Buryat Autonomous *Okrug* with the Buryat Republic to form a larger single Buryat entity. They have also opposed any plans by Moscow to combine the Buryat Republic with Transbaikal *Krai* as a new macro-economic region.

---

[77] Petr Oskolkov, "Merging Russian Regions: Assessing the Reform Before its Second Wave," May 27, 2020, International Center for Ethnic and Linguistic Diversity Studies, Prague, Czech Republic, https://www.icelds.org/2020/05/27/merging-russian-regions-assessing-the-reform-before-its-second-wave/.

[78] Cameron Ross, *Federalism and Democratization in Russia*, Manchester University Press, 2002, p.59.

Some Kremlin proposals for amalgamation have been blocked, most notably the merger of Arkhangelsk *Oblast* and the Nenets Autonomous *Okrug*. In May 2020, the heads of both entities signed a memorandum for unification. Shortly afterward, the local population and a part of the political elite began to organize public protest, and the authorities suspended the merger.[79] Evidently, Moscow miscalculated that the collapse in world oil prices would pressure oil-rich regions, such as the Nenets Autonomous *Okrug*, to seek mergers with other federal subjects. Subsequently, the Nenets Autonomous *Okrug* became the only federal subject to vote against the constitutional amendments in September 2020 to prolong Putin's rule.[80] Any moves to restart the amalgamation through unilateral decisions or a fraudulent referendum can spark fresh protests and the potential growth of the non-governmental Movement for the Defense and Development of the Nenets Autonomous *Okrug*.

Officials in Moscow have voiced proposals for further federal mergers, including combining the Jewish Autonomous *Oblast* with Khabarovsk *Krai* that would further dilute the small Jewish population without bringing any tangible economic benefits.[81] Another scheme envisaged merging the Republic of Tatarstan with

---

[79] Petr Oskolkov, "Merging Russia's Autonomous Entities: Ethnic Aspect," June 15, 2020, International Center for Ethnic and Linguistic Diversity Studies, Prague, Czech Republic, https://www.icelds.org/2020/06/15/merging-russias-autonomous-entities-ethnic-aspect/.

[80] Paul Goble, "Some in Arkhangelsk 'By Hook or Crook' Again Seeking to Promote Amalgamation with Nenets AD," November 21, 2020, http://windowoneurasia2.blogspot.com/2020/11/some-in-arkhangelsk-by-hook-or-crook.html.

[81] Paul Goble, "'Unifying Two Poor Regions Only Doubles Poverty,' Birobidzhan Residents React to Latest Amalgamation Idea," May 10, 2021, http://windowoneurasia2.blogspot.com/2021/05/unifying-two-poor-regions-only-doubles.html.

Ulyanovsk *Oblast* to create a Volga-Kama *Oblast*, but this was strongly opposed by Tatars. New constitutional provisions also enable Moscow to establish directly subordinated "federal territories" from one or more federal subjects.[82] Fears abound that such permutations could be used to eliminate non-Russian republics or partition and amalgamate parts of them into predominantly ethnic-Russian *oblasts* and *krais*. The first such "federal territory" was created in Sochi, on the Black Sea coast, carved out of Krasnodar *Krai*, where regional and local officials had minimal input. Moscow is reportedly planning to create another larger federal territory in the North Caucasus to include nine districts that were part of Stavropol *Krai*, one from the Kabardino-Balkar Republic, and two from the Karachai-Cherkess Republic. One major goal would be to further undermine Circassian national solidarity across the northwestern Caucasus. Local administrations would reportedly be abolished and the region placed under the authority of a single federal territory—the Caucasus Mineral Waters Resort Region.

A new push for amalgamation became evident in the summer of 2021. Moscow reportedly aimed to reduce the number of federal units to 41 and eliminate several non-Russian republics as well as the economically weaker Russian *oblasts* and *krais*.[83] Other official proposals included merging predominantly ethnic-Russian regions in central Russia, especially those with declining populations. A plan developed by Deputy Prime Minister Marat Khusrullin envisaged a

---

[82] Paul Goble, "Moscow's Plan to Carve New Federal Territory Out of Portions of Stavropol Kray, Kabardino-Balkaria and Karchayevo-Cherkessia Angering Regional Officials," December 27, 2020, http://windowoneurasia2.blogspot.com/2020/12/moscows-plan-to-carve-new-federal.html.

[83] Paul Goble, "Moscow to Use Agglomerations to Cut Number of Federal Subjects by More than Half by 2030, Source Says," June 14, 2021, http://windowoneurasia2.blogspot.com/2021/06/moscow-to-use-agglomerations-to-cut.html.

process of amalgamation by forming "inter-regional agglomerations" based around major cities. The first four agglomerations would be centered on Moscow, St. Petersburg, Kazan and Krasnodar. This could initially involve the combination of Moscow and Moscow *Oblast*, Saint Petersburg and Leningrad *Oblast,* Tatarstan with parts of the Mari El Republic, and Krasnodar *Krai* with the Adygei Republic.

If applied, such plans could become models for the combination of other federal subjects over the next decade. Borders between existing federal subjects would then be eliminated and the heads of those federal subjects that were absorbed would lose their remaining powers. The process is intended to eliminate the so-called "*matryoshka*" regions such as the Nenets Autonomous Okrug within Arkhangelsk *Oblast,* and the Yamalo-Nenets and Khanty-Mansi autonomous *Okrugs* in Tyumen *Oblast*. Such an initiative is certain to further alienate both officials and populations in the affected regions, especially in the absence of genuine consultations or democratic referenda. Large corporations linked with the Kremlin would primarily benefit from the new arrangements, while numerous small cities and rural areas will experience further depopulation as residents move to agglomeration centers in search of jobs. Nonetheless, the Kremlin remains mindful that eliminating all authority from the *okrugs* can stir opposition to the regional authorities that have absorbed them and exacerbate resentments against Moscow.

In the Pacific region, in the summer of 2021, the minister for the development of the Far East and the Arctic, Alexei Chekunkov, proposed dividing the territory into four provinces—Transbaikal, Border, Ostrovnaya, and Northern—thereby overriding existing federal subjects.[84] The local population and regional authorities were

---

[84] Georgy Kulakov, "'Четвертование' Дальнего Востока," July 21, 2021, http://region.expert/provinces/.

not consulted over such unification plans and the proposed addition of another bureaucratic layer controlled from Moscow. In a genuinely federal system, freely elected parliaments, governments, and regional governors would seek to develop beneficial inter-regional cooperation that was not imposed from above.

Nonetheless, the amalgamation of some federal subjects may also prove perilous for Moscow if it creates larger regions seeking greater autonomy and eventual independence, especially in Siberia and the Pacific zone. Some officials have proposed merging Primorski *Krai*, Khabarovsk *Krai*, Sakhalin *Oblast*, and Kamchatka *Krai* into a single super-region.[85] If enacted, Moscow's policies will also deepen the divisions between rich and poor regions, as officials plan to concentrate investment in about 20 federal subjects and up to 30 municipalities. Poorer regions will increasingly rely on federal subsidies and experience greater poverty, depopulation, and long-term decline. Even in the wealthier entities, economic investment will be largely concentrated in the capitals and larger cities and neglect the smaller towns and rural areas.

Another method for promoting amalgamation is to give all federal subjects a uniform name of "region" and a single legal status.[86] Such proposals by high officials would enable the renaming of ethnic republics and simplify the amalgamation process through a reduction in the number of entities. However, any renewed push for federal amalgamation under whatever formula could boomerang against the

---

[85] Georgy Kulakov, "'Перенарезка' регионов начнется с Дальнего Востока?" June 21, 2021, http://region.expert/far-east-division/.

[86] Paul Goble, "All of Russia's Federal Subjects Must be Called Regions, Kaplenkov Says," October 12, 2021,

http://windowoneurasia2.blogspot.com/2021/10/all-of-russias-federal-subjects-must-be.html.

Kremlin, where some nations would sense an opportunity for reunification. Proposals to fold the Republic of Adygea with the predominantly ethnic-Russian Stavropol *Krai* led to mass protests in Adygea's capital of Maikop in April 2005, and the move was suspended.[87] Unification initiatives will encourage Circassian (Adyg) demands for the merger of several republics in the North Caucasus containing substantial Circassian populations, including Adygea, Karachaevo-Cherkessia and Kabardino-Balkaria, together with parts of Krasnodar *Krai* and Stavropol *Krai*. Federal border changes and other integrationist moves would also embolden irredentism across the country. For instance, the Republic of Bashkortostan could seek to recover the Orenburg corridor from Orenburg *Oblast*, thus enabling the Middle Volga republics to establish a foreign border—with Kazakhstan.

Federalization Proposals

Russia's crisis is not simply economic and generated by growing disparities between Moscow and the federal regions, it is also political, as evident in deepening opposition to Moscow's governance. Resistance to unpopular unilateral decisions when it assumes mass protests, as witnessed in Khabarovsk in 2020–2021 and Shiyes near Arkhangelsk in 2019, challenges the authority and legitimacy of the central government.[88] It undercuts the credibility of state propaganda, especially as alternative sources of information are available. And it raises doubts about Putin's capabilities despite the constitutional referendum in June–July 2020 on extending his presidential terms. Widespread discontent with the Kremlin's handling of the COVID-

---

[87] *The Territories of the Russian Federation 2020*, London: Routledge, 2020, p.128.

[88] "Eco-Protestors Fight Moscow's Attempt to 'Trash' Russia's North," September 12, 2019, https://www.pri.org/stories/2019-09-12/eco-protesters-fight-moscow-s-attempt-trash-russia-s-north.

19 pandemic exacerbated indignation over a range of government policies. And protests in one region can be imitated in others, especially if they include thousands of citizens openly and peacefully resisting law enforcement. An opinion poll conducted by the independent Levada Center in the summer of 2020 indicated that almost half of Russians supported the Khabarovsk protests, while only 17 percent opposed them, and a third were willing to stage similar demonstrations in their own regions.[89]

Russian citizens in numerous areas, regardless of nationality, view Moscow as an imperial capital and themselves as the residents of dependent colonial territories.[90] Regionalists often perceive Moscow as a state within a state, in which Muscovites live in privileged economic conditions and from which the elite rules its colonies. The ethnic-Russian nation, having assimilated numerous non-Russians to varying degrees, is also less politically united than many officials admit. A growing number of Russian citizens in the regions have also lost trust in United Russia and other officially approved political parties to represent their interests. They resent the official ban on regional parties that could better represent citizens and the restricted authority of local governments.

Programs have been issued by several regionalist groupings to implement a more genuine democratic federalism, in which the rights of each subject are acknowledged through federal-regional partnerships. One such proposal for "refederalization" was produced by a regionalist group in Ingria, in northwest Russia, in November

---

[89] "Nearly Half of Russians Support Anti-Kremlin Protests in Far East – Poll," July 28, 2020, https://www.themoscowtimes.com/2020/07/28/nearly-half-of-russians-support-anti-kremlin-protests-in-far-east-poll-a70999.

[90] "Три империи: российская, коммунистическая, мафиозная," October 30, 2020, http://www.kasparov.ru/material.php?id=5F9AE07E2FFE9.

2020.[91] Mikhail Voitenkov, representing the regionalists of Ingermanland (the historic name of the St. Petersburg region), asserted that all federal subjects should become republics and retain 90 percent of the taxes they collect, thus giving them greater economic self-determination and opportunities for local development.

In March 2020, a group of activists announced plans to establish a Federative Party of Russia by convening a constituent congress.[92] By October 2020, the party attracted participants from 13 regions, elected a central board, declared its preparations to organize branches in all federal subjects, and adopted a preliminary party program.[93] It focused on "economic federalism" that would boost development by decentralizing decision-making, investing in new technologies, and reducing dependence on raw materials exports. It also issued a statement in support of upholding genuine federal principles, decentralizing power, and amending the Constitution."[94] Federative Party leaders asserted that they were not regionalists or separatists but federalists, advocating for an effective state structure in which each region would be economically strong and competitive, with inviolable borders and a negotiated accord with the center for the division of powers. The Federative Party claimed that Russia's systemic parties and most of the opposition were Moscow-centric and had limited

---

[91] "Два проекта возрождения федерализма," 22 November 2020, http://region.expert/2projects/.

[92] Paul Goble, "Leaders of New Federative Party Outline Its Program," March 7, 2020, https://windowoneurasia2.blogspot.com/2020/03/leaders-of-new-federative-party-outline.html.

[93] "Первый съезд Федеративной партии и ее экономическая программа," October 13, 2020, http://region.expert/fedparty1/.

[94] "Два проекта возрождения федерализма," November 22, 2020, http://region.expert/2projects.

commitments to the regions.[95] It supported horizontal connections and equal treaties between the regions, which were isolated from each other under the current system and needed permission from Moscow to conduct any inter-regional projects. In order to build a genuine federation, the party asserted that it was essential to adopt a new Federal Treaty voluntarily signed by freely elected regional authorities.

Moscow cracked down on the Federative Party's activities. It was prohibited from registering for any elections, its founders were either banned from standing in the September 2021 *Duma* ballot, threatened with prosecution, or forced to flee abroad.[96] The party leader, Oleg Khomutinnikov, was pressured to leave Russia under threat of criminal prosecution. Other non-registered parties espousing authentic federalism have included the Russian Party of Freedom and Justice, headed by Maksim Shevchenko, a movement for the Self-Determination for the Peoples of Russia, led by political activist Ayrat Dilmukhametov in Bashkortostan, and the Russian ethno-federalist Association of Popular Resistance. In August 2020, Dilmukhametov was sentenced to nine years in prison after calling for a "new federalism."[97]

The program of the New People Party (NPP), established by a Kremlin-linked oligarch for the September 2021 *Duma* elections,

---

[95] Paul Goble, "All Russia's Systemic Parties and Most Opposition Ones Remain Moscow-Centric, Federative Party Head Says," May 9, 2021, http://windowoneurasia2.blogspot.com/2021/05/all-russias-systemic-parties-and-most.html.

[96] "Лидер Федеративной партии покинул Россию," July 9, 2021, https://region.expert/out_empire/.

[97] "9 лет строгого режима за федерализм," August 24, 2020, http://region.expert/airat9/.

advocated for federalism and decentralization, including a greater retention of local taxes by the regions.[98] Its platform mimicked that of the independent Federative Party, which was banned from running in elections, and seemed intended to allow Kremlin loyalists to defuse a potentially explosive political issue. By enticing voters who seek greater regional autonomy, the NPP was designed as a public pressure valve controlled by state officials. However, such an initiative can escape Moscow's grasp by stimulating genuine demands for decentralization and signals that support for political devolution is more widespread than the authorities acknowledge.

Notable distinctions exist between regionalist and federalist proposals that may increasingly impact on Russia's future. If democratic federalism and inter-regional equality are rejected by Moscow, regionalist demands are likely to gain broader traction in several parts of the country. Regionalism signifies far-reaching autonomy and local sovereignty, while federalism ensures that elements of that sovereignty are yielded to the central government and horizontal links are forged with other federal units. A democratic federation faces a precarious balancing act in ensuring equal representation for all regions to maintain their loyalty to the state and, at the same time, avoiding policies that will be viewed as exploiting richer regions to uphold the economies of poorer ones. Federalists are not separatists, but some Russian regionalists and non-Russian ethno-nationalists may be pushed toward such positions by restrictive central government policies. Proponents of a genuine federation argue that without federalism the country is likely to disintegrate and if Moscow obstructs regional appeals for a devolution of powers such demands will escalate toward calls for separate statehood.

---

[98] Vadim Shtepa, "How New Are the 'New People' in Russia's Parliament?" *Eurasia Daily Monitor*, Vol. 18, Issue 152, October 6, 2021, https://jamestown.org/program/how-new-are-the-new-people-in-russias-parliament/.

Russian federalists will need to focus more attention on building a broad consensus on the necessity of decentralization and regional empowerment to drive economic development. Tying economic growth with regional autonomy is likely to gain more adherents in both richer and poorer regions. Proposals have been voiced that the regions should be responsible for tax gathering, in which the federal units would keep what they collect and transfer a fixed portion to Moscow.[99] Local authorities are in a much better position to use tax revenues to develop their regions. However, officials in Moscow remain cognizant that such a tax system instituted by the Union Republics contributed to dismantling the Soviet Union.

The anti-regime opposition remains divided on the question of federalism, with decentralists arguing that only autonomy and authentic federalism can save the country from rupture, while centralists believe that federalism would be the harbinger of Russia's disintegration. The latter's position underscores the fundamental weakness of the Russian state, where even democrats are convinced that it will collapse if authority is devolved to local and regional governments. In the closing years of the Soviet Union, liberal intellectuals and politicians ignored the forces of regionalism and ethnicity in their pursuit of democratization.[100] Some Russian liberals have even proposed the liquidation of the national republics to equalize them with the non-ethnic *krais* and *oblasts.* Such positions collide with proposals by regionalists and federalists, whether Russian or non-Russian, to elevate the prerogatives of regional entities so that all subjects of the federation have equal status.

---

[99] Martin Nicholson, *Toward a Russia of Regions*, Adelphi Paper No.330, International Institute for Strategic Studies, Oxford University Press, 1999, p.35.

[100] Vladimir Shlapentokh, Roman Levita, and Mikhail Loiberg, *From Submission to Rebellion: The Provinces Versus the Center in Russia,* Westview Press, 1997, p.85.

For many regionalists, the most effective alternative to dictatorial centralism is the transformation of all federal entities into republics with commensurate rights for each in a more symmetrical structure. Nonetheless, leaders of several ethno-national republics have claimed that their entities are entitled to special constitutional status that enhance the rights of indigenous populations that have suffered centuries of state discrimination. In such an arrangement, the republican constitutions should take precedence over federal laws. In effect, they are seeking a confederal arrangement, in which constituent units surrender minimal prerogatives to the center and the state structure is based on treaties or contracts that delegate any powers from the subjects to the center.

Russian nationalists anxious about keeping the country intact seek to elevate predominantly Russian federal *krais* and *oblasts* into republics and provide them with the same status in the Federation as non-Russian republics. Such proposals may find common ground with non-Russians seeking a more authentic federalism.[101] Russian regions that are not republics, such as Khabarovsk *Krai,* may push for the same status as the non-Russian republics and for a genuine federal structure. This could help develop a common multi-ethnic agenda against the centralist imperial state which has pursued a policy of division and domination. The Kremlin has tried to extinguish demands for greater symmetry between federal subjects by asserting that any referenda on the issue in *krais* and *oblasts* would be unconstitutional.[102]

---

[101] "Самоопределение народов России как платформа нового федерализма," August 3, 2020, https://www.idelreal.org/a/30758362.html.

[102] "Кремль отказал регионам России в праве на референдум о самоопределении," March 16, 2021, https://lenta.ru/news/2021/03/16/referendum/.

Some ethno-nationalist activists have called for the creation of a single large Russian Republic within the Federation that would unite the 46 predominantly Russian *oblasts* and *krais*, the three federal cities, and the Jewish Autonomous *Oblast.*[103] While this could be viewed as an attempt to give Russian regions equal status with the ethno-national republics, it may also be considered an attempt at ethno-national dominance, whereby the non-Russian republics would be demoted to second-class status next to a giant Russian ethnic republic that controls the central government and its resources. Nevertheless, some ethnic leaders may actually welcome such a development because it would help convince the non-Russian republics to push for full sovereignty or outright secession.

Federalists and regionalists contend that in addition to strengthening the regions vis-à-vis Moscow, local municipal governments must also gain more authority to check any anti-democratic moves by regional governments. Some local activists have campaigned for restoring direct local elections of governors, mayors, and other local authorities.[104] For instance, in September 2020, opposition parties in Yekaterinburg circulated petitions asking local assemblies to vote on restoring elected mayors and requested a referendum on this issue at the election commission of Sverdlovsk *Oblast.* Such initiatives are likely to be repeated in other regions.

The mass protests in Khabarovsk during 2020 and 2021, despite hundreds of detentions, fines, and arrests, together with the support they received elsewhere in the country, indicated that anti-centralist

---

[103] "В России предлагают создать "Русскую республику" со столицей в Екатеринбурге," February 24, 2021, https://www.idelreal.org/a/31119719.html.

[104] Paul Goble, "Russian Opposition Presses for Elected Mayors, Opening Larger Issue of Elections for Regional Heads," September 28, 2020, http://windowoneurasia2.blogspot.com/2020/09/russian-opposition-presses-for-elected.html.

positions are becoming more widespread. An increasing number of citizens perceive the value of decentralization and local control over resources and finances. Various ideas have been floated on how the revived republics and regions will function, what exact powers and decisions will remain with the federal center, and what representation ethnic majorities and minorities will have in each federal unit. Despite the swelling interest in local democracy, Moscow does not permit any open public debate on these essential questions but seems to believe that it can indefinitely suppress such ideas through censorship and punishment.

Discussions about new regional parties are also evident among activists, despite the legal ban against them. In addition to focusing on local problems, proposals have been voiced for a new federative treaty or a freely elected Federation Council that is not subject to Kremlin control. The longer such demands are ignored or denounced as illegitimate, the more radical they are likely to become.[105] Moscow also fears increasing horizontal links between federal subjects in demanding their constitutional rights or even joint campaigns for decentralization. It has pursued policies to divide and isolate federal units from each other and from any neighboring state, as it fears an internal common front against the Center and an external source of attraction for the regions and republics. A nightmare scenario for the Kremlin would be simultaneous large-scale protest actions in several major cities and regional capitals demanding regional autonomy. Moscow could become overstretched and incapable of suppressing numerous prolonged demonstrations for fundamental political reforms.

---

105 Paul Goble, "Separatism Doesn't Threaten Russia But Will If Kremlin Fails to Listen to Regions, Yarulin Says," August 1, 2020, https://windowoneurasia2.blogspot.com/2020/08/separatism-doesnt-threaten-russia-but.html.

Regional Alienation

The real danger to the Putin regime and to Russia's state integrity will not come from known political opponent but from spontaneous movements in several regions that can spark a wider conflagration. There is a long history of regional protests against Moscow's policies, and several regions declared independence when the Tsarist empire collapsed and the Bolsheviks seized power in October 1917, before they were subdued by the Red Army. During the protracted collapse of the Soviet Union, several regions of the Russian Soviet Federative Socialist Republic (RSFSR) were the first to stage demonstrations against Muscovite centralism. In the late 1980s, mass protest actions against the government began in the regions and autonomous republics.[106] For instance, in April 1986, thousands of Yakuts marched under the slogan "Yakutia for the Yakuts." Such actions were followed by demonstrations and strikes in Vorkuta, in the Komi Republic, and several other regions. Russian regionalist historian Andrei Degtyanov believes this pattern is now being repeated, with protests in Khabarovsk, Shiyes, Ryazan, and elsewhere.[107] This fanning out of protests across Russia and their transformation from single-issue campaigns to political challenges is more threatening to the survival of the regime and the continuity of the state than any street rallies in Moscow.[108]

---

[106] Paul Goble, "As at End of Soviet Times, Mass Actions Beginning in Regions Not in Moscow, Degtyanov Says," August 5, 2020, https://windowoneurasia2.blogspot.com/2020/08/as-at-end-of-soviet-times-mass-actions.html.

[107] "Новое народничество," August 3, 2020, http://region.expert/new-people/.

[108] Paul Goble, "Russian Protests Shift from Big Cities to Hinterlands, Laying 'Depth Charge' under State, Gorevoy Says," August 26, 2020, https://windowoneurasia2.blogspot.com/2020/08/russian-protests-shift-from-big-cities.html.

Opposition to specific government decisions has been mounting, including the appointment or replacement of regional governors, the altering of intra-federal borders, the proposed amalgamation of federal units, the dumping of trash without public consultation, and numerous other unilateral moves by state officials. Disaffection with government policies is underpinned by spreading public resentment that Moscow exploits its *de facto* colonies by appropriating regional resources while neglecting local economic development. As a result, a growing number of citizens will not only become frustrated if their protests are ignored or subdued, they will also start looking for alternative political solutions.

Economic Ingredients

Economic factors can mobilize or contribute to stirring nationalist and regionalist sentiments, as was evident in several autonomous republics in the early 1990s. This can include exasperation over economic mismanagement, falling living standards, spreading unemployment, growing income and wealth disparities, discrimination in hiring policies, and elite nepotism. Protests can occur where income inequalities become most pronounced, particularly in major cities and the richer oil- and gas-producing regions. A growing number of residents in republics such as Komi are outraged that despite working hard for many years in regions rich in natural resources, they ended up in poverty.[109] The government could alleviate some of the public acrimony by increasing taxes on the rich and adopting a more populist economic strategy to help the poor, but this would contribute to alienating its most loyal elite backers.

---

109 Sofia Bogatkina, "Сам ты ошибка!» В Коми активист вышел на пикет после высказывания спикера Госдумы о национальных республиках," November 11, 2021, https://7x7-journal.ru/news/2021/11/11/sam-ty-oshibka-v-komi-aktivist-vyshel-na-piket-posle-vyskazyvaniya-spikera-gosdumy-o-nacionalnyh-respublikah.

An additional source of economic resentment is asymmetrical government spending and the favoring of politically useful regions. In a prime example, the cost of absorbing the newly annexed Crimea after 2014 led to cuts in programs to other regions. This included shelving the construction of a bridge across the Lena River to link Yakutsk, the capital of the Sakha Republic, with the Amur–Yakutsk railway.[110] Large-scale state projects are also viewed with skepticism and increase regional resentments. Defense Minister Sergei Shoigu, who was placed in charge of state plans to develop Siberia, has raised the idea of establishing several large cities in the region with a million inhabitants in each.[111] He posited that they would become attractive for Russian citizens and neighbors in developing Siberia. The first such metropolis would merge Vladivostok, Artem, and additional urban agglomerations to form the capital of the Far Eastern Federal District.

In essence, such plans are a modernized version of the Soviet mega-projects, and in this case based on the extraction and processing of specific resources such as rare-earth minerals, aluminum, timber, coal, and chemicals. The assumption behind these grandiose schemes is that substantial financing will be available and that qualified specialists and workers can be attracted to Siberia, even though the region has lost almost 20 percent of its population since the Soviet dissolution and contains less than 20 million residents. The Siberian cities proposal neglects the necessity of repairing dilapidated regional infrastructure, ignores declining urban areas, and pays little attention

---

[110] Rensselaer Lee and Artyom Lukin, *Russia's Far East: New Dynamics in Asia Pacific and Beyond*, Boulder, London: Lynne Rienner Publishers, p.91.

[111] Sergey Sukhankin, "Russia's 'Re-Exploration' of Siberia and the Far East: Tools, Plans, Ambitions (Part One), *Eurasia Daily Monitor*, Vol. 18, Issue 161, October 25, 2021, https://jamestown.org/program/russias-re-exploration-of-siberia-and-the-far-east-tools-plans-ambitions-part-one/.

to funding, investment, economic competitiveness, attraction for Russian workers, or foreign involvement.[112] In reality, economic stagnation, unpaid wages, poor working conditions, the raising of the retirement age, and increases in social taxes from workers' pay have already provoked labor protests in various cities and regions. Workers in a broad variety of economic branches have staged hundreds of protest actions in a majority of Russia's regions.[113] Links between the political opposition, regionalist activists, and protesting workers could become a combustible combination against the Putin regime, especially during times of economic hardship, when there is little prospect of improvement.

Ethnic Dimensions

Declining living standards and other social ailments can spark anti-government protests, strengthen ethnic assertiveness, and provoke inter-ethnic conflicts. For instance, after the decrease in migrant workers by over two and a half million during 2020, or almost a quarter of the total, several industries and regional governments pressed Moscow to enable their return, as the migrants were willing

[112] Sergey Sukhankin, "Russia's 'Re-Exploration' of Siberia and the Far East: Tools, Plans, Ambitions (Part Two), *Eurasia Daily Monitor*, Vol. 18, Issue 162, October 26, 2021, https://jamestown.org/program/russias-re-exploration-of-siberia-and-the-far-east-tools-plans-ambitions-part-two/.

[113] Ivan Sytkh, "Россия: почему растет число трудовых конфликтов и протестов," May 13, 2021,

https://russian.eurasianet.org/россия-почему-растет-число-трудовых-конфликтов-и-протестов.

to engage in menial work that many Russian citizens avoided.[114] However, rising unemployment among Russians generated resistance to such polices and increasingly assumed an ethnic dimension, especially as almost three quarters of migrant workers were non-Slavic Central Asians. Local workers claimed that corporations employed immigrants in order to keep Russians' wages low. Such sentiments can increase xenophobia and racism and enable Russian nationalist parties to recruit followers.

Periodic clashes between ethnic Russians and migrant workers from the North Caucasus and Central Asia in the country's largest cities have become a persistent trend.[115] Before the 2022 international sanctions began to impact on the Russian economy, non-Russian laborers formed an increasing share of the population in many urban neighborhoods and in some instances, they comprised nearly half of the local population. Many have not integrated into Russian society and preferred to live separately, thereby feeding into ethnic-Russian prejudices against migrants who refuse to assimilate. In some unsafe city neighborhoods, ethnic Russians complain about police indifference and have formed self-defense units. Vigilantism in migrant neighborhoods provides opportunities for radicalism and an escalation of violence that the security services will find difficult to control.

Economic stagnation in several federal regions also has an ethnic dimension. The exodus of ethnic Russians from the non-Russian

---

[114] Paul Goble, "Calls for Return of Non-Russian Migrant Workers Divides Business, Government, and Unemployed Russians," January 7, 2021, http://windowoneurasia2.blogspot.com/2021/01/calls-for-return-of-non-russian-migrant.html.

[115] Paul Goble, "Ethnic Russians in Moscow Forming Self-Defense Units Against Non-Russian Migrants," *Eurasia Daily Monitor*, Vol.18, Issue 170, November 9, 2021, https://jamestown.org/program/ethnic-russians-in-moscow-forming-self-defense-units-against-non-russian-migrants/.

republics has accelerated in the past two decades. The outflow has been spurred by numerous factors, including fewer economic prospects, the allure of Moscow and other large cities in inner Russia, growing indigenous ethnic identification and discrimination against Russians, and local resentment of what is widely perceived as centuries of Russian colonialism. Most national republics have experienced a steady growth in the share of titular ethnicities and their in-migration from other regions. Falling numbers of ethnic Russians raises the self-confidence of ethnic leaders and intensifies demands for autonomy and self-determination.

The demographic decline of ethnic Russians poses challenges for the country's social, political, and territorial cohesion and will encourage movements for autonomy, secession, and independence. According to census figures between 1989 and 2010, in 14 of the 21 republics (excluding the occupied Ukrainian territory of Crimea) the ethnic-Russian population has steadily decreased proportionally to the titular nationality. In 13 republics, ethnic Russians form less than half of the total population. In nine republics, ethnic Russians form less than a third of the total population. In 11 republics, the ethnic-Russian population is smaller than that of the titular nationality. The shrinkage of ethnic Russians looks set to continue and could be further revealed following the October–November 2021 census. However, some observers contend that the results of the census will be falsified to satisfy Kremlin demands and may not disclose the true extent of contraction in the ethnic-Russian population.[116]

The ethnic-Russian shrinkage has been most evident in the republics of the North Caucasus. In Chechnya, following the two Russo-Chechen wars in the 1990s, the ethnic-Russian population fell

---

[116] "Всероссийская перепись населения: чем опасна фальсификация данных," November 15, 2021, https://www.dw.com/ru/perepis-naselenija-rossii-chem-opasna-falsifikacija-dannyh/a-59801766?maca=rus-tco-dw.

dramatically from over 23 percent in the 1989 census to 3.6 percent in 2002 and 1.9 percent in 2010. In Ingushetia, the ethnic-Russian share of the population dwindled from over 23 percent in 1989 to only 1.1 percent in 2002 and 0.8 percent in 2010. Russians in Dagestan have constituted a small minority for decades, but the speed of decline has increased since 1989, when it stood at just over 9 percent. In 2002, it decreased to 4.6 percent, and in 2020, it fell to 3.6 percent.

In the western part of the North Caucasus, ethnic-Russian numbers have been higher and the decline more gradual in each of the ethnic republics. In Kabardino-Balkaria, their share of the total population was under 32 percent in 1989, dropping to 25.1 percent in 2002 and 22.5 percent in 2010. Similarly, in Karachaevo-Cherkessia, the proportion fell from over 42 percent in 1989 to 33.6 percent in 2002 and 31.6 percent in 2010. In North Ossetia–Alania, the steady decline meant that ethnic Russians made up 30 percent of the population in 1989, 23.1 percent in 2002 and 20.8 percent in 2010. Even in Adygea, where the indigenous population has been smaller than in other North Caucasus republics, ethnic-Russian numbers have reduced from 68 percent in 1989 to 64.4 percent in 2002 and 63.6 percent in 2010.

In three Middle Volga republics, the ethnic-Russian minority has either declined more steadily or stabilized at a low level. In Chuvashia, it dipped from 26.6 percent in 1989 to 26.5 percent in 2002 and slightly increased to 26.9 percent in 2010. In Tatarstan, it fell from 43.2 percent in 1989 to 39.4 percent in 2002 and rose slightly to 39.7 percent in 2010. In Bashkortostan, ethnic Russians constituted 39.2 percent of the population in 1989, 36.3 percent in 2002, and 36.1 percent in 2010. Other republics have also witnessed a Russian exodus and a growth in the indigenous population. In Kalmykia, Russian numbers dropped from just under 37 percent in 1989 to 33.5 percent in 2002 and 30.2 percent in 2010. Russians in Tuva have always constituted a minority, and their proportion declined significantly from 32 percent in 1989 to 20.1 percent in 2002 and 16.3 percent in

2010. In Sakha, a narrow Russian majority of 50.3 percent in 1989 fell to a minority of 41.1 percent in 2002 and 37.8 percent in 2010.

Even in republics where the titular nation does not form a majority, the ethnic-Russian population has been steadily decreasing. In Mordovia, ethnic Russians numbered 60.8 percent in 1989 and only 53.4 percent in 2010. In Buryatia, the total decreased from almost 70 percent in 1989 to 67.8 percent in 2002 and 66.1 percent in 2010. In Altai, the drop was from 60.4 percent in 1989 to 57.4 percent in 2002 and 56.6 percent in 2010. In Mari El, ethnic-Russian numbers have stood consistently at just over 47 percent. In two republics, the percentage of Russians increased by small margins. In Khakassia, it rose from 79.4 percent in 1989 to 80.2 percent in 2002 and to 81.7 percent in 2010. In Udmurtia, it increased from just under 59 percent in 1989 to 60.1 percent in 2002 and 62.2 percent in 2010. Only in two republics has the rise in ethnic Russians proved more significant. In Komi, it increased from just under 58 percent in 1989 to 59.5 percent in 2002 and to 65.1 percent in 2010. In Karelia, the portion of Russians in the wider population rose from 73.6 percent in 1989 to 76.6 percent in 2002 and 82.2 percent in 2010.

In six former Autonomous *Okrugs* (AO), the-ethnic Russian population was falling before their merger with neighboring *oblasts* and *krais*. In Agin-Buryat AO, the Russian share declined from 40.8 percent in 1989 to 35.1 percent in 2002. In Koryak AO, it fell from 62 percent in 1989 to 50.5 percent in 2002. In Taimyr AO, ethnic Russians dwindled from 67 percent in 1989 to 58.6 percent in 2002 and 50 percent in 2010. In Ust-Orda Buryat AO, Russian numbers dropped from 56.5 percent in 1989 to 54.4 percent in 2002. In Evenk AO, the fall was from 67.5 percent in 1989 to 61.9 percent in 2002 and 59.4 percent in 2010. In all these districts, the indigenous ethnic population grew. Only in Komi-Permyak AO did the number of ethnic Russians slightly increase from 36.1 percent in 1989 to 38.1 percent in 2002, before the *okrug's* merger into Perm *Krai*.

In three of the four still-existing Autonomous *Okrugs,* the ethnic-Russian share of the population has remained steady or slightly increased through in-migration. In Chukotka, where major natural resources are lacking that would attract migrant workers, the Russian share of the population decreased from 66.1 percent in 1989 to 51.8 percent in 2002 and only marginally increased to 52.5 percent by 2010. In contrast, the Khanty-Mansi Autonomous *Okrug* and the Yamalo-Nenets Autonomous *Okrug*, both within Tyumen *Oblast*, are the main oil- and gas-producing regions where the ethnic-Russian share of the population has risen. In Khanty-Mansi AO, 66.3 percent of the residents were Russians in 1989, 66 percent in 2002, and 68.1 percent in 2010. In Yamalo-Nenets AO, Russians formed 59.2 percent in 1989, 58.8 percent in 2002, and 61.7 percent in 2010. In Nenets AO, part of Arkhangelsk *Oblast*, the number of ethnic Russians has hovered between 65.8 percent in 1989, 62.4 percent in 2002, and 66.1 percent in 2010. In addition, both Khanty-Mansi and Yamalo-Nenets have witnessed a steady rise in the non-Russian and non-Slavic population of migrants from the North Caucasus, especially from Dagestan.[117]

In some *krais* the overall population has continued to decrease, especially in Altai, Zabaikalski, Primorski, Khabarovsk, Kamchatka and Perm. A number of *oblasts* outside of inner Russia have also witnessed significant population declines except in the major cities, including Arkhangelsk, Murmansk, Kurgan, Magadan and the Jewish Autonomous *Oblast*. Despite Moscow's initial projections, the markedly reduced proportion of ethnic Russians, together with Ukrainian and Belarusians, has not been compensated by an influx of Russian migrants from the North Caucasus, Central Asia, the Baltic

---

[117] Denis Sokolov, "Ugra, the Dagestani North: Anthropology of Mobility Between the North Caucasus and Western Siberia," in Marlene Laruelle (Ed.), *New Mobilities and Social Changes in Russia's Arctic Regions*, London: Routledge, 2017, pp.176–193.

States, or other former Soviet territories.[118] Moscow is also unable to attract significant numbers from core Russia to its distant northern and eastern regions, which are experiencing infrastructural decay and shortages of goods and amenities. The planned development of the Northern Sea Route across the Arctic, particularly ports and other infrastructure, is supposed to revitalize the High North regions and increase the incoming population. However, the results will depend on sustained government investment and the region's long-term profitability that could attract workers and specialists.

Resurgent Communities

The ethnically defined Union Republics and Autonomous Republics established by the Soviet authorities in the 1920s and 1930s were intended to give each major nationality a stake in the "construction of Socialism." Instead, they proved to be an incubator of nationalism that, to varying degrees, resisted the consolidation of Soviet identity based on Russian language and culture. The Soviet policy of "national in form, Socialist in content" was formulated on the premise that a common Soviet identity promoted by Communist Party control in each republic would supersede and eventually replace ethno-nationalist identity. However, local ethnic institutions, language use, ethnic identification in internal passports, and the creation of ethno-territorial administrative units served to strengthen ethnic self-definition and limited the de-nationalizing impact of Sovietization and russification.

In some instances, state policy helped to consolidate ethnic categories from an amalgamation of tribal or clan groups and assigned them

---

[118] A.G. Manakov, "Spatial Patterns in the Transformation of the Ethnic Structure of the Russian Population Between the 1959 and 2010 Censuses," *Geography and National Resources*, August 2019, https://doi.org/10.1134/S1875372819020021.

specific territories. This served to develop a distinct ethno-national identity, as was the case with the Khakass after the 1920s and various groups in the Middle Volga region who began to identify as Tatars, Bashkirs, or Chuvash.[119] Yet the attempt to forge a *Homo Sovieticus* that would transcend national and ethnic identities collapsed alongside the Communist system and the Soviet Union. Following the Soviet implosion, ethnic elites in several autonomous national republics in the Russian Federation embarked on a process of solidifying national identities based on ethnic principles and legitimate territorial units. Ethnic self-assertion has been facilitated by the existence of 20 republics named after titular nationalities (not including Dagestan and occupied Crimea, both of which have non-ethnic designations), and four autonomous *okrugs* and one autonomous *oblast* also named after titular nationalities.

Paradoxically, instead of forging common citizenship, the Soviet Union unintentionally institutionalized sub-state political units and strengthened ethnic and regional identities that mushroomed after the collapse of Communism. Political elites in several Russian autonomous republics viewed the collapse of the USSR as an opportunity to increase their power.[120] They benefited from the resurgence of ethno-nationalist movements, often led by students and intellectuals, who mobilized significant sectors of the population to strengthen ethnic distinctiveness and gain increasing independence from Moscow. Sovereignty demands in several republics, including Chechnya, Tatarstan, Tuva, Bashkortostan and Sakha, revolved around economic grievances among the titular nations, such as

---

[119] Dmitry P. Gorenburg, *Minority Ethnic Mobilization in the Russian Federation*, Cambridge University Press, 2003, p.270.

[120] Dmitry P. Gorenburg, *Minority Ethnic Mobilization in the Russian Federation*, Cambridge University Press, 2003, p.2.

perceived subordination to Russians.[121] These were adroitly promoted by nationalist groups to push for republican sovereignty and secession. Even where certain ethnic groups benefited from affirmative actions within titular republics, they resented the degree of central control exerted by Moscow and Russian ethnic hegemony across the country.

Putin's accession to power paralyzed much of the sovereignty process but failed to extinguish it. The formation of ethnic-based political parties was prohibited, ethnic minority representation in the State *Duma* and other elected bodies has been limited, and consultative mechanisms that would enable ethnic inputs into decision-making became largely impotent. However, ethnic leaders can harness numerous resentments over material inequalities, discrimination, and falling living standards. This may also foster inter-group conflicts, with claims of Russian dominance and the second-class status of indigenous populations. A new generation of political and cultural leaders will seek a more extensive role for titular nations in controlling republican resources and involvement in regional politics. They are rediscovering facts about Moscow's imperial and colonial history and highlighting the injustices perpetrated by Russian rulers and colonists during the conquest of Siberia, the High North, and the Pacific regions. By urging a national, linguistic, and cultural revival and greater republican sovereignty, they will become the new national elites that can mobilize the population, especially once the vulnerabilities of the central authorities become starker.[122]

---

[121] Elise Giuliano, *Constructing Grievance: Ethnic Nationalism in Russia's Republics*, Cornell University Press, 2011, p.5.

[122] Dmitry P. Gorenburg, *Minority Ethnic Mobilization in the Russian Federation*, Cambridge University Press, 2003, p.233.

Abbas Gallyamov, a former Putin speechwriter, is convinced that anger over Russia's consolidation as a centralized state is ripening among national elites, intelligentsia, and ethnic activists and will become manifested when the government starts to weaken during a crisis.[123] Throughout Putin's rule, leaders of various national groups have been dismayed by the underfunding of cultural activities, threats to eliminate or merge federal units, the downgrading of titular language rights in the ethnic republics, and constitutional amendments defining Russian as the language of the "state-forming nation." In October 2021, the federal Foundation for the Preservation and Study of Native Languages was closed, indicating declining state involvement in preserving indigenous languages and identities. State authorities also threaten to undermine the "indigenous" status of native peoples in the High North and Siberia by defining Russian settlers, colonizers, and administrators as equally "indigenous." Although this is designed to weaken distinct national identities, it will serve to stiffen resistance against Moscow. Proposals have also been voiced to allow citizens to register two nationalities in the census in the event of mixed marriages. This would allow officials to reduce the number of non-Russians by simply listing "Russian" for those declaring two nationalities or favoring certain non-Russian groups over others. All of these stipulations can be used to discriminate against specific nations in pursuit of russification and homogenization.

An increasing marginalization of non-Russian languages in the educational system has been accompanied by patriotic statist indoctrination and mono-cultural assimilation.[124] Proposals have

---

[123] Ramazan Alpaut, "Центр давит на регионы. Ожидать ли бунта?" November 8, 2021, idelreal.org/a/31547247.html.

[124] Federica Prina, *National Minorities in Putin's Russia: Diversity and Assimilation*, Routledge Contemporary Russia and Eastern Europe Series, Routledge: London and New York, 2016, p.146.

been made to further reduce the status of non-Russian languages by defining Russian as the sole state language and other languages in non-Russian republics as only being "official" for the titular population. In practice, this would enhance russification with much reduced state support for native languages. To downgrade the status of ethnic republics, some officials contend that all languages other than Russian should have equal status as "official" or "regional" languages even if they are not linked with any sub-state formation.[125]

An underlying current of state prejudice and paternalism toward non-Russian ethnicities, especially outside their titular republics, contributes to the sense of subordination and grievance. The revival of ethnic identities is visible in reclaiming a distinct history, monument building, celebrating national anniversaries, the nativization of street signs and place names, and various other forms of symbolic politics. "Linguistic activism" is becoming more commonplace in protest against various government restrictions, including the repressive language law, requirements that all students seeking higher education must take the unified educational examination in Russian, federal cuts in publishing and translating non-Russian literature, reduced publication of textbooks in non-Russian languages, and the closure of local schools.

Intellectuals and cultural figures among various ethnic groups are speaking out against what is perceived as escalating russification and ethnic assimilation. The closing of many rural schools as a cost-cutting measure has outraged indigenous people, as this threatens the survival of their languages and distinct identities. Large-scale school closures in places such as the Komi Republic reduces instruction in

---

[125] Paul Goble, "Bondarenko Wants Russian to be the State Languages and All Others Republic or Not to be Labelled 'Official,'" March 29, 2021, http://windowoneurasia2.blogspot.com/2021/03/bondarenko-wants-russian-to-be-state.html.

non-Russian languages and furthers Russian assimilation.[126] In several locations, activists, including teachers and parents, have campaigned for maintaining local schools and elicited broad public support, with the authorities eventually backing down. Even such small successes can mobilize people to expand their campaigns for national rights.

Moscow's Manipulations

Moscow has pursued a policy of dismantling or reducing the size of several ethnic groups either by supporting linguistic schisms and cultural diversity within specific communities or by trying to create a super-ethnos to dilute national identities. One notable case involves relations between Tatars and Bashkirs in two Middle Volga republics. The Kremlin has manipulated and highlighted claims by some nationalists in both ethnicities that their populations have been assimilated by the other ethnic group. The primary objective is to divide the two nations, reduce the number of self-identifying Tatars, and curtail demands for sovereignty and potential statehood by Tatarstan.

In marked contrast, in the Republic of Mordovia, Moscow has sought to diminish distinctions between the Moksha and Erzya peoples by emphasizing an overarching Mordovian identity.[127] The goal is to undercut the activism of the two Finno-Ugric nations by promoting identity disputes. The two nations have different languages and reside

[126] Paul Goble, "Komis Fighting School Consolidation and Its Negative Impact on Their Lives and Language," September 5, 2021, http://windowoneurasia2.blogspot.com/2021/09/komis-fighting-school-consolidation-and.html.

[127] V.K. Abramov, "мордовское Национальное движение," Mordovian State University, 2020, Saransk, Russia.

in distinct territories—the Moksha primarily in the western part of the republic and the Erzya in the east.[128] The Erzya, in particular, are renowned for their activism and assertiveness, even though the population is approximately half that of the Moksha, who have greater institutional control in the republic. While the local authorities have tried to eliminate the Erzyan language from public life, the Erzyan organization Mastor has called for a distinct Erzyan national district within Mordovia and rejects the Mordovian appellation.[129] In recent years, the precipitous fall of the Russian population in Mordovia has also encouraged Moscow to play on ethnic divisions between Moksha and Erzya. The Moksha-Erzya population in the republic increased from 31 percent in 2002 to 40 percent in 2010 and over 50 percent in 2021, leaving ethnic Russians as a minority.[130] In addition, there are compact Erzya populations in several districts of nearby Samara *Oblast* and Orenburg *Oblast*.

In the North Caucasus, Russian authorities have pursued the division of the Circassian and the Karachai-Balkar communities. The Circassian (Adyg) nation was traditionally formed from twelve major tribes represented as stars on the national flag. The Russian state divided and compartmentalized them in several federal subjects, including the republics of Adygea, Kabardino-Balkaria, and

---

[128] "The Finno-Ugric Separatist Trends in Russia," Robert Lansing Institute for Global Threats and Democratic Studies, Dover, UK, November 11, 2020, https://lansinginstitute.org/2020/11/11/the-finno-ugric-separatist-trends-in-russia/.

[129] Federica Prina, *National Minorities in Putin's Russia: Diversity and Assimilation*, Routledge Contemporary Russia and Eastern Europe Series, Routledge: London and New York, 2016, p.35.

[130] Paul Goble, "Ethnic Divisions among Those Moscow Counts as Mordvins Withstand Divide-and-Rule Policies, Unity Drives and Repression," October 26, 2019, https://windowoneurasia2.blogspot.com/2019/10/ethnic-divisions-among-those-moscow.html.

Karachaevo-Cherkessia. The Shapsug Circassians also possessed an administrative district, the Shapsug National *Raion* within the Azov–Black Sea *Krai*. The *krai* was split in 1937 between Krasnodar *Krai* and Rostov *Oblast*, and the Shapsug National *Raion* was abolished after World War II. Following the Soviet collapse, Shapsug activists have campaigned for the reinstatement of the national *raion* but with no success.

A process of national reawakening has been evident among Circassians both inside Russia and abroad.[131] Activists assert the importance of a common ethnonym, including the self-identification of Circassians as one nation in the 2021 census rather than as one of their sub-ethnic categories. Civil organizations in several republics campaigned for their compatriots to adopt a common Circassian ethnic name. Circassian activists assert that there are twelve Circassian sub-ethnic communities, including those outside their home republics, in Stavropol *Krai* and North Ossetia.[132] They have lobbied for the return of Circassians from the diaspora, where about 90 percent live as a consequence of Tsarist expulsions in 1864. They are also pushing for the revival and development of a unified language, the use of the Latin alphabet instead of Cyrillic to undercut

---

[131] Paul Goble, "Circassians in the Homeland and Abroad Being Transformed by the Internet, Kabard Says," September 15, 2020. https://windowoneurasia2.blogspot.com/2020/09/circassians-in-homeland-and-abroad.html.

[132] Valery Dzutsati, "Advocates Across North Caucasus Demand Reclassifications of Local Ethnic Groups," *Eurasia Daily Monitor*, November 16, 2021, Vol. 18, Issue 174, https://jamestown.org/program/advocates-across-north-caucasus-demand-reclassifications-of-local-ethnic-groups/.

russification, and the creation of a distinct Circassian national republic in the North Caucasus.[133]

Even officials in Moscow have admitted that the creation of a Greater Circassia has significant support in the North Caucasus and abroad.[134] Approximately 720,000 Circassians live in the North Caucasus and an estimated 6 million in the diaspora, including 1.5 million in Turkey. Russian government officials are concerned that the influx of Circassians from abroad will change the ethnic balance in the republics, reinforce a common Circassian identity, and stimulate calls for statehood and independence. Moscow's fears of a Circassian revival are evident in further moves to divide the nation by establishing pro-Moscow Circassian organizations, intensifying control over existing associations, and ensuring that only loyalists are appointed to preside over the North Caucasus republics.[135] Some regional officials are also an obstacle to unifying the Circassians nation because an administrative rearrangement between republics could entail a loss of employment and privileges for local bureaucrats.

The Karachai and Balkars are similarly divided, between the republics of Karachaevo-Cherkessia (KCR) and Kabardino-Balkaria (KBR), despite identifying themselves as a single Turkic people with a

---

[133] Adel Bashqawi, *The Circassian Miracle: The Nation Neither Tsars, Nor Commissars, Nor Russia Could Stop,* Xlibris, 2020, p.442.

[134] Paul Goble, "'Greater Circassia Project has Real Support in Caucasus and Abroad,' Russian Scholar Says," November 9, 2020, http://windowoneurasia2.blogspot.com/2020/11/greater-circassia-project-has-real.html.

[135] Adel Bashqawi, *The Circassian Miracle: The Nation Neither Tsars, Nor Commissars, Nor Russia Could Stop,* Xlibris, 2020, p.462.

common language and small dialectical differences.[136] According to the 2010 Russian census, there are 125,000 Balkars in the KBR and 218,000 Karachais in the KCR. The two groups have formed inter-regional organizations to promote a common Turkic identity, the most significant being Elbrusoid. Disputes over the delineation of borders and land ownership have been evident between the KCR and KBR that could pit Circassian and Turkic populations against each other and bring into question the separation of both nations in different republics. In the event of deepening state fractures, Moscow would undoubtedly try to manipulate the Circassian-Turkic divisions to its advantage, and the onus will be on local leaders to prevent an escalation of disputes and the formation of territorial entities that would satisfy both populations.

Invigorated Identities

A process of both regional and ethno-national revival is evident in Siberia, the Urals, the Pacific region, and the High North. The renaissance of regional traditions is widening distinctions with Muscovites even among people viewed as Russians, Ukrainians, Belarusians and Poles who have undergone russification after settling in these regions several generations ago and developing unique local identities. Language and even dialect is often a major barometer of regional identity, even within the Russian ethnic corpus. This is evident among Siberians, Far Easterners, Cossacks, and among certain groups in European Russia, as in Ryazan, an *oblast* only 200

---

[136] "Один народ, две вершины," September 25, 2020, http://caucasustimes.com/ru/odin-narod-dve-vershiny/.

kilometers away from Moscow.[137] Fearful of linguistic diversification, regional identification, and flourishing ethnogenesis, Moscow enforces a standard Russian language. In some instances, this has generated opposition where regional activists view language as vital in promoting regional identification, including a Ryazan language and culture with a history of independence from Moscow.[138]

Ethnic Russians who do not strongly identify themselves within a single cultural framework with co-ethnics in European Russia, due to generations of separate existence, admixture with other cultures, absorption of non-Russian lifestyles, and the development of distinct regional dialects, can also advocate for sovereignty, as has been evident in Siberia. Several of Russia's federal units possess the natural resources and favorable locations to become autonomous and even independent economically once they curtail their exploitation by Moscow. Trade and investment from neighboring European and Asian countries can also significantly develop republics and regions, such as Kaliningrad, Karelia, Tuva, Sakha, Magadan, and other parts of Siberia and the Pacific region.

The economic dimension for local populations and regional elites can prove a strong pull toward statehood in resource-rich regions of the High North, Siberia, and the Pacific provinces. Public resentments have escalated that Moscow has failed to provide acceptable living standards for some of the richest regions of Eurasia, while local elites may calculate that they stand to benefit directly by controlling the export of local resources upon achieving independence. In particular,

---

[137] Paul Goble, "Even Ryazan Russians, Near Moscow, have a Distinctive Dialect," November 6, 2020, http://windowoneurasia2.blogspot.com/2020/11/even-ryazan-russians-near-moscow-have.htmll.

[138] "Основы Рязанского суверенитета," November 4, 2020, http://region.expert/ryazan-language/.

the Siberian Federal District, consisting of twelve federal subjects, is endowed with 85 percent of the country's reserves of lead and platinum, 80 percent of coal and molybdenum, 71 percent of nickel, 69 percent of copper, 44 percent of silver, and 40 percent of gold.[139]

Moscow's abject failure to realize Siberia's full economic potential to the benefit of its residents has been evident for generations. In a recent example of grand ambitions that deliver little in practice, a state decree issued in 2014 announced the creation of an "Arctic Zone of the Russian Federation" as a single territorial unit.[140] It incorporated parts of several federal subjects under the centralized supervision of the federal-level State Commission on Arctic Development to manage the region's resources and ensure economic development. However, as with many aspirational state projects, the initiative lacked sustainability, it triggered competition for scarce finances and labor, and amplified resentments among leaders of federal subjects and cities left out of Moscow's plans.

Over time and with deepening alienation from the imperial center, regional identities among populations officially viewed as ethnic Russian become solidified and can acquire novel ethnic dimensions. Local and regional symbols, including flags, coats of arms, monuments, historic locations, and notable personalities are

---

139 "Siberian Separatism: Whether Federal Center Can Hold Remote Regions," Robert Lansing Institute for Global Threats and Democratic Studies, Dover, UK, October 27, 2010,

https://lansinginstitute.org/2020/10/27/siberian-separatism-whether-federal-center-can-hold-remote-regions/.

140 Nadia French, "A Second Opportunity? Mechanisms of Renewed Russia's Arctic Colonization,"

The Polar Connection, March 28, 2017, http://polarconnection.org/russian-arctic/.

important markers of identity and have been rediscovered by local activists in a process reminiscent of ethnogenesis. Since the collapse of the Soviet Union, some regions have registered success in forming or reviving distinct quasi-ethnic identities, especially where these have been supported by ambitious governors or political elites. This has included the Pomor identity in Arkhangelsk *Oblast* that played a role in the Shiyes protests and opposed the amalgamation with the Nenets Autonomous *Okrug*.[141] The Pomors are a Russian sub-ethnos settled around the White Sea and culturally and linguistically distinct from the ethnic-Russian majority, but they have not been officially recognized as a self-standing nation and were denied any distinct institutional representation. Despite Moscow's attempts to stifle Pomor identity, an indeterminate number of people continue to identify as Pomors.

The Cossack population has experienced a significant renaissance since the demise of the Soviet Union and demonstrates the process of ongoing ethnic development despite Moscow's suppressive efforts. The authentic Cossacks in the Russian Federation consist of between three to five million people who trace their ancestry to the thirteen Cossack hosts of the Tsarist period.[142] Many consider themselves to be a distinct ethnic group with their own culture, language, traditions, and elected leadership (*atamans*). They are not agents of the state, unlike groups calling themselves "Cossacks" who have been sponsored by the regime as paramilitary units to suppress dissent.

---

141 Paul Goble, "Pomor 'Nation Building' in 1990s Shows What a Concerted Government Effort Can Achieve, Russian Critic Says," October 6, 2020, http://windowoneurasia2.blogspot.com/2020/10/pomor-nation-building-in-1990s-shows.html.

142 Paul Goble, "Cossackia: No Longer an Impossible Dream?" *Eurasia Daily Monitor*, Vol. 16, Issue 23, February 21, 2019, https://jamestown.org/program/cossackia-no-longer-an-impossible-dream/.

Independent Cossacks have become more active in celebrating their heritage and reviving traditions that were suppressed under communism. While some Cossacks believe they are a subgroup within the ethnic-Russian nation and should have cultural autonomy, others claim the status of a separate and distinct nation that must construct its own state, federation, or confederation of Cossack republics. The main Cossack hosts include the Astrakhan, Don, Transbaikal, Bashkir-speaking, Kalmyk-speaking, Ukrainian-speaking, Kuban, Orenburg, Orthodox, Russian, Siberian, Terek, Ural and Ussuri. Although Cossacks are dispersed throughout the country, the largest concentrations of Don, Kuban, and Terek Cossacks live in southern Russia, adjacent to the North Caucasus. The secession of the North Caucasus republics can embolden Cossack leaders to push for their own statehood.

The results of the 2021 census could create new frictions between Moscow and authentic Cossacks. Although in past censuses Cossacks have been counted as a distinct nationality, they could now declare more than one nationality and may be listed as ethnic Russians with a Cossack sub-division rather than a separate nation, as the authorities exhaustively seek to increase the number of ethnic Russians. The census listed 13 different Cossack hosts (*voiska)* as separate nationalities with the evident intent of further dividing the Cossack population.[143] Cossack activists also feared that census organizers would include Cossacks within the Russian nation if they identified in terms of the Russian language or Christian Orthodox religion. Cossacks who view themselves as a distinct nation are likely to doubt

---

[143] Росстат при переписи населения будет учитывать национальность "казак,"

panram.ru/news/society/rosstat-utverdil-pri-perepisi-naseleniya-natsionalnost-donskoy-kazak-i-kazak/ and Paul Goble, "To Keep Number of Cossacks from Growing, Moscow Introduces Multiple Cossack Identifications for Census," April 23, 2021, http://windowoneurasia2.blogspot.com/2021/04/to-keep-number-of-cossacks-from-growing.html.

the veracity of census numbers; and this grievance against Moscow can itself strengthen their sense of separate identity.

Religious Affiliations

Religious affiliation has become an increasingly salient marker of national identity, even if it does not entail religious zeal or even regular participation in religious rituals. This is particularly evident among Muslim populations in the North Caucasus, the Middle Volga, and regions in the Urals. Historically, Islam united different ethnic groups in the North Caucasus in liberation movements against Russian imperialism.[144] In the 19th century, Imam Shamil forged a union between Circassian, Chechen, Balkar, Ingush, Karachai and Dagestani leaders to resist Russia's imperial forces. Shamil was able to establish an independent Imamate in the 1840s and 1850s based on Sufi Islam and Sharia law until it was crushed by Tsarist troops. Another attempt to create a pan-ethnic state in the North Caucasus was made during the collapse of the Russian Empire in World War I. The founding of a sovereign Mountainous Republic of the North Caucasus was declared in March 1917 and lasted until January 1921. This confederation included seven national units, including Dagestan, Chechnya, Ingushetia, Ossetia, Circassia, the Nogai steppes, and with claims to Abkhazia. While the Mountainous Republic was based on secular principles, a theocratic Emirate of the North Caucasus was also established in 1919, modeled on Shamil's Imamate but dismantled by the Bolsheviks in February 1920.[145]

---

[144] Elena Pokalova, *Chechnya's Terrorist Network: The Evolution of Terrorism in Russia's North Caucasus,* Santa Barbara, California: Praeger, 2015, p.x.

[145] Elena Pokalova, *Chechnya's Terrorist Network: The Evolution of Terrorism in Russia's North Caucasus,* Santa Barbara, California: Praeger, 2015, p.11.

The period of Chechnya's independence in the 1990s also witnessed attempts to promote insurgent movements across the North Caucasus based on a Muslim religious revival and liberation from Russian rule, including the Islamic Nation and the Caucasus Confederation. The Insurgent Army of Imam Shamil and the Special Purpose Islamic Regiment also became active in fostering revolts in Dagestan.[146] A Congress of the Peoples of Chechnya and Dagestan was convened in Grozny with the goal of liberating the entire Caucasus from Russia's rule and the establishment of an Islamic state across the region. The Caucasus Emirate (CE), declared after Russia's forces crushed Chechnya's statehood in 1999, promoted the creation of a multi-ethnic Islamic state. In the broader North Caucasus, Muslim populations are generally conservative, traditionalist, and unwilling to be controlled by Kremlin appointees or institutions.

Moscow's relations with Buddhist populations, including Tuvins, Buryats, and Kalmyks, has deteriorated under Putin's rule. This was evident during the expulsion of a Buddhist community from a monastery on the Kachkanar mountain in Sverdlovsk *Oblast* by the Russian Orthodox Yevraz organization, which claimed possession of the property.[147] The Moscow Patriarchate stood behind the takeover to demonstrate the dominance of Orthodoxy over other religions. Buddhism is viewed with growing suspicion among state officials because it is closely tied with national identity and distinctiveness from ethnic Russians and can reinforce calls for republican sovereignty.

---

[146] Elena Pokalova, *Chechnya's Terrorist Network: The Evolution of Terrorism in Russia's North Caucasus,* Santa Barbara, California: Praeger, 2015, pp.78–79.

[147] Paul Goble, "Relations between Moscow and Russia's Buddhists Deteriorating," January 28, 2021,

http://windowoneurasia2.blogspot.com/2021/01/relations-between-moscow-and-russias.html.

In the High North, Siberia, and the Pacific regions, traditional autochthonous religions are playing a growing role in self-identification and national reawakening among indigenous peoples. Leaders of several ethnic groups have called for protecting traditional holy places as well as the local environment by expanding areas with restricted industrial development. This has been the case in the Yamalo-Nenets Autonomous *Oblast*, where development is currently constricted to about 10 percent of the territory but where activists seek to expand the protected zones.[148] Resistance will further spread, as the Moscow Patriarchate has decided to revive the Orthodox Missionary Society and intensify proselytizing among the numerically small peoples of the North.[149] According to the Moscow Patriarchate, missionary intervention is needed to counter "the romanticization of neo-pagan cults" and its influence among Orthodox populations.

Local leaders in republics where traditional religions are widely practiced, such as Mari El in the Middle Volga, are promoting the education of children in native belief systems and oppose the proselytization efforts of the Russian Orthodox Church. The Centralized Religious Organization of Mari Traditional Religion is seeking recognition as an all-Russian religious group because many of

---

[148] Paul Goble, "Call for Protecting Holy Places of Northern Peoples Puts the Latter on Collision Course with Moscow," March 8, 2021, http://windowoneurasia2.blogspot.com/2021/03/call-for-protecting-holy-places-of.html.

[149] Paul Goble, "Moscow Patriarchate to Step Up Missionary Work among Numerically Small Peoples of the North," July 26, 2021, http://windowoneurasia2.blogspot.com/2021/07/moscow-patriarchate-to-step-up.html.

its adherents live outside the Mari El Republic.[150] This has created conflicts with Moscow and republican officials. Mari traditional religion, with its extensive priesthood, holy sites, and rituals, forms the most organized "pagan" movement among indigenous people in Russia. Fearing the revival of ethnic identity among the Finno-Ugric nations, Moscow-appointed officials in Mari El have accused the traditional religious organization of playing into the hands of "nationalist radicals." The Kremlin is also staunchly opposed to growing links between Finno-Ugric nations in Russia and the three independent Finno-Ugric states—Estonia, Finland and Hungary—because it will stimulate their self-assertiveness and nurture international support.

Protestant congregations have also expanded in parts of Siberia, the Far East, and the Northwest. In particular, Adventist, Baptist, Lutheran, and Pentecostal churches are gradually superseding Christian Orthodoxy in numbers and could become an escalating source of conflict with both the Orthodox Church and the Russian state.[151] The Kremlin has responded by forging a covenant with the Moscow Patriarchate to curtail and repress any proselytizing Christian denominations that compete with the state-sponsored Orthodox Church, including Jehovah's Witnesses, the Church of Scientology, and numerous Protestant congregations.[152] The authorities consider these smaller religions as "undesirable" and a

---

[150] Paul Goble, "Mari Pagans Seek Registration as All-Russian Religious Organization But Face Major Obstacles," July 11, 2021, http://windowoneurasia2.blogspot.com/2021/07/mari-pagans-seek-registration-as-all.html.

[151] Mischa Gabowitsch, *Protest in Putin's Russia,* Malden, MA: Polity Press, 2017, p.187.

[152] Lincoln E. Flake, *Defending the Faith: The Russian Orthodox Church and the Demise of Religious Pluralism,* Verlag: Stuttgart, 2021, pp.223–231.

threat to Russian culture, security, and territorial integrity. In October 2021, a new law went into effect allowing the government to close down almost all Protestant groups and threatening other denominations.[153] Official claims that Orthodoxy is the basis of Russian identity and culture will further alienate non-Orthodox populations opposed to assimilationist pressures.

Autonomy Aspirations

Any number of factors can fuel calls for autonomy and even separation from Russia in various federal regions, whether economic, political, ethnic, or cultural. Among them is a growing sense of alienation from the Moscow elites, a corrupt and arrogant federal administration, rich oligarchs favored by the Kremlin, and in many federal subjects a duplicitous regional establishment. Such charges against officialdom have been encapsulated in Aleksei Navalny's anti-corruption campaign. Resentments are also generated at a local level by regional "power verticals" that often replicate the centralized state structure.[154] For instance, taxes collected in the regions predominantly benefit the federal government, the regional governments receive a small share, while districts and municipalities are deprived of funds and citizens suffer.

In the early 1990s, power struggles within the local political elite and with new political players helped to determine the extent of separatist

---

[153] Paul Goble, "Moscow Set to Restrict All Religious Activity It Doesn't Already Control, Bishop Bendas Says," September 25, 2021, http://windowoneurasia2.blogspot.com/2021/09/moscow-set-to-restrict-all-religious.html.

[154] Kirill Strakhov, "Налоги петербуржцев – городу, а не Москве!" September 9, 2021, http://region.expert/spb-taxes/.

demands that federal subjects made on Moscow.[155] Regional authorities could again find themselves in a position of having to respond to public resentments and expectations or face growing opposition and unrest. Protests over regional governors may have various causes, whether in supporting or opposing the nominees. In Khabarovsk *Krai*, citizens opposed the arbitrary replacement by Moscow of the popular governor Sergei Furgal. In stark contrast, politicians in the Kalmyk Republic, including members of United Russia, called for the replacement of the regional governor, Batu Khasikov, because of his mishandling of the pandemic.[156] Some analysts have also speculated that the Kalmyk incident may indicate the fracturing of the United Russia party.

Several potential regionalists with genuine local support belong to the major parties, including Furgal in Khabarovsk *Krai* from the Liberal Democratic Party of Russia (LDPR) and Oleg Mikhailov, the head of the Communist Party of the Russian Federation (KPRF) in the Komi Republic. He accused Moscow of pursuing a "colonial policy" toward the regions and was one of the organizers of the protest movement against the construction of a landfill in Shiyes in Arkhangelsk *Oblast* in 2020. Such figures with a measure of genuine local support could become more influential as Russia's crisis deepens.

Governors and local authorities will feel more frustrated with Moscow in the wake of stringent economic sanctions imposed on Russia for its attack on Ukraine by concluding that the center again abandoned them during a national emergency. Grievances grew during the

---

[155] Elise Giuliano, *Constructing Grievance: Ethnic Nationalism in Russia's Republics*, Cornell University Press, 2011, p.185.

[156] Paul Goble, "Kalmyk Head has So Mishandled Pandemic that Even His United Russia Comrades are Calling on Putin to Oust Him," November 8, 2020, http://windowoneurasia2.blogspot.com/2020/11/kalmyk-head-has-so-mishandled-pandemic.html.

COVID-19 pandemic when the Kremlin provided little leadership or assistance and the federal subjects struggled to contain the mass infections, with some imposing severe restrictions and obligatory vaccinations. Charges of state neglect embolden citizens to act more independently from Moscow. The extensive falsification of general elections in September 2021 in favor of United Russia also contributed to local resentments. Some reports disclosed that the Kremlin ordered governors to ensure a result of 70 percent, while the real rating of United Russia stood at only 27 percent.[157] The ban on independent or opposition candidates from standing in local and national elections makes official balloting redundant in the eyes of many people and has intensified the focus on extra-systemic opposition.

In the local elections in September 2019 and September 2020, hundreds of local officials across Russia were elected under the "smart voting" strategy developed by Navalny.[158] It identified and campaigned for candidates most likely to defeat rivals from the ruling United Russia party. Navalny calculated that gaining local government seats would help the opposition to expose fraudulent elections and expand public opposition to Putin. On September 19, 2021, elections also took place for 12 governors and 39 regional parliaments. Some regional activists nominally joined the systemic parties permitted by the Kremlin in order to be elected to regional parliaments but were determined to adopt positions radically at

---

[157] Private interview with Vadim Shtepa, Editor in Chief, Region.Expert, Tallinn, March 2021.

[158] "With 'Smart Voting' Strategy, Russian Opposition Takes Aim at Putin's 'Party of Crooks and Thieves'," September 8, 2019, https://www.rferl.org/a/russia-smart-voting/30153235.html.

variance with Moscow's policies.[159] Such developments have been particularly visible in Khabarovsk *Krai* and the Komi Republic.

Russian officials have justified the appointment rather than the election of regional governors as a way of preventing ethnic conflicts, especially in the most volatile regions such as the North Caucasus and precluding the emergence of "ethnic enclaves." Such paternalistic explanations denigrate locals as being incapable of self-government without a firm hand from Moscow, and they increase perceptions among non-Russians that they are viewed as subordinate citizens. Moscow has also cracked down on municipal legislators, fearing that they could become a fulcrum of opposition to the Kremlin. In March 2021, police arrested some 150 lawmakers representing 56 regions when they gathered in Moscow for the first-ever national Forum of Municipal Deputies.[160] Their goal was to spend two days debating about local elections and grass-roots campaigning. Municipal legislatures have provided a platform for regime opponents and independent politicians to try and erode the Putinist political monopoly and were perceived as a grievous threat during an election year.

Protest Generators

Public grievances can accumulate over a prolonged period, and protest actions can be triggered by a sudden or unexpected event that

---

[159] Paul Goble, "September Vote for Regional Parliaments Likely to Produce New Generation of Opposition Politicians, Shtepa Says," July 9, 2021, http://windowoneurasia2.blogspot.com/2021/07/september-vote-for-regional-parliaments.html.

[160] https://www.washingtonpost.com/opinions/2021/03/18/russian-authorities-just-arrested-an-entire-conference-hall-full-people-i-was-one-them/.

causes widespread outrage. Street protests have been organized against various unpopular government measures, despite the prohibition on gatherings and the mass presence of police. For instance, in September 2018, large rallies were held in 33 Russian cities, from Kaliningrad to Vladivostok, against government moves to raise the retirement age for men from 60 to 65 and for women from 55 to 63. Many of the protestors called for Putin's resignation.[161] Over a thousand people were arrested by the security services. According to various polls, about 90 percent of Russians opposed the plan. The raising of the retirement age generated even wider public disquiet than was evident in street rallies, as it affected poor elderly people, a core group of Putin backers. Reportedly, the State Pension Fund was running out of money and Moscow did not want to divert funds from other sources.

Moscow's failed nerve agent poisoning of Navalny in August 2021 and his subsequent arrest in January 2021, after returning to Russia following hospital treatment in Germany, sparked a storm of protests across the country. Despite police attacks, 300,000 people staged street demonstrations in over 150 cities and towns in several dozen regions, from Pskov on the Estonian border to Sakhalin on the Pacific coast.[162] The rallies were unexpectedly large in some cities, including Vladivostok, Irkutsk, Krasnodar, Tver, Barnaul, Perm, Voronezh and Ufa. Although the arrest of Navalny served as a trigger, demonstrators voiced an assortment of local grievances and anger at falling living

---

[161] "'Hundreds' Detained As Kremlin Opponents Protest Pension-Reform Plan On Election Day," *Radio Free Europe/ Radio Liberty*, September 10, 2018, https://www.rferl.org/a/russians-vote-in-local-elections-as-police-detain-pension-reform-protesters/29479717.html.

[162] Paul Goble, "Latest Protests Far More Massive and Determined than Those of 2011-2012, Navalny Aide Says," January 27, 2021, http://windowoneurasia2.blogspot.com/2021/01/latest-protests-far-more-massive-and.html.

standards, high unemployment, and Moscow's mishandling of the COVID-19 pandemic. The major demands of regional protestors included the election of independent local administrations and the equitable distribution of budgetary funds.[163] The protests took place without official permission, and participants faced greater fines than on previous occasions, indicating that the public may become more willing to take risks. Moscow and its regional representatives were largely caught by surprise by the size of protests even in bitterly cold conditions in cities such as Chelyabinsk and Yakutsk.[164] Another troubling indicator for the Kremlin was that some demonstrators were willing to use violence against police in response to their attacks on peaceful protestors.[165]

Activists who began their protests with a focus on a single issue, such as pollution, mismanagement or corruption, will broaden their agenda and increasingly challenge the foundations of the centralized system. Inter-regional solidarity between protestors has also been evident. For example, environmental protests in Arkhangelsk *Oblast* and political protests in Khabarovsk *Krai* were supported by representatives of other regions who backed their demands. Until recently, there has been no organized inter-regional network or

---

[163] "Россия, но не Московия: Что такое уральская идентичность и почему Екатеринбург," February 11, 2021, https://novayagazeta.ru/articles/2021/02/11/89164-rossiya-no-ne-moskoviya.

[164] Paul Goble, "Kremlin's Men in Regions Caught Unawares by Massive Protests Outside of Moscow," January 27, 2021, http://windowoneurasia2.blogspot.com/2021/01/kremlins-men-in-regions-caught-unawares.html.

[165] Paul Goble, "Putin Regime's Use of Force Against Navalny Demonstrators May Lead the Latter to Respond in Kind, Martynov Says," January 26, 2021, http://windowoneurasia2.blogspot.com/2021/01/putin-regimes-use-of-force-against.html.

political party to synchronize regional protests. The unregistered Federative Party views itself as an inter-regional project to help coordinate public demands, but it is prohibited from participating in elections.[166] Nonetheless, some Federative Party representatives took part in the September 2021 elections as self-nominated independent candidates.

The positions and policies of local governors will come under increasing question when Moscow has diminishing financial resources to disperse to federal subjects. Regional governors appointed by the Kremlin may be faced with a stark choice as public disaffection mounts. They can either continue to implement Moscow's repressive and exploitative policies and face growing domestic opposition and even revolt, or they can resist pressures from the Kremlin and transform themselves into genuine leaders pushing for local interests vis-à-vis the federal center. As turbulence escalates, local governors could be swept out of power unless they commit themselves to strengthening the position of their republics and regions.

Protest actions can take place in response to a broad range of local issues and can snowball from single causes into wider political demands. The most evident examples in Russia are campaigns for environmental protection. Protests against environmental degradation, toxic pollution, and ecological neglect helped to spur nationalist movements in the Soviet Union during the 1980s, and such concerns are again gaining prominence.[167] They proved to be a

---

[166] Private interview with Vadim Shtepa, Editor in Chief, Region.Expert, Tallinn, March 2021.

[167] Paul Goble, "Ecological Protest in Russia Becoming Political, EKA Environmental Movement Head Says," November 4, 2020,

training ground for independent organizers and gave a sense of empowerment to participants. Given Russia's ecological deterioration, government neglect, and slender budgets, environmentalism can become a trigger for mass mobilization and cross-regional activism. People are more likely to protest environmental issues if they directly affect local communities in tangible ways.[168] When a localized environmental disaster occurs, citizens invariably blame officials and industrial plants and suspect official cover ups.

During the course of one year, between August 2019 and August 2020, the Center for Social and Labor Rights reported that citizens organized 482 environmental protests, second only to gatherings focused on political and civil rights.[169] Regionalist and nationalist attitudes rise where the local population sees itself as defending its land from major companies backed by outsiders from Moscow. Growing prospects also exist for alliances between protesters and regional officials against outside business interests tied to Moscow. Protest organizers realize that to be successful the movement has to become political and challenge officialdom, as it has in various European states. For example, during the Shiyes protests in 2019 against the dumping of trash in Arkhangelsk *Oblast*, citizens sought

---

http://windowoneurasia2.blogspot.com/2020/11/ecological-protest-in-russia-becoming.html.

[168] András Tóth-Czifra, "How Russia's Environmental Issues Increase Risks for the Kremlin," December 2, 2020, Institute of Modern Russia, https://imrussia.org/en/analysis/3212-how-russia's-environmental-issues-increase-risks-for-the-kremlin.

[169] Paul Goble, "In Last Year Alone, Russians Organized Nearly 500 Environmental Protests," September 3, 2020, https://windowoneurasia2.blogspot.com/2020/09/in-last-year-alone-russians-organized.html.

to nominate local candidates who supported them and cast protest votes when their representatives were ignored.

The shipments to Shiyes were to include highly hazardous waste and food products that would emit toxic gases such as hydrogen sulfide and methane. The gases can poison the atmosphere for many kilometers in all directions, and toxic filtrates would enter the region's water supply, affecting the 250,000 residents of Syktyvkar, the capital of the Komi Republic only 90 kilometers away.[170] Shiyes is the tip of a much larger problem, as Moscow is not building processing plants but looking for new regional waste disposal sites regardless of local opposition. According to the Russian Audit Chamber, 32 federal subjects will run out of dumping space by 2024, and 17 by 2022.[171] Moscow plans to deposit some of the most dangerous radioactive, chemical and biological waste in four regions—the Udmurt Republic, the Altai Republic and two predominantly ethnic-Russian *oblasts*, Kirov and Kurgan.[172] Activists in all four federal subjects have pledged to protest government plans.

The inability of state officials to handle the extensive forest fires in Sakha and other parts of Siberia during the summer of 2021 will

---

[170] Yelena Solovyova, "Protests in Shiyes: How a Garbage Dump Galvanized Russia's Civil Society," *The Moscow Times*, July 6, 2019, https://www.themoscowtimes.com/2019/07/06/protests-shiyes-how-garbage-dump-galvanized-russias-civil-society-a66289.

[171] Paul Goble, "More than a Third of Russia's Regions Face 'Critical' Shortage of Trash Dumps," September 30, 2020, http://windowoneurasia2.blogspot.com/2020/09/more-than-third-of-russias-regions-face.html.

[172] Paul Goble, "Moscow Now Wants to Dump Radioactive Trash in Four Regions, Sparking New Outrage," July 28, 2020, https://windowoneurasia2.blogspot.com/2020/07/moscow-now-wants-to-dump-radioactive.html.

mobilize new environmentalist protest movements.[173] Moscow's attempts to blame the regional authorities have had little impact, as everyone knows that the federal center controls the purse strings and directs policy. Such protests can quickly expand beyond ecological issues and against the central government, similarly to the wave of ecological activism that helped to fuel the collapse of the Soviet Union. In response to the escalating number of environmental disasters and greater media coverage, local demonstrations have mushroomed. They include protests over oil spillages, disposal of radioactive waste, construction on historical or ecologically valued areas, and destruction caused by river dams. Finally, environmentalists are concerned that the authorities do not observe basic safety rules when it comes to Russia's contracted import of radioactive from Europe—either for its transportation or storage.

Ecologically minded groups in several regions are intensifying their campaigns to hold referenda on critical environmental problems while spreading awareness of government dereliction.[174] Some activists have raised the prospect of forming a federal-wide green party or declaring "ecological sovereignty" in some regions, despite the fact that such initiatives will be outlawed by the regime.[175] Ecology has also taken on ethno-national dimensions because so many natural

---

[173] "Цена вранья и умолчания: лесные пожары в Сибири и Якутии грозят народными бунтами," August 10, 2021, https://newizv.ru/article/general/10-08-2021/tsena-vranya-i-umolchaniya-lesnye-pozhary-grozyat-narodnymi-buntami.

[174] Paul Goble, "Referenda Efforts Consequential Even If Russian Officials Block Them, Toth-Czifra Says," December 13, 2021, http://windowoneurasia2.blogspot.com/2021/12/referenda-efforts-consequential-even-if.html.

[175] "Протесты в регионах порождают новую популярную партию. Мешают две вещи," December 24, 2019, https://ura.news/articles/1036279372.

resources are located in non-Russian areas.[176] In the Republic of Bashkortostan, state plans to destroy Kushtau Mountain in order to develop its soda reserves sparked protests because of the peak's symbolism for Bashkirs. In August 2020, thousands of protestors organized marches and roadblocks to prevent attempts to bulldoze the area. An assortment of people from different ethnic groups, religious affiliations, and political convictions gathered to defend Kushtau and lined up in a human chain with a huge flag of the republic.[177] For several days, hand-to-hand fights took place with local security forces, with protestors increasingly calling for free elections to install a regional government that would support popular demands.

In November 2020, the Congress of the Karachai People in the Karachai-Cherkess Republic sent an open letter to Putin demanding that the construction of a new mining and processing plant be stopped because it could result in significant damage to people as well as the environment. The project was launched despite the lack of local consultations or environmental impact studies. Protests against polluted water that threaten human health were evident around the country throughout 2021, including in Kamchatka *Krai,* Altai *Krai,* Tambov *Oblast*, Chelyabinsk *Oblast*, and the Republic of Dagestan.[178]

---

[176] Paul Goble, "Environmental Protests in Russian Federation Becoming Not Only Political but Ethnic," November 10, 2020, http://windowoneurasia2.blogspot.com/2020/11/environmental-protests-in-russian.html.

[177] Vadim Sidorov, "Башкортостан: от борьбы за Куштау — к борьбе за Республику Вадим Сидоров," August 18, 2020, http://region.expert/kushtau/.

[178] Paul Goble, "Russia May Face Water Revolts in This Century, Slabunova Says," October 11, 2020, http://windowoneurasia2.blogspot.com/2020/10/russia-may-face-water-revolts-in-this.html; Paul Goble, "Russia Seriously Threatened by Critical Lack of Clean Water, Danilov-Danilyan Says," October 8, 2021, windowoneurasia2.blogspot.com/2021/10/russia-seriously-threatened-by-critical.html.

Official estimates in 2019 indicated that 21 million people did not have access to tested water and state efforts to resolve such problems have proved ineffective. Millions of citizens become sick without even realizing the source of their illness. Contaminated water is taken directly from rivers or reservoirs or piped through aging pipelines, while water treatment facilities are increasingly inadequate. Fixing these dangers through substantial infrastructural investments is not a priority for the Kremlin. Water revolts could spread across the country as a rallying cry against more comprehensive government neglect and incompetence.

The regime has cracked down on some of the environmentalist protests, claiming that they were financed from abroad and instructed by Western intelligence services to undermine Russia's economic development.[179] Between 2012 and 2021, Russia's justice ministry placed 29 environmental groups on its list of "foreign agents" allegedly financed by enemy governments. Mass protests in Serbia to protect the environment and prevent the opening of a lithium mine in Western Serbia may provide further inspiration for Russian activists.[180] Serbia has been hailed by the Kremlin as a close ally and an Orthodox Slavic bastion in the Balkans. While the regime of President Aleksandar Vučić has established a one-party monopoly over political life, Serbia still possesses a vibrant civil society, and the extent and persistence of protests in November and December 2021 had an impact on government policy. In January 2022, to defuse the

---

[179] Paul Goble, "Environmentalist Actions Not Always Innocent, Threaten Russian Economy, and Must be Countered, Moscow Officials Say," November 25, 2020, http://windowoneurasia2.blogspot.com/2020/11/environmentalist-actions-not-always.html.

[180] Sasa Dragojlo, "Serbia Eco Protests to Continue Despite Backdown Over Disputed Laws," December 10, 2021, *Balkan Insight*, https://balkaninsight.com/2021/12/10/serbia-eco-protests-to-continue-despite-backdown-over-disputed-laws/.

demonstrations, Belgrade canceled all mining licenses for the Rio Tinto company, which was supposed to develop the mine.[181]

A number of policies have aggravated relations between the regions and the Center. For instance, Moscow has called on the richer regions to help subsidize the poorer ones and it has restricted direct foreign connections for federal subjects, calculating that this would reduce their dependence on Moscow and boost local autonomy. But decaying infrastructure means that residents of enormous regions, such as Siberia and Russia's Pacific rim, will become even more separated from European Russia, a trend that encourages autonomist and independence initiatives. Local resistance will further escalate if some of Russia's most volatile regions begin to coordinate their demands and push toward genuine federalism. Simultaneous actions by numerous federal units would weaken Moscow's attempts to extinguish each initiative, as happened during the unraveling of the Soviet Union. A number of regionalist organizations are active abroad and could build a local base if Moscow's control weakens. They include the Free Idel-Ural movement and activists from Bashkortostan and Kalmykia represented by the Self-Determination of the Peoples of Russia (SOCR) platform, whose main focus is the geopolitical reorganization of the Russian Federation.[182]

Border disputes between federal units could also animate nationalist and regionalist fervor against Moscow. Although the Kremlin has periodically manipulated some disputes to its advantage, such

---

[181] Dušan Stojanović, "Serbia Scraps Planned Rio Tinto lithium Mine after Protests," *Associated Press*, January 20, 2022,

https://apnews.com/article/technology-business-europe-belgrade-environment-d1ded8849cedddbdd356262f3e425207.

[182] "Между распадом и рефедерализацией," December 7, 2020, https://www.idelreal.org/a/30987951.html.

conflicts can also escape its control. Land shortages, water scarcity, and competition over natural resources can spark struggles within or between federal regions. The North Caucasus in particular is prone to such disputes through a combination of scarcity of arable land, agrarian overpopulation, unclear property rights, and historical claims to land by formerly deported ethnic populations.[183] Republics in the North Caucasus have delineated less than a quarter of their common borders, which could provoke more territorial disputes and even armed conflicts as Russia's crisis deepens.[184]

The Republic of Ingushetia has witnessed the most dramatic recent regional dispute. In September 2018, Ingushetia's head, Yunus-Bek Yevkurov, forfeited 10 percent of the republic's territory in a secret deal with the head of the Chechen Republic, Ramzan Kadyrov, sparking months of protests against Yevkurov and Kadyrov, as well as against Moscow, which supported the agreement.[185] Yevkurov avoided holding a referendum as required by the republic's constitution and arrested some of the thousands of Ingush who demonstrated against the deal. His replacement, Makhmud-Ali Kalimatov, an ethnic Ingush but closely tied with Moscow, deepened the crisis by failing to release detained protestors and refusing to meet with respected members of Ingush society. Instead of spreading public fear, the imprisonment and show trials of seven protestors created

---

[183] V. A. Kolosov, et al., "Transformation Policies and Local Modernization Initiatives in the North Caucasus," in Derek Averre and Kevork Oskanian (Ed), *Security, Society and the State in the Caucasus*, Routledge, 2019, p.86.

[184] "Регионы Северного Кавказа внесли в госреестр менее 23 процентов границ," January 3, 2021, https://www.kavkaz-uzel.eu/articles/358250/.

[185] Paul Goble, "Kalimatov has Compounded Yevkurov's Betrayal of Ingushetia, Activists Say," September 27, 2020, http://windowoneurasia2.blogspot.com/2020/09/kalimatov-has-compounded-yevkurovs.html.

political martyrs and will further alienate Ingush society from the state, including both Moscow and the government it implanted in the capital Magas.[186]

In some cases, Russia may witness the revival of opposition to previous border changes between federal units. A prime example is the demand for recreating the "Kudymkar corridor" located between the six republics of the Middle Volga and the Arctic Sea regions populated largely by Finno-Ugric peoples.[187] In 2005, Moscow redrew the borders and eliminated the Kudymkar corridor and folded the Komi-Permyak Autonomous *Okrug* into Perm *Krai*. The Middle Volga or Idel-Ural republics, thereby, lost their land bridge to the Arctic just as earlier they forfeited their bridge to Kazakhstan with the creation of Orenburg *Oblast*. Both territorial linkages can become a priority for an emerging Volga-Ural confederation.

Unresolved territorial disputes between federal subjects are commonplace in Russia and can surface on unpredictable occasions. Some may be provoked by the government to pursue its divide-and-rule policies; some may be ignited through social protests based on historical grievances; and in other cases, border disputes may be fanned by ambitious local officials. In January 2021, the leadership of the Tuva Republic issued territorial claims against two neighbors,

---

[186] Paul Goble, "Ingush Seven Trial 'a Theater of the Absurd' Leaving Ingush Indifferent to the Fate of Russia, Chemurziyev Says," January 17, 2021, http://windowoneurasia2.blogspot.com/2021/01/ingush-seven-trial-theater-of-absurd.html.

[187] Paul Goble, "The Kudymkar Corridor – Another Problem Moscow Created but Now Must Worry About," April 27, 2019, https://windowoneurasia2.blogspot.com/2019/04/the-kudymkar-corridor-another-problem.html.

Krasnoyarsk *Krai* and Irkutsk *Oblas*t.[188] This was widely seen as a desperate attempt by the governor of Tuva, Sholban Kara-ool, to win support from the population and prevent Moscow from sacking him. His efforts failed, and he was replaced in April 2021, as Russian Defense Minister Sergei Shoigu, a native Tuvan, held considerable political influence in the republic.[189] Nonetheless, the Tuva case indicates that governors may pursue policies that are at odds with Moscow's instructions and more in line with popular demands.

In several instances, lingering territorial claims are upheld by populations who were deported by the Soviet regime and were not allowed to reclaim all their territory when returning from exile. The Chechen and Ingush cases are the starkest examples, as some of their lands were transferred to neighboring republics and regions. Moscow's intervention in such disputes can further aggravate conflicts if officials are seen to be favoring either side. The most equitable solutions would require peaceful negotiations between the disputants without Kremlin interference, but Moscow is unwilling to allow such inter-regional solutions, as this too would weaken its stranglehold over the federal structure.

---

[188] Paul Goble, "Territorial Disputes among Russia's Federal Subjects Must Be Decided Not by Moscow or Unilateral Action but by Negotiations, Sidorov Says," January 21, 2021, http://windowoneurasia2.blogspot.com/2021/01/territorial-disputes-among-russias.html.

[189] "Putin's Dismissal: Tuva Leader Change," Warsaw Institute, April 8, 2021, https://warsawinstitute.org/putins-dismissal-tuva-leader-change/.

4.

Chronicle of Turmoil

Regional unrest in the multi-national Russian Federation will be propelled by an accumulation of grievances. Public resentments are evident over economic stagnation, infrastructural decay, government corruption, Moscow's exploitation of regional resources, attacks on national language rights, unaccountable Kremlin appointments of regional governors, and threats to eliminate or merge federal units. The regime has also broken the unwritten "social contract," adapted from Soviet times, whereby the state guarantees steady material welfare in return for political passivity. Although the government was largely able to deliver higher living standards in the first decade of Vladimir Putin's presidency, several economic shocks have undermined Russia's economic performance, and the future looks bleak. Revolt is more likely in a society in which rising expectations of material well-being over the past two decades, especially among a more educated and ambitious younger generation, have been thwarted by repeated failures in official policy and where there is no realistic plan to overcome mounting domestic problems especially in the midst of potentially prolonged international economic sanctions.

At the core of unrest will be a growing conviction that without Moscow's control and exploitation, the republics and regions will be more capable of ensuring economic and political progress and forging constructive connections with each other and with foreign partners.

In some regions, such as the North Caucasus and the Middle Volga, simmering frustrations with Moscow can reach a boiling point. In December 2021, in a heated video conference with the Presidential Human Rights Council, Putin rejected a proposal by renowned film director Alexander Sokurov to let Russian regions secede if they no longer want to be part of the state.[1] Putin warned of a repeat of the bloody wars in a collapsing Yugoslavia during the 1990s and revealed that there were 2,000 territorial claims nationwide that should be treated "very seriously" as they could divide up Russia. To assess the prospects for fragmentation of the Russian Federation, it is important to chronicle recent political and social turmoil in each major part of the country and its historical antecedents, even though this listing is far from exhaustive.

North Caucasus

The genesis of armed insurrection in the North Caucasus against Russian rule in the modern era dates back to the closing years of the Soviet Union and the crushing of Chechnya's independence. On April 26, 1990, Soviet President Mikhail Gorbachev signed a law that in effect made Autonomous Republics (AR) equal with Union Republics (UR). The legislation stated that in the event that URs seceded from the Soviet Union, the ARs had the right to secede from the URs and remain in the USSR.[2] By default, Chechnya and all other ARs obtained equal status with the Russian Soviet Federative Socialist Republic (RSFSR) and were empowered to secede and claim independence. When the Soviet Union itself was dismantled in December 1991, the only choice was between remaining within the newly formed Russian

---

[1] http://kremlin.ru/events/president/news/67331/videos, December 9, 2021.

[2] Christoph Zürcher, *The Post-Soviet Wars: Rebellion, Ethnic Conflict, and Nationhood in the Caucasus*, New York: New York University Press, 2007, pp.35–36.

Federation or forming separate independent states that would be opposed by the government in Moscow.

Several North Caucasus republics benefited from the power vacuum after the Soviet collapse to reach for political independence. Although Chechnya was the only previous AR within the RSFSR that took that step in the early 1990s, others may have emulated Chechnya if the project had been successful and Moscow had not staged an intensive military onslaught against the republic's statehood. In November 1990, the Chechen-Ingush Autonomous Republic adopted a declaration of state sovereignty as a Union Republic. But after the dissolution of the USSR in December 1991, the republic split into two—the Chechen Republic of Ichkeria and the Republic of Ingushetia—following a referendum that same month. In February 1994 the Ingush Republic passed a new constitution that did not envisage independence but membership in the Russian Federation. The North Ossetian Autonomous Republic declared its sovereignty in June 1990, the Kalmyk Autonomous Republic in October 1990, and in June 1991 the Adygea Autonomous *Oblast* achieved the status of an Autonomous Republic within the RSFSR. Dagestan voted against the new Russian federal constitution in December 1993, adopted a republican constitution in July 1994, and created a State Council as the supreme executive body representing the republic's 14 largest ethnic groups.[3]

In Chechnya, the nationalist politician Dzhokhar Dudaev was elected President in October 1991 and an independent Chechen Republic of Ichkeria (ChRI) was proclaimed on November 2, 1991. In effect, Chechnya declared its independence from the USSR, which was in the process of dissolving, and refused to sign the federative treaty that established the Russian Federation in December 1991. Russia's then-

[3] *The Territories of the Russian Federation 2020*, London: Routledge, 2020, p.165.

President Boris Yeltsin asserted that he would use all means to reverse Chechnya's secession and launched the first war against the new state in December 1994.[4] Russian forces captured the capital Grozny following an intensive bombing campaign, in which approximately 25,000 civilians perished. Although vastly outnumbered, Chechen forces defeated the Russian military and retook Grozny during August 1996. On August 25, 1996, a peace agreement between Russia and Chechnya was concluded in the city of Khasavyurt in Dagestan, and a formal treaty was signed in Moscow on May 12, 1997. The accords declared Chechnya to be a sovereign entity and a subject of international law. Russia *de facto* recognized Chechnya as an independent state even though the implementation of all attributes of statehood was formally deferred for five years.

Under Dudaev's successor, Aslan Maskhadov, a quasi-independent Chechnya that was decimated by the Russian military onslaught was internationally isolated and economically blockaded by Moscow. This contributed to intensifying institutional weaknesses, lawlessness, clan conflicts, and economic decline.[5] The ambitions of competing military field commanders and a fragmented political leadership were not conducive for establishing a centralized state structure. Salafist radicals also created their own military units and expanded their influence in competition with Chechen Ichkerian nationalists who had led the struggle against Russia's neo-imperialism. Maskhadov, who was elected President in January 1997, was increasingly unable to control internal security or the incursions of armed Salafist units into Dagestan seeking to instigate an anti-Russian Islamic rebellion across

---

[4] Mark Kramer, "Guerrilla Warfare, Counterinsurgency and Terrorism in the North Caucasus: The Military Dimension of the Russian – Chechen Conflict," *Europe-Asia Studies*, Vol. 57, No. 2, March 2005, pp.209–290.

[5] James Hughes, *Chechnya: From Nationalism to Jihad*, Philadelphia, Pa: University of Pennsylvania Press, 2007, p.63.

the North Caucasus. This attempt to build a Salafist Caucasian Caliphate provided a valuable pretext for a new Russian military intervention.

The newly appointed Russian Prime Minister Vladimir Putin violated legal principles and treaty obligations with Grozny by launching the Second Chechen War in October 1999.[6] Moscow managed to divide the Chechen resistance by forging links with selected field commanders and coopting them into a new government. With overwhelming numbers, Russian forces captured the capital Grozny in February 2000 and terminated Chechen independence, driving the government and parliament into exile. Estimates of civilian and combatant deaths ranged from 60,000 to over 150,000. While many secular Chechen officials were isolated abroad, the *jihadists* increased their influence. In the summer of 2002, an emergency meeting of the remnants of the Chechen government and armed forces adopted a multi-ethnic and religious-based campaign, with the goal of expanding the insurgency across the North Caucasus.

On October 5, 2003, Imam Akhmad Kadyrov was installed as Chechnya's President by the Russian government. When he was killed by insurgents in April 2004, his son Ramzan Kadyrov became Putin's special protégé and the new President of the Republic of Chechnya.[7] More than 200,000 Chechens fled to Western Europe and acquired an increasing voice in the Chechen movement opposing Kadyrov. Many young Chechens in the diaspora supported the revival of the Ichkerian state. However, in October 2007, soon after rebel military leader Doku Umarov assumed the presidency of the outlawed Ichkerian Republic, he announced the creation of the Caucasus Emirate (*Imarat Kavkaz*)

---

[6] Tony Wood, *Chechnya: The Case for Independence*, London, New York: Verso, 2007, p.120.

[7] John Russell, "Kadyrov's Chechnya—Template, Test or Trouble for Russia's Regional Policy?" *Europe-Asia Studies*, Vol. 63, No. 3, May 2011, pp.509–528.

that no longer focused solely on Chechnya's statehood but on pan-Caucasian independence. His ambition to spread the insurgency throughout the region and even to Tatarstan and Bashkortostan was calculated to stretch Russia's security forces more thinly. In addition, he sought to position the North Caucasus insurgency within a global Islamist movement fighting against the enemies of the Muslim faith and tried to enlist international support for his campaign.[8]

Moscow and Grozny struck an alliance with traditional Sufi clergy and the *tariqas* (Sufi brotherhoods) in their common struggle against the Salafists.[9] Kadyrov used Sufi Islam to prove his credentials as a Chechen patriot and to pursue an Islamic conservative revival. He presided over a Sufi form of Islamization in meshing political, religious, and social life in Chechnya. Although Moscow has tried to pose as the defender of traditional Sufi Islam against radicals inspired by foreign ideologies, in effect Chechnya became a distinct territory that no longer observed the principles of Russia's secular system.[10] This may increasingly challenge the unity of the Russian state especially if Kadyrov seeks to promote the Chechen model to other Muslim regions in the North Caucasus as the federal structure comes under increasing stress.

---

[8] Elena Pokalova, *Chechnya's Terrorist Network: The Evolution of Terrorism in Russia's North Caucasus*, Santa Barbara, California: Praeger, 2015, pp.160–162.

[9] International Crisis Group, "The North Caucasus: The Challenges of Integration (II), Islam, the Insurgency and Counter-Insurgency," Moscow, Russia: International Crisis Group, *Europe Report* No. 221, October 19, 2012, http://www.crisisgroup.org/~/media/Files/europe/caucasus/221-the-north-caucasus-the-challenges-of-integration-ii-islam-the-insurgency-and-counter-insurgency.pdf, p.13.

[10] Domitilla Sagramoso and Akhmet Yarlykapov, "Caucasian Crescent: Russia's Islamic Policies and its Responses to Radicalization," in Robert Bruce Ware (Ed.), *The Fire Below: How the Caucasus Shaped Russia*, New York: Bloomsbury, 2013, pp.74–76.

An inadequate government response to the COVID-19 pandemic exacerbated social and economic tensions in the North Caucasus and created conditions for a future social explosion, while traditional social organizations and Islamic groups challenge Moscow's appointees in several republics.[11] Unrest could be sparked by intensified territorial disputes where borders have not been fully demarcated, as between Chechnya and Ingushetia, Chechnya and Dagestan, or Ingushetia and North Ossetia. Local resentments have been aggravated by escalating unemployment levels and reductions in Moscow's subsidies to regional governments. People are increasingly turning to traditional social organizations, including Islamic structures and clan organizations such as *teips*, to address their problems, and to émigré communities through the internet.

Moscow's extensive repression in the northeastern part of the North Caucasus may have reduced the level of Islamist terrorism, but it also served to alienate large sectors of the population.[12] This policy was undergirded by the reorganization of the North Caucasus Federal Military District into the Southern Federal Military District in 2010, aimed at intensifying the counterterrorism campaign. Such offensives increased the sense of insecurity among those affected and further radicalized young people against the state. Insurgency attacks reached

---

[11] Paul Goble, "Year 2020 in Review: Pandemic Exacerbated Problems Across North Caucasus and Set Stage for More Conflict," *Eurasia Daily Monitor*, Vol. 18, Issue 2, January 5, 2021,

https://jamestown.org/program/year-2020-in-review-pandemic-exacerbated-problems-across-north-caucasus-and-set-stage-for-more-conflict/.

[12] Julie Wilhelmsen, "Russian Governance of the North Caucasus: Dilemmas of Force and Inclusion," in Derek Averre and Kevork Oskanian (Ed), *Security, Society and the State in the Caucasus*, Routledge, 2019, p.38.

their peak during 2010–2013.[13] The authorities engaged in various "preventive measures," including frequent police checks and detention of members of extended families on suspicion of assisting insurgents as well as crackdowns on Salafi groupings on the assumption that they all produce and harbor terrorists. Official Islamic structures have also been used to repress Salafis, thereby creating rifts within the Islamic communities.

Kadyrov has benefited from Moscow's hardline policy by eliminating all dissent to his rule and using Sufi institutions to repress Salafi groups. In essence, Kadyrov, his clan, and his paramilitary units (*kadyrovtsy)* were co-opted and corrupted by Moscow to eliminate Islamist insurgents and any nationalist pro-independence opposition. However, the Chechen model is not readily applicable to other North Caucasus republics, especially to those without clear ethnic majorities. For instance, the complex multi-ethnic structure in Dagestan would derail any attempts by a mono-ethnic paramilitary force to impose mass repression and eliminate an insurgency. Instead, such offensives would provoke inter-ethnic clashes that Moscow would be hard pressed to disentangle and subdue.[14]

Insurgency violence has continued to simmer in the North Caucasus although at a lower level than in the 2000s, following the outflow of thousands of Islamist *jihadists* to the Islamic State rebellion in Syria and Iraq and with a more effective disruption of terrorist networks by

---

[13] Emil Aslan Souleimanov, *The North Caucasus Insurgency: Dead or Alive?* US Army War College, Strategic Studies Institute, February 2017, p.54.

[14] Emil Aslan Souleimanov, *The North Caucasus Insurgency: Dead or Alive?* US Army War College, Strategic Studies Institute, February 2017, p.66.

Russia's counter-insurgency forces.[15] Nonetheless, the sense of grievance and retribution against officials and security forces responsible for quelling activists and violently repressing their families has persisted. As a result, in the coming years, the insurgency could reignite in several republics, where the political system is increasingly viewed as unjust, corrupt and repressive.[16]

Insurgency and terrorism may also be propelled by seasoned fighters returning from *jihadist* battlefronts in Syria, Iraq, Afghanistan and elsewhere. Kadyrov became especially concerned that the Taliban takeover of Afghanistan, following the withdrawal of US troops in the summer of 2021, would have an impact on Chechnya. The Taliban had recognized the Chechen Republic of Ichkeria in 2000, and Kadyrov calculated that Kabul would support an independent Chechnya alongside his ouster. The Chechen branch of the significantly weakened Caucasus Emirate congratulated the Taliban on their victory and pledged that this will inspire militant Islamists in their struggle for an independent Emirate in the North Caucasus.[17]

According to Russia's Prosecutor General's portal, the total number of terrorism-related crimes in the North Caucasus in the first ten months of 2021 stood at 1,906, with Dagestan accounting for 457,

---

[15] Valery Dzutsati, "Year 2020 in Review: Internal and External Challenges Mount for Moscow in the Northeast Caucasus," *Eurasia Daily Monitor*, Vol. 18, Issue 1, January 4, 2021, https://jamestown.org/program/year-2020-in-review-internal-and-external-challenges-mount-for-moscow-in-the-northeast-caucasus/.

[16] Emil Aslan Souleimanov, *The North Caucasus Insurgency: Dead or Alive?* US Army War College, Strategic Studies Institute, February 2017, p.13.

[17] Aslan Doukaev, "Taliban's Return to Power Draws Mixed Reaction From Chechen Factions," *Eurasia Daily Monitor*, Vol.18, Issue 135, September 8, 2021, https://jamestown.org/program/talibans-return-to-power-draws-mixed-reaction-from-chechen-factions/

Chechnya for 115, Ingushetia for 99, Kabardino-Balkaria for 59, and Stavropol *Krai* for 55.[18] Moscow has not released detailed numbers since then. "Terrorist crimes" included actual attacks, involvement or the provision of assistance in such attacks, public calls or public justification for terrorist activities, intentionally supplied false information about them, and the formation or participation in illegal armed groups. In October 2021, Russia's National Anti-Terrorism Committee (NAK) reported that over a three-year period, law enforcement agencies and intelligence services thwarted 29 terrorist attacks, eliminated 84 militants, identified 59 terrorist cells, and arrested 379 collaborators in the North Caucasus.[19]

Incidents of terrorist and insurgent offensives included the killing of six armed militants by Chechen security forces in January 2021. They were allegedly led by Aslan Byutukayev, a close associate of Doku Umarov, the late leader of the Caucasus Emirate.[20] Four alleged Islamist militants were killed by security forces in Grozny in October 2020, and two officers of the National Guard also died in the shootout.[21] Chechen officials claimed they killed two other militants in the west of the republic, and another shooting of police officers took place in December 2020. It proved difficult to verify if the "militants"

---

[18] http://crimestat.ru/offenses_table.

[19] "В Москве прошло заседание Национального антитеррористического комитета," October 12, 2021, http://nac.gov.ru/nak-prinimaet-resheniya/v-moskve-proshlo-zasedanie-nacionalnogo-26.html.

[20] "Kadyrov Says Six Armed Militants Killed In Chechnya," January 20, 2021, https://www.rferl.org/a/kadyrov-says-six-armed-militants-killed-in-chechnya/31055416.html.

[21] "Chechen Officials Say Four 'Militants' Killed In Grozny," October 13, 2020, https://www.rferl.org/a/chechen-officials-say-four-militants-killed-in-grozny/30890556.html.

were Islamist guerrillas, members of an organized criminal gang, or armed political opponents of the Kadyrov regime. That same month, authorities in Dagestan reported that police killed two men after they opened fire on law enforcement officers.

Other republics in the North Caucasus are also not immune from terrorist threats and attacks. In December 2020, a suicide bomber detonated a device in the village of Uchkeken, in the Karachai-Cherkess Republic, killing himself and injuring six police officers.[22] On March 11, 2021, government forces in Makhachkala, the capital of the Republic of Dagestan, killed a suspected rebel plotting a terrorist assault on government agencies.[23] Russian security forces reportedly conducted a "counter-terrorism operation" in a central area of the city for the first time since 2016. In June 2021, security forces killed two terrorists planning attacks in Moscow and in Astrakhan *Oblast*, north of Dagestan on the Caspian coast.[24]

On September 30, 2021, five alleged members of the Islamic State were given long prison sentences for plotting terrorist attacks in Moscow.[25] They had reportedly formed an "undercover group" in the Moscow region intending to bomb police facilities and an educational

---

[22] "Suicide Bomber Injures Six People In Russia's North Caucasus," December 11, 2020, https://www.rferl.org/a/north-caucasus-suicide-bombing-/30995684.html.

[23] Valery Dzutsati, "Makhachkala Experiences First Special Operation in Five Year," *Eurasia Daily Monitor*, Vol.18 Issue 47, March 23, 2021, https://jamestown.org/program/makhachkala-experiences-first-special-operation-in-five-years/.

[24] "Russia Says Foiled IS Attacks in Moscow, South," *The Moscow Times*, July 1, 2021, https://www.themoscowtimes.com/2021/07/01/russia-says-foiled-is-attacks-in-moscow-south-a74401.

[25] "Пятеро сторонников ИГ получили до 25 лет колонии за подготовку терактов в Москве," September 30, 2021, https://www.interfax.ru/moscow/794461.

establishment. In the same month, counter-terrorist forces killed two militants and discovered a cache of weapons during a raid in Dagestan's Buinaksk region.[26] The Federal Security Service (FSB) also arrested two members of the radical Islamist group Katibat Tawhid wal-Jihad (KTJ) in the Siberian city of Krasnoyarsk. They were accused of promoting terrorist ideology and recruiting Krasnoyarsk residents to participate in destructive activities.[27] On October 1, 2021, the FSB arrested a man in Karachaevo-Cherkessia on charges of plotting a bomb attack on the instructions of the Islamic State.[28] Police allegedly seized bomb-making devices and mobile correspondence with "members of terrorist structures." The planned targets were law enforcement personnel in Cherkessk, the republic's capital.

Public protests against government policy have also periodically erupted in the North Caucasus. A mass demonstration of 2,000 people took place in Vladikavkaz, the capital of North Ossetia–Alania, on April 20, 2020, against pandemic-related restrictions imposed by local authorities and the lack of emergency financial support to compensate for job losses. Moreover, protesters demanded the resignation of the regional government. Local police refused to forcefully disperse the crowds, so the authorities deployed security forces from outside the republic, and dozens of protestors were detained. Over the coming

---

[26] "Russia Says 2 Militants Killed in Anti-Terror Raid," September 10, 20121, https://www.themoscowtimes.com/2021/09/10/russia-says-2-militants-killed-in-anti-terror-raid-a75017.

[27] "Сотрудники ФСБ задержали в Красноярске двух вербовщиков террористов," September 15, 2021, https://www.interfax.ru/russia/790400.

[28] "ФСБ предотвратила теракт в Карачаево-Черкесии," October 1, 2021, https://www.interfax.ru/russia/794713.

months, at least 14 protesters were found guilty of taking part in mass disorders and sentenced to between four and six years in prison.[29]

Various administrative moves to restrict self-government have faced opposition not only among citizens but even among some local legislators. In September 2020, the Popular Assembly of the Republic of Ingushetia rejected proposals to eliminate the republic's Constitutional Court, viewing this as a violation of its constitution, engineered by Moscow.[30] Such decisions will result in fresh protests if the Kremlin insists on disbanding the Court that many Ingush consider to be an important defense against decisions that undermine their national institutions.

The governors of Ingushetia appointed by Moscow have also endeavored to control and pressure local Muslim leaders to agree with their policies and help pacify the population.[31] Such measures have largely failed, and tensions have escalated between the muftiate and the head of the republic, Makhmud-Ali Kalimatov, who brought in an ethnic Russian to head the ministry for nationality affairs, which also supervises religious groups. This was viewed as a blatant foreign imposition over the Muslim community. Ingush authorities have also brought in militia members from outside the republic to help repress demonstrations, as they believed the local police were unreliable in

---

[29] "More Jailed in Russia's North Ossetia for COVID-Related Protests," November 12, 2021, https://www.rferl.org/a/north-ossetia-jailed-covid-protests/31558846.html.

[30] "Парламент Ингушетии вернул законопроект об упразднении Конституционного суда республики," September 22, 2020, https://fortanga.org/2020/09/kalimatov-nazad/.

[31] Paul Goble, "Magas Effort to Control Ingush Muslim Leadership Deepening Divide between People and Powers, Mutsolgov Says," October 6, 2020, http://windowoneurasia2.blogspot.com/2020/10/magas-effort-to-control-ingush-muslim.html.

cracking down on their own people. Such short-sighted moves help convince the local population that they are merely a colony of Russia.

Indigenous people across the North Caucasus have become more assertive regarding their identity and history and can communicate more effectively through the internet. They are also more willing to counter Moscow's distorted history of the region and to resist the central government.[32] In particular, Circassian (Adyg) groups across the northwest Caucasus have mobilized in several federal units, including the Adygea Republic, the Kabardino-Balkar Republic (KBR), and the Karachai-Cherkess Republic (KCR). Circassians in Russia and in the *diaspora* mark May 21 as the anniversary of the mass murders and expulsions of their ancestors from the Caucasus by Tsarist forces in 1864, after a century of resistance to Russian conquest. This Day of National Rebirth signals a revival of national activism for Circassian rights and eventual independence.

In March 2019, Circassian activists gathered in the KCR capital Cherkess and formed a Coordinating Council of Circassian Public Activists to defend their national republics, achieve international acknowledgement of what they consider a Tsarist genocide in the 1860s, defend their language and education, and promote their common identity.[33] Public rallies have also become more commonplace. During 2021, Circassian demonstrations took place in several cities despite government repression. The largest rally was in

---

[32] Paul Goble, "Moscow's Misrepresentations about Colonial War in Caucasus Set the Stage for New Violence, Khakuasheva Says," December 13, 2020, http://windowoneurasia2.blogspot.com/2020/12/moscows-misrepresentations-about.html.

[33] Adel Bashqawi, *The Circassian Miracle: The Nation Neither Tsars, Nor Commissars, Nor Russia Could Stop,* Xlibris, 2020, pp.430–431.

Nalchik, the capital of the KBR, in which 2,000 people participated.[34] In September 2021, two new independent Circassian organizations—the Circassian (Adyg) Historical-Geographic Society and the Unified Circassian Media Space—were created in the KBR with plans to study and defend Circassian history, restore Circassian topographic names, and help ensure the survival and growth of the Circassian language and identity.[35] The reduction of textbooks in non-Russian languages, a move that fosters linguistic russification, has sparked protest actions by parents and activists in the KBR. Residents have met with republic officials to convince them to supply Circassian-language textbooks for schools.[36]

Circassian activists focused on the 2021 census by petitioning for all the major subdivisions or traditional tribes to declare themselves as

---

[34] Paul Goble, "Circassian Genocide Anniversary Must Be Not Only a Day of Remembrance but Also a Day of National Rebirth, Activists Say," May 23, 2021, http://windowoneurasia2.blogspot.com/2021/05/circassian-genocide-anniversary-must-be.html.

[35] Paul Goble, "Two New Circassian Organizations Take Up Cudgels for that Nation's History, Language and Toponymy, Windows on Eurasia," September 10, 2021, http://windowoneurasia2.blogspot.com/2021/09/two-new-circassian-organizations-take.html.

[36] Paul Goble, "Moscow Finds Another Way to Kill Non-Russian Education by Not Printing Textbooks," October 3, 2021, windowoneurasia2.blogspot.com/2021/10/moscow-finds-another-way-to-kill-non.html;

Paul Goble, "Circassian Language Textbook Crisis Deepens; Many Suspect Moscow Behind It," October 18, 2021, http://windowoneurasia2.blogspot.com/2021/10/circassian-language-textbook-crisis.html.

Circassians (native Adygs).[37] Such an initiative encourages the rediscovery of Circassian history and the revival of Circassian identity that has been divided and distorted by the Tsarist, Soviet, and Russian regimes. On October 3, 2021, leaders of eight Circassian groups in the KBR issued an appeal to their kindred across the North Caucasus to use their self-designation in the census and not the alien one that Moscow has imposed on them.[38] Circassian mobilization can serve as a model for other nations to assert their identities and ethnonyms and to challenge existing borders and administrative arrangements. Russian officials may try to falsify the census results, but if the alterations become obvious, they can provoke protests and convince more Circassians that they need a unified republic or an independent state to effectively defend their nation.

Activists are also pushing for the return of Circassians from the Middle East, to where thousands fled from Tsarist oppression. The Circassian population inside Russia totals about 720,000, but outside Russia the number is estimated at over 6 million, with the largest concentrations in Turkey, Jordan, and Syria.[39] Moscow has strictly restricted Circassian immigration from the Middle East, fearful that this would strengthen calls for national unity and eventual independence. Regardless of the limited return of Circassians to their native lands, an increasing number of young people are unearthing

---

[37] "Черкесы – все те, кто на родном зовут себя «адыгэ», – к Переписи населения РФ," February 14, 2021, https://adygplus.blogspot.com/2021/02/blogpost_14.html?mc_cid=ae535bcbd7&mc_eid=4655fb8220.

[38] Paul Goble, "Circassians See Russian Census as Real Chance to Unite Their Nation," *Eurasia Daily Monitor*, Vol.18, Issue 156, October 14, 2021, https://jamestown.org/program/circassians-see-russian-census-as-real-chance-to-unite-their-nation/.

[39] Adel Bashqawi, *The Circassian Miracle: The Nation Neither Tsars, Nor Commissars, Nor Russia Could Stop*, Xlibris, 2020, p.638.

their common roots. This will invigorate demands for the restoration of a single Circassian republic, whether within the Russian Federation or as a separate independent state. Circassian demands have also helped to stimulate activism among two divided Turkic nations in the northwest Caucasus, the Balkars in the KBR and the Karachais in the KCR. Calls for Circassian unification and self-determination will embolden calls for Balkar-Karachai amalgamation in a single state and could raise demands for further border changes in the western part of the North Caucasus.

Some of Dagestan's distinct nations are also becoming revitalized. The ethnic-Lezgin movement *Sadval* in Dagestan was active during the 1990s, advocating for the creation of an independent state combining parts of southern Dagestan and northern Azerbaijan, and its goals can be revived as disaffection with the central and regional governments escalates. Dagestan is also witnessing religious radicalization.[40] Over 1,800 Dagestanis reportedly joined anti-government Islamist groups during the war in Syria. Dagestan's officials claim that around 1 percent of the republic's population of around 3.1 million, according to estimates in 2021, sympathized with their fighting compatriots. Independent experts believe those numbers are much higher and that extremist religious views are growing. According to polls conducted in 2019, 14.5 percent of high school students and 9 percent of teachers expressed support for Dagestanis joining the Islamic State. Dagestani officials admit the government is losing the ideological battle for the hearts and minds of the younger generation.

Territorial disputes in the North Caucasus are also a source of discontent and growing opposition to Moscow. Ingushetia is embroiled several border conflicts with neighboring republics. The

---

[40] Aslan Doukaev, "Dagestani Leadership Struggles With Countering Islamic State's Propaganda Offensive," June 4, 2021, https://jamestown.org/program/dagestani-leadership-struggles-with-countering-islamic-states-propaganda-offensive/.

most volatile has been with North Ossetia–Alania over Prigorodny Rayon, from which approximately 60,000 Ingush fled or were expelled by paramilitary units during the October–November 1992 war; 600 Ingush civilians perished during those hostilities. Ingush activists have demanded the return of the district to Ingushetia, and periodic clashes have taken place. In November 2021, there were several skirmishes between Ossetians and Ingush in Prigorodny as well as in the Ossetian capital of Vladikavkaz.[41] Tensions remain high between Ossetian residents and those Ingush refugees who have returned, particularly to the rural parts of Prigorodny. The Ingush population does not feel protected, because it is not adequately represented in local government or in law enforcement agencies.

A prime source of recent resistance in Ingushetia to Moscow's policies has been the border changes arranged between former Ingushetian head Yunus-Bek Yevkurov and Chechnya's leader, Ramzan Kadyrov.[42] It appeared that in return for quashing anti-Putin dissent in Chechnya, the Kremlin permitted Kadyrov to pursue irredentist claims against neighboring republics. Such a "divide and rule" approach was also intended to prevent the development of a pan-Caucasian front against Russian rule. In the September 2018 agreement, the Ingush government surrendered about 103 square miles of its territory to Chechnya, and the deal sparked two years of street protests in Ingushetia.

---

[41] Valery Dzutsatii, "Ossetian-Ingush Tensions Escalate Into Series of Clashes," *Eurasia Daily Monitor,* Vol. 18, Issue 183, December 8, 2021, https://jamestown.org/program/ossetian-ingush-tensions-escalate-into-series-of-clashes/.

[42] "Съезд представителей тейпов потребовал восстановить территориальною целостность Ингушетии," November 11, 2019, https://fortanga.org/2019/11/sezd-predstavitelej-tejpov-potreboval-vosstanovit-territorialnoyu-tselostnost-ingushetii/.

The border dispute remained a live question during the imprisonment and show trials of seven protest leaders following a street demonstration in March 2019. In December 2021, the protesters were given prison sentences of between seven to nine years on charges of organizing an extremist organization and violence against security officials.[43] They were also accused of working with various Ingush organizations in forming a "shadow government" to overthrow the current administration in Magas. Although no evidence surfaced of any crimes committed by the protesters, their trial was supposed to dissuade others from openly resisting the republican regime. However, the prolonged trial had the reverse effect by underscoring the arbitrary nature of Russia's justice system and the persecution of innocent civilians. The authorities also raided the homes of members of the independent Ingush Congress of National Unity.[44]

While Moscow and its regional proxies have sought to undermine Ingushetia's secular nationalists through imprisonment, Ingush religious leaders are becoming more active in defending the national interests of the republic. Further conflicts and protests can erupt over Chechen government claims to sections of the Sunzha and Malgobek *rayons* in Ingushetia, which were once part of the Chechen Autonomous *Oblast* in the 1920s. An additional source of resentment in Ingushetia has been Moscow's plans to construct a Russian military facility without consultation with Ingush leaders and which would take more land away from the republic. Other federal border changes without legal foundation and against the interests of the Ingush nation

---

[43] "Russia: Quash Sentences Against Ingush Protest Leaders," Amnesty International, December 15, 2021, https://www.amnesty.org/en/latest/news/2021/12/russia-quash-sentences-against-ingush-protest-leaders/.

[44] "Ingush Activists Under Pressure After Protests Over Chechnya Border Deal," Radio Free Europe/ Radio Liberty, April 3, 2019, https://www.rferl.org/a/ingush-activists-under-pressure-after-protests-over-chechnya-border-deal/29858984.html.

have included transfers of two districts to North Ossetia and three districts to Stavropol *Krai*. Ingushetia was given nothing in exchange for these losses.

In Dagestan, debates about adjusting the border with Chechnya could spark mass protests, as happened in Ingushetia, and with the prospect of escalating violence. Chechen officials have demanded the restoration of Aukhovsky *Rayon* to Chechnya, from which it was separated after the mass deportations of Chechens to Central Asia by the Soviet regime in February 1944. Dagestani leaders remained under pressure from Moscow to forge an agreement with Grozny but were divided on how to proceed and whether to surrender or exchange any territories.

Internal ethnic disputes are also evident in Dagestan, primarily over land and resources. For instance, restlessness is growing among the Kumyks, a Turkic-speaking nation in northern Dagestan, with protests against new laws governing land use and restricting herding practices in the mountains.[45] The republican authorities have additionally allowed businesses and representatives of other ethnic groups to move into the highland areas and precluded the return of Kumyk herders. Kumyk activists have demanded that control over pastureland is returned to the municipalities. Land shortages, rural overpopulation, and the lack of consultations with citizens by the republican government will animate protests and inter-ethnic conflicts in various parts of Dagestan.

Territorial disputes are evident in other regions bordering the North Caucasus. In the Kalmyk Republic on the Caspian coast, the

---

[45] Paul Goble, "Kumyks See New Daghestan Land Law Threatening Their Nation's Survival and Begin to Protest," June 12, 2021, http://windowoneurasia2.blogspot.com/2021/06/kumyks-see-new-daghestan-land-law.html.

independent Congress of the Kalmyk People has claimed portions of the neighboring and mostly ethnic-Russian Astrakhan *Oblast* as part of Kalmyk territory.[46] Sizeable areas of Astrakhan and parts of the Republic of Dagestan, including Nogayski *Rayon*, belonged to the Kalmyk Autonomous Soviet Socialist Republic before Stalin's deportations of the Kalmyk population to central Siberia in 1943, while other lands were transferred to Kalmykia. The current dispute can radicalize young Kalmyks, who have a long list of complaints against the republic's head appointed by the Kremlin. A general agreement exists between the Kalmyk government and opposition that the republic needs to acquire land back from Astrakhan *Oblast* but no consensus on the extent of those territories. The government in the capital Elista seeks the transfer of 4,000 square kilometers of largely unpopulated terrain, while the Kalmyk Congress wants the return of 11,500 square kilometers with a population of some 77,000 people who are mostly ethnic Russians and Cossacks. Tensions have also escalated between Kalmyk society and Moscow as a result of outsiders being emplaced by the Kremlin in key governing positions in the republic.[47]

In May 2021, the third Chuulhn Congress, the highest representative body of the Oirat-Kalmyk nation, convened in Elista, with representatives from the Kalmyk Republic, Moscow and Mongolia.[48] The meeting was precipitated by an accumulation of social, economic, and environmental problems that are driving the republic deeper into

---

[46] Todar Baktemir, "'Восстановление исторической справедливости.' О чем спорят Калмыкия и Астраханская область," June 8, 2021, idelreal.org/a/31292962.html.

[47] Marybek Vachagayev, "Неизвестные калмыки: кто они – европейские буддисты?" July 9, 2021, kavkazr.com/a/31346080.html.

[48] Alla Hurska, "Kalmykia: Russia's Emerging Powder Keg?" *Eurasia Daily Monitor*, Vol.18, Issue 128, August 11, 2021, https://jamestown.org/program/kalmykia-russias-emerging-powder-keg/.

destitution. Kalmykia is one of the ten poorest federal subjects and suffers from one of the largest outflows of working-age adults in Russia. The republic is also experiencing prolonged water shortages: much of the water is unsuitable for human consumption because of insufficient purification facilities. Only 7.4 percent of the population has access to quality drinking water. Prolonged droughts and desertification have damaged local agriculture, on which many Kalmyks depend. The Chuulhn Congress asserted that the crisis of federalism in Russia had resulted in Kalmykia completely losing its independence and accused Moscow of a hidden ethnocide of Oirat-Kalmyks. It demanded an end to repression against representatives of the Oirat-Kalmyk people and the restoration of the republic as a democratic law–bound state within the Russian Federation. Moscow's denial of republican autonomy can mobilize Kalmyks to push for outright independence.

Additional flashpoints for the Kremlin bordering the North Caucasus include the Kuban region, which straddles most of Krasnodar *Krai* and parts of the Adygea Republic, the Karachai-Cherkess Republic and Stavropol *Krai*. Putin's calls for the federalization of Ukraine after the 2014 seizure of Crimea and parts of Donbas backfired domestically in some Russian regions. In particular, a movement emerged in the Kuban demanding autonomy for the territory. Further pressure by Moscow to divide Ukraine by recognizing the independence of regions carved out by Russian military forces in Donetsk and Luhansk *oblasts* can encourage similar demands for "special status" or sovereignty within Russia's regions. A Kuban Republic has been proclaimed on the internet, with its own flag and a supposed mandate to represent the Cossacks of Kuban.[49]

---

[49] Alexander Podrabinek, "Russian Separatism: The Hotbeds of Tension," August 29, 2014, https://imrussia.org/en/analysis/politics/797-russian-separatism-the-hotbeds-of-tension.

Middle Volga

The six Middle Volga republics consist of Tatarstan, Bashkortostan, Chuvashia, Mordovia, Udmurtia, and Mari El. Three are Finno-Ugric republics (Udmurtia, Mari El, and Mordovia). Finno-Ugric languages form the third-most-populous ethno-linguistic group in Russia after Slavic and Turkic. Komi and Karelia are the other two Finno-Ugric republics, and the Khanty-Mansi Autonomous *Okrug*–Yugra is also a titular Finno-Ugric entity. According to the 2010 census, the Turkic-speaking Tatars form the second-largest nation in Russia, numbering some 5.3 million, of which approximately two million reside in the Republic of Tatarstan, forming 53.2 percent of the population. Soviet policy divided the Tatar population, fearing Tatar domination of the Volga-Ural region. Only a quarter of Tatars were included within the Tatar Autonomous Soviet Socialist Republic when it was established in May 1920, with many Tatars left in the neighboring Republic of Bashkortostan and in other regions of Russia.[50]

Tatarstan's leaders were frustrated that despite having a larger territory and titular population than Estonia, they could not achieve independence when the USSR disintegrated. The Tatar Autonomous Republic declared its sovereignty as a Union Republic in August 1990, rejected the Federation Treaty in March 1992 that undergirded the Russian Federation, and adopted its own republican constitution in November 1992. Despite pressure from Moscow, Tatar authorities did not annul their sovereignty declaration but signed a bilateral treaty with the federal government and claimed that a genuine federation required decentralization and shared sovereignty between the center and federal subjects. Tatar leaders did not push for secession and outright independence from Russia, calculating that this could result in military intervention by Moscow. However, they have remained

[50] Katherine E. Graney, *Of Khans and Kremlins: Tatarstan and the Future of Ethno-Federalism in Russia*, Rowman & Littlefield: Lexington Books, 2009, p.10.

determined in their quest for sovereignty and this could turn to a pro-independence position if either Moscow formally annuls their progress or the Russian federal state starts to fracture.

Periodic protests have been staged in the capital Kazan, demanding an enhanced status for the Tatar language and other markers of Tatar distinctiveness. One important symbol of national reawakening is to commemorate formerly banned anniversaries, such as Russia's imperial conquests. Despite Moscow's opposition, Tatar nationalist activists mark the anniversary of the occupation and sacking of Tatarstan's capital Kazan by the Muscovite army of Ivan the Terrible in 1552 with a Memorial Day on October 15 for the Tatar defenders. The Muslim Spiritual Directorate (MSD) of Tatarstan has also become involved by holding annual prayers for those who died fighting Russia's imperial force. The transformation of a Tatar national holiday into a wider Muslim commemoration can inspire other Islamic societies to honor their history of resistance to Moscow and boost the status of Tatarstan as a Muslim center.[51]

The State Council of Tatarstan was pressured by the Kremlin to amend the republic's constitution to bring it in line with that of the amended Russian federal version. Kazan agreed to eliminate its constitutional court following Moscow's ruling but replaced it with a constitutional council inside the parliament. Moscow's insistence on replacing the position of Tatarstan's President with the term "head," as in other national republics, has been steadfastly resisted. The right of a federal subject to call its senior official President was not eliminated in Tatarstan nor the naming of its legislature as the State

---

[51] Paul Goble, "Tatarstan to Have a Muslim Holiday in Memory of Those who Fell Fighting Ivan the Terrible in 1552," May 30, 2021, http://windowoneurasia2.blogspot.com/2021/05/tatarstan-to-have-muslim-holiday-in.html.

Council.[52] All other republics dropped the title of President following Moscow's demands, but it has remained a source of pride for Tatars and a marker of their distinct status in the Federation. In January 2021, the procuracy of Tatarstan released an official letter stating that the head of the republic can no longer be called President, a move opposed by the Tatar government and people.[53] In November 2021, Tatarstan's parliament backed amendments to the bill on public administration declaring that Russia's regions should be guided by their own constitutions together with their historical and national traditions when selecting the official title for heads of republics. This would allow Tatarstan to maintain its head as a "President."

Moscow's persistent pressures sets the stage for direct conflict with Kazan and could further undermine support for the United Russia party in national and local elections. In October 2021, Russia's justice ministry closed down the All-Tatar Public Center (a.k.a. the Tatar Social Center), accusing the group of extremism. The Center was the oldest Tatar public organization, and by declaring it "extremist" Moscow will further radicalize the population. In reality, the Center was a bastion of moderation within Tatar nationalism and focused on maintaining Tatar language and history. The Tatar government has also demanded that Moscow enable Tatar speakers outside of the republic to have access to Tatar-language schools and maintain their national traditions.

---

[52] "Татарстан не хочет отдавать президентский пост В республике готовятся к изменению региональной конституции," December 29, 2020, https://www.kommersant.ru/doc/4636481.

[53] Paul Goble, "Tatarstan Procuracy Says Kazan Must Stop Styling Republic Head as President," January 21, 2021, http://windowoneurasia2.blogspot.com/2021/01/tatarstan-procuracy-says-kazan-must.html.

In countering Moscow's offensive to reduce the number of self-declared Tatars, five hundred Tatar representatives from across the Russian Federation met in Kazan in September 2021 to develop plans for reversing the decline in the size of the Tatar population in the Russian census.[54] According to participants, mixed marriages and pressure from non-Tatar regional officials have resulted in a lower count of the number of Tatars outside of Tatarstan, where the majority lives. Younger people are also becoming increasingly involved in defending their national rights and distinct ethnic identities. For instance, on November 6, 2021, activists of the Azatlyk Union of Tatar Youth held a demonstration in Kazan under the slogan "if we can defend Tatarstan, we will be able to defend other republics as well."[55]

The Bashkort Autonomous Republic declared its sovereignty in October 1990 and in December 1993 voted against accepting the new Russian federal constitution while adopting a new republican constitution.[56] Provisions that republican legislation takes precedence over federal laws were rescinded after Putin became President. Bashkir nationalism has continued to simmer, and in May 2020, Moscow engineered a ban on the Bashqort group, which promotes the nation's language and culture. This was part of a broader campaign to stifle any national resurgence among non-Russians in the Middle

---

[54] Paul Goble, Tatars from Across Russia Meet in Kazan to Plan How to Limit Decline in Size of Tatar Nation in Census," September 26, 2021, http://windowoneurasia2.blogspot.com/2021/09/tatars-from-across-russia-meet-in-kazan.html.

[55] Paul Goble, "'If Tatars Can Defend Tatarstan, They Can Defend Other Republics as Well,' Nabiullin Says," December 27, 2021, http://windowoneurasia2.blogspot.com/2021/12/if-tatars-can-defend-tatarstan-they-can.html.

[56] *The Territories of the Russian Federation 2020*, London: Routledge, 2020, p.197.

Volga republics.[57] Bashqort came under increasing attention after staging several rallies challenging the policies of both local and federal authorities, especially the abolishment of mandatory indigenous language classes in national republics.[58] Bashkortostan also witnessed clashes in August 2020 between environmental activists and workers of the Bashkort Soda Company seeking to engage in limestone mining on the ecologically unique Kuhstau Hill. [59]

Moscow has promoted divisions within the Tatar nation in order to reduce its size in the national census and to assimilate groups that it does not recognize as Tatar. Mounting disputes revolving around ethnic identity can also precipitate more vocal demands for sovereignty as a form of self-assertion and self-defense. The case of Tatar and Bashkir identity is significant, as some Tatar nationalists claim that their co-ethnics in Bashkortostan were forcibly "Bashkirized" during Tsarist and Soviet times.[60] The claim is rejected by Bashkortostan's leaders, but it sharpens feelings of national pride

---

[57] "Старейшую татарскую общественную организацию могут объявить экстремистской и закрыть," January 15, 2021, https://www.turantoday.com/2021/01/tatar-public-center-charge-extremism.html; Paul Goble, "All-Tatar Social Center (VTOTs) Faces Liquidation for 'Extremism'," January 17, 2021, http://windowoneurasia2.blogspot.com/2021/01/kazan-wants-to-liquidate-all-tatar.html; Paul Goble, "Ufa Court Bans Bashkort National Organization as Extremist," May 24, 2020, https://windowoneurasia2.blogspot.com/2020/05/ufa-court-bans-bashkort-national.html.

[58] "Russian Court Bans Prominent Group Promoting Ethnic Bashkir Rights," May 22, 2020, https://www.rferl.org/a/russian-court-bans-prominent-group-promoting-ethnic-bashkir-rights/30629173.html.

[59] "The Battle for Russia's Kushtau Hill," August 17, 2020, https://www.rferl.org/a/the-battle-for-russia-bashkortostan-kushtau-hill/30788099.html.

[60] Paul Goble, "New Kazan Study Expands Debate on Bashkirization of Tatars," January 18, 2021, http://windowoneurasia2.blogspot.com/2021/01/new-kazan-study-expands-debate-on.html.

and distinctiveness among both nations and is exploited by Moscow to the detriment of both parties. Some officials continue to promote the re-identification of Tatars as Bashkirs to boost the Bashkir share of the population. There is an element of insecurity in Bashkortostan, as Bashkirs form only 30 percent of the population, while Russians stand at 36 percent and Tatars at 25 percent. Such moves have created tensions with Tatarstan, with some Tatars condemning officials in Ufa, Bashkortostan's capital, for promoting an "artificial" nation of Bashkirs, while some Bashkirs denounce Tatars for an imperial mindset. Bashkort officials and intellectuals also claim the Mishar population in the republic as a separate nation with close ties to Bashkirs rather than being a Tatar sub-ethnos. Fears persist that the Mishar dispute may also animate mutual territorial claims between Bashkortostan and Tatarstan.

On the other hand, there are examples of cooperation between independence activists in Tatarstan and Bashkortostan. Two leading nationalist organizations—Azatlyk (The Union of Tatar Youth) and the Bashkort Kuk Bure (The Heavenly Wolf)—have reportedly merged their agendas and called for unity among other Turkic-speaking and Finno-Ugric groups, including the Chuvash, Udmurt, and Mari.[61] Latent support for autonomy and independence have periodically been manifest in the other Middle Volga republics. Chuvashia declared its sovereignty in October 1990 and voted against the federal constitution in December 1993. Udmurtia declared sovereignty in September 1990 and passed a republican constitution in December 1994. Mari El declared sovereignty in October 1990 and adopted a republican constitution in June 1995. Mordovia declared

---

[61] Peter Eltsov, *The Long Telegram 2.0: A Neo-Kennanite Approach to Russia*, Lanham: Lexington Books, 2020, p.121.

sovereignty in December 1990 and passed a republican constitution in September 1995.[62]

National revivalist movements have been active in the Middle Volga, including the Mari Society (*Mari Ushem*), which established chapters in several towns in the Mari El Republic in 1990. The movement has been hounded by the Russian authorities, as with other national renaissance groups and independent socio-cultural organizations. Moscow's limitations on the use of local languages have also spurred protests across the Middle Volga. In September 2019, the self-immolation of Albert Razin, an Udmurt activist and scientist, in opposition to Russia's new language law, generated solidarity among the Finno-Ugric nations.[63]

One can expect increasing pressure on the Orenburg *Oblast,* which was carved out in 1925 as a majority-ethnic-Russian region to separate Bashkortostan from Kazakhstan and deny Bashkortostan and Tatarstan the status of Union Republics because they did not possess external borders. Without such borders, they did not formally possess the constitutional right to secede when the Soviet Union disintegrated. Some activists in the region have demanded that Bashkortostan reclaim the "Orenburg corridor" and the right to independence.[64] The Free Idel-Ural movement, which campaigns for the independence and union of the six Middle Volga republics, has

---

[62] *The Territories of the Russian Federation 2020,* London: Routledge, 2020, pp.201, 203, 207, 215.

[63] "The Finno-Ugric Separatist Trends in Russia," Robert Lansing Institute for Global Threats and Democratic Studies, Dover, UK, November 11, 2020, https://lansinginstitute.org/2020/11/11/the-finno-ugric-separatist-trends-in-russia/.

[64] Paul Goble, "Idel-Ural Activists Call on Bashkortostan to Recover Orenburg Corridor in Upcoming Border Talks," December 27, 2018, https://windowoneurasia2.blogspot.com/2018/12/idel-ural-activists-call-on.html.

called for the return of Kuvandyk and Gaysky districts in Orenburg *Oblast* to Bashkortostan.[65] This would restore Bashkortostan's border with Kazakhstan.

According to officials, armed Islamist activity has been evident in the Middle Volga. In November 2020, five alleged members of the Hizb ut-Tahrir group, labeled as extremist and banned in Russia, were detained in Tatarstan and charged with propagating "terrorist ideas" among Tatarstan's Muslims.[66] Hizb ut-Tahrir is based in London and seeks to unite Muslim countries into an Islamic caliphate, but it claims that its methods are peaceful. A few days earlier, six people were detained for an attempted terrorist attack against a police station in the town of Kukmor, Tatarstan.[67]

Moscow's proposals for federal amalgamation and municipal agglomeration have provoked opposition in several regions and republics. In Mari El, there are fears that its capital Yoshkar-Ola will be neglected while Kazan, in neighboring Tatarstan, will be favored.[68] Some Mari organizations, including the national rebirth movement Mari Ushem, contend that such moves will destabilize the republic and threaten the survival of the Finno-Ugric nation. Conversely, some

---

[65] Ramazan Alpaut, "Начните с Оренбургского коридора!" Хуснуллину ответили из "Свободного Идель-Урала," https://www.idelreal.org/a/31227964.html.

[66] "Five Alleged Members Of Banned Hizb Ut-Tahrir Islamic Group Arrested In Tatarstan," November 6, 2020, https://www.rferl.org/a/five-alleged-members-of-banned-hizb-ut-tahrir-islamic-group-arrested-in-tatarstan/30933743.html.

[67] "Six Detentions Made Over 'Attempted Terrorist Act' In Tatarstan," November 2, 2020, https://www.rferl.org/a/six-detentions-made-over-attempted-terrorist-act-in-tatarstan/30926574.html.

[68] Paul Goble, "Neither Maris nor Tatars Happy about Amalgamation via Agglomeration Plan," June 21, 2021, http://windowoneurasia2.blogspot.com/2021/06/neither-maris-nor-tatars-happy-about.html.

Tatar leaders in Mari El have welcomed the proposal, as it would initiate the unification of the two republics, while Tatars in Tatarstan are opposed because it would increase financial burdens on Kazan. Steps toward amalgamation can spark ethnic conflicts between Tatars and Mari. In June 2021, the ten largest public organizations in Mari El, including civic and environmental activists and military veterans, released an open letter to President Putin and Prime Minister Mishustin denouncing the idea of territorial changes.[69] They asserted that this would damage the national rights of indigenous peoples and reverberate in other republics and regions by energizing support for secessionism and raise prospects for social explosions.

Northwest

Several regions of Northwest Russia have a notable history of attempted autonomy and statehood. Karelia was an independent principality contested between Sweden and Novgorod before falling under Swedish control in the 16th century. It was subsequently annexed by Muscovite Russia in 1721. The Karelia region was disputed between Russia and Finland after the collapse of the Tsarist empire during World War I. The Republic of Uhtua, or East Karelia, was established in July 1919. The Provisional Government of Karelia located its capital in the town of Uhtua, and the quasi-state formed an alliance with Finland with the goal of unification. In March 1920, a Congress of representatives of 11 Karelian counties declared that the region was seceding from Russia. The new state was recognized by Finland in May 1920 but was overrun by the Red Army and the government fled to Finland.

[69] Paul Goble, "Mari El Groups Warn of Social Explosion if Moscow Proceeds with Amalgamation Plans," July 3, 2021, http://windowoneurasia2.blogspot.com/2021/07/mari-el-groups-warn-of-social-explosion.html.

The Karelian region was absorbed and folded by the Bolsheviks into the Karelian Autonomous Soviet Socialist Republic within the Russian Soviet Federative Socialist Republic. Some Finnish and Karelian activists continued to campaign for independence and unification with Finland, and a united Karelian government was formed in exile. During the subsequent Russo-Finnish war, Finnish troops occupied parts of Karelia in late 1921 but were defeated by the Red Army in January 1922. An East Karelian uprising against Soviet rule was quelled by March 1922. A Karelo-Finnish Soviet Socialist Republic (KFSSR) was formed between 1940 and 1956 before its incorporation as an Autonomous Republic within the Russian Soviet Federative Socialist Republic. Moscow's objective during this period was to absorb Finland itself into the USSR as a distinct Union Republic. If the KFSSR had existed as a Union Republic in 1991 it would have had the right to secede and form a separate state or unify with an independent Finland.

In the current Russian Federation, "Free Karelia" is a regionalist movement based on multi-ethnic principles that stresses decentralization and local self-government.[70] It also seeks to develop ties with other Russian and European regions. It has criticized Russia's centralized system that inhibits Karelia's development, appropriates its resources, and appoints its government. Karelia is the only non-Russian Republic in which the language of the titular nationality is not the official state language. Lack of such status generates resentment among Karels who view this as blatant discrimination, russification, and assimilation. Karelians have also written their language in the Latin script since the late 1980s, thus facilitating relations with Finland, which Moscow strenuously seeks to prevent.

---

[70] http://www.free-karelia.org/eng/About.aspx.

The Kremlin fears the development of a united front among Finno-Ugric nations and closer links with Finland and Estonia in particular. One of its methods is to twist history by depicting Finns as aggressors who committed genocide against Slavic Russians during World War II.[71] The goal has been to mobilize Russians against any expressions of regionalism and independence in the republics of Karelia, Komi, Mordovia, Mari El, and Udmurtia. According to the "Free Karelia" movement, Russia's centralized system has collapsed in the past and can do so again. The organizers only agree for Karelia to remain part of the Russian state if it is reformed into a genuinely democratic federation. Otherwise, "Free Karelia" considers itself as a legitimate body to initiate a republican referendum and transform Karelia into an independent state or to join Finland.[72]

During the Civil War in the collapsing Tsarist empire, Finnish activists established a Republic of North Ingria in the southern section of the Karelian Isthmus, in what are currently the Priozersky *Raion* and Vyborgsky *Raion* of Leningrad *Oblast*. The overall aim was to incorporate the territory within Finland, which itself had proclaimed independence from Russia in 1917. The Ingrian initiative lasted for less than a year, between 1919 and 1920, before the region was forcefully incorporated into the Russian Soviet Republic (RSR)—renamed in 1922 as the Russian Soviet Federated Socialist Republic (RSFSR), within the USSR. In the post-Soviet era, Ingermanland regionalists have supported the merger of St. Petersburg and Leningrad *Oblast* into a single federal subject with the status of a

---

[71] Paul Goble, "Moscow's Playing Up of Finnish Camps in Karelia about More than Distracting Attention from Stalin's Far Larger GULAG There," August 24, 2021, http://windowoneurasia2.blogspot.com/2021/08/moscows-playing-up-of-finnish-camps-in.html.

[72] Alexander Podrabinek, "Russian Separatism: The Hotbeds of Tension," August 29, 2014, https://imrussia.org/en/analysis/politics/797-russian-separatism-the-hotbeds-of-tension.

republic under the historical name of Ingria (Ingermanland).[73] Some activists have revived calls for an independent Ingria as the fourth Baltic republic if Moscow does not allow for genuine federalism and would include St. Petersburg as the capital.[74] In September 2021, Ingrian activists opened an Ingria House in the nearby Estonian city of Narva.[75] They launched a regular "Ingria Without Borders" podcast and with the support of local authorities pledged to disseminate information and host meetings on Ingermanland and its aspirations.

A number of independent principalities existed in what is now northwestern Russia before Moscow emerged as an expansionist regional power in the 14th century. These included Novgorod, Vladimir-Suzdal, Tver, Ryazan, Vologda and Pskov. Each of these regions are *oblasts* in the current federation. The rediscovery of pre-imperial local histories can become a source of inspiration for new movements pushing for autonomy and self-determination. In particular, the history of the Novgorod Republic remains a serious challenge to Muscovite imperialism and is gaining more attention in parts of northwest Russia. This medieval East Slavic state existed from the 12th to 15th centuries between the Gulf of Finland and the Ural Mountains and contained much of modern-day northern Russia. Novgorod was a thriving trading center with democratic traditions and a strong sense of identity, before it was defeated in battle and annexed by Moscow in 1478. Alexander Nevsky, the prince of

---

[73] "Чего хотят ингерманландские регионалисты?" July 29, 2021, https://www.trtrussian.com/mnenie/chego-hotyat-ingermanlandskie-regionalisty-6178367.

[74] Peter Eltsov, *The Long Telegram 2.0: A Neo-Kennanite Approach to Russia*, Lanham: Lexington Books, 2020, p.142, and Pavel Mezerin, "9 июля – День Независимости Ингерманландии," July 9, 2021, https://region.expert/ingria102/.

[75] "В Нарве открылся Дом Ингрии," September 7, 2021, http://region.expert/ingria-house/.

Novgorod and Grand Prince of Kyivan Rus, and one of the mythified figures of "Russian" history, fought for Novgorod not Muscovite Russia during battles with Swedish and German invaders in the 13th century.[76]

During the collapse of the Tsarist empire, regionalist movements sprung up in Russia's northwest but were suppressed by the Bolsheviks. Since the demise of the Soviet Union, local activists have delved into regional history and rediscovered their non-Muscovite roots. The traditions of the Novgorod Republic undermine the Kremlin narrative that Russians need a statist authoritarian system because they are incapable of democratic self-government. References to the former state are, therefore, routinely denounced by pro-regime apologists as "Novgorod separatism."[77] A revival of political activism in Pskov *Oblast*, next to the Latvian and Estonian borders, also cannot be discounted. It could call upon the historical precedent of the Pskov Republic, which became independent from the Novgorod Republic in the 14th century, until its conquest by the expanding Muscovite empire in the early 16th century. Activists in Vologda *Oblast* could similarly rekindle claims to sovereignty based on the region's history before absorption by Muscovy in the 14th century. In May 1993, the local authorities declared a Vologda Republic but were rebuked by the Kremlin.[78]

---

[76] Peter Eltsov, *The Long Telegram 2.0: A Neo-Kennanite Approach to Russia*, Lanham: Lexington Books, 2020, p.70.

[77] "Реаниматоры новгородского сепаратизма против первого русского базилевса Иоанна Третьего!" February 19, 2021, https://materik.ru/analitika/reanimatory-novgorodskogo-separatiz/.

[78] Vladimir Shlapentokh, Roman Levita, and Mikhail Loiberg, *From Submission to Rebellion: The Provinces Versus the Center in Russia*, Westview Press, 1997, p.109.

Kaliningrad

The final status of Kaliningrad *Oblast*, on the eastern Baltic coast, remains undetermined and contestable. It is Russia's only exclave territory and is wedged between two NATO and EU countries, Poland and Lithuania, with its own coastline. Its geographical position and isolation from the rest of Russia are positive factors that would help facilitate and encourage secession and statehood. Despite their *de facto* control of the *oblast*, the Soviet Union and the Russian Federation have never held a *de jure* title to its final status through a peace treaty.[79] Under the Potsdam Agreement between the Allied powers in April 1946, the region was stripped from Germany and incorporated into the Russian Soviet Federated Socialist Republic (RSFSR), a constituent republic of the USSR. However, the Allies decided that the area would not be immediately legally transferred to the Soviet Union but simply placed under its administration pending a final peace treaty. The creation of two German states—the Federal Republic of Germany and the German Democratic Republic (West and East Germany, respectively) after World War II—precluded the signing of the peace treaty until 1990. The Final Settlement was signed in September 1990, paving the way for German unification. However, questions about the legal status of Kaliningrad were not resolved, as rights to the territory were not transferred either to the Russian Federation or the Soviet Union, which dissolved a year later. The region's annexation by Russia has not been made explicit in any legally binding document, because "administration" does not equal "annexation" under international law.

In 1993, several political leaders in Kaliningrad *Oblast* tried to obtain the status of an autonomous republic but were thwarted by Moscow.

---

[79] Raymond A. Smith, "The Status of the Kaliningrad Oblast Under International Law," *Lithuanian Quarterly Journal of Arts and Sciences*, Vol. 38, No.1, Spring 1992, http://lituanus.org/1992_1/92_1_02.htm.

In the 1990s, the Baltic Republican Party legally existed, seeking to transform Kaliningrad *Oblast* into a fully independent Baltic republic. The party was subsequently suppressed, but when Russia's economic problems escalate and frustrations mount, its support for statehood and liberation from Kremlin imperialism can be quickly revived.[80] Many local residents have visited neighboring European Union states and can readily compare political freedoms and economic opportunities in Poland and Lithuania with repressive and stagnant conditions inside Russia. Kaliningrad retains a significant potential for protests provoked by Kremlin policies, as was evident in January 2010 when over 12,000 people participated in a "march of dissent" in the capital city.[81] A mass popular movement in 2009–2010 precipitated the removal of the unpopular governor, Georgy Boos, who was not reappointed to a second term by the Kremlin.[82] The protests indicated that sustained and extensive pressure on the regime can yield results without necessarily precipitating mass repression. The movement suffered from a lack of organization and, after the removal of Boos, the regime focused on dividing the campaign and coopting or discrediting its leaders in its customary subversive fashion.

The protests were sparked by a confluence of factors, including the termination of Kaliningrad's special economic status that promoted business, travel, and exchanges with neighboring EU states, the imposition of tighter political and economic controls by Moscow, and

---

[80] Mikhail Feldman, "БРП: история с продолжением," November 19, 2020, http://region.expert/brp-2/ and "Янтарный край – Балтийская Республика или заложник кремлевской империи?" July 8, 2021, http://region.expert/baltic_republic/.

[81] *The Territories of the Russian Federation 2020,* London: Routledge, 2020, p.107.

[82] Karine Clément, "From 'Local' to 'Political': The Kalininigrad Mass Protest Movement of 2009-2010 in Russia," in Kerstin Jacobsson (Ed.) *Urban Grassroots Movements in Central and Eastern Europe,* Routledge, 2015, pp.163–193.

the global financial crisis of 2008, which severely impacted on the *oblast*. During the 1990s, the exclave was considered a pilot project in the EU's program of regional integration, and its residents traveled abroad without visas. But under Putin, the region was turned into a military base to confront NATO, and the rights of local residents were drastically limited. Additionally, Boos was viewed as an outsider imposed by the Kremlin to exploit the region's resources for Moscow's benefit while stifling the *oblast's* economic development.

Several incidents in Kaliningrad have dented Moscow's depiction of the region as a loyal Russian territory. In March 2021, security agencies arrested a Kaliningrad citizen on terrorism charges after he was detained allegedly in possession of materials for constructing a bomb and literature attacking "Russia's organs of executive and legislative power," while actively recruiting accomplices.[83] Russian nationalists have also complained that the political elites in Kaliningrad are enabling the region's Germanization by promoting German culture, education and tourism.[84] Such initiatives purportedly provide a wedge for NATO inroads to gradually detach Kaliningrad from Russia. Officials in Moscow have demonstrated that they share such concerns and are prepared to replace the *oblast* leaders with stricter loyalists.

A pro-Western Belarus would also challenge Moscow's control over Kaliningrad.[85] The only land routes from Russia to the exclave of

---

[83] "ФСБ задержала россиянина за подготовку теракта "из ненависти к власти," March 4, 2021, https://www.mk.ru/incident/2021/03/04/fsb-zaderzhala-nenavidyashhego-vlast-rossiyanina-za-podgotovku-terakta.html.

[84] Paul Goble, "Kaliningrad Elites Selling Out Russia for German Money, Shulgin Says, June 24, 2021, http://windowoneurasia2.blogspot.com/2021/06/kaliningrad-elites-selling-out-russia.html.

[85] Paul Goble, "Kaliningrad is Why Moscow Must Control Minsk, Russian Commentator Says," September 1, 2020, https://windowoneurasia2.blogspot.com/

Kaliningrad traverse either Latvia and Lithuania, both NATO members, or through Belarus and Lithuania or across Belarus and Poland, also a NATO member. The exclave can be supplied by sea and by air, but moving heavy weapons and materiel by those routes is both expensive and time consuming. If Minsk were to veer away from its Russia orbit, Moscow's links with Kaliningrad would weaken, and this could reactivate the region's autonomist movement.

Crimea

Crimea was illegally seized by Moscow in February 2014 with limited Ukrainian military resistance and declared a republic within the Russian Federation. Moscow employed its special forces, disguised military personnel, and pro-Moscow local proxies to capture the peninsula. Then it staged a fraudulent referendum on Crimea's incorporation into Russia in March 2014. The occupation regime banned all political opposition and ethnic-based organizations, including the Mejlis, the executive representative body of the Crimean Tatars, as "extremist organizations." Russian officials claimed that the Mejlis maintained links with Ukrainian intelligence services and engaged in sabotaging natural gas pipelines and organizing protests against the proxy Crimean government.

Since Crimea's occupation by Russian forces, over 10,000 Tatars have been forced to flee their homeland and hundreds of people suffered various abuses at the hands of Moscow's implanted authorities, including beatings, arbitrary arrests, and falsified convictions on

---

2020/09/kaliningrad-is-why-moscow-must-control.html, and Sergey Sukhankin, *The Belarus Factor in Kaliningrad's Security Lifeline to Russia*, January 29, 2021, https://jamestown.org/program/the-belarus-factor-in-kaliningrads-security-lifeline-to-russia/

terrorism charges.[86] Human rights groups have criticized Moscow and its local surrogates for locking up dozens of Crimean activists as religious extremists. Crimean Tatars have also complained that much of their land has been confiscated by the new pro-Moscow administration.[87] The local authorities also banned "foreigners," including Ukrainians, from owning land by applying Russian laws in Ukrainian territory.

Resistance to Moscow's rule has continued on the peninsula and will strengthen as Russia weakens and is distracted by multiple internal crises. In January 2021, three Crimean Tatars were sentenced to lengthy prison terms on charges of membership of a banned Islamist group plotting to seize power on the peninsula.[88] They were found guilty of membership in Hizb ut-Tahrir, an Islamist group that is designated as terrorist and banned in Russia but is legal in Ukraine. This follows a pattern of arrests and imprisonment for opponents of the Russian occupation, which the Ukrainian authorities have consistently condemned as politically motivated. In August 2021, Russia's Southern District Military Court sentenced four men in Crimea to prison on charges of participating in a cell of Hizb ut-Tahrir.[89] They were accused of organizing activities in the city of Alush, engaging in propaganda, recruiting locals, and conducting meetings. As with other occupied territories, information about the

---

[86] https://unpo.org/related/news/7871.

[87] Ivan Zhilin and Arden Arkman, "Крым их," March 20, 2021, https://novayagazeta.ru/articles/2021/03/20/krym-ikh.

[88] "Russian Court Jails Three Crimean Tatars On Extremism Charges," January 12, 2021, https://www.rferl.org/a/russian-court-jails-three-crimean-tatars-on-extremism-charges/31043360.html.

[89] "Russian Court Sentences Four Men on Extremism Charges in Crimea, "*RIA Novosti*, Moscow, August 16, 2021, BBC Monitoring.

extent of human rights abuses and of local resistance is tightly censored by Moscow and its local proxies.

Inner Russia

Inner European Russia has not been immune from regionalist, autonomist, and even separatist movements. Several waves of regionalism have swept across inner Russia since the 19th century, in which local identities were resurrected, pre-Mongol and pre-Muscovite history rediscovered, and support for decentralization and federalism revived.[90] Localism and regionalism have mushroomed throughout Europe in recent years, and such aspirations are likely to spread to the core of the Russian imperial state and fortify regional opposition to authoritarian centralism. If outlying republics and regions move toward secession, regions in inner Russia may be motivated to pursue their own autonomy and sovereignty.

In inner Russia, various post-Soviet autonomy initiatives have included the declaration of a Voronezh Republic in Voronezh *Oblast*, the Leningrad Republic in Leningrad *Oblast*, the Neva Republic in the city of St. Petersburg, and the Central Russian Republic formed from 11 *oblasts* and centered in Oryol *Oblast*.[91] Autonomous Cossack movements also mushroomed after the Soviet rupture, demanding the formation of special military units and, in some cases, comprehensive territorial autonomy. Don Cossacks pushed for a sovereign republic within the Russian Federation. In the North Caucasus, three Cossack republics were proclaimed in the Karachai-

---

[90] Susan Smith-Peter, "The Six Waves of Russian Regionalism in European Context, 1830-2000," in Edith W. Clowes, Gisela Ersblöh and Ani Kokobobo, *Russia's Regional Identities: The Power of the Provinces*, 2020, pp. 15–43.

Cherkess Autonomous *Oblast* prior to its elevation to the status of a republic—Batalapashinsk, Abazin and Zelenchuk-Urup.[92]

The Kremlin fears a Belarus-like mass protest scenario during regularly defrauded elections in various parts of Russia, especially in Moscow and St. Petersburg.[93] The large-scale falsification of ballot results can prove provocative and bring to the forefront new charismatic leaders. In addition, the extensive use of force against protesters may not ultimately work, and the Kremlin is keeping a close eye on longer-term post-election developments in Belarus as an experiment in social control. A nightmare scenario for the Kremlin would unfold if protests in various major cities in inner Russia coalesce and help spark rallies in numerous regional capitals, with Moscow increasingly viewed as an oppressor even in Moscow *Oblast*.[94] The Kremlin exploits the notion that any regional protests are "anti-Moscow" in order to stir resentments in the capital against the protesters and thereby dismiss their demands as unwarranted. However, such messages may ultimately have the reverse effect by focusing on the capital as the source of the country's deepening and multiplying crises.

---

[92] Vladimir Shlapentokh, Roman Levita, and Mikhail Loiberg, *From Submission to Rebellion: The Provinces Versus the Center in Russia*, Westview Press, 1997, p.113.

[93] Paul Goble, "Belarus-Induced Fears Not Pandemic Driving Kremlin to Criminalize Politics, Davydov Says," December 24, 2020, http://windowoneurasia2.blogspot.com/2020/12/belarus-induced-fears-not-pandemic.html.

[94] "Москва нам не враг!," August 7, 2020, https://www.gumilev-center.ru/moskva-na-ne-vrag/.

Urals

The Urals region, stretching from the Arctic to Central Asia, has long experienced regionalist movements seeking genuine autonomy or even a separate republic. During the Russian Civil Wars, in 1916–1926, a regionalist government operated in the Urals and opposed Bolshevik rule. In July 1993, following the collapse of the Soviet Union, the Regional Council of the city of Yekaterinburg, the administrative center of Sverdlovsk *Oblast* in the Urals, announced the establishment of a Urals Republic with its own government, constitution and currency.[95] Local politicians understood sovereignty as ensuring their constitutional equality vis-à-vis the ethnic republics and as a net benefit for economic development by helping to realize the region's capacities.[96] They aired various economic grievances against the federal center and sought control over natural resources, a free economic zone, reduced taxation, and an independent foreign economic policy. The Urals Republic began as an initiative to reorganize the federation with equal status for all subjects and to strengthen a pan-Russian identity, but it evolved into a regional sovereignty movement. Opponents of the movement viewed it as a threat to the integrity of the Russian Federation.[97]

The idea of sovereignty if not secession from Russia after the Soviet collapse became highly popular in Sverdlovsk *Oblast*, and many residents believed that the Urals possessed sufficient natural resources

---

[95] Peter Eltsov, *The Long Telegram 2.0: A Neo-Kennanite Approach to Russia*, Lanham: Lexington Books, 2020, pp.123–124.

[96] Yoshiko M. Herrera, *Imagined Economies: The Sources of Russian Regionalism*, Cambridge University Press, 2007, p.203.

[97] Yoshiko M. Herrera, *Imagined Economies: The Sources of Russian Regionalism*, Cambridge University Press, 2007, pp.212–213.

and industry to sustain significant autonomy and even independence.[98] In a referendum held in April 1993, 84 percent of the population of Sverdlovsk supported the creation of the Urals Republic.[99] Five other regions in the Urals worked together with the Sverdlovsk leadership to form this autonomous entity and asserted that the region had a sufficient economic base.[100] The Sverdlovsk *Oblast* council (*soviet)* adopted a constitution for the Urals Republic in October 1993, but the initiative was obstructed by Moscow. In November 1993, then-President Yeltsin dissolved the council and fired the head of its administration, Eduard Rossel.

Despite Yeltsin's moves, Rossel remained widely popular locally and served as the governor of Sverdlovsk *Oblast* between 1991 and 2009. Rossel also formed a movement called Transformation of Russia based on the notion that only the empowerment of regions could ensure national progress.[101] Even though Yekaterinburg voiced no immediate plans for secession, its brazen political activism shocked Moscow, which feared similar initiatives elsewhere in the federation. In Chelyabinsk *Oblast,* some activists also called for the creation of a Southern Urals Republic. Such initiatives indicated that some regional administrations resented the federal asymmetry in which ethnic

---

[98] Mark Lipovetsky, "The Strange Case of a Regional Cultural Revolution," in Edith W. Clowes, Gisela Ersblöh and Ani Kokobobo, *Russia's Regional Identities: The Power of the Provinces,* 2020, p.146.

[99] Cameron Ross, *Federalism and Democratization in Russia,* Manchester University Press, 2002, p.24.

[100] Susan Smith-Peter, "The Six Waves of Russian Regionalism in European Context, 1830-2000," in Edith W. Clowes, Gisela Ersblöh and Ani Kokobobo, *Russia's Regional Identities: The Power of the Provinces,* 2020, p.30.

[101] Vladimir Shlapentokh, Roman Levita, and Mikhail Loiberg, *From Submission to Rebellion: The Provinces Versus the Center in Russia,* Westview Press, 1997, p.154.

republics were able to extract more concessions from Moscow than *krais* or *oblasts*.

The Russian Federation has also confronted sub-regional, district, or even city separatism, where residents demand that their city join a different federal unit. For instance, the city of Chaykovsky, established in 1955 to support the development of a hydro-electric dam, has petitioned to leave Perm *Krai* and join the Udmurt Republic, where they have more trust in the local authorities and with which they already have better transportation links.[102] In the USSR, borders between Union Republics were changed nearly 200 times and those between regions or Autonomous Republics were shifted even more frequently due to demographic, political, or economic calculations. Paradoxically, Kremlin support for the amalgamation of some federal units could increase local demands for potentially advantageous border adjustments, territorial exchanges, or even federal mergers that are not favored by Moscow, especially where this strengthens non-Russian national republics such as Udmurtia.

Citizens' actions over concrete local issues have also been evident in the Urals region. Protests against state policy have taken place in Yekaterinburg on several occasions regarding plans to build an Orthodox cathedral in the center of the city and eliminate a popular park.[103] Similar protests have occurred in the city of Irkutsk, the administrative center of Irkutsk *Oblast* in southern Siberia, over building plans by the Orthodox Church without any public

---

[102] Paul Goble, "Chaykovsky Residents Want Their City to be Part of Udmurtia Not as Now in Perm Kray," November 26, 2020, http://windowoneurasia2.blogspot.com/2020/11/chaykovsky-residents-want-their-city-to.html.

[103] Matthew Luxmoore, "Russian Officials Suspend Controversial Church Plan As Putin Suggests Polling Public," May 16, 2019, https://www.rferl.org/a/yekaterinburg-church-protest-putin-suggests-poll-update/29944742.html.

consultations.[104] In Yekaterinburg, thousands of demonstrators drew support from various parts of Russia, and officials eventually temporarily halted construction after Putin asserted that residents should be consulted. Activists complained that the park was one of the few green recreation spaces left in the city and wanted the Orthodox cathedral to be moved elsewhere. The Yekaterinburg and Irkutsk protests illustrated that the public can be mobilized in opposition to state policy and that the Orthodox hierarchy does not possess the unassailable social authority that it claims.

High North

The "numerically small peoples" of Russia's European High North and of northern and eastern Siberia were conquered through often ruthless colonization campaigns during Tsarist times.[105] Until the collapse of the Soviet Union in 1990, these societies had few opportunities to assert native rights to their land and to pursue their traditional occupations. Under Communist social engineering, they were forcibly sedentarized, collectivized and deprived of genuinely autonomous institutions, with no freedom of speech, assembly, or information. Since the Soviet demise, local activists have demanded genuine autonomy in order for their distinct communities to survive, including the designation of certain territories for their exclusive use and the exclusion of industrial enterprises and central state bodies that destroy their land and livelihoods. Some have even called for the

---

[104] Shpak Klim, "Привет Екатеринбургу!": Жители Иркутска выступают против храма на месте сквера," August 25, 2021, sobesednik.ru/obshchestvo/20210825-privet-ekaterinburgu-ziteli-irkutska.

[105] James Forsyth, *A History of the Peoples of Siberia: Russia's North Asian Colony, 1581–1990*, Cambridge University Press, 1992, pp.28-47.

creation of "reservations" modeled on the US system, with tribal self-government and land ownership.[106]

Several efforts were made to form distinct republics in the High North shortly after the creation of the Russian Federation in 1991 but were ignored or subdued by Moscow.[107] These included the Pomor Republic in Arkhangelsk *Oblast* and the Nenets Republic in the Nenets Autonomous *Okrug*. In March 1994, then-President Yeltsin suspended a resolution by the Nenets government to hold a referendum on the formation of a distinct Nenets Republic.[108] A 1999 law "On the guarantees of the rights of indigenous small-numbered peoples of the Russian Federation" confirmed indigenous status on ethnic group not exceeding 50,000 people. Members of 46 officially acknowledged groups were entitled to earlier retirement, preferential access to natural resources, and the right to alternative military service. However, authentic self-government and local control of resources were disallowed even for the larger nationalities.

The Nenets (or Samoyeds) are the most numerous of all legally designated "numerically small" indigenous peoples of northern Russia, estimated at about 44,000 in the 2010 census and with a growing percentage moving from traditional occupations in rural areas into various urban jobs. They have also established organizations, such as the Yasavey Association, to promote Nenets culture, language and traditions. By obtaining the status of a federal

---

[106] James Forsyth, *A History of the Peoples of Siberia: Russia's North Asian Colony, 1581-1990*, Cambridge University Press, 1992, p.416.

[107] Vladimir Shlapentokh and Joshua Woods, *Contemporary Russia as a Feudal Society: A New Perspective on the Post-Soviet Era*, 2007, New York, Springer. p. 105–106.

[108] *The Territories of the Russian Federation 2020*, London: Routledge, 2020, p. 120.

subject, the national *okrugs* inhabited by indigenous groups such as the Nenets can maintain direct official connection with the federal government, control a regional budget, and are represented in federal legislative bodies. All these advantages disappear once Moscow decides to merge national *okrugs* with another federal subject. Ethnic groups interpret such absorption as a loss of status and distinct identity; this sparked protests in several previously merged *okrugs* during the 2000s.[109]

Protests have also taken place over Moscow's unilateral appointments of regional governors, as evident in the Khanty-Mansi Autonomous *Okrug*–Yugra in February 2010. In ethnic republics and autonomous districts, the federal government is increasingly perceived as arrogant and dismissive of local concerns. For instance, protests in Shiyes in Arkhangelsk *Oblast* and in the Komi Republic during 2020 illustrated that far more was at stake than simply blocking the building of a trash dump for waste from Moscow. They highlighted a loss of trust in the central and local authorities. Demonstrators did not believe that officials would abide by pledges that the dump would be cleaned despite sustained local opposition.[110] They remained on the site to monitor the company responsible for cleaning up any damage. Although the police eventually arrested a number of protesters and closed their encampment, opposition to the government will become more widespread if it fails to fully clean up the Shiyes site and follows through on plans to open new trash dumps in the region. The

---

[109] Petr Oskolkov, "Merging Russia's Autonomous Entities: Ethnic Aspect," June 15, 2020, International Center for Ethnic and Linguistic Diversity Studies, Prague, Czech Republic, https://www.icelds.org/2020/06/15/merging-russias-autonomous-entities-ethnic-aspect/.

[110] Paul Goble, "Shiyes Protesters Refuse to Leave Until Area of Planned Dump for Moscow Trash Fully Restored," December 21, 2020, http://windowoneurasia2.blogspot.com/2020/12/shiyes-protesters-refuse-to-leave-until.html.

persistent rallies attracted people from across Russia in solidarity with the demonstrators.[111] They also sparked an initiative for free elections in parts of the High North and the creation of authentic social movements, such as the New Republic in the Komi Republic.[112]

By promoting the development of the city of Murmansk, in Murmansk *Oblast*, on the Kola Peninsula, at the expense of the rest of the High North, Moscow can provoke new protests in this extensive region.[113] In August 2020, Deputy Prime Minister Yury Trutnyev announced the creation of a Foundation for the Development of the Arctic, to be funded by tax revenues from government-supported Arctic projects. He wanted all the money earmarked for the development of Murmansk as an ice-free port with nothing left over for the rest of the region. The plan could also indicate that Moscow is creating an Arctic Federal *Oblast* or Northern *Krai* that will remove the last vestiges of decision-making from the federal subjects along the Arctic coast. This will generate fresh tensions between officials and residents.

Environmental degradation and restricted land use are propelling indigenous alienation from Moscow. Russia's High North contains

---

[111] Paul Goble, "Shiyes Protesters' Victories Affecting Entire Region," November 2, 2020, http://windowoneurasia2.blogspot.com/2020/11/shiyes-protesters-victories-affecting.html.

[112] Sofia Bogatkina, "Сам ты ошибка!» В Коми активист вышел на пикет после высказывания спикера Госдумы о национальных республиках," November 11, 2021, https://7x7-journal.ru/news/2021/11/11/sam-ty-oshibka-v-komi-aktivist-vyshel-na-piket-posle-vyskazyvaniya-spikera-gosdumy-o-nacionalnyh-respublikah.

[113] Paul Goble, "Moscow's Failures to Consider All Sides of Issues Mean Arctic Likely to Become Another Khabarovsk, Stanulevich Says," August 10, 2020, https://windowoneurasia2.blogspot.com/2020/08/moscows-failures-to-consider-all-sides.html.

some 85 percent of the country's gas deposits and 15 percent of its oil reserves, and the extensive exploitation of these resources without consultation with indigenous inhabitants has destroyed their hunting, trapping, fishing, and pasture lands and threatened their traditional way of life. Although a 1992 presidential decree promised "clan-based communities" preferential rights to drilling and logging licenses, in practice these measures were not implemented.[114] Laws are frequently ignored, and residents of remote communities do not have the power or resources to demand the enforcement of their distinct interests. Although indigenous leaders have asserted rights to land and resources, the question of land ownership has been neglected. Russian law emphasizes rights to use lands for "traditional activities," but it does not allow for unrestricted ownership by indigenous peoples.[115] Disputes have persisted between natives and Russian companies in dozens of locations that affect reindeer pastures, fishing locations, ancestral burial grounds, and sacred religious sites. For instance, the Nenets have experienced regular confrontations with *Gazprom* and Norilsk Nickel over the disruption of their livelihoods.[116] Khanti native rights groups have also campaigned to keep the energy industry out of the few remaining unspoiled sections of their traditional lands.[117]

---

[114] Anna Reid, *The Shaman's Coat: A Native History of Siberia*, New York: Walker and Company, 2002, p.195.

[115] Gail Osherenko, "Indigenous Rights in Russia: Is Title to Land Essential for Cultural Survival?" *Georgetown International Environmental Law Review*, April 2001, https://web.archive.org/web/20110511104207/http://www.allbusiness.com/legal/international-law/1112279-1.html.

[116] Marlene Laruelle, *Russia's Arctic Strategies and the Future of the Far North*, London: Routledge, 2014, p.38.

[117] Anna Reid, *The Shaman's Coat: A Native History of Siberia*, New York: Walker and Company, 2002, p.54.

In November 2012, the central government suspended the work of the Russian Association of Indigenous Peoples of the North (RAIPON), which was founded in 1990 to represent 42 indigenous groups and gained permanent membership in the multi-national Arctic Council.[118] Due to governmental neglect, dilapidated infrastructure, and shrinking spending on social services, unemployment and poverty levels among indigenous populations have worsened. Unemployment is almost twice that of the general Russian population, and incomes are two to three times lower.[119] Inadequate health care contributes to high infant mortality, life expectancy below the national average, and numerous ailments, including tuberculosis, viral hepatitis, intestinal infections, and upper respiratory infections. The Kremlin has also waged a campaign to undermine indigenous cultures by introducing laws to weaken language use and increase state control over orthography. Such assimilationist maneuvers are backfiring against Moscow and stiffening local resistance, as the younger generation rediscovers their heritage and traditions.

The outflow of ethnic Russians from the High North in recent decades has strengthened the sense of local and regional patriotism among indigenous nations and descendants of original Russian settlers. It has also nurtured a greater sense of collective identity in the towns and cities to which they have gravitated.[120] Over half of the "historically indigenous" people in the High North and Siberia are estimated to live

---

[118] "RAIPON's Suspension: Just or Just Opportune?" *Cultural Survival*, December 8, 2012, https://www.culturalsurvival.org/news/raipons-suspension-just-or-just-opportune.

[119] Who are the Indigenous Peoples of Russia?" *Cultural Survival*, February 19, 2014, https://www.culturalsurvival.org/news/who-are-indigenous-peoples-russia.

[120] Nikolay Petrov, "Depopulation of Russia's Asian North and Local Political Development," in Marlene Laruelle (Ed.), *New Mobilities and Social Changes in Russia's Arctic Regions*, London: Routledge, 2017, p.16.

in cities. Their numbers are supplemented by the "historically rooted" peoples, or descendants of early Russian and other settlers.[121] In an indication of growing anxiety, Russian nationalists claim that outside powers are planning to exploit divisions between indigenous communities and ethnic Russians in Siberia and the High North.[122] However, what they most fear is closer cooperation between the two communities in pursuit of regional self-determination.

As Russia's internal turmoil deepens, leaders among the northern peoples will look more closely at the Canadian model of autonomy as exemplified by the territory of Nunavut and among other Inuit populations across northern Canada. However, Canada is a genuine democracy that allows for political devolution and local autonomy. Without such prospects in an authoritarian Russia, the only alternative would be moves toward independence. The progress of Greenland toward statehood and independence from Denmark will also be closely monitored in Russia's High North, Siberia, and the northern Pacific regions.

Siberia

Residents of Siberia are traditionally known for their more independent spirit than the rest of imperial Russia, as they did not experience serfdom and the region was renowned for its religious diversity, in which several dissenting religious groups settled,

---

[121] Vera Kuklina and Natalia Krasnoshtanova, ""The Urbanization of Indigenous Peoples of Northeastern Siberia," in Marlene Laruelle (Ed.), *New Mobilities and Social Changes in Russia's Arctic Regions*, London: Routledge, 2017, pp.104, 105.

[122] Vladimir Stanulevich, "Спасти нельзя погубить: о коренных народах на Ямале, в НАО и Якутии, regnum.ru/news/society/3381878.html.

including Protestants.[123] Many settlers were escaping despotism and serfdom in European Muscovy. Regionalist intellectuals underscore the pioneering spirit of Siberians and the development of a distinct Siberian identity, comparing it with the state-building movements in the English colonies of North America, Canada, Australia, and New Zealand. Settlers from Ukraine and other parts of the Russian empire, together with Cossack mutineers, often disregarded the central government in St. Petersburg and viewed Siberia as a separate territory.[124]

Ethnic Ukrainians played a key role in the conquest and development of Siberia and the Pacific territories, and several "wedges" *(klinya)* of concentrated Ukrainian communities are recognized to this day. Ukrainian activists defined the large Ukrainian population in southern Siberia and the Pacific region as the "Green Wedge" or as Ukraine's Far Eastern colonies. In the Amur and Pacific Maritime regions, Ukrainians formed a rural majority and maintained their national identity and traditions. The 1989 Soviet census recorded about a third of the population of Tyumen *Oblast,* over 600,000, people as ethnic Ukrainians; and when the USSR expired in 1991, Kyiv opened a consulate there, and the community established a national cultural autonomy.[125]

---

[123] Paul Goble, "Siberia isn't Russia Even in Religious Terms -- and Moscow is Worried," October 30, 2020, http://windowoneurasia2.blogspot.com/2020/10/siberia-isnt-russia-even-in-religious.html.

[124] James Forsyth, *A History of the Peoples of Siberia: Russia's North Asian Colony, 1581-1990*, Cambridge University Press, 1992, p.199.

[125] Paul Goble, "Ukrainian 'Wedge' Regions East of Urals Declining in Size but Still Numerous," *Eurasia Review*, January 4, 2011, https://www.eurasiareview.com/04012022-ukrainian-wedge-regions-east-of-urals-declining-in-size-but-still-numerous-oped/.

Under Putin's dominion, the Ukrainian population in Russia has steadily decreased, through death, out-migration, assimilation and repression. The number stood at over 4.3 million in 1989 but fell to just under 2 million in the 2020 census. In the ongoing crackdown to constrict Ukrainian activism throughout the Russian Federation, in August 2020 authorities in Omsk *Oblast* disbanded the regional public organization "Siberian Center of Ukrainian Culture—Gray Wedge."[126] In 2010, the Federal National Cultural Autonomy of Ukrainians in Russia was liquidated, and in 2012, the Association of Ukrainians in Russia was prohibited. Nonetheless, the Ukrainian population has displayed resilience to russification and will rapidly revive when state repression is eased or ended. The full-scale Russian invasion of Ukraine in February 2022 will also have an impact on Ukrainian communities in Russia and could engender more pronounced opposition to the regime and actions in support of Kyiv and Ukraine's statehood.

Other nations are also becoming more active in Siberia. For instance, Siberian Tatars are increasingly outspoken in asserting their distinct identity and affirming pride in the existence of a Siberian khanate before the Tsarist conquest.[127] This is fanning fears among officials in Moscow that the Tatars could become one of the sparks for a broader Siberian independence movement. Several other native Siberian peoples resisted Russian conquest and colonization for prolonged periods, including the Buryats, Tuvans, Yakuts, Koryaks, and Chukchi. During the mass unrest in the 1905 revolution and the

---

[126] Petro Kraliuk, "Ukrainians of the Gray Wedge, why are the Russian Authorities at War with them?" *Ukrainian Echo*, September 29, 2020, www.homin.ca/news.php/news/22737/group/28.

[127] Paul Goble, "Moscow Increasingly Alarmed by 'Siberian Tatar Nationalism'," October 23, 2020, http://windowoneurasia2.blogspot.com/2020/10/moscow-increasingly-alarmed-by-siberian.html.

collapse of the Tsarist empire during World War I, political leaders in several indigenous national communities declared autonomy or full independence from Russia. These included Sakha-Yakut nationalists and an assortment of political groups who proclaimed Yakutia (the largest entity in Siberia) as an independent state in February 1918.[128] The Bolsheviks overthrew the Yakut government in July 1918 and imposed a Communist regime.

The Tungus Republic, or the Provisional Tungus Central National Government, existed between July 1924 and May 1925. Formed from eastern parts of Sakha-Yakutia and the Okhotsky *Raion* of Khabarovsk *Krai,* the republic declared separation from Soviet Russia and national independence.[129] In February 1918, an independent Altai Republic was declared in southern Siberia by various anti-Bolshevik groups and Altai Turkic nationalists; this entity lasted until 1921. Some activists also declared a Confederated Republic of Altai between 1917 and 1920, as a pan-Mongol construct. The Buryat Mongol population in southern Siberia retained much of its homeland during Tsarist and Soviet occupation and maintained a strong sense of pan-Mongol national identity. As Tsarism disintegrated, this group called for Buryat national autonomy within a single continuous territory along the Mongolian border. In June 1918, leaders of the Tuva nation also demanded independence or unification with Mongolia. The Bolsheviks turned Tuva into a puppet state that was fully annexed by the Soviet Union in 1944 as part of the RSFSR.

In addition to ethno-national movements, Siberian regionalism has traditionally been viewed as an anti-colonial struggle. It included the

---

[128] James Forsyth, *A History of the Peoples of Siberia: Russia's North Asian Colony, 1581-1990*, Cambridge University Press, 1992, pp.231–232.

[129] *P. E. Antonov, Тунгусское восстание: ошибок можно было избежать, Yakutsk: Ilin, 1995.*

Siberian patriot (*sibirskie patrioty*) and regionalist (*oblastnik*) movements in the 19th century that promoted local cultures, customs, dialects, and identities. Some local patriots argued that Siberia should have the right to secede from the Russian empire.[130] Even among non-separatists there was growing support for regional autonomy, led by a number of Russian authors.[131] In August 1905, the Siberian Regional Union was formed in Tomsk in South-Central Siberia, calling for a regional parliament with broad decision-making powers. Tomsk and Irkutsk became the major centers of these autonomist movements, and their leaders were arrested as separatists seeking to create a new country modeled on the United States of America.

Regional governments were formed during the post-Tsarist Civil War, between 1917 and 1922. Regionalist movements focused on decentralization and self-determination and envisioned the formation of two distinct regions—Western and Eastern Siberia.[132] A congress held in October 1917 passed the "Declaration on the Regional Status of Siberia," and new institutions of governance were formed.[133] In January 1918, the Tomsk-based Provisional Siberian Government was established and challenged Bolshevik rule not as a White Russian monarchist formation seeking to recreate the Russian empire but as a

---

[130] Susan Smith-Peter, "The Six Waves of Russian Regionalism in European Context, 1830-2000," in Edith W. Clowes, Gisela Ersblöh and Ani Kokobobo, *Russia's Regional Identities: The Power of the Provinces,* 2020, p.17.

[131] Vladimir Shlapentokh, Roman Levita, and Mikhail Loiberg, *From Submission to Rebellion: The Provinces Versus the Center in Russia,* Westview Press, 1997, pp.50–51.

[132] Ivan Sablin, *The Rise and Fall of Russia's Far Eastern Republic, 1905-1922: Nationalisms, Imperialisms, and Regionalisms In and After the Russian Empire,* Routledge, 2019, pp.40–41, 84.

[133] Peter Eltsov, *The Long Telegram 2.0: A Neo-Kennanite Approach to Russia,* Lanham: Lexington Books, 2020, p.123.

regionalist initiative for self-determination supported by socialists and liberals. The underlying goal was to establish the "Siberian Union of Free States." Another Siberian Republic was founded on July 4, 1918, and it lasted until November 1918. Some Russian intellectuals called either for Siberian territorial autonomy or the secession of Siberia from the Russian empire, just as the US colonies declared independence from the British empire in 1776. They argued that to be successful, Siberia also needed to free itself from the imperial metropolis and its colonial policies. Siberian autonomist movements included the Siberian Regional Council, established by the local intelligentsia, and the Union of Siberian Federalists created in December 1917 and calling for an autonomous "Great Siberia."[134]

When the Soviet Union imploded in the early 1990s, several ethnic republics in southern Siberia pushed for greater autonomy. The Khakass Autonomous *Oblast* declared sovereignty in July 1991 as an Autonomous Republic and adopted a republican constitution in May 1995. The Tuva Autonomous Republic declared sovereignty in December 1990, demanded the status of a Union Republic, and adopted its republican constitution in October 1993 with the right to secede from the Russian Federation. The Buryat Autonomous Republic declared sovereignty in October 1990, adopted the name Republic of Buryatia in 1992, and passed a republican constitution in March 1994. The independent pan-Mongolist Buryat-Mongol People's Party continued to operate throughout the 1990s. The Gorno-Altai *Oblast* was renamed as an Autonomous Republic in October 1990 and declared itself a distinct Union Republic of the Soviet Union in July 1991. However, it was only recognized by Moscow as the Altai Republic within the Russian Federation in March 1992. In northern Siberia, a separate Yakut-Sakha Republic outside of

---

[134] James Forsyth, *A History of the Peoples of Siberia: Russia's North Asian Colony, 1581-1990*, Cambridge University Press, 1992, pp.229, 231.

Russia was proclaimed in April 1990 and a new republican constitution was promulgated in April 1992.[135]

Regionalist and non-ethnic autonomist movement were also visible during the collapse of the Soviet Union at the end of the 1980s and early 1990s. Regionalists in Tomsk *Oblast* formulated a Constitution of the Tomsk Region, and a Party of Siberian Independence was established in the city.[136] In July 1993, the regional assembly in Amur *Oblast* unilaterally declared the territory a republic. Other initiatives included the Yenisei Republic in Irkutsk *Oblast*, the Siberian Republic in Novosibirsk *Oblast* and the Chukotka Republic, which was declared by the legislature in the Chukotka Autonomous *Okrug* in February 1991.[137] Regional activism was also pronounced in Chita *Oblast*, which was merged with the Agin-Buryat Autonomous *Okrug* in 2008 to form the Zabaykalsky *Krai*.[138] Regionalism remains strong in other territories, including Krasnoyarsk *Krai*, as manifested in substantial votes for those regional branches of the major federal parties that managed to maintain a degree of independence.[139] In August 2014, a planned "March for the Federalization of Siberia" in Novosibirsk, around the slogan of "Stop Feeding Moscow!" was forbidden by the local authorities; its organizers were arrested and all reporting on the

---

[135] *The Territories of the Russian Federation 2020*, London: Routledge, 2020, pp.260, 264, 286, 290.

[136] Vladimir Shlapentokh, Roman Levita, and Mikhail Loiberg, *From Submission to Rebellion: The Provinces Versus the Center in Russia*, Westview Press, 1997, p.108.

[137] *The Territories of the Russian Federation 2020*, London: Routledge, 2020, p.318.

[138] Yoshiko M. Herrera, *Imagined Economies: The Sources of Russian Regionalism*, Cambridge University Press, 2007, pp.34-35.

[139] Nikolay Petrov, "Depopulation of Russia's Asian North and Local Political Development," in Marlene Laruelle (Ed.), *New Mobilities and Social Changes in Russia's Arctic Regions*, London: Routledge, 2017, pp.24–25.

initiative was banned by Russia's state media watchdog *Roskomnadzor*.[140]

In an indication of Moscow's concern about the growth of regional self-identification, Siberian and other regional identities are omitted from the list of officially approved nationalities. The central government fears that allowing people to identify themselves as Siberians will further distance them from the Russian ethnos, just as the American and other independent national projects emerged during and after their separation from imperial Britain. The interest in regional history, culture, dialect, and identity continues to expand among residents, and a "Siberian consciousness" is visible and based on self-reliance, regional solidarity, and collective action.[141] Participation in ecological and other local movements helps to mobilize residents for specific causes, and this generates support for campaigns on a broader range of demands at local and region-wide levels, such as improved healthcare and education, lower energy costs, and genuine representation in local governments. In addition, over the generations, Russian settlers in Siberia, the High North, and the Pacific regions intermarried and assimilated with indigenous populations; in several cases, this resulted in the emergence of new national identities, including the Kamchadals in Kamchatka *Krai*, the

---

140 Alexander Podrabinek, "Russian Separatism: The Hotbeds of Tension," August 29, 2014, https://imrussia.org/en/analysis/politics/797-russian-separatism-the-hotbeds-of-tension.

141 Alla Anisimova and Olga Echevskaya, "Siberian Regional Identity: Self-Perception, Solidarity, or Political Claim?" in Edith W. Clowes, Gisela Ersblöh and Ani Kokobobo, *Russia's Regional Identities: The Power of the Provinces,* 2020, pp.189, 194, 196, 197.

Russkoustintsy in the Sakha Republic and the Gurany in Transbaikal *Krai*.[142]

Moscow has attempted to stymie the consolidation of Siberian identity with the active support of the Orthodox Church hierarchy. This campaign has included crackdowns on Protestant groups and other religions outside the four traditional faiths (Christian Orthodoxy, Islam, Buddhism and Judaism). Nonetheless, regional activists have encouraged residents to declare themselves as Siberians in each population census, and local linguists have promoted a distinct Siberian language based on regional dialects.[143] During economic downturns, the economic inequalities and political asymmetries between the center and the regions become starker and focus attention on the economic rights denied by Moscow. Simultaneously, residents perceive a growing colonizing attitude by the center toward Siberia that breeds widespread feelings of injustice and deprivation.[144]

Another factor that generates turmoil is that several Siberian cities have multiple power centers, and the elites have developed greater

---

[142] Paul Goble, "Russian Intermarriage with Indigenous Peoples of Siberia Gave Rise to New Nationalities," December 21, 2021, http://windowoneurasia2.blogspot.com/2021/12/russian-intermarriage-with-indigenous.html; "Какие народы в Азии и Сибири возникли на основе русских?," ZenYandex, December 5, 2021, zen.yandex.ru/media/centralasia/kakie-narody-v-azii-i-sibiri-voznikli-na-osnove-russkih-619c7889f169457c0e38a31c?&.

[143] Alla Anisimova and Olga Echevskaya, "Reading Post-Soviet Transformations of Siberian Identity through Biographical Narrative," *Region: Regional Studies of Russia, Eastern Europe, and Central Asia*, Vol.5, No.2, 2016, pp.127–148.

[144] Alla Anisimova and Olga Echevskaya, "Siberian Regional Identity: Self-Perception, Solidarity, or Political Claim?" in Edith W. Clowes, Gisela Ersblöh and Ani Kokobobo, *Russia's Regional Identities: The Power of the Provinces,* 2020, p.199.

maneuverability.[145] In cities with only a single center of power, the governor or mayor controls all aspects of life, and security forces act under their direction. In the majority of Siberian cities, where various oligarchic groups and diverse elites operate, the police forces are less prepared to be used by one group against another. In such a divided elite environment the population may feel more emboldened to demonstrate. As resources shrink, the loyalty of urban elite coalitions to the federal and regional center will be challenged, and they can encourage protest actions in local power struggles.

In the September 2020 local elections, Tomsk, the administrative center of Tomsk *Oblast*, was dubbed as "the new capital of the Russian opposition" after residents deprived United Russia of its majority in the city *duma*.[146] This gave citizens a sense of empowerment that could be manifest in greater activism against the Putin regime. Numerous grievances against Moscow are visible throughout Siberia. These include cuts in federal funding for the region, Moscow's mishandling of Chinese investments, the inability to control forest fires, floods, and other natural disasters with shrinking financial resources, and anxieties that Kremlin support for Arctic development will reduce financing for parts of Siberia and the Pacific regions.[147] Moscow has also lost much of its ability to use the China threat to keep Siberians

---

[145] Paul Goble, "Rising Number of Protests in Siberia Reflects Diversity of Power Centers among Elites in Many Cities There, Sociologist Says," February 16, 2021, http://windowoneurasia2.blogspot.com/2021/02/rising-number-of-protests-in-siberia.html.

[146] Paul Goble, "Tomsk Set to Become 'New Capital of Russian Opposition,' Polorotov Says," September 28, 2020, http://windowoneurasia2.blogspot.com/2020/09/tomsk-set-to-become-new-capital-of.html.

[147] Paul Goble, "Year 2020 in Review: Siberians Take Center Stage in Russia," *Eurasia Daily Monitor*, Vol.18, Issue 4, January 7, 2021, https://jamestown.org/program/year-2020-in-review-siberians-take-center-stage-in-russia/.

and Far Easterners in line. Paradoxically, the central government has allowed Chinese companies to operate in ways that have turned people against both Moscow and Beijing. Chinese firms despoil some areas by overcutting forests and Moscow profits from such schemes while preventing regional authorities from intervening.

The Republic of Sakha (Yakutia) has become a hub of regional opposition to Moscow. Since the unravelling of the Soviet Union, the republic has witnessed a cultural and national revival amidst growing tensions over Sakha's politically subservient position in the Russian Federation.[148] Sakha's governor, Aysen Nikolaev, a member of United Russia, proved unable to deliver an overwhelming vote for the July 1, 2020, constitutional amendments that allow Putin to serve two more presidential terms until 2036.[149] Of all federal subjects, Sakha cast the largest percentage of negative votes, recorded at 41 percent, although the total was undoubtedly much higher because of the systematic falsification of results. This was a major rebuke for the Kremlin.

In January 2021, the popular mayor of the capital Yakutsk, Sardana Avksentyeva, was reportedly hounded out of office by pressure from Moscow.[150] She had been elected in September 2018 as a non-partisan candidate and defeated the United Russia nominee loyal to Moscow by almost 9 percent. Avksentyeva publicly voted against the Kremlin's constitutional amendments to extend Putin's rule. The amendments also abolished direct elections for city mayors that Avksentyeva won

---

148 Eleanor Peers, "Soviet *Kul'tura* in Post-Soviet Identification: The Aesthetics of Ethnicity in Sakha (Yakuita)," in Joachim Otto Habeck (Ed.), *Lifestyle in Siberia and the Russian North,* Cambridge, UK: Open Book Publishers, 2019, pp.257–293.

149 Paul Gregory, "Why Putin Fears the Shaman's Exorcism," July 18, 2020, https://www.hoover.org/research/why-putin-fears-shamans-exorcism.

150 "The 'Last Free Mayor In Putin's Russia' Steps Down. The Question Is Why," January 13, 2021, https://www.rferl.org/a/yakutsk-mayor-health-ran-afoul-putin-russia-/31045218.html.

in 2018. To avoid potential mass protests similar to those in Khabarovsk in 2020, the authorities did not fabricate criminal charges against her or apply other repressive measures.

Massive wildfires in the Republic of Sakha during the summer of 2021 destroyed huge tracts of forest and contributed to the region's anger at Moscow. Heavy smoke from hundreds of wildfires raged across the region and blanketed dozens of cities, including Yakutsk, and prompted the authorities to declare a state of emergency. Wildfires burned in many regions of Siberia, but Sakha was the worst hit, with over four million hectares of forest affected. A combination of factors contributed to the catastrophe, including Sakha's fast-warming climate, a 150-year-record drought, high winds, and harmful forestry practices whereby regional authorities are not required to extinguish fires in "control zones" while allowing both legal and illegal logging. Local residents frustrated with inadequate government actions to fight the fires established an army of volunteers to help save hundreds of villages and other settlements from devastation.[151] Such self-help groups driven by regional patriotism can become the drivers for social action to gain genuine autonomy for Sakha. Russian state TV channels only offered selective coverage, evidently instructed not to fan the flames of anger against inadequate assistance from Moscow and the late response from the governor to a regional catastrophe. The state media also wanted to avoid publicizing and encouraging self-help initiatives by citizens that can evolve into campaigns for self-determination.

One newsworthy demonstration of opposition to Putin in Siberia has been the protest actions of a Sakha-Yakut shaman, Aleksandr Gabyshev. In May 2020, the authorities tried to silence him through

---

[151] Maksim Pakhomov and Sania Yusupova, "We're Suffering': The Volunteer Army Battling Siberia's Record-Breaking Wildfires," Radio Free Europe/ Radio Liberty, August 12, 2021, https://www.rferl.org/a/siberia-wildfires-russia/31407076.html.

incarceration in a psychiatric hospital. Gabyshev was stopped from completing his walk to Moscow to perform a ritual to purportedly remove Putin from office. He was prevented from delivering "Russia without Putin!" sermons to local people along his journey, and hundreds of his supporters were also detained. In January 2021, Gabyshev announced a third pilgrimage to reach Moscow from Sakha, this time on horseback and by car rather than on foot.[152] He was promptly seized by Russian police and reincarcerated in a psychiatric hospital. In October 2021, Amnesty International declared Gabyshev a political prisoner because he had been subjected to forced psychiatric treatment. Gabyshev's arrest prompted demonstrations in other republics where shamanism is widely practiced, including in the capital of the Buryat Republic Ulan-Ude in September 2019. Demonstrators also expressed anger at the conduct of recent mayoral elections in the city.[153]

In southern Siberia, the Tuva Republic has evolved into a hotbed of separatism. Between 1921 and 1944, Tuva was an independent state along the Mongolian border before being absorbed by the Soviet Union within the Russian Soviet Federated Socialist Republic. According to Russian journalists, in recent years the legal system in the republic has broken down, Russians and their language have been reduced to second-class status, and separatism is rising alongside

---

[152] Paul Goble, "Self-Proclaimed 'Warrior-Shaman' from Sakha Announces Plans for Third March on Moscow," January 15, 2021, http://windowoneurasia2.blogspot.com/2021/01/self-proclaimed-warrior-shaman-from.html.

[153] *The Territories of the Russian Federation 2020*, London: Routledge, 2020, p.287.

demands for the return of territory from neighboring regions.[154] The Russian population has dwindled from 32 percent in 1989 to about 16 percent in the 2010s, with the Tuvan majority standing at over 82 percent. Calls for separation resonated widely after the collapse of the USSR, and some nationalists have laid claim to territories in neighboring Krasnoyarsk *Krai,* Irkutsk *Oblast,* and Mongolia.[155] Nationalist sentiments have been intensified by declining economic conditions and resentment of Moscow's dominance. Waves of violence against Russians and the destruction of Russian-owned property were reported after the collapse of the USSR, and many Russians have since been reportedly coerced to leave the republic.[156] Tuva also faces a potential breakdown in governance, with local clans and organized crime groups in control of much of the republic.

Buryats had developed a strong political consciousness by the end of the 19th century, with a sizeable middle class that supported Siberian regionalism and even Buryat statehood.[157] Buryat aspirations toward autonomy were crushed by the Bolsheviks and throughout the Soviet interlude. However, greater inter-ethnic and inter-tribal unity has been evident in the republic in recent years in opposition to the regional authorities, who have also been attacked by Moscow for

---

[154] Paul Goble, "Russians Flee Tuva as Law Decays, Economy Collapses and Separatism Intensifies, Znak Journalist Says," March 3, 2021, http://windowoneurasia2.blogspot.com/2021/03/russians-flee-tuva-as-law-decays.html.

[155] Elise Giuliano, *Constructing Grievance: Ethnic Nationalism in Russia's Republics,* Cornell University Press, 2011, p.161.

[156] Anna Reid, *The Shaman's Coat; A Native History of Siberia,* New York: Walker and Company, 2002, pp.110–111.

[157] Anna Reid, *The Shaman's Coat; A Native History of Siberia,* New York: Walker and Company, 2002, p.68.

failing to keep the population in check. The COVID-19 pandemic had an especially acute political impact in the Buryat Republic, where the government was widely discredited for its failure to manage the infections.[158] A rising sense of ethno-national identity will encourage the emergence of a coherent political opposition and calls for establishing an independent Buryat state, to include the Buryat Republic with two autonomous Buryat *okrugs* in neighboring regions. Given the multitude of national and regional aspirations, Siberia as a whole can be characterized as a waking giant that could decide the future of the precarious Russian state.

Pacific Region

Russia's "Far East" or Pacific territories have a history of regionalism, autonomism, and separatism and have demonstrated increasing alienation from Moscow and European Russia since the Soviet collapse. The Pacific region was not extensively settled by Russians until the later part of the 19th century, but similarly to the Siberians the newcomers developed a distinct regional identity that can be regarded as an emergent sub-ethnos. Far Easterners are renowned for their individualism, entrepreneurship and self-reliance, and they reportedly become more active when the central government retreats.[159] In terms of state formation, a nominally independent Far Eastern Republic (*Dalnevostochnaya Respublika*—DVR) was established in 1920–1921, following the collapse of the Tsarist Russian

---

[158] Paul Goble, "Pandemic has Brought Buryatia to 'Boiling Point,' Setting Stage for a Single Buryat Nation to Emerge, Ochirov Says," August 6, 2021, http://windowoneurasia2.blogspot.com/2021/08/pandemic-has-brought-buryatia-to.html.

[159] Rensselaer Lee and Artyom Lukin, *Russia's Far East: New Dynamics in Asia Pacific and Beyond,* Boulder, London: Lynne Rienner Publishers, p.65.

empire.[160] The DVR, with its capital in Chita, was approved by Bolshevik leaders as a buffer state and to help defend the Far East from Japanese territorial claims at a time when the Red Army was preoccupied with establishing the Soviet empire in Europe's east. At its largest extent, the DVR included present-day Zabaikalskii *Krai*, Amur *Oblast*, the Jewish Autonomous *Oblast*, Khabarovsk *Krai* and Primorski *Krai*.

Communist leaders utilized Russian-majority nationalism in defending Russian imperial territory from foreign claims. However, the DVR maintained some elements of genuine autonomy until it was fully absorbed into the Russian Soviet Federative Socialist Republic in November 1922. It did not become one of the constituent or Union Republics of the Soviet Union, formally established in December 1922, and was not afforded autonomous status within the RSFSR but was divided between different federal regions. Another quasi-state formation, the Provisional Priamur Government, based in Vladivostok, was an anti-Bolshevik initiative that sought the restoration of an imperial Russia during the Civil Wars of 1917–1922.

After the Soviet rupture, several initiatives were undertaken to create republics in the Pacific region, including the Primorsky Republic in Primorsky *Krai*, with its center in Vladivostok.[161] Demands for decentralization and recreation of the Far Eastern Republic were revived during the first half of the 1990s and have simmered periodically since. Disillusionment spread widely over the lack of domestic and foreign investment in the region, despite early promises of substantial economic development. Unfulfilled expectations and

---

[160] Ivan Sablin, *The Rise and Fall of Russia's Far Eastern Republic, 1905-1922: Nationalisms, Imperialisms, and Regionalisms In and After the Russian Empire*, Routledge, 2019.

[161] Cameron Ross, *Federalism and Democratisation in Russia*, 2003, Manchester University Press, pp.24–25

the persistent economic depression in the region have contributed to periodic protest actions against the central government. Vladivostok experienced mass protests in December 2008, following Moscow's decision to increase import duties on used Japanese cars in order to protect Russia's automobile industry. As demonstrations spread in the city, they revealed widespread indignation over rising prices, failing social services, and the lack of regional self-determination. They also spawned a new political movement, the Fellowship of Proactive Citizens of Russia (TIGR), which demanded the resignation of the transitory Russian President at the time, Dmitry Medvedev, and his government; the initiative spread to several other regions.[162] Mass demonstrations were eventually violently suppressed by elite police units. Vladivostok also earned the reputation as the most opposition-minded large city in the country, based on the results of national elections between 2000 and 2012.[163]

A violent youth group styling itself as the Primorsky Partisans was active during 2010 in Kirovsky *Raion*, near Vladivostok in Primorsky *Krai.*[164] It waged a self-styled guerrilla war against the local police forces, accusing them of corruption, extortion, drug dealing, and brutality, and claimed that they could no longer tolerate the abusive state. Independent public surveys revealed that over 60% of regional respondents were willing to help the Partisans and give them shelter from law enforcement. Although members of the group were caught or killed by police units, those arrested were tried and acquitted,

---

[162] Mischa Gabowitsch, *Protest in Putin's Russia,* Malden, MA: Polity Press, 2017, p.135.

[163] "Индекс оппозиционности крупных городов России,"*Kommersant,* March 12, 2012, www.kommersant.ru/doc/1889330.

[164] Ben Judah, *Fragile Empire: How Russia Fell In And Out Of Love With Vladimir Putin,* Yale University Press, 2013, p.318.

demonstrating that Russia's police force is widely perceived as an organization of gangsters.

The city of Khabarovsk was the center of mass protests throughout much of 2020 against Moscow's unilateral dismissal of the region's governor, Sergei Furgal. In September 2018, he defeated the Kremlin-backed candidate in the Khabarovsk *Krai* gubernatorial elections by 70 percent to 28 percent. Furgal became popular as a responsive administrator and with higher job approval ratings than Putin. On July 9, 2020, a police special forces team kidnapped Furgal and imprisoned him in a Moscow jail on murder charges, which he vehemently denied during interrogations. This sparked several months of street demonstrations by tens of thousands of Khabarovsk residents demanding Furgal's return and protesting against central government directives. Putin responded by appointing an acting governor from outside the region who was poorly received by residents.

Despite the police crackdown in October 2020, after 90 days of protests, the street rallies soon resumed, indicating that state intimidation was losing its long-term impact.[165] In June 2021, public demonstrations intensified as protesters believed that Furgal could die in prison because of poor treatment.[166] In addition to the restoration of Furgal as governor, protesters demanded an end to repression and the release of all political prisoners. Such prolonged protests will contribute to generating greater political activism, with calls to establish a regional political movement despite the ban on such

---

[165] Paul Goble, "Despite Crackdown, Khabarovsk Residents Resume Their Protest," October 12, 2020, http://windowoneurasia2.blogspot.com/2020/10/despite-crackdown-khabarovsk-residents.html.

[166] "В Хабаровске жители вновь вышли на акцию в поддержку Фургала," June 5, 2021, https://www.sibreal.org/a/miting-v-podderzhku-furgala/31291834.html.

localized parties under Russian law. Further economic decline can radicalize protesters and provoke labor actions, workers' strikes or even an "urban guerrilla war," as animosity toward Moscow escalates.[167] The protests in Khabarovsk were not initially targeted at changing the government but simply reinstalling an ousted governor. They were also a means of testing the regime's response and providing a model and encouragement for future public revolts.[168]

Russians in other regions have sympathized with the demonstrators in Khabarovsk and will also demand a real voice in the selection of regional governors. Sympathy demonstrations for Khabarovsk were evident in Vladivostok, Nakhodka, Novosibirsk, Barnaul, Irkutsk and Yuzhno-Sakhalinsk.[169] Activists outside the Pacific region, including in Syktyvkar, in the Komi Republic, also staged protests in support of Khabarovsk residents.[170] Analysts predict that other arrests of regional governors who are considered disloyal but are genuinely popular may be staged by Moscow on the pretext of combating corruption. It was noteworthy that the central government was hesitant in cracking down on mass protests in Khabarovsk in 2020, indicating some anxiety that this could provoke further demonstrations.

---

[167] "Гданьск или Ольстер?" November 17, 2020, http://region.expert/gdansk-or-ulster/.

[168] Paul Goble, "Protesters in Khabarovsk and Belarus May Not Have Won, But Kremlin has Lost in Both, Shevtsova Says," October 3, 2020, http://windowoneurasia2.blogspot.com/2020/10/protesters-in-khabarovsk-and-belarus.html.

[169] "В поддержку хабаровчан и белорусов. Жители регионов вышли на протесты," August 15, 2020, https://www.sibreal.org/a/30785377.html.

[170] "В Сыктывкаре горожане покормили голубей в поддержку Хабаровска и против политики Путина,"October 11, 2020, https://7x7-journal.ru/news/2020/10/11/v-syktyvkare-gorozhane-pokormili-golubej-v-podderzhku-habarovska-i-protiv-politiki-putina.

Paradoxically, such initial reticence could also stir further enmity against Moscow in other parts of the country, such as the North Caucasus, if this is interpreted as favoring Russian ethnics, because similar protests among non-Russians would precipitate a brutal crackdown.

The Chukchi have a long tradition of resistance to Russian conquest and colonization stretching back to the 18th century and despite attempts at mass extermination by Russia's military leaders.[171] Dissatisfaction with Moscow's rule has simmered under the surface for several generations, but the sparsely populated region has lacked a critical mass to demand autonomy or separation. Since 2020, Chukchi activists have become more visible by staging street rallies, writing letters, and using the electronic media in a campaign to prevent former Governor Roman Abramovich from building an economically unnecessary port on the Naglenynyn peninsula. While Abramovich would profit from substantial finances from Moscow, the port would reportedly destroy the herds of reindeer, bears and fish on which the Chukchi rely.[172]

The Kremlin has been promoting an economic arrangement in the Far East that could generate more resistance by creating a single public-private corporation to develop the region.[173] Such an entity

---

[171] Stepan Kostetskiy, "Первая чукотская, Россия годами воевала с чукчами. Почему она не могла победить гордый народ?" May 22, 2021, https://lenta.ru/articles/2021/05/22/chukchi/.

[172] Paul Goble, "No Laughing Matter: Chukchis Protest Abramovich Plan to Get Moscow Money for Unnecessary Port," October 10, 2020, http://windowoneurasia2.blogspot.com/2020/10/no-laughing-matter-chukchis-protest.html.

[173] Paul Goble, "Moscow Adopting East India Company Strategy to Develop Russian Far East," *Eurasia Daily Monitor*, Vol.18, Issue 16, January 28, 2021,

would be stronger than any regional government or local business but is likely to confront significant local opposition as another corrupt venture to exploit local resources. In practice, Moscow has failed to resolve the overarching problems stemming from a decrepit infrastructure and poor regional interconnectivity in most parts of the Pacific region, Siberia and the Arctic. In 2020, the Ministry for the Development of the Far East and Arctic announced the creation of a Russian Far East and Arctic Development Corporation to supervise the economy, administer ports and other facilities, and, in essence, take over the functions of several republican, *krai* and *oblast* governments.[174] As the management of the Corporation will not be answerable to the electorate, it is bound to create new conflicts not only with the public but also with local bureaucrats and government officials. The corruption that the new body would engender will further antagonize regional discontent and could create alliances between regional governors and citizens groups challenging Moscow's rule.

In the fall of 2021, several federal subjects in the Pacific region experienced acute shortages of food, fuel and basic services even though Moscow was profiting from the area's trade with China.[175] This increased popular antagonism toward both the federal and regional authorities. The Kremlin reduced the volume of goods coming into the region from other countries as well as the amount of shipping capacity available to carry food and fuel from the southern parts of the region to the northern and eastern regions. This left many

---

https://jamestown.org/program/moscow-adopting-east-india-company-strategy-to-develop-russian-far-east/.

[174] http://fareaststreet.ru/en/participants/ministry/minvostok.

[175] Paul Goble, "Moscow's Trade With China Leaves Russians in the Far East Hungry, Cold and Angry," *Eurasia Daily Monitor*, Vol.18, Issue 184, December 9, 2021, https://jamestown.org/program/moscows-trade-with-china-leaves-russians-in-the-far-east-hungry-cold-and-angry/.

Siberians and "Far Easterners" facing serious shortages of basic goods amidst a health crisis and declining government services. Their desperation is likely to result in a greater population outflow, weaken Moscow's control over the Pacific region, and open up the area to greater Chinese penetration.

5.

Rupture Scenarios

The Russian Federation confronts an urgent existential paradox that has been intensified as a result of its destructive and prolonged war in Ukraine. It will become starker as the closure of Vladimir Putin's presidential term approaches, regardless of whether it is constitutionally extended through falsified referenda and rigged elections. Centralization and repression without sustained economic growth will increase public opposition and generate turmoil, while liberalization and decentralization can also result in the unravelling of the state. Without political pluralism, economic reform, and regional autonomy, the federal structure will become increasingly unmanageable. However, if genuine democratic reforms were undertaken, several of the country's regions could use the opportunity to secede. The chances for violent conflicts may diminish in the event of systemic reform, although they cannot be excluded, while the prospects for violent conflict substantially increase if reforms are indefinitely blocked.

Political devolution is perceived as weakness by the Kremlin, so that the Putin regime is unlikely to yield to regional demands for administrative decentralization and authentic federalism. As the country slides toward domestic turmoil, expanding sectors of the population will view the existing federal system as illegitimate. A spectrum of domestic scenarios can then materialize that will thrust the country toward rupture, including intensifying intra-elite power struggles, factional strife in the *siloviki* institutions, escalating conflicts between the Kremlin and regional governments, and a breakdown of central controls in several parts of the country. It is instructive to assess the potential impact of each major scenario on state integrity, as well as Moscow's efforts to avert public upheaval, the breakdown of government authority, and federal fragmentation. Each of these scenarios can be developed in greater detail based on more intensive research in each republic and region as the ruptures unfold.

Disruption Scenarios

The power structure in the multi-national Russian Federation looks more fragile than that of the Soviet Union because of over-reliance on the persona of one leader and no predictable and legitimate method of succession. The Kremlin deputy chief of staff Vyacheslav Volodin has asserted that "there is no Russia today if there is no Putin," indicating the profound fear of state collapse inside the presidential administration if Putin were to be incapacitated, ousted, or assassinated.[1] Even discussions about a likely successor to Putin have been condemned by the Kremlin for potentially destabilizing the country's political system.[2] Such assertions are intended to send a strong message to Russia's public and the political elite that without an autocratic tsar-like figure, Russia will cease to exist and its neighbors will divide and devour its territories. Official fears indicate

---

[1] "'No Putin, No Russia,' Says Kremlin Deputy Chief of Staff," *The Moscow Times*, October 23, 2014, https://www.themoscowtimes.com/2014/10/23/no-putin-no-russia-says-kremlin-deputy-chief-of-staff-a40702.

[2] "Putin Says Talk of Succession 'Destabilizes' Russia," *The Moscow Times*, October 14, 2021, https://www.themoscowtimes.com/2021/10/14/putin-says-talk-of-succession-destabilises-russia-a75293.

that Putin may be perceived as the only politician who can contain intra-establishment conflicts and prevent a political war over wealth, power, and access to resources that will contribute to state fracture.[3]

Credibility Crisis

No personalistic regime is permanent: regime succession can rarely be automatically transmitted to another autocrat in the absence of a clear line of political inheritance, as in monarchical systems or in states built around a family dictatorship. In addition, Russia no longer possesses an entrenched and powerful Communist Party apparatus that can ensure a relatively smooth transition of leadership that is considered sufficiently legitimate by elites and the public. Furthermore, a democratic transition through competitive elections is anathema to the ruling clique, as it would inject even more uncertainty over Russia's future. Indeed, the emergence of a democratic system throughout the Russian Federation after Putin's demise may be less feasible now than it was in the 1990s.[4] Expectations for genuine democracy are low, institutions are hollow, alternative political parties are weak, and civil society is comprehensively repressed. It will take time for a coherent political and management elite to emerge at an all-state level, and such a process can be challenged and derailed by autocratic, nationalist, populist, and other anti-democratic forces.

---

[3] Regina Smyth, *Elections, Protest, and Authoritarian Regime Stability: Russia 2008-2020*, Cambridge University Press, 2021, p.211.

[4] Nikolai Petrov, "Myth 16: 'What Comes After Putin Must be Better than Putin,'" Chatham House Report: Russia and Eurasia Program, May 2021, *Myths and Misconceptions in the Debate on Russia. How They Affect Western Policy, and What Can Be Done,* https://www.chathamhouse.org/2021/05/myths-and-misconceptions-debate-russia.

A much more likely prospect is the deepening of fissures inside the political structure, growing challenges to the hierarchy of power, weakening central controls, and widening political cleavages that culminate in state rupture. National identities and ethnic divisions may help fuel separatism in some instances, but secessionist sentiments can also develop within the same ethnos where distinct regions harbor an assortment of grievances against the central government or calculate that separation would be politically and economically beneficial. Initial challenges to state integrity can be gradual and peaceful, although violent scenarios will become more probable when frustrations increase because of strong regime resistance.[5]

The demise of the current Russian Federation is unlikely to follow a single path, unlike that of the Soviet Union, where the fifteen Union Republics became independent states almost by default. In the USSR, the forces of unity and centralization proved inadequate, and the state was abolished by agreement and formalized by the leaders of three emerging states—Russia, Ukraine and Belarus.[6] Nonetheless, the termination of the Soviet Union also involved violence over territories in several republics as well as two highly destructive wars between Russian forces and a *de facto* independent Chechnya during the 1990s. In contemporary Russia, the fracturing of the state is likely to be chaotic, prolonged, sequential, conflictive and, increasingly, violent. It can result in the full separation of some federal units and the amalgamation of others into new federal or confederal arrangements.

---

[5] Matthew Crosston, *Shadow Separatism: Implications for Democratic Consolidation*, London: Routledge, 2004, p.17.

[6] Paul Goble, "Disintegration of Russian Federation Won't Follow a Single or Simple Path, Yakovenko Says," August 25, 2020, https://windowoneurasia2.blogspot.com/2020/08/disintegration-of-russian-federation.html.

If Russia is to transform from an empire into a genuine federal state, the departure of the ethnic republics would be insufficient. Unless this was accompanied by structural democratic reform, the remaining federal units would still be part of an imperial structure, similar to post-Soviet Russia after the secession of the Union Republics. However, moves toward separation by any ethnic republic are likely to provoke demands for self-determination among several regions with ethnic-Russian majorities in opposition to Moscow's continuing dominance. This would significantly weaken the center and lessen the likelihood of maintaining an autocratic state. Instructively, in the early 1990s, 40 percent of the predominantly ethnic-Russian regions pressed for greater autonomy and some veered toward sovereignty similar to the ethnic republics.[7] Enhanced regional activism can be a bargaining tactic for extracting finances or other resources from the Center. However, separatist movements often start with demands for limited autonomy and economic decentralization and then escalate in response to central government actions, vocalized local grievances, and soaring elite and public aspirations.

A key driver of state disintegration would be a military defeat or a prolonged stalemate accompanied by steady economic decline for which the Kremlin is widely blamed domestically. Public acquiescence and regime survival under Putin's rule has been increasingly based on an aggressive foreign policy, territorial revisionism, patriotic militarism, and anti-Western propaganda. Moscow endeavors to use these elements to demonstrate the country's revived grandeur and potency.[8] A major setback or stalemate in war, despite Russia's military capabilities and involving significant casualties would evoke opposition to Putin's policies, propel power struggles to replace him,

---

[7] Yoshiko M. Herrera, *Imagined Economies: The Sources of Russian Regionalism*, Cambridge University Press, 2007, p.4.

[8] Kathryn E. Stoner, *Russia Resurrected: Its Power and Purpose in a New Global Order*, Oxford University Press, 2021, p.24.

stimulate popular revolts against a discredited leadership, and highlight the accumulated failures of the Russian Federation. The Tsarist empire collapsed during a war with imperial Germany in World War I, and the Soviet empire disintegrated in the wake of a failed war in Afghanistan. Vladislav Surkov, the Kremlin's former chief ideologist, may have been correct when he claimed in a programmatic article published in November 2021 that if Russia does not engage in successful imperial expansion, then it will expire as a state.[9]

Putin's power and credibility, along with Russia's survival in its current territorial form, could be the casualty of a long and inconclusive war with Ukraine that results in a broader confrontation with the North Atlantic Treaty Organization (NATO) and economically crippling Western sanctions. Despite overwhelming firepower, Russia's military will be unable to cower the government in the Ukrainian government into submission. The failure to capture Kyiv, Kharkiv, and other key cities in February-April 2022 and the focus on simply expanding control over the Donbas (Luhansk and Donetsk) and two other eastern *oblasts* demonstrated Moscow's military limitations. It also indicated that the Kremlin had abandoned any hope of dominating Kyiv through political, institutional, and economic linkages. A prolonged military quagmire in Ukraine, with mounting losses for Russia's armed forces and a contracting economy, will not be sustainable for Moscow. Ukrainian resistance would be supported through the supply of weapons by neighbors and key Allies such as the United States and the United Kingdom, even if there is no direct confrontation between Russian and NATO troops. Putin's failure to turn Ukraine into a compliant ally will expose the weaknesses of his regime, and this can convince military and security

[9] Paul Goble, "Surkov Says Russia Must Expand or Die, the Most Dangerous of All Possible 'Prescriptions,' Rostovsky Says," January 11, 2022, http://windowoneurasia2.blogspot.com/2022/01/surkov-says-russia-must-expand-or-die.html.

leaders to replace him. Governments that lose wars or cannot win them when they have staked so much on victory invariably collapse in Russia.

Russia's leadership is also fearful of spontaneous public unrest, as witnessed in its overreactions to peaceful street protests and its constant attempts to eliminate all forms of organized opposition. Officials are aware that public opinion polls are not a failsafe barometer of the public mood. They tend to be sparse in many regions of the country, reflect an unwillingness to reveal genuine sentiments, and can swing in unpredictable directions during times of escalating crisis and perceived regime fragility. Additionally, as elections results are falsified by state actors, the public's political preferences cannot be accurately gauged by state officials and this contributes to anxieties within the "power vertical" over the longevity of the current system. What appears to be apathy, avoidance, and even hopelessness among the majority of the population can rapidly spiral into hatred and aggression toward the authorities.[10]

Triggers for Turmoil

Spreading disruption can be fueled by multiple factors and triggered by a major event or a series of rolling crises. This can have strong economic dimensions with a wide array of public grievances, such as a deepening depression, rampant inflation, wage arrears, inadequate housing, environmental destruction, collapsing infrastructure, declining social services, and fast-rising unemployment. Kremlin assurances that economic downturns are merely temporary phenomena will ring increasingly hollow if they are prolonged and

---

[10] Anders Åslund and Leonid Gozman, "Russia after Putin: How to Rebuild the State," *Atlantic Council Report*, February 24, 2021, https://www.atlanticcouncil.org/in-depth-research-reports/report/russia-after-putin-report/.

deep. Even the traditionally pro-government elderly population and residents of small cities, towns, and rural areas will feel increasingly abandoned and cheated by Moscow. Local political actors will accuse the federal government of economic exploitation and highlight the parasitism and arbitrariness of state bureaucrats at the expense of public well-being.

Levada Center polls indicate that citizens increasingly view social and political rights as being interconnected and that improvements in such arenas as health care, education, and infrastructure will only be achieved through major political change.[11] Public indignation over the *status quo* will be generated by an accumulation of political and apolitical factors. Although protests could be spontaneous and initially small scale, they can also rapidly snowball. A core of organized opposition remains in Russia that will contribute to mobilizing and directing the protests and whose networks can link together various single or multiple issue campaigns.[12] If specific local problems cannot be alleviated by the government, then protestors are likely to demand more far-reaching political changes.

The Kremlin may also miscalculate and spark an active backlash by seeking to formally eliminate the last semblance of regional and local autonomy. Mass protests have previously erupted in Russia without much warning and their scale surprised observers, as witnessed in the winter of 2011 and the spring of 2012 in opposition to the rigging of national *Duma* elections. Tens of thousands of ordinary citizens rallied across the country and marched in hundreds of cities, many

---

[11] Paul Goble, "Russians Increasingly View Social and Political Rights as Interlinked, Galkina Says," January 13, 2022, http://windowoneurasia2.blogspot.com/2022/01/russians-increasingly-view-social-and.html.

[12] Regina Smyth, *Elections, Protest, and Authoritarian Regime Stability: Russia 2008-2020*, Cambridge University Press, 2021, pp.79–80.

demanding Putin's ouster and the overthrow of the ruling clique. Grassroots initiatives dealing with a host of local problems also provide fertile soil for the development of larger movements and broader political causes that creates a sense of collective empowerment in challenging the government.[13] For instance, lorry driver strikes in November 2015 against a costly new toll system that eventually encompassed much of Russia were joined by activists of various grassroots movements. They were organized by a trade union that grew out of previous protests—the Interregional Union of Professional Drivers.[14]

Extensive and blatant election falsification to gain parliamentary majorities for United Russia or a clearly fraudulent ballot in 2024 designed to extend Putin's rule could again backfire on the government by releasing pent-up public frustrations. Elections are a focal point for expressing numerous public resentments, whether over economic conditions, political repression, health care, or environmental neglect; and if an accurate result is denied, then the chances for protest escalate. Such demonstrations can also erupt against local officials in regions where major electoral fraud is perpetrated and could be replicated in other federal subjects. A great deal will depend on the size and persistence of demonstrations and the response of police forces and other local security units. Moscow may also face prison revolts because of atrocious conditions and persistent brutality in the prison system. With Russia's police units and internal security forces thinly spread around the country, control could be lost in several localities.

---

[13] Karine Clément, "From 'Local' to 'Political': The Kalininigrad Mass Protest Movement of 2009-2010 in Russia," in Kerstin Jacobsson (Ed.) *Urban Grassroots Movements in Central and Eastern Europe*, Routledge, 2015, p.175.

[14] Mischa Gabowitsch, *Protest in Putin's Russia*, Malden, MA: Polity Press, 2017, p.253.

Although mass street rallies by themselves are unlikely to rapidly overthrow the regime, as in Ukraine in February 2014 or in the various "color revolutions" in Central-Eastern Europe, they would contribute to undermining the legitimacy of the federal administration. They would also strengthen the sense of regional solidarity. Similarly to the collapsing Soviet Union, regional identities can displace political, professional, and even ethnic profiles during a time of political chaos.[15] It is worth remembering that ethnic Russians in several former Union Republics supported and voted for their independence, as evident in eastern Ukraine containing sizeable Russian populations during the December 1991 Ukrainian referendum.[16]

Spreading Ungovernability

Some Russian economists contend that major protest actions are unlikely in the near future because people tend to demonstrate when they think change is possible.[17] The Putin regime has spent the last two decades convincing citizens that there is no viable alternative to the prevailing system, and most people harbor no expectations of improvement or sustained economic growth. Nonetheless, the relationship between protests and economic conditions may be more variable and combustible when society experiences constant decline and not simply "stagnation," when inequalities between rich and poor become increasingly conspicuous, and where official mismanagement

---

[15] Lyudmila Parts, "'How is Voronezh Not Paris?' City Branding in the Russian Provinces," in Edith W. Clowes, Gisela Ersblöh and Ani Kokobobo, *Russia's Regional Identities: The Power of the Provinces*, 2020, p.125.

[16] http://soviethistory.msu.edu/1991-2/the-end-of-the-soviet-union/the-end-of-the-soviet-union-texts/ukrainian-independence-declaration/.

[17] Vladislav Inozemtsev, "Почем бунт лиха: Почему российская бедность не провоцирует протест," July 12, 2021, novayagazeta.ru/articles/2021/07/12/pochem-bunt-likha.

and corruption are combined with severe political restrictions and police repression. No large-scale demonstrations took place in the wake of the fraudulent September 2021 *Duma* elections, due to a mix of state repression, public fear, and a period of demoralization following the January 2021 mass protests against the arrest of opposition leader Alexei Navalny. But this looked like a temporary respite for a regime resting on shallow foundations built around a single personality. A crunch point could materialize during the spring of 2024, when elections are scheduled to extend Putin's presidential term in the midst of intensifying public disaffection and economic distress.

Government reactions to social unrest can prevent, subdue, or accelerate popular resistance and organized political opposition. To avert a revolutionary scenario, the administration may impose a variety of measures, including the provision of urgent but short-lived economic benefits for key sectors of the population, offers of administrative decentralization to several regional centers, selective repression against specific protests, or a mass crackdown in one or more regions intended to signal the Kremlin's capabilities. A program of reform and limited democratization may also be attempted to try and pacify public unrest, but this would also aggravate disputes between the Center and regions, as was the case during the Soviet fragmentation. The limits of republican and regional sovereignty would be tested in trying to forge a workable federation, and several subjects will see an opportunity for pursuing maximalist options during a period of confusion or hesitation at the central level.

Attempts to pacify the most volatile areas of the country through economic incentives and political manipulation could boomerang. Selective economic benefits can provoke resentment in other regions and convince citizens that mass opposition to Kremlin policy can be lucrative by increasing state funding. Political concessions to local leaders and administrative devolution will encourage governors to act more independently and push for more extensive autonomy.

Increased resources and authority for ethnic republics could also enflame Russian ethnic nationalism, driven by animosity against national republics and ethnic groups perceived to be favored by Moscow. This can either increase calls for greater centralization and the elimination and merger of several federal subjects or inflame demands for the creation of a distinct Russian ethno-national republic. Selective repression may also prove ineffective or escalatory by sparking ever-wider resistance that the government is ill prepared to contain. The regime's capabilities to impose mass repression across the country or even in several restless regions simultaneously will prove inadequate. Indeed, the unreliability of state security organs in eliminating open opposition can engender broader unrest.

Strikes and other forms of industrial labor action can break out across several regions, with employees protesting against low or unpaid wages, poor working conditions, rising prices, and falling living standards.[18] Leaders of trade unions who have been coopted by the government would prove powerless to prevent workers' protests and will be seen as part of the privileged establishment. Farmers in some regions can also organize protests against official corruption in land distribution, similarly to the "tractor marches" on previous occasions.[19] In August 2016, several hundred farmers from Krasnodar *Krai*, in southern Russia, were persistently blocked by the police as

[18] "Employees of Russia E-Retail Giant Wildberries Go On Strike," September 16, 2021, https://www.themoscowtimes.com/2021/09/16/employees-of-russia-e-retail-giant-wildberries-go-on-strike-a75067.

[19] Regina Smyth, *Elections, Protest, and Authoritarian Regime Stability: Russia 2008-2020*, Cambridge University Press, 2021, p.186.

they drove toward Moscow to raise awareness about local corruption and theft of farmers' lands.[20]

Spiraling chaos will witness conflicts between state and society, with ebbs and flows of mass protests and police repression. Police attacks on peaceful manifestations can provoke radicalization and more violent responses from some protestors against law enforcement or other regime representatives. It could also outrage wider sectors of society and if Moscow encounters decisive mass resistance to police repression it may waver and retreat in some cities, especially if mass protests erupt simultaneously in several regions and the authorities are overstretched to suppress them all.[21] Protests will also provide opportunities for coordination between different movements, causes, and locations. Kremlin confusion and weakness can lead to a revolutionary situation whereby the state is incapable of maintaining the repression necessary to subdue all public unrest, while a growing number of people are unwilling to live under a failed dictatorial regime.

The Kremlin will also attempt to steer the population toward ethnic scapegoating by depicting a potentially separatist republic or region as an existential threat to Russia and its citizens. This would replicate how Chechnya was demonized by officials when then–Prime Minister Putin launched the second war of reconquest in August 1999. However, the promotion of ethnic and religious prejudices and hatreds would further break down national and social cohesion and convince sizeable segments of the Muslim populations that Russia had

---

[20] Howard Amos, "Angry Farmers Stage Tractor March on Moscow," *The Moscow Times*, August 22, 2016, https://www.themoscowtimes.com/2016/08/22/angry-farmers-stage-tractor-march-on-moscow-a55067.

[21] Private interview with Vadim Shtepa, Editor in Chief, *Region.Expert*, Tallinn, March 2021.

become their existential threat. Moscow will not be able to sustain the survival of the state if it scapegoats particular nations or religions and alienates specific ethnic groups.[22] Such a policy may also prove politically counter-productive by convincing the majority of Russia's citizens that separatist entities should be allowed to secede to avoid bloodshed. The classic "divide and rule" strategy can thereby result in more division and less rule.

The sudden, widespread and, in some cases, violent demonstrations in Kazakhstan in January 2022 generated fear in the Kremlin that the internet could be used in Russia to "recruit extremists and terrorists" and create "sleeping cells of militants" seeking to overthrow the government.[23] According to Putin, social networks that involve Russian citizens in protest actions are a precursor of "terrorist attacks," indicating a profound anxiety about social opposition that cannot be easily monitored or contained. Paradoxically, substantial sectors of the population who supported Putin because he evidently ensured order and predictability will abandon the regime when it appears to be increasingly weak and yielding. If uncertainty and chaos spread in the country and no credible successor emerges in Moscow, sectors of society will look toward local and regional leaders to restore some semblance of order in their cities and regions.

Intensifying Power Struggles

Before the federal structure begins to rupture, Russia will face a prolonged spiral of chaos, ungovernability and accelerating elite power struggles, in which state institutions witness a breakdown in

---

[22] Julia Wilhelmsen, *Russia's Securitization of Chechnya: How War Became Acceptable*, London and New York: Routledge, 2018, p.213.

[23] http://kremlin.ru/events/president/news/67568.

the chain of command, as was evident in the final months of the Soviet Union. Some institutions may cease to function altogether, while regional and central elites compete more vigorously over shrinking financial resources. Kremlin fears will come to fruition regarding the enduring loyalty of the networks of elites who have benefited from presidential control over state assets.[24] Their adherence will dissipate alongside their shrinking economic benefits, and this could herald a series of turf battles, kidnappings, assassinations, and attempts to use the security forces against political and business rivals.

Russia's political stability is based on elite consensus in support of Putin together with sufficient public acquiescence.[25] It is not dependent on popular legitimacy or enduring institutions. Putin has managed to balance competing political, economic, and security factions, while relying on his security service connections and the allegiance of his original Leningrad inner circle, the *Ozera Dacha*. An internal power struggle may be short and swift, with the emergence of a clear winner, whether a reformer or another centralizing autocrat. However, it is more likely to be prolonged, violent, and inconclusive. Putin's ouster will not necessarily end the contest for absolute power or pacify public disquiet. On the contrary, it will intensify political battles and popular turmoil because there is little trust among top officials and minimal public confidence in the ruling elite.

---

[24] Kathryn E. Stoner, *Russia Resurrected: Its Power and Purpose in a New Global Order,* Oxford University Press, 2021, p.22.

[25] John Tefft, "Understanding the Factors That Will Impact the Succession to Vladimir Putin as Russian President," July 2020, https://www.rand.org/pubs/perspectives/PE349.html.

Power struggles can erupt between rival political "clans" or networks, as evident in the composition of the *Duma.*[26] The strongest of these "clans" include state security officials and military personnel (*siloviki*), heads of state corporations, major oligarchs (tycoons), leaders of loyal political parties, industrial lobbies, and regional heads. These conflicts can burst into the open once the consensus around Putin begins to unravel or if the country faces protracted economic decline and growing inter-elite competition for scarcer resources.[27] Contests between political rivals to replace Putin will undermine the "power vertical" and solidify factions within the internal security forces. Police officers in some regions are likely to remain neutral or even join public protests and provide them with weapons once demonstrations against the regime take on a mass form. In the smaller cities in particular, the police are more closely connected with the local population through family and friendship networks.[28]

In some cases, Russia's state security forces may stage terrorist attacks and accuse separatists of the atrocities, as occurred with the bombing of several apartment buildings in the fall of 1999 that were evidently perpetrated by the Federal Security Service (FSB).[29] On that occasion, the bombings were blamed by the Kremlin on radical Muslims,

---

[26] "Новой Госдумой будут руководить девять кланов," October 7, 2021, *Ura.Ru Information Agency*, https://ura.news/articles/1036283216.

[27] Dmitry Travin, Vladimir Gel'man, Otar Marganiya, *The Russian Path: Ideas, Interests, Institutions, Illusions*, Stuttgart: Ibidem Verlag, 2020, p.204.

[28] Paul Goble, "Police in Regions will Avoid Provoking Protesters and May Even Join Them; Those in Capitals Won't, Former Ivanovo Officer Says," February 6, 2021, http://windowoneurasia2.blogspot.com/2021/02/police-in-regions-will-avoid-provoking.html.

[29] John Dunlop, *The Moscow Bombings of September 1999: Examinations of Russian Terrorist Attacks at the Onset of Vladimir Putin's Rule*, Soviet and Post-Soviet Politics and Society, Vol. 110, August 22, 2013.

providing justification for the second anti-Chechen war and helping to propel Putin into the presidency as the alleged savior of Russia's state integrity. Although the goal of such atrocities would again be to generate public fear of terrorism and buttress the position of the regime, it could also backfire if citizens conclude that the authorities can no longer protect them or that the regime itself was responsible for domestic terrorism.

Elite loyalty toward the Kremlin is not based on shared ideology or policy platforms but on raw economic and political advantages that high-level connections bestow. Elements of the elite will lose confidence in the regime if resources for corruption become depleted, international isolation shrinks revenues, and social unrest spreads in the country.[30] In a negative spiral that will further damage Russia's economy, the struggle for power and resources and spreading instability will also make foreign investment less attractive even from countries such as China that are not compliant with Western sanctions. Bureaucratic infighting and the frustrated aspirations of mid-level officials will augment intra-elite pressures and opposition to the regime as well as trigger clashes to replace Putin. The Kremlin cannot bank on the permanent loyalty of the country's elites, as they become increasingly disillusioned by Russia's detachment from global commerce and the diminishing prospects for substantial profits. Sectors of the business elite will fear that their revenues will plummet as the economy deteriorates or that their properties and assets will be confiscated if the regime seeks scapegoats to mobilize and manipulate public support. With a shrinking national economic "pie" the pyramid of state paternalism favoring specific interest groups will

---

[30] Denis Volkov, "Russia in the Mid-2020s: Breakdown of the Political Order," S. Enders Wimbush and Elizabeth M. Portale (Eds), *Russia in Decline*, Jamestown Foundation, March 2017, p.318.

become increasingly unstable.[31] Intra-elite conflicts would revolve around diminishing resources, with some oligarchs and security chiefs seeking to steer social unrest to weaken or eliminate their rivals.

United Russia can splinter, as many regional members of the party did not enlist because of ideological affiliation or political loyalty but for reasons of expediency and opportunism and are likely to abandon it when power struggles weaken the central government. In turn, the three systemic opposition parties—the Communist Party of the Russian Federation (KPRF), the Liberal Democratic Party of Russia (LDPR), and A Just Russia–Patriots–For Truth (SRZP)—will become increasingly dissatisfied with the regime, which expects their loyalty and compliance for certain political and economic privileges. They can adopt a more independent posture in criticizing the Kremlin if their benefits dwindle. Regional branches of party organizations have also proven to be less compliant than national bodies and could break away or challenge Moscow loyalists.[32] This can lead to factionalism, purges, and outright conflicts within United Russia and intensify power battles within the ruling strata. Pro-regime movements funded by Putinist loyalists could also splinter, including youth organizations, veterans groups, sports networks, and various social and cultural associations sponsored by the Kremlin.

Russia's national and regional bureaucracy will likewise become frustrated by the intrusive role of the FSB, which resembles a national extortion racket. Business and local authorities could seek protection against the FSB by forging alliances with other security organs. Indications of intense rivalries have periodically surfaced. For

---

[31] Dmitry Travin, Vladimir Gel'man, Otar Marganiya, *The Russian Path: Ideas, Interests, Institutions, Illusions,* Stuttgart: Ibidem Verlag, 2020, p.135.

[32] Regina Smyth, *Elections, Protest, and Authoritarian Regime Stability: Russia 2008-2020*, Cambridge University Press, 2021, p.208.

instance, during Russia's seizure of Crimea and its takeover of parts of Ukraine's Donbas in the spring of 2014, some "harder liners" in Moscow charged that there was a "fifth column" in the Kremlin consisting of oligarchs and bureaucrats who sought to restrict the takeover of Ukraine and were even conspiring to replace Putin because they were fearful that their assets in Western banks would be confiscated.[33] Clashes among Russia's elites will be exacerbated during public revolts, while disinformation offensives between political rivals, the release of *kompromat* (compromising) materials, and attempts to use the security services or private contractors to dispossess or eradicate competitors will further splinter the Russian establishment.

Moreover, a government crisis in which Putin's control over state institutions diminishes, can provoke feuds between various powerful factions in the FSB and other security organs to install their favored candidate as President.[34] Factional fighting inside the "power institutions" could be a major trigger that undermines the supposed stability of the Putin administration. In the absence of systemic change, a coalition of high officials and security chiefs may stage a "palace coup" and blame the previous regime for Russia's problems. Putin's susceptibility to an internal *putsch* cannot be ruled out if economic and international conditions continue to deteriorate. Nevertheless, such a rotation of the "power vertical" will do little for economic development and can increase social turmoil and even

---

[33] Ilya Yablokov, *Fortress Russia: Conspiracy Theories in Post-Soviet Russia,* Cambridge, UK: Polity Press, 2018, p.177.

[34] Atlantic Council, Dossier Center, "Lubyanka Federation: How the FSB Determines the Politics and Economics of Russia," October 2020, https://www.atlanticcouncil.org/in-depth-research-reports/report/lubyanka-federation/.

trigger civil conflicts and insurrections that culminates in state fragmentation.[35]

When national institutions become unstable, hardline *siloviki* could attempt to seize power and impose an extensive clampdown on any political or public opposition, sideline rivals, and abandon any proposed political reforms. However, moves to replace relatively moderate regional leaders with loyalists could also create opportunities for more radical political actors. Political factions in Moscow may also seek allies among regional elites, as was the case during the Soviet breakdown in the early 1990s. Both Gorbachev and Yeltsin encouraged regional sovereignty to weaken the other's position and enhance his own support base. While Gorbachev courted autonomist movements among republics within the Russian Federation in a maneuver to undermine Yeltsin, Yeltsin supported pro-sovereignty movements at all levels to weaken the central Soviet government.[36] Renewed attempts to manipulate republican and regional leaders will become another precursor for the dissolution of the state.

As power struggles intensify, Russia's military commanders will become increasingly alienated from the Kremlin. This would be especially evident if the military were mobilized to pacify public unrest. This could lead to factional realignments with other power structures against the presidential administration. In the midst of state collapse, the military can also experience a breakdown in the chain of command, with internal mutinies and revolts, especially if conscripts are ordered to quell civil unrest and fire on mass demonstrations. The military could itself fracture along ethnic and religious lines, with

---

[35] Ilan Berman, *Implosion: The End of Russia and What it Means for America*, Washington DC: Regnery Publishing Inc., 2013, pp.123–124.

[36] Yoshiko M. Herrera, *Imagined Economies: The Sources of Russian Regionalism*, Cambridge University Press, 2007, p.144.

potential clashes between different ethnicities and the evacuation of non-Russians from service outside their federal regions. Simmering resentments between Russians and non-Russians in the military and other security forces can easily boil over. In a potential harbinger of future military ruptures, in mid-October 2021, Chechen and ethnic-Russian members of a Russian National Guard (*Rosgvardia*) special forces unit clashed at the Tambukan training center in Stavropol *Krai.*[37] As the federal crisis deepens and the military fractures, various categories of weapons will be acquired by militias, insurgents, and emerging proto states.

Polarization and Radicalism

During its accelerating domestic crisis, the Russian Federation will witness political polarization and radicalization. Immense economic and political stresses can fracture existing multi-national bonds, while growing uncertainty can polarize societies in various directions based around group identity, economic status, or political persuasions. Ethnic consciousness, national group cohesion, and acceptance of a distinct ethno-national leadership tend to strengthen during periods of pressure and uncertainty.[38] This would enable activists to push for far-reaching political demands and bank on widespread public support. It can also lead to scapegoating, a sense of threat, distrust of other ethnic groups, and heighten the potential for inter-ethnic conflicts. Public polarization over the war in Ukraine and the failing policies of the Putin regime will also accelerate conflicts as the economy deteriorates.

---

[37] Valery Dzutsati, "Chechen and Russian Special Forces Clash over Insignia," *Eurasia Daily Monitor,* Vol.18, Issue 165, November 1, 2021, https://jamestown.org/program/chechen-and-russian-special-forces-clash-over-insignia/.

[38] Henry E. Hale, *The Foundations of Ethnic Politics: Separatism of States and Nations in Eurasia and the World,* Cambridge University Press, 2008, p.259.

In an increasingly chaotic Russia, liberals and pan-Russian democrats will prove less capable of mobilizing the public on a national civic platform or an agenda of state preservation. Nationalists will promote the collective paranoia that ethnic Russians are besieged not only from the outside by the West but also from the inside by immigrants, minorities, and separatists. In particular, they will manipulate public fears against migrants and non-Russians in the major cities. Fights between ethnic Russian and non-Russian gangs have taken place in several urban suburbs over the past decade and could expand exponentially as the state weakens, security forces are preoccupied, and some nationalist politicians exploit the public mood by fanning ethnic and religious disputes. Clashes between Russians and non-Russian migrants will become politically destabilizing once self-defense groups arm themselves and no longer respect any police presence.

The democratic and liberal opposition has been stifled under the Putin administration at national and regional levels, and the lack of political party pluralism has buttressed regional authoritarianism and local clientalistic networks. New parties will be formed during Russia's escalating turmoil, with competing liberal democratic, radical leftist, neo-Bolshevik, and ethno-nationalist movements seeking public support. Communists could become emboldened to challenge the regime given their relative success in the September 2021 *Duma* elections and tap into public grievances against income inequalities, falling living standards, and state corruption. Leaders of the KPRF have not turned the party into a social democratic formation. Instead, its ideology revolves around "national communism," in which Stalin's statism based around the ethnic-Russian nation prevails over inter-ethnic internationalism. The Kremlin's rehabilitation of Stalin and his widespread popularity in the country does not transfer into automatic support for the current regime. On the contrary, this can rebound against Putin, who will be widely viewed as a weak imitation pandering to monopolistic capitalists and needing to be replaced with a tougher leader.

Communists and other anti-capitalist groupings could forge links with Russian ethno-nationalists and an assortment of ultra-rightist formations in attempts to further centralize the state, expel immigrants, and downgrade the position of non-Russian republics and non-Russian nations. They can also call for a more combative and expansionist foreign policy. In January 2022, KPRF deputies tabled a resolution in the State Duma proposing that Putin recognize the self-proclaimed Luhansk and Donetsk "people's republics" in Ukraine as independent states prior to their *de facto* absorption by Russia.[39] On the eve of the invasion of Ukraine in February 2022, Putin did indeed recognize them as independent and subsequently claimed that they should include all of the Donetsk and Luhansk *Oblasts*.[40]

Growing populist demands for economic justice in the midst of massive elite corruption and falling living standards are likely to favor radical leftist forces or populist nationalists with a leftist economic agenda. A gap has evidently emerged between the aging generation of pro-Western liberals and a more critical younger generation, many members of which are skeptical of free-market capitalism to ensure economic and social justice. Leftist-populist groups can also form tactical links with ultra-nationalist groups in a strategy of "social revenge" against the elites, especially the stratum of tycoons and Kremlin patronage networks that control the national economy.

---

[39] "Communists Propose Duma Officially ask Putin to Recognize Self-Proclaimed Donbas Republics," *Interfax*, January 19, 2022, https://interfax.com/newsroom/top-stories/73642/.

[40] "Full Putin Speech: Russia Recognizes Luhansk And Donetsk Secession From Ukraine, Warns Kiev Not To Interfere," *RealClear Politics*, February 21, 2022, https://www.realclearpolitics.com/video/2022/02/21/full_putin_speech_russia_recognizes_luhansk_and_donetsk_secession_from_ukraine_warns_kiev_not_to_interfere.html#!

Regional Revivals

As turmoil spreads, a regional resurgence will be evident across the country. Some analysts posit that Russia's hierarchical regime is more fragile than it appears on the surface, as it remains dependent on coopting the loyalty of power elites in a small number of key regions, either those with sizeable populations or with key industries and resources, particularly in the energy field. If the Kremlin begins to lose their support, the "federal vertical" would undergo rapid decay.[41] A major peril of centralization is that the center eliminates or enfeebles other power nodes and can no longer deflect blame from itself during times of crisis and unrest.

The stability and durability of the federal structure will come under increasing pressure, especially when central control diminishes because of internal elite conflicts and budgetary contractions that drastically reduce subsidies to the federal subjects.[42] Governors may become less concerned about Moscow's coercive measures and seek popular legitimacy in their home territories by opting for regional sovereignty. Some governors will also conclude that Moscow's campaign against titular languages in the republics and plans for regional amalgamation will further reduce their authority and even lead to disbanding republican institutions or subjecting them more directly to Moscow. Such developments will raise support among governors and local legislatures for sovereignty and self-determination.

---

[41] William M. Reisinger and Bryon J. Moraski, *The Regional Roots of Russia's Political Regime,* Ann Arbor: University of Michigan Press, 2017, pp.174–175.

[42] Elena A. Chebankova, *Russia's Federal Relations: Putin's Reforms and Management of the Regions*, Routledge Series on Russian and East Europe Studies, Routledge: London and New York, 2010, p.186.

Grievances and demands in the ethnic republics and non-ethnic regions will be driven by an accumulation of negative developments, including sharply rising poverty levels, falling federal financial subsidies, deteriorating local infrastructure, costly and inadequate transportation connections between cities, contested land use between federal and regional authorities, an absence of adequate environmental protection, deteriorating health care services, neglect of significant historical sites, harmful social policies, police brutality, rampant official corruption, and overall public alienation from central decision-making. Simultaneously, it can be positively energized by expectations of material benefits, rising ethno-national status, and international recognition if Moscow's overlordship is reduced or eliminated.

Disparities in regional self-assertion are likely, with leaders in ethnically homogenous republics, resource rich regions, or entities more geographically distant from the capital escalating their demands and fortifying links with nearby foreign states. Regional activists will mount challenges to the legal basis of the federal state and the position of its subjects. Some could seek the full application of federalism or propose new structural arrangements to loosen ties with Moscow, including a confederation or commonwealth. The wealthier regions with greater economic potential and a sizeable export portfolio will demand a radical reduction of the money transferred to the central government or may fully or partially withhold payments. This can be the case with oil-producing regions in Western Siberia or the mineral-rich republic of Sakha.

Power will devolve to the regions when the Moscow-centered vertical begins to splinter and a local crisis precipitates a state-wide avalanche. In the event of major public unrest, regional governors will find themselves in an untenable position. The Kremlin will demand that they suppress local protests, while citizens will press them to fulfill their regional responsibilities. Attempts by regional authorities to use local protests as bargaining chips to gain resources from Moscow may no longer bear fruit if the Center cannot afford to comply and protests escape the control of local officials. Governors can either avoid a crackdown or blame Moscow for a harsh repressive response. Either way, they will fortify local public opinion against the Center. The process will expose the deep-rooted regional resentments against Russia's capital, which is widely viewed as a colonial exploiter with an irredeemably corrupt bureaucracy. People will increasingly identify themselves as residents of a particular region rather than as citizens of an integral Russian state.

Some republican and regional leaders will claim discrimination in the federal structure, which avowedly favors other federal subjects, and demand regress through increased budgetary allocations. Alternatively, they can push for a higher status of autonomy or outright secession. Similarly to federal Yugoslavia on the eve of its disintegration in the early 1990s, several richer regions will voice their resentment at subsidizing the poorer federal subjects and claim they would be better managed and more prosperous if either they separated from the Russian Federation or the poorer regions, such as the North Caucasus, seceded. Separatist movements that contributed to the crumbling of the Soviet communist empire in the 1990s were partly or initially elite projects designed to keep more resources in the hands of republics. Many of the leaders of republican pro-independence movements emerged from the Soviet establishment. In a spiraling schism, when the richer republics and regions push toward separation this will further shrink the federal budget and undermine Moscow's ability to control those federal subjects that depend on state subsidies.

Nationalists, regionalists, and separatists outside the structures of power can mobilize significant segments of the public and pressure regional leaders and legislatures to adopt some of their programs and assert greater autonomy from Moscow. Protests propelled by extensive public indignation against the federal center will not only spread in regional capitals but also to smaller-sized cities. Republican and regional leaders and local legislatures are more likely be perceived as trustworthy and effective in comparison to the federal government if they agree to address local social, ethnic, and economic demands.

Simultaneous mass protests in several regions in the midst of a severe economic downturn will convince local elites to abandon the Kremlin's patronage system and canvas for local support, similarly to developments in the Union Republics during the Soviet collapse. People are likely to defend local governors or city mayors if they are actively trying to improve living conditions. Nonetheless, in many regions, citizens have been even more dissatisfied with the performance of local governments than with the federal center, since they directly affect their lives.[43] During a conflict, the Kremlin may try to position itself as the protector of citizens from corrupt local authorities. However, because governors and other local officials are Moscow appointees and the Center controls the purse strings, such maneuvers are likely to be rejected by the populace.

Regional officials and police forces may react to protest actions in various parts of the country by allowing open displays of frustration and anger against Moscow. This would encourage more demonstrations and an escalation of public self-confidence. At some point, regional elites will conclude that the costs of maintaining loyalty to Moscow outweigh the benefits and will opt for greater regional sovereignty. When local elites no longer trust the Kremlin to assure their political legitimacy and provide necessary resources, they will decide to promote their own power base as authentic republican or regional leaders. Despite the fact that most non-Russian republics regularly deliver overwhelming majorities for United Russia in falsified elections, the loyalty of local elites cannot be taken for granted once the competition for power in Moscow weakens the "federal vertical."

---

[43] Private interview with Kseniya Kirillova, Jamestown Foundation, March 2021.

Public movements and local authorities in different republics, *krais*, and *oblasts* can synchronize their demands toward Moscow once the hierarchy of power splinters and they may form cross-regional linkages to offer mutual support. A knock-on effect would be visible, whereby the success of some federal subjects in gaining greater sovereignty without central government intervention encourages other republics and regions to push for fuller autonomy. Moscow's traditionally divisive policies to provoke conflicts between ethnic groups and disorient the opposition will prove less successful where ethnic republican leaders seek coalitions with representatives of different national groups and assist other entities in pushing for sovereignty.

Republican leaders will also demand control over natural resources and economic assets on their territories, insisting that they have been unfairly exploited by Moscow. Even some ethnic districts, such as the Khanty-Mansi Autonomous *Okrug*–Yugra, in Tyumen *Oblast,* can claim sole ownership over natural resources in regions that supply a substantial proportion of Russia's oil and natural gas revenues. This will lead to calls for local autonomy or for raising the administrative status of particular districts. As the federation loosens, regional governments could stake claims to a variety of economic benefits, including export privileges, tax reductions, and special quotas for local products, as well as direct access to pipelines exporting oil and gas that are currently controlled at the federal level.

Russia will undergo a revival of many of the pro-independence movements that emerged during the collapse of the Soviet Union. In several cases, members of titular ethnic groups will claim the right to play a more dominant role in their republics. Numerous ethnicities can assert indigenous status and residential longevity in their home territories in distinction to recent Russian or other settlers. Ethnic activists will also challenge the dominant Muscovite narrative that all republics voluntary entered the Tsarist Empire, the Soviet Union or the Russian Federation. Ethnic elites will seek public support by asserting that for the smaller nations the republics are their only homeland, while Russians possess a much larger territory outside these republics. Such pronouncements could lead to pressures on members of non-titular groups to leave the republics, particularly ethnic Russians.

Inter-ethnic and inter-religious disputes and even violent clashes can be expected in some parts of the country. In the midst of economic decline and political uncertainty, an assortment of ethno-nationalist movements will emerge, with some seeking scapegoats to mobilize the public. This can incite divisions and conflicts even in relatively tranquil multi-ethnic societies. Members of several non-titular ethnic groups will raise complaints that republican elites have promoted their own nations at the cost of other ethnicities and engaged in minority assimilation. Such allegations could be most evident in the overlapping historical, territorial, and identity claims in the North Caucasus and the Middle Volga, and they can strengthen aspirations toward both the separation and fracture of some republics.

The Kremlin is mindful of promoting Russian ethno-nationalism domestically to dampen discontent over the deteriorating economy, as this would contribute to tearing the country apart. Fanning xenophobia, racism, Islamophobia, and anti-immigrant sentiments could light a fuse Moscow will not be able to extinguish, and the consequences will backfire against the regime. Surveys have consistently indicated that ethnocentric and xenophobic sentiments are widespread in the country and have been bolstered by anti-immigrant attitudes against workers from Central Asia and the North Caucasus.[44] However, the exploitation of such sentiments by state actors and a growth in Russian ethno-nationalism will also rebound

---

[44] Pål Kolstø, "The Ethnification of Russian Nationalism," in Pål Kolstø and Helge Blakkisrud (Eds.), *The New Russian Nationalism: Imperialism, Ethnicity and Authoritarianism, 2000-15,* Edinburgh University Press, 2016, p.40.

against Moscow and provoke anti-Russian sentiments among other nationalities.

Periodic manifestations of mass xenophobia and inter-ethnic violence invariably target migrants from the North Caucasus and Central Asia in the larger Russian cities. For instance, mass riots against the Chechen community took place in the town of Kondopoga in the Republic of Karelia in August–September 2006.[45] In December 2010, following the death of a football fan in a brawl with a gang from the North Caucasus, several thousand nationalists occupied a square in central Moscow waving racist banners.[46] In 2013, after the murder of a Russian ethnic by someone identified as Chechen, several hundred protestors marched on the Chechen district of Pugachev in Saratov *Oblast* and demanded the expulsion of all North Caucasians.[47] In October 2013, the fatal stabbing of an ethnic Russian, allegedly by an Azerbaijani citizen, led to mass rioting in the southern Moscow working-class suburb of Biryulyovo.[48]

Some radical politicians have attempted to capitalize on such violent incidents to boost public support for their xenophobic and racist

---

[45] Claire Bigg, "Russia: Kondopoga Violence Continues Unabated," *Radio Free Europe/ Radio Liberty*, September 6, 2006, https://www.rferl.org/a/1071116.html.

[46] Alexander Verkhovsky and Galina Kozhevnikova, "The Phantom of Manezhnaya Square: Radical Nationalism and Efforts to Counteract it in 2010," Sova Center for Information and Analysis, May 5, 2011, https://www.sovacenter.ru/en/xenophobia/reports-analyses/2011/05/d21561/.

[47] "Mass Protests Continue to Rock Russian Small Town of Pugachev," *TASS*, July 11, 2013, https://tass.com/russianpress/696927.

[48] Yulia Ponomareva, "Tensions Over Migrants Test Politicians," *Russia Beyond*, October 29, 2013, https://www.rbth.com/politics/2013/10/29/tensions_over_migrants_test_politicians_31243.html.

prescriptions.[49] Periodic clashes between ethnic Russians and immigrant workers indicate growing ethnic polarization, xenophobia, and immigrant self-assertion. This exacerbates the danger that local protests in some cities could turn against the government for its allegedly tolerant policy toward migrants.

Islamophobic attitudes are pervasive in Russia and are directed primarily against Muslim migrants from Central Asia and the North Caucasus into the central parts of Russia, as well as resentment against state subsidization of the poorer Muslim-majority republics in the North Caucasus, which allegedly contributes to impoverishing ethnic-Russian-majority regions.[50] Moscow has registered little success in integrating millions of migrants or creating a civic identity that could incorporate and provide them with legal protection.[51] This leaves them prone to discrimination and contributes to generating ethnic conflicts. An escalation of ethnic tensions during times of turmoil can radicalize all sides and ignite riots, pogroms, and clashes with security forces in a number of Russian cities. Radical nationalists may also view these incidents as an opportunity to spark a revolutionary outburst against what they perceive as an insufficiently patriotic or hardline regime.

Fears grew during the winter of 2021–2022 that the lifting of pandemic restrictions will release public frustrations and increase

---

[49] Marlène Laruelle, *Russian Nationalism: Imaginaries, Doctrines, and Politcal Battlefields*, Routledge Series on Russian and East Europeans Studies, 2019, p.166.

[50] Edward Ponarin and Michael Komin, "Imperial and Ethnic Nationalism: A Dilemma of the Russian Elite," Pål Kolstø and Helge Blakkisrud (Eds.), *Russia Before and After Crimea: Nationalism and Identity, 2010-2017*, Edinburgh University Press, 2019, p.59.

[51] Marlene Laruelle, *Russia's Arctic Strategies and the Future of the Far North*, London: Routledge, 2014, pp.62–63.

hate crimes targeting migrants as well as provide fresh ammunition to Russian nationalists.[52] Some people will be searching for scapegoats to channel their anger over social restrictions and economic conditions. Even in regions with higher living standards and steady jobs, ethnic tensions between migrants and longer-term residents can result in conflict. For instance, following massive migrant inflows from the North Caucasus into the oil- and gas-extracting regions of the Yamalo-Nenets and Khanty-Mansi-Yugra Autonomous *Okrugs*, ethnic tensions with ethnic Russians have escalated and far-right nationalism has increased.[53] Further political radicalization, ethnic confrontations, and police crackdowns against migrants can be expected in the event of an economic downturn or a visible weakening of the central government. In addition, terrorist attacks may be staged against transportation and energy infrastructure or other targets, as radical *jihadist* influence becomes more pronounced in several regions among radicalized youths from the North Caucasus and Central Asia.

Rupture Scenarios

The Putinist regime has validated the hypothesis that within its current borders Russia is incapable of transforming into a democracy and unless it disassembles into several independent states, the country

---

[52] Richard Arnold, "Anti-Migrant Rally in Buzhaninovo Raises Specter of Dangerous Russian Nationalism," *Eurasia Daily Monitor*, Vol.18, Issue 149, September 30, 2021, https://jamestown.org/program/anti-migrant-rally-in-buzhaninovo-raises-specter-of-dangerous-russian-nationalism/.

[53] Denis Sokolov, "Ugra, the Dagestani North: Anthropology of Mobility Between the North Caucasus and Western Siberia," in Marlene Laruelle (Ed.), *New Mobilities and Social Changes in Russia's Arctic Regions*, London: Routledge, 2017, pp.182–183.

is destined to remain an autocratic empire.[54] Possible state ruptures of the Russian Federation could span a broad gamut of scenarios over a variable timeline, including a limited fracture, widescale fragmentation, violent separation, and complete state disintegration. These could develop in the midst of spreading unrest in Moscow and other major Russian cities. When protests erupted in Belarus over election rigging in August 2020, President Alyaksandr Lukashenka claimed that if Russia did not assist him to quell the demonstrations, it would soon be faced with a similar scenario.[55] Conspiracy narratives promulgated by Russian state propaganda that Western intelligence services were behind all public protests in order to dismember the country through internal revolts can rebound against the government. Instead of restoring faith in the Kremlin as the guarantor of national unity, they reinforce perceptions of regime mendacity, weakness, and inability to prevent state collapse.

From Fracture to Fragmentation

An initial rupture of the state could involve a limited fracture. A peaceful separation of one or more federal entities can occur where there is little or no prospect of reconciliation with Moscow. In this scenario, the Kremlin accepts such an outcome to avoid mass violence that could spread to other republics and regions. Chechnya is a primary candidate for such a break because the foundations of a separate state already exist and independence was initially achieved during the 1990s. Other republics may declare their sovereignty

---

[54] Peter Eltsov, *The Long Telegram 2.0: A Neo-Kennanite Approach to Russia*, Lanham: Lexington Books, 2020, p.2.

[55] Paul Goble, "If Putin Continues to Copy Lukashenka, Russia will Eventually Explode as Belarus has, Blogger Says," September 10, 2020, http://windowoneurasia2.blogspot.com/2020/09/if-putin-continues-to-copy-lukashenka.html.

without immediately moving toward outright secession, or they may seek to emulate Chechnya's example, especially in the North Caucasus or the Middle Volga. This could resemble the situation in 1990, when all autonomous republics in the RSFSR proclaimed their sovereignty, although at that time they stopped short of secession.

In addition, some regions with a predominantly ethnic-Russian population may demand the status of autonomous republics. This would include *krais* and *oblasts* objecting to an asymmetrical federation amidst growing calls for sovereignty, self-administration, and even secession in parts of Siberia and the Pacific region. During a prolonged and uncertain succession crisis in the Kremlin, regional politicians will endeavor to increase their power and influence and may even calculate that supporting separatism was essential for their political survival. Regional identification in Siberia, the Urals, the Pacific region, and elsewhere will motivate calls for statehood regardless of common origin and language, as witnessed in the former British colonies.

A more widespread fragmentation would occur once the regime itself begins to unravel at the center through a combination of internal power battles and public revolts. This could be sparked by Putin's incapacitation, assassination, sidelining, isolation or sudden natural death. In the less violent scenario, a reformist or quasi-democratic leadership takes over the presidency and even includes some members of the political opposition to placate a frustrated public. However, a rival coup attempt may also be staged by hard-liners seeking to preserve the political structure and either maintain Putin at the helm or replace him with a similar authoritarian figure. Such a scenario could be reminiscent of the failed seizure of power by Soviet hard-liners in August 1991, which triggered the collapse of the Soviet

Union.[56] A coup by Russian statist hard-liners would most probably be resisted in several ethno-national republics, as well as in Moscow, St. Petersburg, and other large cities, although some regional authorities may side with the putschists or decide to wait until there is a clearer outcome.

The federal structure will be a casualty of Russia's intra-elite battles. However, administrative ruptures may not affect the entire country uniformly. Some federal units can push for secession and others for extensive autonomy and confederation, while the federal center is preoccupied with structural and economic reforms to restore some semblance of political stability. Moscow's attempts at pacification will prove costly and ultimately unworkable if unrest and inter-communal conflicts escalate in several locations at the same time. A new or reformed Russian government may promise far-reaching decentralization, genuine federalism, or even a loose confederation and decide not to violently impose state integrity. However, if this is offered at a time when the country is already unravelling, it will be perceived as weakness and serve to escalate demands for political emancipation and independence. Moves toward democratization can enable some federal subjects to secede without violent confrontations, but there will be no guarantees that Moscow will consolidate a system of political pluralism. A broader movement for separation and independence can rapidly spread among federal units. In the economically important regions of Siberia, the Urals, and the High North, Moscow will attempt to prevent secession through economic, political, and security pressures. Some regions may remain relatively peaceful, expecting the Center to regain the initiative and "normalize" the country, but they will be drawn into decisions on separation as the federal structure erodes.

---

[56] Alexander Sungurov, "Russia in Decline: Possible Scenarios," in S. Enders Wimbush and Elizabeth M. Portale (Eds), *Russia in Decline,* Jamestown Foundation, March 2017, p.350.

Violent Centralization

At some critical point, Putin's Kremlin could decide on violent centralization and mass repression to keep the country intact, and this itself would trigger violent responses in several parts of the federation. A floundering regime that has lost its credibility in the midst of economic decline and increasing international isolation would face a combination of power struggles, public revolts, and mutinies within the internal security forces. If legal and passive resistance fails to dislodge the Putin dictatorship, then the only option will be armed resistance—whether through urban warfare or armed partisan movements in the more disaffected regions. In driving the opposition underground, the regime will radicalize several groups that could turn to sabotage, bombings, and assassinations to further disrupt state authority.

The Kremlin may endeavor to mobilize the public through a major military intervention in a rebel republic, claiming that the latter had embarked on "anti-Russian separatism" and endangered the country's territorial integrity and survival. However, following the heavy military losses in Ukraine, the public could prove lukewarm to another major military confrontation. Citizens may prefer that some restive republics are allowed to secede to avoid another prolonged and destructive war. Notably, during the first Russian military intervention in Chechnya (1994–1996) only 25 percent of citizens accepted Yeltsin's justifications of the war as necessary to preserve Russia, and the majority sought to avoid military service.[57] In January 2022, leaders of several indigenous nations, including Tatar, Bashkir, and Erzya, issued a statement condemning Russia's military involvement in the crackdown in Kazakhstan and called on conscripts

---

[57] Vladimir Shlapentokh, Roman Levita, and Mikhail Loiberg, *From Submission to Rebellion: The Provinces Versus the Center in Russia*, Westview Press, 1997, p.161.

and officers to sabotage such deployments.[58] Leaders of the Bashkir national movement *Bashkort* also called on their co-ethnics not to take part in any war against Ukraine.[59] Such assertions illustrate that an internal crackdown by Moscow's forces could generate even more opposition and military mutinies by conscripts across the country.

A breakdown of authority between Moscow and the federal subjects in combination with Kremlin opposition to separation can provoke both violent local resistance and violent reintegration to preserve the state. In some parts of the country, the collapse of central power and a vacuum in regional authority could lead to local security personnel, armed militias, or crime groups seizing control over regional governments and local economies.[60] Alternatively, regional authorities can demand the withdrawal of Russian troops, and in some republics and regions local governors will establish their own military and security units to defend the fledgling states, similarly to the creation of armed forces in the early 1990s in the former Soviet Union Republics, in the separatist enclaves within Moldova, Georgia and Azerbaijan, and in the republics that separated from Yugoslavia.

---

[58] "Indigenous Leaders Call on Nations in Russia to Boycott Crackdown on Protestors in Kazakhstan," *Euromaidan Press*, January 19, 2022, https://euromaidanpress.com/2022/01/09/indigenous-leaders-call-on-nations-in-russia-to-boycott-crackdown-on-protesters-in-kazakhstan/.

[59] "'Not Our War:' Leaders of Bashkir National Movement Call on Countrymen to Boycott Russia's War Against Ukraine," *Euromaidan Press*, January 3, 2022, https://euromaidanpress.com/2022/01/03/bashkir-national-movement-calls-to-boycott-russias-war-against-ukraine/

[60] Paul Goble, "If Putin Regime Collapses, Power More Likely to Fall to Bandits than to Liberal Opposition, Shaburov Says," *Window on Eurasia*, September 13, 2020, https://windowoneurasia2.blogspot.com/2020/09/if-putin-regime-collapses-power-more.html.

Regional capitals buttressed by public support would also block sending military conscripts to other parts of Russia to subdue revolts. Some military units that Moscow may try to deploy against regionalist leaders are likely to mutiny against the center, support officials in their own republics and regions, and defend the local population. Through their resistance to state violence, regional leaders would accumulate increasing power and authority. They will also assert that by seizing full political and military control over the federal subjects they were preventing a descent into lawlessness and anarchy, as Moscow could no longer provide regional security.

During prolonged turmoil and rupture, both Russian ethno-nationalism and statist-imperialism will witness a resurgence and mobilize supporters, just as ethnic and regional separatism mushrooms throughout the country. Nationalists and imperialists could challenge the central government as well as several regional administrations. Some nationalist leaders may marshal pro-regime groups to prevent state fracture, or they may seek to replace the Putinist government with a more explicitly imperialist or ethno-nationalist regime that can salvage state integrity and eliminate opponents. Russian nationalists can be mobilized through systematic attacks on immigrants from the North Caucasus and Central Asia and wholesale expulsions from urban districts. Nationalists will establish militia groups on the pretext of defending Russian ethnics in various republics, resisting regional independence movements, and preventing a meltdown of the state. The conflict will be intensified by religious differences between Muslim and Christian Orthodox populations that can be exploited by militants on both sides. In a display of increasing desperation in trying to keep the country together, the Kremlin may arm, finance, and encourage overtly ethno-nationalist and imperialist Russian organizations.

A growth of terrorism against civilians and government facilities can be expected, as this attracts media attention and erodes government credibility in protecting citizens. For instance, the "urbanization" of insurgencies in the North Caucasus favors terrorism, as guerrillas have a target-rich environment in cities for undermining the government.[61] Arbitrary official repression following terrorist attacks further undercuts government legitimacy and fuels insurrection. Some analysts have noted the growth of nihilist terrorism or "social terrorism," whose primary objective is neither ethnic nor religious but to destroy state institutions. Such groups will be much more difficult to identify and suppress in a fragmenting federation.[62]

Emerging National States

In a scenario of escalating state disintegration, conflicts between Moscow and several republican and regional governments will intensify. Declarations of independence will be issued by a growing number of federal subjects, while Moscow's attempts to subdue them sparks broader resistance across Russia between protestors and security forces and conflicts spread to numerous regional capitals. Security and military units will become thinly stretched and unable to contain a multiplicity of political revolts against Moscow. A declaration of independence in one federal subject can be rapidly repeated in neighboring entities and spread across a wider region.

The 1990s demonstrated that when Russia's central government weakens and power struggles intensify, numerous republics and regions reach for sovereignty and even independence to secure their territories and provide a measure of stability. Political paralysis at the

---

[61] Robert W. Schaefer, *The Insurgency in Chechnya and the North Caucasus: From Gazavat to Jihad*, Santa Barbara, CA: Praeger, 2011, p.22.

[62] Paul Goble, "'Social Terrorism' Displacing Religious and Ethnic Violence in Russian Federation, Analyst Says," *Window on Eurasia*, September 8, 2013, https://windowoneurasia2.blogspot.com/2013/09/window-on-eurasia-social-terrorism.html.

level of the federal center will encourage several republics and regions to issue declarations of independence and organize public referenda. Movements toward self-determination in richer and more economically developed republics such as Tatarstan and Bashkortostan will encourage similar initiatives in neighboring republics. They can voice a spectrum of demands for their future status, including sovereignty, confederation, or outright independence and separate statehood. Such assertions will have a domino effect throughout the country and stimulate other republics and regions to emulate their success.

A number of ethno-national movements will assert historical precedents for statehood by highlighting periods of independence before Russia's imperial conquest and colonization. Tatar nationalists affirm a 1,000-year history of statehood as heirs to the Volga Bulgaria state of the 10th century, the Mongol Golden Horde of the 13th-14th centuries, and the Kazan khanate of the 15th–16th centuries before its conquest by Czar Ivan IV in 1552, during Moscow's early imperial expansion.[63] Tatar leaders can also support the recreation of the Idel-Ural Republic, which existed briefly during the post-Tsarist civil wars, before it was defeated by the Red Army. The republic was proclaimed by a Muslim Congress meeting in the Tatarstan capital of Kazan in December 1917 and existed until April 1918.[64]

Bashkir nationalists contend that they have been living on their home territory since the 6th century, long before the arrival of Tatars and Russians, and they have staged periodic rebellions against Russian

---

[63] Dmitry P. Gorenburg, *Minority Ethnic Mobilization in the Russian Federation*, Cambridge University Press, 2003, p.88.

[64] Jonathan D. Smele, *The "Russian" Civil Wars, 1916-1926: Ten Years That Shook the World*, Oxford University Press, 2017, p.185.

rule as proof of Bashkir commitments to independence.[65] Chuvash nationalists in the Middle Volga zone have asserted direct descent from the Volga Bulgars, whose state structure included the region between the 7th and 13th centuries.[66] Any number of nations with distinct republics can retrace their history to periods of tribal independence or autonomy before the Muscovite conquest, occupation, and colonization, including the Karelians, Udmurts, and the Moksha and Erzya in Mordovia. Some Mari tribes in the Middle Volga united with the Tatars against Muscovite encroachment before the forces of Ivan the Terrible conquered Kazan in 1552. The Mari continued their struggle against invading Russian forces under their own leadership in the Cheremisian Wars, between 1553 and 1580.

Ethnic leaders in Dagestan highlight that the region was a separate khanate seized by Russia in the early part of the 19th century following a series of wars with Persia. Other nations in the North Caucasus treasure their histories of independent statehood or sovereign tribal confederations before the offensives of Tsarist Russian armies in the 19th century, including Circassians, Chechens, Ingush and Ossetians. Kalmyk nationalists claim the Kalmyk Khanate as a stable state structure established through two treaties with Russia in 1655 and 1657, following the dissolution of the Golden Horde.[67]

Khakass nationalists underscore the existence of two medieval Khakassian states between the 6th and 13th centuries and between the 15th and 17th centuries, before the Mongol invasions and Russian

---

[65] Dmitry P. Gorenburg, *Minority Ethnic Mobilization in the Russian Federation*, Cambridge University Press, 2003, p.96.

[66] Dmitry P. Gorenburg, *Minority Ethnic Mobilization in the Russian Federation*, Cambridge University Press, 2003, pp.103–104.

[67] Mairbek Vatchagaev, "Неизвестные калмыки: кто они – европейские буддисты?" July 9, 2021, https://www.kavkazr.com/a/31346080.html.

conquests and colonization, respectively.[68] Altai and Buryat leaders can also point to periods of national semi-autonomy under the Mongol and Chinese empires. Tuvan leaders assert that their republic was a fully independent state in the first part of the 20th century, after centuries of either Mongol or Chinese rule and before Russia's unilateral annexation. In eastern Siberia, the Chukchi have a long history of self-determination and independence throughout the Tsarist empire, while their payment of compulsory tribute to the Russian state could not be enforced. There was only a limited Russian presence on their territories and attempts to organize administrative units failed until after the Bolshevik takeover of the Russian empire during the civil wars of 1916–1926.[69]

Activists in several other nations in the High North, Siberia, and the Pacific region may demand their own autonomous regions with greater control or higher revenues from valued resources on their territories, including oil, natural gas, gold, uranium, mercury, and other minerals. A number of indigenous peoples can claim the right to self-determination under the United Nations Charter, the International Covenant on Civil and Political Rights, and the 2017 United Nations Declaration on the Rights of Indigenous Peoples.[70] They will affirm legal rights to their traditional territories and resources and to administrative self-determination. They could proceed further by asserting statehood, according to the United

---

[68] Dmitry P. Gorenburg, *Minority Ethnic Mobilization in the Russian Federation*, Cambridge University Press, 2003, p.109.

[69] Yuri Slezkine, *Arctic Mirrors: Russia and the Small Peoples of the North*, Ithaca: Cornell University Press, 1994, p.105.

[70] *Indigenous Peoples Human Rights Defenders Field Handbook on Human Rights Documentation and Advocacy*, Asia Indigenous Peoples Pact (AIPP) Foundation, Chiang Mai 50210 Thailand, 2015, https://www.iwgia.org/images/handbookhrdip-aipp.pdf.

Nations General Assembly 1960 Declaration on the Granting of Independence to Colonial Countries and Peoples, and appeal for international support in its implementation.[71] Even nations in Russian-majority *krais* and *oblasts* can claim indigenous status prior to the Russian conquest and colonization as grounds for self-determination and independence from the current federal subjects.

Arising Regional States

The Russian Federation can also unravel along regional lines rather than simply according to ethno-republican boundaries. Residents of resource-rich regions or with strong local identities could push for independence based on inclusive multi-ethnic principles and an internal administrative arrangement acceptable to the majority of the population. Such plans would pose a serious challenge to Russia's unity.[72] Some predominantly ethnic-Russian regions have previously created the rudiments of statehood under strong and quasi-autocratic leaders, and such initiatives can be revived. The most notable example was the short-lived Urals Republic in 1993, consisting of six *oblasts*—Sverdlovsk, Perm, Chelyabinsk, Tyumen, Kurgan and Orenburg.[73]

A number of other embryonic or temporary state structures based on regional identity have existed on the territory of the current Russian Federation, and some local activists may seek their revival or use them as historic precedents for claiming legitimate statehood. These include

---

[71] https://cdn.un.org/unyearbook/yun/chapter_pdf/1960YUN/1960_P1_SEC1_CH5.pdf.

[72] Peter Eltsov, *The Long Telegram 2.0: A Neo-Kennanite Approach to Russia*, Lanham: Lexington Books, 2020, pp.124–125.

[73] Matthew Crosston, *Shadow Separatism: Implications for Democratic Consolidation*, London: Routledge, 2004, p.81.

the Siberian Republic and the Far Eastern Republic, whose territorial span would encompass several current *krais* and *oblasts*. In addition, smaller entities could be rekindled, such as the Kuban People's Republic (KPR), an anti-Bolshevik formation proclaimed in February 1918, which sought unification with the independent Ukrainian People's Republic during the post-Tsarist civil war. It was established on the territory of the Kuban region along the Black Sea in present day Krasnodar *Krai*. The KPR existed for 21 months, before its military forces were defeated by the Red Army in November 1919.

During the post-Tsarist civil wars, Siberian regionalists, who claimed a distinct identity and sought to emulate the American War of Independence in their own struggle against Russian colonial rule, established a provisional government for an Autonomous Siberia in January 1918, but the formation was eliminated by the Bolsheviks.[74] Nonetheless, a significant sector of ethnic Russians may support the sovereignty or secession of regions in which they have ancestral roots and have few ties with Moscow or European Russia regardless of their common language. In addition, a sizeable proportion of Russians living in the ethnic-based republics are likely to endorse their independence. For instance, in March 1992, 47 percent of Russians in Tatarstan voted in favor of sovereignty in a public referendum in which over 62 percent of all residents backed republican sovereignty.[75]

Predominantly Russian ethnic regions can emerge by default as sovereign and independent units during the federal collapse. Additionally, Russian ethno-nationalists will claim that Russians have been discriminated against in the Soviet Union and in the Russian

---

[74] Jonathan D. Smele, *The "Russian" Civil Wars, 1916-1926: Ten Years That Shook the World*, Oxford University Press, 2017, pp.69–70.

[75] Elise Giuliano, *Constructing Grievance: Ethnic Nationalism in Russia's Republics*, Cornell University Press, 2011, p.46.

Federation and need their own single national republic or a federation of Russian republics to restore their ethnic identity and statehood. Some nationalists will also welcome the separation of predominantly non-Russian republics in order to ensure greater ethnic homogeneity and eliminate state subsidies to poorer federal subjects. During a federal fracture, a Republic of Siberia could be one of the first entities to proclaim its independence.[76] Some activists can claim the Khanate of Sibir in southwestern Siberia before its conquest by Moscow in the late 16th century as a historical precedent and a nucleus for pan-Siberian statehood. The large Ukrainian population in the Far East may also seek greater regional autonomy and closer links with Ukraine. Descendants of Ukrainians and other nations, including Tatars and Chuvash, who were deported to or settled in southern Siberia and the Pacific territories, have undergone a process of cultural and linguistic rejuvenation since the Soviet decomposition.[77]

Ethnic and Regional Rivalries

Secession based on ethno-national principles could also spark internal disputes between majority and minority groups or with an ethnic-Russian population seeking to remain within a single all-encompassing federation. Some republican leaders or movements supporting secession from Russia may also campaign for territorial acquisitions and the amalgamation of neighboring regions containing ethnic kindred.

---

[76] Andrei Piontkovsky, "Life After Decline," in S. Enders Wimbush and Elizabeth M. Portale (Eds), *Russia in Decline,* Jamestown Foundation, March 2017, p.296.

[77] Artem Rabogoshvili, "Ethnicity on the Move: National-Cultural Organizations in Siberia," in Joachim Otto Habeck (Ed.), *Lifestyle in Siberia and the Russian North,* Cambridge, UK: Open Book Publishers, 2019, pp.295–329.

The Ethno-Russian Question

As the fault lines widen, Putin or his successor can turn to Russian ethno-nationalism to try and maintain Kremlin control, prevent the secession of Russian-majority regions, and preserve a core Russian state. Even where resistance to Moscow is manifest among Russian populations in several regions, by tapping into ethnic identity and sparking inter-ethnic conflicts, Moscow may undercut moves toward separatism in some federal subjects. However, this will also boomerang against the regime by strengthening anti-Russian radicalism. Even in Moscow and other large cities, inter-ethnic clashes can be generated by numerous factors, including racism and discrimination, police brutality, and minority and religious radicalization.

The deliberate pursuit of ethnic divisions through violence would resemble developments in a collapsing federal Yugoslavia during the 1990s. It is worth remembering that the "Yugoslav scenario" was varied, with only limited military skirmishes in Slovenia, a small guerrilla war in Macedonia, a short NATO bombing campaign in Serbia, and no armed conflicts in Montenegro. In marked contrast, the wars in Croatia, Bosnia-Herzegovina, and Kosova took the lives of tens of thousands of people and displaced millions more. Different parts of the Russian Federation could follow these diverse scenarios with outright war between the center and some republics and regions. Moscow can emulate Serbia in the 1990s by mobilizing ethnic Russians to carve out ethnically homogenous regions from rebellious republics. It can mobilize, fund, arm, and direct militia groups and volunteer movements, as in Slobodan Milošević's Yugoslavia, to kill, plunder, and terrorize non-Russian populations. Various ethno-nationalist revolutionary movements advocating violence against non-Russians could be recruited, and some already have experience in violent attacks against ethnic minorities and political opponents.[78] Returning fighters from Ukraine and other conflict zones can gravitate toward internal territorial and ethnic battlegrounds.

In the midst of outright conflict with Moscow, the process of de-russification can intensify in some former federal subjects. New governments will seek to protect a burgeoning identity and independent statehood and avoid being drawn back into a "Russian world." In some cases, this could involve purging ethnic Russians from significant political positions, confiscating Russian-owned businesses, and even expelling Russian populations viewed as a potential fifth column for Muscovite subversion. "Ethnic cleansing" operations could also be conducted by the central government as well as by some republican regimes in order to ensure ethnic homogeneity or to seize territory and create larger states.

Russia can experience a number of civil wars, reminiscent of the period between 1917 and 1926, during the collapse of the Tsarist empire and following the Bolshevik seizure of power.[79] Several of these conflicts were in essence wars of national liberation to restore or establish states independent from the Russian empire. Such struggles can include guerrilla wars against the central government or against regional governments loyal to Moscow. The Kremlin will find its security forces too thinly stretched to handle simultaneous liberation wars across the country and may only be able to maintain control over Moscow, St. Petersburg, and the core *oblasts* of European Russia.

---

[78] Robert Horvath, "Ideologue of Neo-Nazi Terror: Aleksandr Sevastianov and Russia's 'Partisan' Insurgency," in Pål Kolstø and Helge Blakkisrud (Eds.), *Russia Before and After Crimea: Nationalism and Identity, 2010-2017*, Edinburgh University Press, 2019, pp.163–180.

[79] Jonathan D. Smele, *The "Russian" Civil Wars, 1916-1926: Ten Years That Shook the World*, Oxford University Press, 2017.

A smaller Russia may not necessarily gravitate toward democracy and regional cooperation. It could evolve into an aggressive power, just as Putin's Russia has proved to be more internationally assertive and imperialist than the Soviet Union under Gorbachev. Nonetheless, its military capabilities would be significantly reduced, its geopolitical aspirations narrowed, and it would be focused on ensuring state survival rather than territorial expansion. In the midst of the escalating conflicts, competing factions with distinct ideologies or regional programs could claim to be the legitimate national governments of a new Russian state.[80] The country could then face a Libyan, Iraqi, or Syrian scenario, with competing political forces fighting over disputed territories, economic resources, and political authority in a greatly shrunken Russia.

North Caucasus Cauldron

The North Caucasus is particularly vulnerable to ethnic-based separatism, inter-republican territorial conflicts, internal power struggles, and inter-ethnic disputes within and between several republics. Moscow views the region as a perpetual flashpoint and does not trust the leaders of any republic, including Chechnya's President Ramzan Kadyrov who exacerbates public alienation from Moscow.[81] In Chechnya, there are at least three positions on relations with Russia: nationalists seeking confederacy or full independence, Islamic separatists supporting a pan-Caucasian Emirate that would purportedly guarantee the independence of each constituent republic,

---

[80] Remarks by Russian activists at a Jamestown Foundation Roundtable on "The Future of Russia's Federation: Reform or Rupture?" Jamestown Foundation, September 9, 2021.

[81] Remarks by Russian activists at a Jamestown Foundation Roundtable on "The Future of Russia's Federation: Reform or Rupture?" Jamestown Foundation, September 9, 2021.

and a group around Kadyrov or not involved with either the nationalists or Islamists who calculate that it is counterproductive to immediately demand sovereignty and prefer to play a longer game until Russia weakens sufficiently and starts to abandon the North Caucasus.

Relations between Moscow and Grozny are based on a personal deal in which Kadyrov is Putin's vassal who maintains Chechnya within the Russia Federation and represses all dissent. In return, Moscow provides lucrative state subsidies or reverse "tributes" that the center must pay to a subject to maintain his fealty. When Kremlin rule weakens and federal payments dramatically decline, Kadyrov will find himself in a precarious position and will no longer be able to buy the loyalty of the major Chechen clans. If Kadyrov concludes that the central government is retreating and he cannot depend on federal funding, he will revive the option of Chechnya's independence. Chechnya has largely existed outside Russia's legal system and has its own security and police forces loyal to Kadyrov, although their long-term loyalty remains in question.[82] Kadyrov has established a harsh authoritarian regime, but this could be turned into a state-building project based on a synthesis of Chechen nationalism and traditionalist Sufi Islam.

Alternatively, if Kadyrov dies or is incapacitated, the current structure, based upon the personal loyalty of the Chechen leader to Putin, could unravel and Moscow would be faced with tens of thousands of heavily armed Chechens pushing for independence. Even with Kadyrov in power, the republic can descend into civil war fueled by economic decline, clan rivalries and warlordism. Kadyrov

---

[82] Valery Dzutsev, "Experts Warn Moscow's North Caucasus Policies Exacerbate Regional Instability," *Eurasia Daily Monitor*, May 1, 2013, Vol. 10, Issue 82. For predictions about a Third Chechen War that would oust Russian forces from the region see Lauren Goodrich and Peter Zeihan, *A Crucible of Nations: The Geopolitics of the Caucasus*, A Stratfor Book, Austin, TX, 2011, pp.109–110.

may also seek to distract attention by provoking armed conflicts with neighboring Ingushetia or Dagestan over regions of both republics claimed by Grozny. Kadyrov could use his paramilitary army (*kadyrovtsy*), estimated in size from 5,000 to 20,000 combatants, to reassert Chechnya's statehood. He is currently the only republican head who controls the local security services and has called for the removal of all federal troops from Chechnya. A declaration of independence could help appease those clans who resent Kadyrov's authoritarian system and his loyalty to Moscow.

Some analysts contend that Kadyrov's authoritarian regime is stealthily moving toward independence and that his "state within a state" could serve as a model for other North Caucasus republics.[83] The belief has also grown among Chechen leaders that they could pursue a Greater Chechnya that would incorporate parts of Ingushetia and Dagestan, and with a strategic link to the Caspian Sea.[84] Kadyrov has called for the restoration of the Chechen-majority Aukhov *Raion* in Dagestan. After the deportation of the Chechen population in February 1944 to Central Asia, the district was renamed Novolaksky and populated with Laks from other regions of Dagestan, while a part of Aukhov *Raion* was transferred to Kazbekovsky *Raion* and populated by Avars. After returning from deportation, Chechen leaders sought to restore Aukhov *Raion* and relocating Laks and Avars elsewhere. Dagestan's Chechens have demanded that the Dagestani government resettle them in towns where they lived before their deportation.[85] Grozny may also insist that the *raion* be incorporated

[83] Charles King and Rajan Menon, "Prisoners of the Caucasus – Russia's Invisible Civil War," *Foreign Affairs*, Vol. 89, No. 4, July/August 2010, p.30.

[84] Roland Dannreuther and Luke March, "Chechnya: Has Moscow Won?" *Survival*, Vol. 50, No. 4, August–September 2008, p. 06.

[85] Mairbek Vatchagaev, "Dagestan Is Enmeshed in Another Round of Ethnic

in the Chechen Republic, from which it was separated during the 1944 deportations; this, too, can spark armed conflicts.[86]

Several other disputes have simmered in areas where Chechens have territorial claims, including with Kumyk, Lak, Avar and Cossack populations. Avars charge Chechnya's government with irredentism and interpret calls for a united Chechen–Dagestani state as disguised attempts to annex territory. Meanwhile, Kumyk villages have protested against Lak resettlement and the creation of Novolaksky *Raion* on what they consider their ancestral lands.[87] Kumyks historically inhabited most of Dagestan's lowlands. After the mass migration of other groups from the mountains to the plains, they became dispersed minorities on territories they consider to be their ethnic homeland. In particular, Dagestan's Khasavyurt *Raion*, bordering Chechnya, is rife with territorial disputes between Chechens, Kumyks, Laks, Avars and Andys.[88]

Several republics could face ethno-territorial splintering. Dagestan is the prime contender for fracture along ethnic lines. Numerous factors can generate conflict, including rivalry between the two leading ethnicities, the Avars and Dargins; dissatisfaction with the ethnic

---

Confrontation," *Eurasia Daily Monitor*, Vol. 10, Issue 39. March 1, 2013.

[86] "The North Caucasus: The Challenges of Integration (1) Ethnicity and Conflict," International Crisis Group, *Europe Report*, No. 220, October 19, 2012, Moscow, Russia, http://www.crisisgroup.org/~/media/Files/europe/caucasus/220-the-north-caucasus-the-challenges-of-integration-i-ethnicity-and-conflict.pdf, p.20.

[87] "The North Caucasus: The Challenges of Integration (1) Ethnicity and Conflict," International Crisis Group, *Europe Report*, No.220, October 19, 2012, Moscow, Russia, http://www.crisisgroup.org/~/media/Files/europe/caucasus/220-the-north-caucasus-the-challenges-of-integration-i-ethnicity-and-conflict.pdf, p.21.

[88] Mairbek Vatchagaev, "Kumyk Leader Murdered in Dagestan," *Eurasia Daily Monitor*, Vol. 10, Issue 79. April 26, 2013.

distribution of top government positions; disputes over land ownership; rifts between mountain and lowland nationalities, particularly between Avars and Kumyks; and the grievances of nations divided by current borders.[89] Under the Soviet and post-Soviet systems, Dagestan has been officially jointly administered by 14 ethnicities. The destabilization of Dagestan could lead to the resumption of campaigns for national autonomy among several ethnic groups. Renewed fears of ethnic fragmentation arose in response to the transition to a presidential system in early 2006 and the disbanding of the 14-member State Council, in which each of the 11 titular ethnic groups, together with Russians, Azeris and Chechens, were represented. Kremlin nominations of regional governors has stirred resentments among various ethnic leaders.[90]

Given the number of nationalities and overlapping settlement patterns, a territorial division of Dagestan seems improbable, but such an attempt by any one group could provoke a chain reaction of conflictive claims.[91] In 2015, Kumyk activists established a Kumyk Cultural National Autonomy to campaign for self-determination. The Kumyk organization *Tenglik* has sought local autonomy, and more ambitious members have called for a separate Kumyk Republic within the Russian Federation. Tenglik has campaigned to turn Dagestan into a federation with full territorial autonomy for each nationality in its historical homeland. Avars and other groups oppose this initiative,

---

[89] Moshe Gammer, "The Road Not Taken: Daghestan and Chechen Independence, *Central Asian Survey,* June 2005, Vol. 24, No. 2, pp.97–108, http://dx.doi.org/10.1080/02634930500154701.

[90] Edward C. Holland and John O'Loughlin, "Ethnic Competition, Radical Islam, and Challenges to Stability in the Republic of Dagestan," *Communist and Post-Communist Studies*, 43, 2010, www.elsevier.com/locate/postcomstud, p. 300.

[91] Svante E. Cornell, "Conflicts in the North Caucasus," *Central Asian Survey,* 1998, Vol. 17, No. 3, http://dx.doi.org/10.1080/02634939808401045, p.433.

as they believe demographic size is more relevant than historical origins. The Nogays remain opposed to any encroachment on their land by people from the mountain regions. Their grievances have also revived calls for autonomy. *Birlik*, the Nogay national movement, supported the creation of a Nogay autonomous entity combining parts of northern Dagestan with co-ethnics in the Republic of Chechnya and Stavropol *Krai*. Dargin militants have also demanded a separate homeland inside Dagestan. In response, the Dagestani government has regularly affirmed that internal administrative borders are permanent.[92]

Ethnic contests in the North Caucasus and elsewhere place Moscow in an unenviable position of either favoring one side in a dispute and alienating rivals, attempting mediation, or avoiding involvement and thus undercutting its influence in the region. The outbreak and escalation of inter-communal clashes in Dagestan will make the region increasingly ungovernable. A cohort of influential political activists and religious leaders no longer recognize Russia's jurisdiction in the republic. Even an official Russian report in 2005 produced for the Kremlin revealed that Dagestan faced a process of fragmentation and the emergence of several ethnic entities and Salafist enclaves in some mountain areas.[93]

The Circassian and Turkic nations in the North Caucasus can accelerate their aspirations to unite in one republic and redraw the borders of the Kabardino-Balkar and Karachay-Cherkess republics. Circassians across the region can also demand unification with the

---

[92] "Russia's Dagestan: Conflict Causes," International Crisis Group, *Europe Report* No.192, Makhachkala, Dagestan, June 3, 2008, http://www.crisisgroup.org/~/media/Files/europe/192_russia_s_dagestan_conflict_causes.

[93] Robert Bruce Ware and Enver Kisriev, *Dagestan: Russian Hegemony and Islamic Resistance in the North Caucasus,* Armon, New York: M.E. Sharpe, 2010, pp.191–195.

Republic of Adygea and the recreation of a Shapsug Circassian entity in the Sochi region of Krasnodar *Krai.* Circassian populations are scattered in other parts of Krasnodar *Krai,* much of which formed part of an independent Circassian state before the Tsarist conquest, the mass expulsions of indigenous peoples, and the Russian and Cossack colonization in the 19th century.

Kabardino-Balkaria and Karachaevo-Cherkessia remain locked in a dispute over several thousand acres of pastureland.[94] Conflicting claims to this land could turn into an ethno-national dispute between Turkic and Circassian groups in both republics, potentially demanding a redrawing of borders along ethnic lines. The dispute is compounded by an increasing scarcity of arable land, limited border demarcations between the North Caucasus republics and adjoining regions, and the willingness of republican authorities to support the land demands of farmers. In 1991, Balkar leaders declared their sovereignty and secession from the Kabardino-Balkar Republic; they announced the founding of a separate Balkar Republic within the Russian Federation. This move was overwhelmingly approved in a referendum in December 1991.[95] The Kabardins subsequently declared a Kabardin Republic in January 1992. Both initiatives were opposed and suppressed by Moscow. Karachai and Cherkess leaders also pushed for a rupture of Karachaevo-Cherkessia into two separate republics, and such initiatives will be re-energized as the Russian state fragments.

---

[94] Paul Goble, "Last Two Bi-National Republics in Russia on Brink of Fateful Territorial Dispute," June 25, 2021, http://windowoneurasia2.blogspot.com/2021/06/last-two-bi-national-republics-in.html.

[95] Elena Pokalova, *Chechnya's Terrorist Network: The Evolution of Terrorism in Russia's North Caucasus,* Santa Barbara, California: Praeger, 2015, p.19.

Multiple Regional Disputes

A plethora of territorial, ethno-national, religious and resource disputes are evident in several other parts of the Russian Federation. These could either be exploited by the Kremlin to try and control its federal subjects or become explosive ingredients when the federation starts to unravel. Such feuds revolve around historical losses, population expulsions, territorial claims, confiscated economic resources, official discrimination, and non-recognition of distinct national identities.

The Cossack population in the wider North Caucasus is becoming more assertive in claiming traditional territories and even a separate republic and state structure in the region. This could engender competing territorial claims with neighboring nations. During the post-Tsarist civil war in 1916–1926, there were repeated battles between the Red Army and various Cossack hosts, some of which established quasi-independent states such as the Don Republic with its capital in Novocherkassk in southern Russia, currently in Rostov *Oblast*. Popular uprisings by the Kuban, Orenburg, Terek, Transbaikal and other Cossack hosts were denounced as separatism by the Bolsheviks.[96] Several Cossack hosts have experienced a renaissance of tradition and identity since the dissolution of the Soviet Union, and another state collapse will provide an opportunity for territorial independence.

In several instances, the nominal ethnicity in specific republics has much of its ethnic kindred residing in neighboring federal units. Its leaders could claim the territories on which they form sizeable and compact populations, contending that an injustice was perpetrated when internal federal borders were established under the Soviet

---

[96] Jonathan D. Smele, *The "Russian" Civil Wars, 1916-1926: Ten Years That Shook the World*, Oxford University Press, 2017, p.50.

system and perpetuated in the Russian Federation. For instance, although ethnic Bashkirs in the Republic of Bashkortostan form only 30 percent of its population, significant numbers reside in neighboring Chelyabinsk, Orenburg and Sverdlovsk *oblasts*. Proposals have been voiced to exchange territories with Orenburg *Oblast*, including a fifty-kilometer portion with sizeable Bashkir and Tatar populations. This would also provide Bashkortostan with an external border with Kazakhstan. However, unilateral claims to neighboring territories could trigger assertions by some regions to parts of Bashkortostan where Bashkirs are in the minority.

Some territories in Siberia with sizeable ethnic-Russian populations can campaign for mergers with neighboring regions. The most notable is the heavily Russian-populated southern part of Sakha Republic that could push for separation and absorption by neighboring Khabarovsk *Krai*.[97] In the High North of European Russia, the Nenets Autonomous *Okrug*, within Arkhangelsk *Oblast*, and the Yamalo-Nenets Autonomous *Okrug*, part of Tyumen *Oblast*, can seek unification to form a single Arctic entity. In southern Siberia, along the borders of Kazakhstan and Mongolia, the Altai Republic will have an opportunity to pursue a merger with Altai *Krai* and form a larger sovereign republic, even though ethnic Russians constitute the majority of the population in the *krai*.

In other cases, former autonomous *okrugs* absorbed by neighboring *krais* and *oblasts* will seek to restore their previous status. Residents of the disbanded Koryak Autonomous *Okrug* have called for a referendum to secede from Kamchatka *Krai*, with which the district was amalgamated in 2005, and restore their status as a distinct federal

---

[97] Anna Reid, *The Shaman's Coat: A Native History of Siberia*, New York: Walker and Company, 2002, p.136.

subject.[98] Koryaks complain that pledges that the district would retain special status have not been fulfilled while the economy has nosedived and unemployment has spiked since the merger with Kamchatka *Krai*. Similar initiatives can be expected with demands for separating the resource-rich Khanty-Mansi Autonomous *Okrug*–Yugra from Tyumen *Oblast*.

The potential for conflict is not confined to areas with overlapping ethnic and territorial claims. For instance, in a newly emerging controversy in the High North, Moscow has selected a handful of "prioritized" regions for substantial federal support, particularly Murmansk *Oblast*, the Novaya Zemlya archipelago in Arkhangelsk *Oblast*, and the Taymyr peninsula in Krasnoyarsk *Krai*. This decision will generate disputes if local elites in neighboring regions with a paucity of natural resources or less strategically situated along the Northern Sea Route vent their frustrations with being excluded. The initiative can sharpen inter-regional rivalries and propel centrifugal forces across the Russian Arctic.[99] The Yamalo-Nenets and the Khanty-Mansi-Yugra Autonomous *okrugs* may seek to separate from Tyumen *Oblast*, as inter-elite rivalries and contestation over natural resources accelerate without Moscow's mediation or control.

---

[98] "Готовы к решительным действиям» – аборигены грозят выходом Корякии из состава края - Все подробности,"October 20, 2020, https://kam24.ru/news/main/20201020/77178.html.

[99] Sergey Sukhankin, "Russia's New 'Arctic Offensive': Do the Benefits Outweigh the Costs? (Part One),"

Eurasia Daily Monitor, Vol.18, Issue 27, February 17, 2021, https://jamestown.org/program/russias-new-arctic-offensive-do-the-benefits-outweigh-the-costs-part-one/.

After the Rupture

Moscow has established a precedent for separatism, territorial adjustments, and border changes in the former Soviet Union republics, including Russia itself, by annexing Crimea and recognizing South Ossetia and Abkhazia, the breakaway territories of Georgia, along with the Ukrainian Donbas regions of Donetsk and Luhansk, as independent states. Such precedents can be used to justify and legitimize Russia's territorial partition, particularly in the North Caucasus, South Siberia, the Northwest, and other regions with international state borders. Republics or regions can also declare their independence regardless of their geographical location or the final fate of the Russian Federation, just as the RSFSR declared independence in June 1990, before the Soviet Union was officially dissolved in December 1991.

Support by Russian state-generated propaganda for the independence of various regions in European countries, including Scotland and Catalonia, can also rebound against the Kremlin by making citizens more cognizant of the possibility of secession that can be applied in Russia itself. Aspiring countries that emerge from a fracturing Russian Federation are unlikely to gain rapid international recognition. Some may evolve into "frozen states" with unresolved internal ethnic and territorial conflicts or even become embroiled in external disputes with neighbors. The process of fracture could lead to a number of destabilizing scenarios, whether through spillovers of armed conflicts, refugee outflows, territorial wars, energy, transportation, and trade disruptions, or various military incursions. However, it can also result in the creation of several viable states with a higher degree of political stability than the Russian Federation, a sufficient economic base, a favorable geographic location, and governments committed to international cooperation.

Diverse Proto States

Statehood is an important condition for the preservation and development of national identity. The proto states and other entities that emerge from the Russian Federation will not be uniform in their internal political systems and administrative structures. Several could develop into embryonic democracies with newly formed political parties competing for office as the republican or regional institutions achieve independence from the defunct "federal vertical." They will seek workable models of sovereignty and may look toward the three Baltic States (Estonia, Latvia, Lithuania) and other post-Soviet countries for assistance and guidance.

New autocrats may emerge in some former federal units, and a few may resemble mini-Russias, with corrupt authoritarian local leaders constructing personalistic fiefdoms through control of the legislature, law enforcement, and the judicial system, combined with internal repression and media censorship. They may also invent or exaggerate the extent of internal and external threats in order to pose as the staunch defenders of the integrity of the new state. Because of prolonged Putinist repression, in the majority of regions there is limited organized democratic opposition that could challenge local autocrats.

In parts of the North Caucasus, the traditional ethno-clanship system of self-government will gain strength and replace Moscow-appointed regional administrations. In some former autonomous republics, local leaders could construct ethnocratic states curtailing the rights of non-natives. Secession can also lead to intra-elite power struggles based on rival patronage networks within the fledgling states if stability and representative government cannot be ensured by the regional administration. Some aspiring proto states could impose various restrictions on minority leaders fearing calls for sub-regional secession, partition, or amalgamation with another emerging entity or with regions that remain in a truncated Russia. Moves toward independence will become a test of strength for regional identity and multi-ethnic co-existence in a number of ethnically mixed territories. Some regions, such as Astrakhan *Oblast,* which are renowned for their multi-culturalism, may prove more resilient to exclusivist ethno-centric politics.

Internal differences over political representation, minority rights, resources and budgets will become evident in several embryonic states. This could lead to various models of representation in state institutions in efforts to engender consensus and commitment to the new country. However, some republics may witness ethnic discrimination, purges, expulsions, or the voluntary exodus of non-titular nationalities, including Russians, as the new leaders seek to create more ethnically homogenous entities. Many nascent states will also face economic problems when Moscow's federal allocations, however inadequate, are terminated. Moreover, business operations and foreign investments will be discouraged if there is persistent political uncertainty, social unrest, ethnic conflicts, official corruption, and organized criminality.

Religious affiliation can also become a source of dispute, and the Russian Orthodox Church may itself fracture into several autocephalous churches at the regional level, emulating the achievement of independence by the Ukrainian Orthodox Church in January 2019. Several attempts have already been registered in forming separate Russian Orthodox Churches, whether in opposition to the alleged ecumenism of the Moscow Patriarchate or the corruption and lavish lifestyle of the Patriarch. These include the Russian True Orthodox Church and the Russian Orthodox Autonomous Church, as well as the Old Believers, who separated from the Muscovite Church in the 17th century. Some Cossack Orthodox congregations will also seek independence from the Muscovite Church, as the Patriarch loses authority because of his ties with the failed regime.

Political debates will materialize between proponents of presidential and parliamentary systems, with some favoring a strong executive during a time of transition toward statehood and others fearing another descent into dictatorship without comprehensive parliamentary oversight. Similar developments were evident in the former republics of the Soviet Union. Nonetheless, several post-Russia statelets could become more democratically oriented, business friendly, and receptive to international investment, especially those bordering democratic foreign states. They could also guarantee broad ethnic representation in government institutions in order to provide key constituencies with a stake in the new state and support its independence. However, each developing country will confront the enormous task of reconstruction and economic stabilization and will need significant international diplomatic and material support. Assistance is more likely to be forthcoming for fledgling states that are able to ensure a relatively stable and predictable political, social, and legal environment or those that possess resources and industries that can attract foreign investment.

Disputes between some post-Russia states could escalate toward armed clashes in which the control of nuclear weapons, military equipment, energy infrastructure, or critical resources could become a major source of contention. A core state based around Moscow and Saint Petersburg is much more likely to retain Russia's nuclear weapons systems, although some other entities may also endeavor to acquire them as a potential form of defense against any Muscovite resurgence. However, it would be misleading to assume that a fractured Russian state will generate conflict and chaos in all directions, as claimed by Kremlin propaganda. In a more peaceable scenario, developing states may follow the example of post-colonial Africa by maintaining the previous administrative boundaries in order to avoid persistent conflicts over territories and minorities where virtually every state possesses some claim against neighbors. Such a solution may be pursued by several governments regardless of whether the proto states develop as democracies or autocracies.

New Federations

The dismantling of Moscow's rule can also encourage the emergence of pan-regional and pan-republic associations, although these will not encompass the entire country. Such initiatives could evolve into federal or confederal state structures. A precursor of such a process was visible in the 1990s with the development of eight inter-regional associations spanning most of the Russian Federation that were subsequently subdued by Yeltsin.[100] The most significant was the Siberian Agreement, based in Novosibirsk and including 19 regions with the objective of coordinating economic activities between western and eastern Siberia. Moscow resisted any moves toward forging agreements with a single Siberian unit, as it was fearful of fortifying an extensive pan-regional identity and encouraging Siberian separatism. The Urals Republic, declared in 1993 and which involved several federal subjects, could also become an inspiration for a new confederal arrangement between former *oblasts, krais,* and national republics. In 2003, the "Urals Republican Movement" in Yekaterinburg once again proclaimed that the establishment of a Urals Republic was a key objective.

In the contemporary post-Muscovite setting, regional initiatives will move beyond economic cooperation toward political association. They may pursue a federative option, in which several neighboring regions decide to join together in one state but in a decentralized structure and remain receptive for other former federal subjects of Russia to enlist. In such an arrangement, the new capital could be located in one of the major regional cities and further diminish Moscow's influence. Several neighboring republics and regions could also forge looser confederal agreements, especially where there is a

---

[100] Vladimir Shlapentokh, Roman Levita, and Mikhail Loiberg, *From Submission to Rebellion: The Provinces Versus the Center in Russia,* Westview Press, 1997, pp.197–198.

common history of cooperation and each party would benefit from subsuming some of their sovereignty to a central government in which they would have equal representation. Both federalism and confederalism would contribute to a more effective defense against any future attempts at imperial revisionism by Moscow.

In the Middle Volga region, the Idel-Ural State can be revived. This was a short-lived independent republic proclaimed in March 1918 in Tatarstan's capital Kazan; it asserted the unification of Tatars, Bashkirs, Chuvash, and other peoples in that region and their liberation from the Russian empire. The entity included present-day Tatarstan, Bashkortostan and Orenburg *Oblast*, with some activists even claiming part of the Caspian Sea coastline. It was overthrown by the Bolsheviks, who declared the Tatar-Bashkir Soviet Socialist Republic in April 1918. A present-day incarnation of a Middle Volga union promoted by the Free Idel-Ural movement would include the republics of Tatarstan, Bashkortostan, Chuvashia, Mari-El, Udmurtia, and Mordovia—the latter renamed as Erzyano-Moksha in recognition of the two constituent nations.[101]

The Free Idel-Ural organization was established in Ukraine in 2018 by emigres from the Middle Volga. Moscow declared it a threat to Russia's security and integrity. Tatarstan also has a government-in-exile based in Europe and the US. The new Idel-Ural state is envisaged as a confederation in which each republic would maintain its own domestic and foreign policy. Some activists have proposed a larger confederation to include the Komi Republic, Perm *Krai*, and Orenburg *Oblast* to give the new state a foreign border with Kazakhstan. Some Bashkir activists have expressed fears that an Idel-Ural state would be dominated by Tatars, whereas a broader federation could limit the predominance of any constituent national group. The Free Idel-Ural organization in exile has proposed that each

[101] https://tatar-toz.blogspot.com/2020/01/the-patriots-of-idel-ural-are.html.

republic pursue an independent domestic and foreign policy but that the proposed federation would share a single currency and tariff zone and a joint army to defend all external borders.

Inter-republican initiatives can also include the revival of the independent Mountainous Republic of the Northern Caucasus that existed between 1918 and 1922, before the Bolshevik seizure of the entire territory. This confederal republic included seven constituent states—Dagestan, Chechnya, Ingushetia, Ossetia, Circassia, Abkhazia, and the Nogai steppes. During the Soviet collapse, attempts were made to revive the Mountainous Republic; and an Assembly of the Mountain Peoples of the North Caucasus was convened in August 1989 and renamed as the Confederation of the Mountain Peoples of the Caucasus. In October 1990, it was declared as a successor state to the Mountain Republic of 1918 and as separate from the Russian Federation.[102] In November 1991, representatives from 14 peoples of the North Caucasus signed a treaty formally founding the Confederation. It was not based on Islamic religious principles but on multi-ethnic solidarity and opposition to Russian imperialism and colonialism. A modern version of the Mountain Confederation could also include the republics of Karachay-Cherkess, Kabardino-Balkar and Adygea, together with part of Krasnodar *Krai*.

In northern Siberia, Sakha would become the largest state, extracting itself from the Russian Federation with its own Arctic coastline, ports, and significant energy and mineral resources. With an astute political leadership, it could benefit from the expanding Northern Sea Route and significantly develop its trading potential with the Asia-Pacific region as well as with southern Siberia and China.[103] Other northern

---

[102] Elena Pokalova, *Chechnya's Terrorist Network: The Evolution of Terrorism in Russia's North Caucasus*, Santa Barbara, California: Praeger, 2015, p.22.

[103] Marlene Laruelle, *Russia's Arctic Strategies and the Future of the Far North*, London: Routledge, 2014, pp.207–208.

regions along the Arctic Ocean may follow Sakha's example on the global stage, including the Komi Republic, the Nenets Autonomous *Okrug*, and the Yamalo-Nenets Autonomous *Okrug*. In addition, some regional links previously initiated by Moscow could escape central control. For instance, the "Union of Cities in the Arctic and High North" established by the Kremlin in the early 1990s and involving several dozen cities, can become a vehicle for asserting regional identity and more autonomous decision-making.[104]

Russia's fracture will encourage indigenous rights movements in the High North, Siberia, and the Pacific region to play a more prominent role in shaping governing institutions. Indigenous organizations have generally opposed the transfer of land rights to individuals who can be tricked or enticed into selling land cheaply to Russian state companies. They have preferred various forms of communal indigenous management of land and resources. With the prospect of statehood, full ownership of lands traditionally used by indigenous peoples would facilitate self-determination and enable residents to determine the scale of industrial development.[105]

A parallel development to republican independence would be the emergence of sovereign Russian majority regions, some of which federate or confederate to create new state structures. Such an entity or entities could stretch across European and Asian Russia even while excluding non-Russian ethnic republics. This would finally signal the emergence of an ethnic-Russian national state, although its political

---

[104] Genevieve Parente, "Shaping Russia's New Arctic: The Union of Cities in the Arctic and High North," Marlene Laruelle (Ed.), *New Mobilities and Social Changes in Russia's Arctic Regions*, London: Routledge, 2017, pp.30–43.

[105] Gail Osherenko, "Indigenous Rights in Russia: Is Title to Land Essential for Cultural Survival?" *Georgetown International Environmental Law Review*, April 2001, https://web.archive.org/web/20110511104207/
http://www.allbusiness.com/legal/international-law/1112279-1.html.

composition and the prerogatives of the central government are likely to generate competition and even conflict between regional leaders and the administrations in Moscow or St. Petersburg.

Russia's liberal political opposition is unlikely to support the country's rupture and disintegration or its reformulation into several new states. However, it will not possess sufficient domestic or international influence to prevent such a scenario once the country enters a phase of social turbulence and structural dissolution. Some democratic exiles may return in the midst of the crisis to try and steer the country toward a democratic transformation, but they will be overshadowed by far-reaching demands for de-imperialization and decolonization. The vast majority of the tens of thousands of professionals, entrepreneurs and graduates who have emigrated over the past two decades are unlikely to return to an uncertain future. The core of European Russia experienced a major exodus at the outset of the February 2022 war against Ukraine and included professionals and businessmen who felt that Russia no longer offered them any prospects.[106] Concurrently, some non-Russian populations could decide to relocate or return to the new proto states arising from the failed Russian Federation. This could include Circassians, Chechens, and other North Caucasians, and more recent émigrés eager to contribute to the independence of embryonic independent states, such as Tatarstan, Bashkortostan, Tuva, Buryatia, and Sakha.

---

[106] https://www.cnn.com/2022/03/30/europe/russia-ukraine-brain-drain-graphics-intl-cmd/index.html.

6.

Neighborhood Impact

Escalating instabilities and growing fractures in the Russian Federation will have an impact on all neighboring countries. Some states will be vulnerable to spillovers of conflict or subject to Moscow's provocations designed to divert attention from domestic upheaval in Russia. Other countries stand to benefit from Russia's weaknesses and cleavages by easing their security concerns, expanding their influence, and even regaining territories lost to various iterations of the Muscovite imperium.

A total of 35 republics, *krais* and *oblasts* in the Russian Federation share a frontier with 14 foreign countries. Before the collapse of the Soviet Union, 12 federal subjects of the Russian Soviet Federative Socialist Republic (RSFSR) had land borders with Norway, Finland, Poland, China, Mongolia and North Korea. With the establishment of an independent Russian Federation in December 1991, the administrative boundaries of another 23 of Russia's federal subjects gained international borders.[1] In sum, ten *oblasts*, one *krai*, and one republic border Kazakhstan; six republics and one *krai* border

[1] Martin Nicholson, *Toward a Russia of Regions*, Adelphi Paper No.330, International Institute for Strategic Studies, Oxford University Press, 1999, pp.49–50.

Georgia; five *oblasts* border Ukraine; three *oblasts* border Belarus; two *oblasts* border Estonia; Lithuania, Latvia and Poland border one *oblast*; and Azerbaijan borders one republic. In addition, several federal subjects that do not currently share borders with foreign countries have long-standing ethnic, religious, cultural, and linguistic connections either with Russia's immediate neighbors or with nearby states.

Frontiers with former Soviet Union republics are often "soft," with little permanent demarcation and control, thus making them susceptible to competing territorial claims. Moreover, long-standing historical, ethnic, religious and tribal links will encourage some neighboring states to play a prominent role in the kindred regions of an unstable Russia, whether to influence political developments, prevent violence, or forestall economic collapse. Some capitals may also recognize kindred entities within the fraying Russian Federation as independent entities, contribute to state-building, and even push for unification and absorption.

Diversions and Opportunities

In efforts to conceal an internal crisis and to mobilize the public against an alleged foreign adversary, Moscow can engage in various military or sub-military provocations against its neighbors. Putinism is designed to manufacture enemies with whom it constantly struggles in order to sidetrack attention from its failures. Ongoing assertiveness along the North Atlantic Treaty Organization's (NATO) Eastern Flank could develop into several outright conflicts with NATO allies or partners. The Kremlin has been careful in its foreign interventions not to provoke a direct NATO response and experience a military defeat. However, it can become more emboldened where it encounters little resistance to an initial provocative action, or it may miscalculate and overreach in its ambitions. When Western governments publicly acknowledge Russia's domestic ruptures and impending demise, Moscow will desperately try to prove them wrong and is more likely to engage in risky policies and miscalculations.[2] In such a scenario, the Kremlin could engineer several international crises, some simultaneous, that would also rebound negatively on Russia's internal conditions.

One major focus of Putin's counter-rupture offensive will be to instigate more aggressive postures among the secessionist entities in Europe's east. Although these breakaway regions claim they are independent states that control their territories and have functioning economies and governmental institutions, they are ultimately militarily and economically dependent on their patron—the Russian Federation.[3] One option for the Kremlin in reanimating support for Putin at a time of domestic unrest would be the outright annexation of Abkhazia and South Ossetia from Georgia, of Transnistria from Moldova, and of the Donetsk People's Republic and the Luhansk People's Republic from Ukraine. However, this could provoke resistance in Abkhazia in particular. Abkhazian leaders have opposed outright political and economic integration with Russia despite signing several agreements, indicating that they view the relationship as primarily based on security protection from Georgia and financial subsidization from Moscow.

Alternatively, some separatist regimes sponsored by the Kremlin may feel more vulnerable if Russia is preoccupied internally and could provoke armed conflicts with the countries from which they separated in order to increase Moscow's military protection and political integration. A Russian retreat or the curtailment of economic subsidies to the separatist entities could lead to political instability,

---

[2] Private interview with Enders Wimbush, Jamestown Foundation, March 2021.

[3] Tomáš Hoch and Vincenc Kopeček (Eds.) *De Facto States in Eurasia*, Routledge Contemporary Russia and Eastern Europe Serries, London and New York, 2020.

political struggles, factional wars, and even the collapse of some statelets.[4] They remain heavily dependent on Moscow for their survival and have no other significant sponsors or outlets. This will also encourage the fractured states—Georgia, Ukraine and Moldova—to regain their lost territories through economic pressure or outright military intervention. They would calculate that Moscow is focused on domestic problems, as during the Soviet bloc collapse, and not be capable of waging a new war.

In the case of Abkhazia and South Ossetia any ensuing conflicts could also spill over the border into Russia's North Caucasus, with different republics and militias supporting South Ossetian and Abkhazian independence in order to buttress their own claims to statehood. Additionally, North Ossetia's leaders can seek unification with South Ossetia to form a larger independent state, while contending that South Ossetia has already declared its independence and is recognized as such by Russia.[5] Such moves are likely to exacerbate territorial conflicts between North Ossetia and Ingushetia and heighten tensions with neighboring Chechen and Circassian populations.

The Kremlin may calculate that domestic turmoil necessitates a more assertive approach toward neighboring states. This could temporarily divert attention from public disaffection by arousing patriotic sentiments and gain Moscow some temporary international leverage. But despite calculations that the creation of a threatening foreign enemy or the annexation of new territories will disarm domestic opposition, Putin's attempted empire building will eventually backfire at home. Instead of deflecting from domestic woes, a foreign offensive can both concentrate and exacerbate public anger.

---

[4] Huseyn Aliyev, "Explaining De Facto States' Failure," in Tomáš Hoch and Vincenc Kopeček (Eds.) *De Facto States in Eurasia*, Routledge Contemporary Russia and Eastern Europe Serries, London and New York, 2020, p.257.

[5] https://www.britannica.com/place/South-Ossetia.

The "Crimea consensus," following the annexation of the peninsula from Ukraine in 2014, largely subsided by the close of the decade, and citizens questioned the cost of incorporation for Russia's budget. A Levada Center poll in April 2019 revealed that a clear majority of Russians believed that Moscow's foreign policies worsened the country's economy and standards of living.[6] Sustained public support for foreign interventions, including the full-scale war in Ukraine launched in February 2022, will prove even more challenging for the regime at a time of economic depression. A costly, prolonged and bloody war that further impoverishes and isolates the country and produces a growing number of casualties will help convince wide sectors of the Russian population that the only viable solution is the ouster of the Putin regime.

Growing unrest, power struggles, and fractures in the Russian Federation are likely to reverberate around its borders. NATO allies and partners need to closely monitor rising tensions in several neighboring regions inside Russia and prepare for developments that could challenge their own security. Although the Helsinki Final Act declares that the borders of Europe are inviolable, it does not confirm that they are necessarily final. Article 1 indicates that the participating states "consider that their frontiers can be changed, in accordance with international law, by peaceful means and by agreement."[7] Logically, the current borders of the Russian Federation cannot be considered permanent and in case of a state crisis they can be altered

[6] Mike Eckel, "Poll: Majority of Russians Support Crimea Annexation, But Worry About Economic Effects," Radio Free Europe/ Radio Liberty, April 3, 2019, https://www.rferl.org/a/poll-majority-of-russians-support-crimea-annexation-but-worry-about-economic-effects/29859570.html.

[7] Conference on Security and Cooperation in Europe Final Act," Helsinki 1975, https://www.osce.org/files/f/documents/5/c/39501.pdf.

by mutual consent between the separating region and the federal government.

While the Russian constitution does not explicitly prohibit unilateral secession by any federal subject, such restrictions are implicit in several of its provisions. Separation is also not overtly permitted in the constitution. However, article 66, section 5 of the document affirms that the status of a federal subject "may be changed upon mutual agreement of the Russian Federation and the subject of the Russian Federation and according to the federal constitutional law."[8] Moreover, border changes can transpire and new states can emerge regardless of constitutional provisions but because of a breakdown in central authority, intense centrifugal pressures, threats of violence, state collapse, civil war, or foreign invasions.

The fragmentation of Russia can either increase or reduce confrontations with specific neighbors, including NATO members and former Soviet republics that are NATO partners.[9] Moscow is likely to intervene in cases where it sees its imperial holdings imminently imperiled, and this can draw Western states into more direct confrontations with Russia. However, the Kremlin will be less capable of handling several simultaneous secessionist initiatives when state authority is receding and the loyalty of military units and security forces cannot be guaranteed.

International Recognitions

Russia's devolution from a failed state to a collapsing state will impact outside its current frontiers. The Russian Federation contains several

---

[8] http://www.constitution.ru/en/10003000-01.htm.

[9] Andrei A. Kovalev, *Russia's Dead End: An Insider's Testimony from Gorbachev to Putin*, Potomac Books/ University of Nebraska Press, 2017, p.310.

major cross-border nations that either have a kindred state or a co-ethnic population in a neighboring country. As aspirant states reach for greater autonomy and sovereignty, they will seek mutual recognitions with other post-Russian entities, diplomatic recognition by nearby states and other capitals, and membership in multi-national organizations. Several disaffected federal units may gravitate toward particular neighbors, especially those with long-standing ethnic, linguistic, historic, economic, or religious attachments. This can generate conflicts between Moscow and the states involved and draw other Western countries into regional confrontations with the Kremlin, even while its controls weaken throughout the federation.

Ethnic republics with a largely homogenous ethnic or religious population may have better perspectives for international recognition especially if internal conflicts remain limited.[10] For instance, Tatarstan has already laid the groundwork for its international diplomacy, having opened 17 missions abroad during the 1990s, before the Putin crackdown on republican sovereignty. These included all the former Soviet republics, the United States, Turkey, Germany and France.[11] Economic development can also favor independence. For instance, Tatarstan and Bashkortostan possess modern hydrocarbon industries and relatively diversified economies, including sizeable manufacturing and agricultural sectors.

Emerging states that have kindred "mother countries" as neighbors, such as Finland, will also benefit from their international diplomatic support. Some entities may seek the status of protectorates vis-à-vis neighboring powers and particularly with co-ethnic states or petition

---

[10] Remarks by Russian activists at a Jamestown Foundation Roundtable on "The Future of Russia's Federation: Reform or Rupture?" Jamestown Foundation, September 9, 2021.

[11] Matthew Crosston, *Shadow Separatism: Implications for Democratic Consolidation*, London: Routledge, 2004, p.63.

to create a joint-state or confederation. Nonetheless, disputes over history, identity, and statehood could also materialize between a new state and an older ethnic kindred state, such as Mongolia. This could factionalize domestic politics into competing parties that either seek full independence, confederation or amalgamation. Some new republican or regional governments will appeal for the presence of international peacekeepers or other military forces to help ensure national security and public safety during the transition to statehood. However, aspiring states are unlikely to call on Moscow for "peacekeepers," as they would be widely viewed as an occupying force seeking to stifle independence.

Heads of several federal subjects in Russia have focused on attracting foreign investments, and this can provide them with springboards to establish relations abroad.[12] After the USSR collapsed, a number of regional leaders initiated such contacts but were reined in by the Yeltsin government, which increasingly feared disintegration. Some regions and ethnic republics have retained their room for maneuver, particularly in the economic arena. For instance, Tatarstan's leaders regularly travel abroad or meet with representatives of foreign states to enhance their independence. Buryatia has developed links with Mongolia, and the Finno-Ugric republics pursue contacts with Finland, Estonia and Hungary together with diaspora populations. It is worthwhile to explore a plethora of cross-border connections that will gain traction as Russia's rupture unfolds.

---

[12] Paul Goble, "Heads of Russian Republics, Krays and Oblasts Remain Active Abroad, Stremoukhov Says," November 3, 2020, http://windowoneurasia2.blogspot.com/2020/11/heads-of-russian-republics-krays-and.html.

Norway and Denmark

A weakened Moscow will find itself in an increasingly precarious position when asserting its maritime claims in the Arctic region. This can revive disputes with Norway and potentially benefit Oslo over the delimitation of state boundaries in the Barents Sea, the Arctic Archipelago of Svalbard, and other maritime areas where Russia currently claims fishing rights and access to oil and natural gas resources.[13] Denmark can also reassert its claims to the Lomonosov Ridge, an underwater ridge of continental crust in the Arctic Ocean that Moscow has unilaterally declared to be an extension of Russian territory. Copenhagen maintains that the Ridge is an extension of Greenland, an autonomous territory and one of the three constituent countries within the Kingdom of Denmark.

In addition to maritime and territorial contests, the status of Greenland may feature in the calculations of several of Russia's federal subjects.[14] Greenland's self-government with local control over natural resources, the judicial system, law enforcement, national borders, and other domains, could serve as an example for several Siberian and High North entities, including the Sakha Republic, the Komi Republic, the Nenets Autonomous *Okrug*, and the Yamalo-Nenets Autonomous *Okrug*, as well as for regions seeking genuine autonomy, such as Khabarovsk *Krai* and Chukotka *Okrug*. Greenland's majority Inuit population also has ethnic, linguistic and cultural ties with the Yupik population in Chukotka *Okrug*. An

---

[13] Andreas Østhagen, "How Norway and Russia avoid Conflict over Svalbard," The Arctic Institute, June 19, 2018, https://www.thearcticinstitute.org/norway-russia-avoid-conflict-svalbard/.

[14] Mininnguaq Kleist, "Greenland Self-Government and the Arctic," in Dawn Alexandrea Berry, Nigel Bowles, and Halbert Jones (Eds.) *Governing the North American Arctic: Sovereignty, Security, and Institutions*, Palgrave Macmillan, 2016, pp.247–252.

autonomous status for the northern regions of the dissolving Russian Federation could become a stepping stone toward full independence and statehood. Since Greenland's referendum on enhanced autonomy in November 2008, the Danish government only retains control over Greenland's foreign affairs, defense, and monetary policy. This could become an initial model for several of Russia's current northern territories.

Norwegian, Swedish, and Finnish authorities have expressed concern over the status of the Finno-Ugric speaking Sámi people on the Kola peninsula of Murmansk *Oblast* and favor developing closer ties with their own Sámi populations. Unlike in Norway, Sweden, and Finland, the small Sámi community in Russia has little practical control over land and natural resources on which they have been dependent for subsistence.[15] Laws that are supposed to ensure their rights are rarely implemented and vast traditional areas have been destroyed by mining and smelting activities, oil, natural gas, and mineral exploration, timber and commercial fishing industries, oil spills that affect fishing and hunting activities, as well as pipelines and roads that restrict access to reindeer calving grounds and sacred religious sites.

Finland

Moscow's sharply intensified military assault on Ukraine in 2022 generated a sense of insecurity in all bordering countries and, specifically, heightened calls for NATO membership in Finland and Sweden. But the war or a potential escalating political crisis in Russia may also raise support in both states for the national rights of the

[15] Gail Osherenko, "Indigenous Rights in Russia: Is Title to Land Essential for Cultural Survival?" *Georgetown International Environmental Law Review*, April 2001, https://web.archive.org/web/20110511104207/http://www.allbusiness.com/legal/international-law/1112279-1.html.

Finno-Ugric populations in the Russian Federation. The World Congress of Finno-Ugric Peoples are political summits, usually attended by presidents of the world's three Finno-Ugric-majority countries—Finland, Estonia and Hungary—as well as Finno-Ugric representatives from the Russian Federation. The Congress has adopted a more assertive position in recent years in support of Russia's Finno-Ugric nations, and the Kremlin has tried to curtail such connections but with limited success. Moscow's opposition indicates a fear of international linkages, especially with Finland and Estonia, given that the "historic goal" of the Congress is to develop and defend national identity, languages and cultures, promote cooperation among Finno-Ugric peoples, and "ensure the right of all Finno-Ugric peoples to self-determination."[16]

Moscow has tried to control the Finno-Ugric nations in Russia and limit ties with kindred countries by establishing an official Association of Finno-Ugric Peoples of the Russian Federation. This state-supervised organization has accused Finland, Estonia, and Hungary of seeking to "patronize and control" Finno-Ugric movements, and it disparaged the Finno-Ugric World Congress as "an instrument of interference in the internal affairs of the Russian Federation."[17] Although the Kremlin controls regional officials and officially registered ethno-national organizations, it will find it increasingly difficult to block independent contacts between ethnic groups and compatriots in kindred states.

---

[16] Paul Goble, "Internet Defeats Moscow's Efforts to Undermine Finno-Ugric Unity, Congress Organizers Say," June 18, 2021, http://windowoneurasia2.blogspot.com/2021/06/internet-defeats-moscows-efforts-to.html.

[17] Vadim Shtepa, "Kremlin's Geopolitical Fears Divide Finno-Ugric Peoples," *Eurasia Daily Monitor*, Vol.18, Issue 100, June 23, 2021, https://jamestown.org/program/kremlins-geopolitical-fears-divide-finno-ugric-peoples/.

Helsinki has been especially focused on the Karelian and Ingermanland populations; and as Russia weakens, Finland can revive its historical claims and ethnic links to the Karelian Republic. The Karelo-Finnish Soviet Socialist Republic (KFSSR) was established by the Soviet government in March 1940 and incorporated territory captured from Finland during the First Soviet-Finnish war, including the Karelian Isthmus and Ladoga Karelia. Almost the entire Karelian population of some half a million was evacuated or expelled to Finland, and the KFSSR was settled by Russians and other outsiders. Finland regained most of the Karelian territories in 1941 during the Second Soviet-Finnish war, but Moscow recaptured them by the end of the hostilities in September 1944 and transferred the Karelian Isthmus to Leningrad *Oblast.* In July 1956, the Karelo-Finnish Union Republic was incorporated into the Russian Soviet Federative Socialist Republic (RSFSR) as the Karelian Autonomous Soviet Socialist Republic (KASSR). By losing its Union Republic status, Karelia was disqualified from having the right to secede from the Soviet Union when the USSR collapsed in 1991.

Finnish nationalists will also become more vocal in claiming several border regions captured by the Soviet Union in the wake of World War II, including Salla, Repola and Porajärvi. Some activists will become even more ambitious in advocating for a "Greater Finland" to include not only the Karelian Republic but also Murmansk *Oblast* and the northern portion of Leningrad *Oblast.* Such aspirations to politically unite the Finno-Ugric speaking peoples of northwest Russia with their "mother country" have been voiced periodically since the collapse of the Tsarist empire and after the disintegration of the Soviet Union but until now with limited political success or public support.[18]

---

[18] Henrik Meinander, *A History Of Finland*, Oxford University Press, 2020, pp.180, 191, 203.

Estonia

A provocation involving ethnic Russians or Russian speakers in Estonia could be staged by Moscow to justify an incursion to protect an allegedly endangered community and to stir patriotic feelings in Russia. Undercover Russian agents and disinformation outlets may seek to inspire or exploit separatist sentiments among elements of the Russian minority in eastern Estonia, especially in the municipality of Narva and the broader Ida-Viru County containing a Russian-speaking majority of 71.2 percent.[19] Operatives could also try to stir ethnic conflicts in the capital Tallinn, which has a sizeable Russian population of some 36 percent. Such maneuvers would test both Estonia's preparedness for subversion and conflict, as well as Western cohesion in deterring Russia's military and sub-military incursions. However, with Russia itself spiraling toward domestic conflict, territorial partition to join the federation will lose its appeal among Russian minorities residing in stable and prosperous states.

In an alternative scenario, as the Russian state degenerates, Estonia can reassert its ownership of border territories south of Lake Peipus that were unilaterally transferred to Pskov *Oblast* in the RSFSR at the end of World War II, when Estonia was forcibly incorporated into the USSR. Some Finno-Ugric activists in the Russian Federation also complain that the three independent Finno-Ugric states (Finland, Estonia and Hungary) are not doing enough to campaign for their rights and aspirations in Russia, because they are fearful of provoking Moscow. Such fears will abate during Russia's spreading domestic crises. The Estonian government has consistently spoken up for the rights of Finno-Ugric nations in Russia and offered exile for activists persecuted by Moscow. Tallinn will become more assertive when regional unrest swells in Russia. Estonia's administration is likely to pursue closer contacts with activists in neighboring Ingria as well as

---

[19] https://www.stat.ee/en/find-statistics/statistics-by-theme.

with the Finno-Ugric republics, autonomous regions, and national leaders in the High North, the Middle Volga, and the Urals region.

Latvia

Moscow has tried to exploit the regionalist Latgal question in Latvia to undermine the central government in Riga. The Latgals form over 65 percent of the population in the Latgale region of eastern Latvia, which, according to the 2011 census, totaled 304,000 inhabitants.[20] They are predominantly Roman Catholics and speak a distinct dialect of Latvian. The region also has a sizeable ethnic-Russian minority of some 24 percent, concentrated in its largest city, Daugavpils. Some officials in Moscow have promoted the idea that Latgals should be recognized as a distinct nation and Latgalia should be detached from Latvia and united with Russia. The Kremlin calculates that by promoting such a scenario it can better leverage the Latvian government and limit its NATO involvement.[21] Russia's media outlets have been pushing the notion that NATO intends to expand a small training center in Latvia into a military base in Latgale and that such developments are opposed by the local population because they would provoke conflicts with Russia. Unrest in Russia can tempt the Kremlin to incite a conflict inside NATO territory, and Latvia may be viewed as a potentially softer target than its neighbors.

Paradoxically, Russia's aggression will also boomerang against it when its weaknesses become evident and the regime is distracted on multiple internal and external fronts. In defending itself against

---

[20] https://www.citypopulation.de/en/latvia/admin/LV005__latgale/.

[21] Paul Goble, "Moscow Again Wants to Play Latgal Card, This Time against NATO in Eastern Latvia," December 30, 2020, http://windowoneurasia2.blogspot.com/2020/12/moscow-again-wants-to-play-latgal-card.html.

Russia's subversion, Riga has enhanced its territorial defense strategy and is training more intensely with Euro-Atlantic allies. In the event of Russia's rupture, Latvia could also revive its claims to parts of Pskov *Oblast*, particularly the Pytalovsky *Raion* that was known as Abrene County before its unilateral transfer to the RSFSR and Latvia's forcible annexation in the Soviet Union at the close of World War II.

Lithuania

The final status of Kaliningrad *Oblast*, a region along the Baltic coast separated from Germany and occupied by the Soviet Union after the Second World War, will be questioned during Russia's internal turmoil. The region's uncertain legal standing can be challenged by neighboring Lithuania and Poland and generate irredentist claims by nationalists in both states. Lithuania's claim to Kaliningrad would be based upon both ethnic and historical grounds.[22] Vilnius could argue that the first people to hold sovereignty over the region were ethnic Lithuanians and the closely related original Baltic Prussians. Additionally, the pre-1945 population outside the cities of the *oblast* was largely of Lithuanian origin. If the status of Kaliningrad were to be altered, then Vilnius could have a strong argument for assimilating all or parts of the eastern portion of Kaliningrad, historically designated as "Lithuania Minor."

Russian officials have expressed fears that Lithuania and Poland have contingency plans for absorbing Kaliningrad in the event of a conflict

---

22 Raymond A. Smith, "The Status of the Kaliningrad Oblast Under International Law," *Lithuanian Quarterly Journal of Arts and Sciences*, Vol. 38, No.1, Spring 1992, http://lituanus.org/1992_1/92_1_02.htm.

between Russia and NATO.[23] Such a move would eliminate Moscow's military presence on the frontiers of both countries, as Russia does not directly border either state. In the event of a collapse of Moscow's control over Kaliningrad, the region could benefit from becoming a province of Lithuania with a measure of autonomy and the unchallenged "right of return" for any native Kaliningraders or Königsbergers from Germany and elsewhere. By acquiring Lithuanian citizenship, the current population would benefit from EU funding, reconstruction, investment, freedom of movement, and greater job opportunities.

The Kremlin could seek to shift attention away from Kaliningrad by applying pressure on the Baltic states and test NATO's reaction to an incursion in Estonia, Latvia, or Lithuania in an alleged defense of Russian ethnics. Such assertive moves could convince Poland and Lithuania working in tandem with some NATO allies to stage a counter-offensive in Kaliningrad, degrade Russia's military infrastructure, occupy the exclave, sever Moscow's connections, and stage elections for a new regional administration. This could be preceded or followed by a regional referendum to determine whether Kaliningrad discards its current Bolshevik-era name and if it should deciare independence and statehood, acquire a special territorial status linking the region with both Poland and Lithuania, or if it should be partitioned and absorbed by both countries. Potential claims by Germany to Kaliningrad (Königsberg), based on its historical possession as East Prussia, could also be raised.

---

[23] Paul Goble, "Lithuania and Poland Want to 'Recover' Kaliningrad, Russian Analysts Say," *Eurasia Daily Monitor*, Vol.18, Issue 166, November 2, 2021, https://jamestown.org/program/lithuania-and-poland-want-to-recover-kaliningrad-russian-analysts-say/.

Poland

Moscow operates on the deeply rooted historical fear that it remains in intense competition with two former imperial powers—Poland and Turkey—over the control of territories and states in their immediate neighborhood. These two powers evidently also represent Roman Catholicism and Islam in a centuries-long conflict with Russian Orthodoxy. Moscow's attack on Ukraine and the turmoil in Belarus following the defrauded elections in August 2020 unmasked the historic rivalry between Poland and Russia over the states that lie between them. Russian state propaganda depicted the Polish government as promoting coups in Kyiv and Minsk intended to tear both countries away from "Mother Russia" and expanding Polish influence. In reality, the contest in the region is not between two imperial projects, but a struggle between two strategic concepts—a centralized Russian dominion that subordinates neighbors, and voluntary multi-national confederations embodied in the EU and the NATO-anchored transatlantic alliance.

Russia has been the dominant power in the broad region between the Baltic and Black seas since the Muscovite expansion in the 18th and 19th centuries. At the end of the 18th century, the Tsarist Empire, in league with the Kingdom of Prussia and Habsburg Austria, carved up the Polish-Lithuanian Commonwealth and absorbed and assimilated the people of Belarus and Ukraine. Soviet Communists expanded the empire after collaborating with Nazi Germany to divide up the eastern half of Europe and further enlarged their territorial gains at the end of World War II. Moscow finally lost Poland as a satellite state when the Soviet bloc collapsed in 1989, and Poland was one of the first countries to recognize the independence of Belarus and Ukraine after the Soviet Union disintegrated in December 1991.

For Poland, NATO and EU membership and a strategic partnership with the US are cornerstones for the defense of its independence. Warsaw has also endeavored to secure and stabilize its eastern borders by helping immediate neighbors move closer toward European institutions, and it promotes multi-national efforts across Central-Eastern Europe. This includes the Three Seas Initiative to enhance economic and infrastructural connections between the Baltic, Adriatic, and Black seas.[24] No Polish government or any significant political party harbors neo-imperial aspirations to absorb, partition, or suborn Belarus or Ukraine. On the contrary, since the rejection of Soviet Communism, Warsaw has campaigned for the freedom of independent states to enter the multi-national institutions of their choice.

Fearing a long-term loss of influence, the Kremlin has tried to restrict Poland's influence among countries that Moscow does not recognize as fully independent. Because of inadequate leadership and Russia's subversion, both Belarus and Ukraine failed to develop stable democratic systems and competitive market economies after the Soviet demise that would have consolidated their independence and helped move them closer to the EU. In Ukraine, two popular revolutions, in 2004 and 2014, tried to break the stranglehold of corrupt officialdom and Russia's dominance; but the country continues to face an uphill struggle to ensure economic development and political stability. In Belarus, an authoritarian system controlled by President Alyaksandr Lukashenka disqualified the country from closer ties to the EU, but it also temporarily acted as a shield against full dominance by Moscow. The Kremlin did not intervene militarily in Belarus, because the country's leaders did not aspire to either EU or NATO membership. Nonetheless, some Russian forces were emplaced in Belarus at the outset of Russia's expanded war against Ukraine in February 2022 in order to threaten the opening of a northern front against Kyiv.

---

[24] https://www.3seas.eu.

Poland has been active in drawing its eastern neighbors closer to the EU through a number of initiatives, including the Eastern Partnership Program (EaP).[25] But the impact has been limited because unlike in the Western Balkans, the EU has not offered the prospect of membership. In Belarus, Warsaw's influence has been restricted by the Lukashenka administration, which feared pluralism and democratization that could dislodge it from power. However, in recent years, Warsaw and its three Baltic neighbors (Lithuania, Latvia, and Estonia) have tried to deepen diplomatic and economic ties in order to help defend Belarusian independence from an increasingly belligerent Russia, even at the cost of partially legitimizing Lukashenka. Such initiatives were largely derailed following the police crackdown on mass protests against election fraud in August 2020, culminating in new EU sanctions against Minsk.

If the crisis in Belarus reignites and deepens, the Kremlin will depict Poland as a growing regional threat and a conduit for American influence in order to justify its escalating political, economic, and security interventions. Although Polish democracy has suffered setbacks under the Law and Justice (*Prawo i Sprawiedliwość)* government, the country's political pluralism, civil liberties, and economic opportunities are a source of attraction for young Belarusians, tens of thousands of whom live and work in Poland. The country also hosts opposition activists and journalists hounded by Minsk, and the *Nexta* Telegram channel, housed in Poland and run by exiled Belarusians, was at the vanguard in recording and encouraging anti-Lukashenka demonstrations.

No government in Warsaw can ignore Poland's security by distancing itself from its eastern neighbors and remaining passive if Belarus

---

[25] European Union External Action Service, https://eeas.europa.eu/diplomatic-network/eastern-partnership_en.

merges with an expanding Russia. To bring Belarus closer to Western institutions despite the official crackdown, Warsaw has promoted an EU mini "Marshall Plan" consisting of at least one billion euros in financial assistance to help rebuild the country, but its proposals have not been accepted in Brussels.[26] Poland fears that a tighter Russia-Belarus Union State, the construction of Russian bases on Belarusian soil, and the integration of the Russian and Belarusian militaries would generate new threats along Poland's eastern borders. It could also draw NATO into a more direct confrontation with Russia.

An additional possibility is a Polish intervention in Belarus if Russia begins to weaken and there is either a violent crackdown by the Lukashenka regime against the Polish minority in western Belarus or escalating civil unrest and armed clashes that threaten to spill over Poland's borders. According to the 2019 census, the Polish minority in Belarus is officially listed as numbering 288,000, although Warsaw claims there are over a million Poles in the country. Poles form the second-largest ethnic minority in the country after ethnic Russians, at around 3.1 percent of the population, and they are more heavily concentrated in Belarusian *oblasts* bordering Poland and Lithuania. According to the 2009 census, Russians are the largest ethnic minority, number nearly 707,000 people, and account for approximately 7.5 percent of the population.[27]

Some analysts believe Poland would need a defense in depth in Belarus against any prospective Russian offensive.[28] This should involve preparations for active intervention in Belarus if Russian

---

[26] "Poland Wants EU to Pledge at Least 1 Billion Euros to Stabilize Belarus," September 17, 2020, https://www.reuters.com/article/idUSKBN2681JP.

[27] http://catalog.ihsn.org/index.php/catalog/4377/download/56821.

[28] Jacek Bartosiak, "Belarus as a Pivot of Poland's Grand Strategy," December 2020, https://jamestown.org/program/belarus-as-a-pivot-of-polands-grand-strategy/.

forces were to use Belarusian territory to plan a breach of Poland's borders. By extending the battlefield deep into the enemy's territory, it would severely complicate Russia's planning and combat operations. The resilience of Poland and its regional allies against Russian forces would need to be augmented by a credible national defense and the rapid response of the larger NATO allies in case of attack. According to proponents of an Intermarium bloc of states between the Baltic and Blacks seas, NATO allies and partners must commit themselves to much more extensive defense spending and the acquisition of effective modern equipment to curtail Russia's current military advantages.

Belarus

Several developments could destabilize Belarus and impact on Russia and NATO neighbors. Moscow may seek to replace Lukashenka with a more predictable and compliant pro-Moscow leader, either if Minsk veers toward the West or if fresh protests erupt that the regime is hard pressed to subdue. Putin can push toward a more integrated Union State or even a complete merger between Russia and Belarus, but this could precipitate resistance within Belarusian society and some elements of the political and security establishment and culminate in a Russian military intervention. The Putin regime fears political pluralism in Belarus for two reasons—it would drive the country closer to the West and steer it out of the Russian orbit, and it could have a ripple effect in encouraging public uprisings in Russia itself. Moscow has expected Lukashenka to stifle any peaceful protests and prepare new elections that could potentially favor another presidential candidate acceptable to Putin and to the majority of citizens.[29] Moscow may even seek to transform Belarus from a presidential to a parliamentary system of government in which parties funded and assisted by the Kremlin predominate.[30] Russian officials are also weighing the costs and benefits of tighter institutional integration between the two states but are uncertain whether that could spark more intense Belarusian resistance.

Moscow can use the pretext of an increase of US and other NATO forces in Poland and the three Baltic States to claim that its military intervention in Belarus is intended to defend the country from an imminent Alliance attack. The permanent presence of Russian troops in Belarus would raise prospects that Moscow could engineer border incidents in order to close the Suwałki Corridor between Poland and Lithuania and link up with its forces in Kaliningrad. Moscow may also claim to be defending the Belarusian population in Poland's Podlaskie Voivodship, bordering western Belarus, as part of its obligation within the Union State. A more extensive Russian military intervention in Ukraine could additionally embroil Belarus in the hostilities and further the process of military integration between Russian and Belarusian forces.

Putin's support for Lukashenka in the aftermath of mass anti-regime protests in the summer of 2020 signaled deep fears that his ouster could rebound against the regime in Russia. If Lukashenka's removal

---

[29] Keir Giles, "Russia Can Use Both Hard and Soft Power to Prop Up Lukashenko." International Center for Defense and Security, Estonia, https://icds.ee/en/russia-can-use-both-hard-and-soft-power-to-prop-up-lukashenko/.

[30] Vladimir Socor, "Russia's Regime-Change Experiment in Belarus Runs Into Difficulties (Part One)," *Eurasia Daily Monitor*, Vol.17, Issue 140, October 7, 2020, https://jamestown.org/program/russias-regime-change-experiment-in-belarus-runs-into-difficulties-part-one/.

was perceived to be the result of public pressure, it could inspire Russian citizens to try and emulate the mass demonstrations in Minsk. Anti-Lukashenka protests helped to shine a spotlight on Russia's population, as they provided a nearby barometer of potential public responses to massive election fraud in Russia itself because of the closeness of the two countries.[31] According to opinion surveys, younger Russians sympathized with the protesters who were aggrieved by Lukashenka's authoritarianism and falsification of elections. This indicates that large-scale public opposition in Belarus will have reverberations in Russia, as the population grows more frustrated and impoverished and prospects for emigration recede. Expressions of solidarity by protestors in Khabarovsk in Russia's Pacific region with demonstrators in Minsk during August and September 2021 were viewed with trepidation by the Kremlin.[32]

Regardless of the risk, Moscow may push Belarus to unite with Russia as alleged evidence of Putin's successful statesmanship. This could also provide Putin with an alternative leadership position after his current Russian mandate expires—as President of the combined Union State. Nonetheless, some Russian analysts are convinced that Russia itself could be destabilized by Belarus if it tries to absorb the

---

[31] Paul Goble, "Belarusian Events have Eclipsed Pandemic in Minds of Russians, Levada Center's Volkov Says," September 8, 2020, https://windowoneurasia2.blogspot.com/2020/09/belarusian-events-have-eclipsed.html.

[32] Andrey Makarychev, "The Minsk–Khabarovsk Nexus: Ethical, Performative, Corporeal," *New Perspectives*, January 3, 2021, https://doi.org/10.1177/2336825X20984336.

country.[33] Most Belarusians seek to retain a separate state and would view amalgamation as foreign occupation. In the event of a merger, those Belarusians who protested against Lukashenka will direct their anger and frustrations against Moscow. An institutional, economic, and political annexation of Belarus could prove damaging for the Putin regime not only because of Belarusian resistance but because, unlike the patriotic sentiments that were released during the absorption of Crimea, it could spark protests against state policy in Russia itself, in which the Kremlin would be viewed as an aggressor against a "fraternal" people.

By helping Lukashenka subdue mass protests, the Kremlin endeavored to make Minsk more dependent on Russia and further undercut links with the West. However, the fusion of Belarus and Russia would also prove economically costly for Moscow, especially if Belarus and Russia remain under Western sanctions. In seeking to maintain power, Lukashenka will benefit from ongoing tension and conflict between Russia and the West. He is an asset to the Kremlin during times of confrontation with Washington and the EU because of his anti-Western moves. Lukashenka himself may attempt to stir further animosities so that his position is not undervalued in the Kremlin and he is not ousted and replaced. In an alternative scenario, another mass uprising in Belarus that succeeds in overthrowing Lukashenka cannot be discounted, particularly if the security forces or military units mutiny against enforcing mass repression. If the regime is replaced by a pro-Western one, it would have a major geopolitical impact as Minsk may reject many of the close linkages with Russia developed during Lukashenka's tenure.

---

[33] Paul Goble, "Absorbing Belarus Would Give Russia Another Unstable Region and Add to Moscow's Problems, Belanovsky Says," September 4, 2020, https://windowoneurasia2.blogspot.com/2020/09/absorbing-belarus-would-give-russia.html.

If Belarus were to adopt a more pro-Western foreign policy and seek to extract itself from the Union Treaty with Russia, this would also have an impact on Russia's Kaliningrad *Oblast*. Land routes from Russia to Kaliningrad either traverse NATO members Latvia and Lithuania, or across Belarus and through Lithuania or Poland. Moscow can supply the exclave with military support by sea and air, but moving heavy weapons is expensive and slow. A pro-Western pivot by Minsk could result in the denial of access and transit for Russian troops across Belarusian territory or the use of Belarusian air bases in the event of armed conflict between Russia and NATO. This would leave Kaliningrad *Oblast* more exposed and vulnerable to NATO strikes. It could also weaken the Kaliningrad economy, which is dependent on transportation routes across Belarus for the export of manufactured goods to Russia proper. Worsening economic conditions in the *oblast* will also result in growing anti-Moscow moods akin to the developments that occurred in Kaliningrad in 2009–2010.

Belarus's democratic transformation and pro-Western orientation would energize pro-Western autonomist and separatist movements in Kaliningrad *Oblast* and several *oblasts* bordering Belarus, including Pskov, Smolensk, and Bryansk.[34] As democratic pluralism becomes closely linked with establishing close connections with Western states and institutions, this will challenge the viability of the Putinist political system and the survival of the Russian Federation. When Kaliningrad autonomism and separatism gains popular backing and some measure of international support, this can become a catalyst for other independence movements among Russia's restive republics and regions.

[34] Sergey Sukhankin, "The Belarus Factor in Kaliningrad's Security Lifeline to Russia," January 29, 2021, https://jamestown.org/program/the-belarus-factor-in-kaliningrads-security-lifeline-to-russia/.

Ukraine

Ukraine is the most likely target not only in the cause of Russia's imperial restoration but also to help prevent an internal implosion in the Russian Federation. An independent and democratic Ukraine integrating into pan-European institutions would be viewed as a major defeat by Moscow because it could serve as an example for Russian citizens to overthrow a failed authoritarian regime. As a result, Kremlin pressures on Ukraine have continued with the aim of neutralizing or destabilizing the state. This multifaceted pressure campaign culminated, on February 24, 2022, with a full-scale military re-invasion of Ukraine, initially apparently aiming to occupy the entire territory; yet following several weeks of military setbacks, Moscow downgraded its interim goal to only further partitioning the country. Military preparations for this attack were initiated in the spring of 2021 and continued into the winter of 2021–2022.[35] By early February 2022, an estimated 135,000 Russian troops were stationed near the Ukrainian border and in the occupied Ukrainian territories of Donetsk, Luhansk, and Crimea. Following the Zapad 2021 exercises involving Russian and Belarusian forces, held in September 2021, much of Russia's military equipment materiel was left near the borders of Ukraine to enable the rapid mobilization of combat units for offensive action against Kyiv. Russian forces also conducted large-scale command and staff exercises near the Ukrainian frontier and in joint exercises with the Belarusian military in February 2022. Meanwhile, the Kremlin's rhetoric against Kyiv remained consistently threatening and combative.

---

[35] Howard Altman, "Russian Troop Movements Show Wider Conflict Is Possible, Top Ukraine Official Says," November 10, 2021, https://www.militarytimes.com/flashpoints/2021/11/10/russian-troop-movements-show-wider-conflict-is-possible-top-ukraine-official-says/.

In addition to its full-scale invasion, capture of more territory, and attempt to overthrow the democratic government in Kyiv, Moscow blocked or seized Ukrainian ports along the Azov and Black Sea coastlines, from Mariupol to Odesa, while using Crimea as a bridgehead for its operations. Having built up its maritime capabilities, Moscow was in a strong position to ward off any countermeasures to open sea-lanes and free Ukrainian ports. In addition to gaining control over the North Crimean Canal to supply water to Crimea, the goal has apparently been to strangle Ukraine economically, promote social instability, and weaken the government in Kyiv. Moscow simultaneously sought to engage in extensive cyberattacks to, for instance, take down much of Ukraine's electric grid, the banking system, and other critical components of the country's economy and governmental agencies. However, Ukrainian cyber defense capabilities, which have grown and improved significantly since 2014, prevented these Russian measures from having critical or long-lasting effects. Nonetheless, without continued strong Western support, Ukraine risks becoming more vulnerable to conceding to Russia's territorial and political demands.

The extensive Russian military intervention in Ukraine can expedite the demise of the Putin regime and hasten Russia's state rupture. Although Moscow has clear military superiority to heavily damage and overrun portions of Ukraine, it cannot indefinitely occupy its major cities and expect installed local governments to have popular legitimacy. During the first four months of the full-scale war, Ukrainian morale has been high in defending their territory. The population draws on a combination of the legacy of guerrilla war against Soviet occupation in the 1940s and early Ukrainian tactical victories against the invading Russian forces in the winter and spring of 2022, including the defense of Kyiv. At the same time, Ukraine's military today is considerably better organized and armed than it was at the beginning of the Russian invasion of February 2014.

Russia's large-scale military assault on Ukraine in February 2022 led to a series of increasingly more onerous Western sanctions that have impacted the Russian economy, including a freeze on Russia's central bank assets to prevent it using the $630bn (£470bn) of reserves it has in foreign currencies, the exclusion of major Russian banks from the SWIFT payment settlement system, the termination of the Nord Stream Two gas pipeline from Russia to Germany, EU plans to ban all imports of Russian oil by the end of 2022, and the sanctioning of leading "oligarchs" and the majority of key Russian companies, including energy conglomerates. Moscow's intervention also convinced NATO to significantly bolster its military presence along its Eastern Flank and the US to provide increasing security assistance to Poland, Romania, Lithuania, Latvia and Estonia.

A prolonged war in Ukraine can be expected to damage Putin domestically and engender elite disputes and power struggles to unseat him. Such conflicts would preclude a smooth transition of power in the Kremlin in 2024. Regimes that lose wars or cannot win them outright when they have staked so much on victory invariably collapse in Russia, as evident during World War I and the Cold War. The direct and extensive Russian intervention in Ukraine will ultimately prove less domestically beneficial for Putin than the capture of Crimea. It has already proven costly in terms of casualties and resources because of sharp, longer-term Ukrainian resistance and resolute Western opposition. The slaughter of Ukrainian civilians has exposed the falsified historical and ideological narratives repeated by the Kremlin that Russians and Ukrainians are the same people. For those ethnic Russians who believe such claims, it means Moscow is murdering its own people and Putin is committing fratricide. This will contribute to delegitimizing his rule and the credibility and longevity of the regime.

Following the state-sponsored patriotic euphoria in Russia generated by the annexation of Crimea and the port city of Sevastopol, the Kremlin failed to inform citizens how expensive this occupation would be in practice. Prior to the outbreak of the 2022 large-scale war, the subsidization of Crimea amounted to about 70 percent of the peninsula's budget and exceeded the payments allocated by Moscow to any other federal subject.[36] In addition, the water shortage crisis continued to grow more severe because Crimea lost access to water supplies from Ukraine's mainland and could not provide sufficient quantities for agricultural needs, industry, and households.

Kyiv has continued to press for the return of Crimea and will be emboldened both by Russian battlefield losses and subsequent cleavages forming inside the Russian Federation. Ukrainian President Volodymyr Zelenskyy's "Crimea Platform" was designed to maintain diplomatic pressure on Moscow.[37] It involved high-level meetings with international leaders to bring constant attention not only to the illegality of Russia's occupation but also to the persistent human rights abuses faced in particular by the Tatar population. According to Vladislav Inozemtsev, returning Crimea to Ukraine could have the same impact on the Russian Federation that recognizing Baltic independence did on the USSR by rapidly leading to state disintegration.[38] When the Balts restored their independence in the early fall of 1991, the other Union Republics quickly followed. Paradoxically, the loss of illegally occupied Crimea and Sevastopol

---

[36] Stefan Hedlund, "The Costs of Annexing Crimea Keep Rising for Russia," *Geopolitical Intelligence Services*, August 12, 2021, https://www.gisreportsonline.com/r/russia-crimea/.

[37] Diane Francis, "'Crimea is Ukraine': Kyiv Summit Sends Powerful Message to Vladimir Putin," *Ukraine Alert*, Eurasia Center, Atlantic Council, August 30, 2021.

[38] Paul Goble, "Returning Crimea to Ukraine Could Have Same Impact on Russia Recognizing Baltic Independence Did for USSR, Inozemtsev Says," December 14, 2020, http://windowoneurasia2.blogspot.com/2020/12/returning-crimea-to-ukraine-could-have.html.

could spark demands for separation in several of Russia's republics and regions.

Some Russian ethno-nationalists have viewed the two separatist entities in Ukraine's Donbas as "Russian national states" that can unify other Russian-speaking Ukrainian regions and also serve as "an experimental platform for Russia's future."[39] Although this "Russian Spring" ideology failed to inspire the creation of a *Novorossiia* (New Russia) confederation by separating other regions from Ukraine, it may still carry some resonance among ethno-nationalists seeking to transform the Russian Federation into a Russian nation-state. This will become especially evident when the country starts to fracture and nationalists seek to create a more "ethnically pure" Russian entity. Putin exploited the existence of the proxy regimes in Donetsk and Luhansk as a *casus belli* to spark Russia's wider war with Ukraine, mendaciously claiming that Russian-speakers were subject to "genocide." Paradoxically, asserting independence for regions in neighboring states such as Ukraine and Georgia can also encourage separatist movements inside the Russian Federation.[40]

As Russia weakens and is distracted on multiple fronts, ambitious Ukrainian nationalist movements are likely to call for the incorporation of the Kuban region on the northeast shore of the Black Sea and other areas containing sizeable Ukrainian populations currently inside the Russian Federation. Since Moscow's partial partition of Ukraine, the Ukrainian parliament has paid increasing

---

[39] Konstantin Skorkin, "Merge and Rule: What's In Store for the Donetsk and Luhansk Republics," Carnegie Moscow Center, March 16, 2021, https://carnegie.ru/commentary/84089.

[40] Vadim Shtepa, "Putin Opens Pandora's Box for Russian Regionalism, *Eurasia Daily Monitor,* Volume: 19 Issue: 72 May 17, 2022, https://jamestown.org/program/putin-opens-pandoras-box-for-russian-regionalism/.

attention to the Ukrainian diaspora in Russia and also campaigned for civil and national rights for various non-Russian populations.[41] The 2010 Russian census revealed that 1.9 million Ukrainians lived in the Russian Federation, with sizeable numbers in several Siberian and Far Eastern regions including Tyumen *Oblast*, Omsk *Oblast*, and Primorsky *Krai*. Ukraine's claims to the historic Kuban, including Krasnodar *Krai* and parts of Stavropol *Krai*, could also encourage independence and irredentist movements in nearby areas, such as Kalmyk claims to large parts of Astrakhan *Oblast*. The potential domino effect of rebellion across southern Russia would severely narrow Moscow's access to the North Caucasus, the Caspian and the Black Sea.

Moldova

Moscow is the patron of separatist entities in Moldova, Ukraine, and Georgia and could use them to spark conflicts with national governments that are moving closer to Western institutions. The self-declared Transnistrian Moldovan Republic (TMR) inside Moldova has been a client fiefdom for Russia since the armed clashes in 1992 between Moldovan forces and Transnistrian separatists aided by Moscow.[42] The status of the breakaway territory, with an ethnic

---

[41] Ramazan Alpaut, "Спасти народы России от Кремля. Депутаты Украины просят обсудить нарушение прав в России," April 24, 2021, https://www.idelreal.org/a/31220447.html?mc_cid=485272860d&mc_eid=4655fb8220.

[42] Agnieszka Miarka, "Transnistria as an Instrument of Influence of the Russian Federation on the Security of Moldova in the Second Decade of the 21st Century—Selected Aspects," *Communist and Post-Communist Studies*, Volume 53, Issue 2, June 2020, https://online.ucpress.edu/cpcs/article abstract/53/2/61/110702/Transnistria-as-an-Instrument-of-Influence-of-the?redirectedFrom=fulltext.

Russian population of some 30% percent and with pronounced pro-Moscow loyalties, has not been settled. The Kremlin exploits the separatist dispute to help neutralize any aspirations by the government in Chisinau to join the NATO alliance. Transnistrian leaders have also petitioned for incorporation in the Russian Federation, although such demands are coordinated with the Kremlin to pressurize Moldova into granting the region political concessions.

Moscow possesses additional leverage over Chisinau by supporting the authorities in the autonomous region of Gagauzia in southern Moldova, whose leaders have been staunchly pro-Russian. It can thereby threaten Moldova's territorial integrity and blunt its aspirations for Western institutional integration. The Kremlin is also positioned to manipulate the Transnistrian and Gagauz questions beyond Moldova's borders and precipitate conflicts between Moldova, Ukraine, and Romania. This could be expanded to challenge the status of Ukraine's southern Bessarabia and Danube delta regions. Such a scenario can lay the groundwork for a Russian intervention on the pretext of defending Transnistria, Gagauzia, or other Russian-speaking or pro-Moscow populations in Moldova and Ukraine. This can include the creation of other separatist entities inside Ukraine, particularly in the Budjak or Bessarabian region along the Black Sea coast bordering Moldova and Romania, to further undermine the government in Kyiv.

After Moldovan President Maia Sandu called for the withdrawal of Russian peacekeepers from Transnistria in November 2020, Igor Strelkov, a former leader of the Donetsk proxy separatists warned that if Moscow evacuates its troops from the entity, ethnic Russians will flee the country and Moldova will escape Russia's orbit.[43] As with

---

[43] Paul Goble, "If Russian Peacekeepers Leave, Russians Will Flee Transdniestria, Strelkov Says," November 24, 2020, http://windowoneurasia2.blogspot.com/2020/11/if-russian-peacekeepers-leave-russians.html.

Ukraine and Georgia, Chisinau will benefit significantly from Russia's internal unrest and any lessened capabilities by the Kremlin in sponsoring separatist enclaves in Moldova. Above all, it will be in a better position to regain and reincorporate its Transnistrian territories and increase its control over Gagauzia, as both entities will forfeit their patron in Moscow.

Romania

Soviet acquisitions of Romanian territory after World War II primarily affect relations between Ukraine and Romania over the northern Bukovina and southern Bessarabian regions. However, the Moldovan question continues to loom large in Romanian identity, history and regional policy. Any lessened support by Moscow for the separatist entity in Transnistria would encourage Chisinau to retake these territories and potentially pull Romania into the ensuing conflict. A rupture of the Russian Federation and any attendant contraction of its foreign policy offensives could encourage Bucharest to push for closer relations and even a federation, confederation, or union with Moldova. A lessened threat of Russian intervention in Ukraine and the return of occupied territories could also reduce regional desputes and benefit both Kyiv and Bucharest in improving bilateral relations and revoking any latent territorial claims. Without Moscow's manipulation of ethnicity, regionalism, and separatism in Moldova and Ukraine, Romania could become another gateway for closer EU and NATO ties for both states.

Turkey

Turkey will become a major player when Russia's crisis accelerates, with expanding influence in several regions adjacent to the Russian Federation and among Turkic-speaking nations inside Russia. Ankara has promoted the Cooperation Council of Turkic-Speaking States (Turkic Council), headquartered in Istanbul and initially composed of members Azerbaijan, Kazakhstan, Kyrgyzstan, Turkey, and Uzbekistan. Turkmenistan received observer status in the Turkic Council at its eighth summit in November 2021, when it was renamed as the Organization of Turkish States (OTS).[44] Turkmenistan's decision to relinquish its strictly neutral status was made in the wake of the Taliban victory in Afghanistan and amidst fears of regional instability. The US withdrawal from Afghanistan provided Turkey with a larger political and security opening in the region. Ashgabat's refusal to join the Moscow-led Collective Security Treaty Organization (CSTO) antagonized the Kremlin, as it demonstrated that Turkmenistan was veering toward the "Turkic world" and further away from Russia.

The Azerbaijan-Armenia war in the summer of 2020 proved strategically beneficial for Ankara and raised its influence among Turkic-speaking people in the Caucasus, Central Asia, and inside the Russian Federation. Turkey's growing presence will undercut Moscow's role in regions with large Islamic populations.[45] The "Susha Declaration," signed by Turkish President Recep Tayyip Erdoğan and Azerbaijani President Ilham Aliyev on June 15, 2021, outlined joint initiatives to modernize the Azerbaijani armed forces and work together on defense industry projects. It affirmed Ankara's role as a guarantor of Azerbaijan's borders, pledged mutual assistance in the

---

[44] Paul Goble, "Turkmenistan Appears Set to Move Away from Neutrality, Giving Turkey a Major Boost," September 17, 2021, http://windowoneurasia2.blogspot.com/2021/09/turkmenistan-appears-set-to-move-away.html.

[45] "Как Россия проиграла во второй карабахской войне,"November 10, 2020, https://www.vedomosti.ru/opinion/articles/2020/11/10/846462-rossiya-proigrala?mc_cid=f224cb05de&mc_eid=4655fb8220.

event of a threat or attack by a third country, and raised the prospect of establishing Turkish military bases in Azerbaijan.[46] Ankara also planned to establish a "civil defense mechanism" in the OTS to help coordinate and assist in each country's domestic security, a process that could be expanded to include Turkic-speaking entities emerging from a contracting Russia.

Such initiatives deepened consternations in Moscow that Turkey was becoming more ambitious in promoting the "Turkic World." Ankara's assertiveness feeds into the Kremlin narrative of an "Anaconda ring," according to which the West led by the US seeks to encircle and strangle Russia with hostile states and unresolved conflicts in order to eventually partition the country.[47] Turkish military support for Ukraine, particularly the supply of Bayraktar unmanned combat vehicles, confirmed Moscow's conspiracy theories.

In addition to condemning Turkey as a NATO wedge into Moscow's zone of influence, Russian analysts regularly warn about the threat of pan-Turkism or Turkey's Eurasianism. They contend that Ankara is not only seeking to establish a union of Turkic states to expand its influence but also an association of Turkic nations, including those

---

[46] "Shusha Declaration Ascertains Turkey, Azerbaijan's Borders," June 18, 2021, https://www.dailysabah.com/politics/diplomacy/shusha-declaration-ascertains-turkey-azerbaijans-borders.

[47] Rahim Rahimov, "Russia, Turkey Compete to Entice Azerbaijan Into Their Geopolitical Plays," Eurasia Daily Monitor, Vol.18, Issue 114, July 19, 2021, https://jamestown.org/program/russia-turkey-compete-to-entice-azerbaijan-into-their-geopolitical-plays/ and https://euvsdisinfo.eu/report/west-has-anti-russian-plan-named-anaconda-ring/?mc_cid=05ce3c5da9&mc_eid=4655fb8220.

inside the Russian Federation.[48] Moscow has frequently criticized such an initiative but remains anxious that open condemnation will provide it with greater attention.[49] Russian officials also express concern that Turkey will join the GUAM states and expand its influence in several neighboring regions.[50] The GUAM Organization for Democracy and Economic Development was established in October 1997 by the governments of Georgia, Ukraine, Azerbaijan, and Moldova as a political, economic, and strategic alliance designed to strengthen the independence and sovereignty of these states vis-à-vis Russia.

Russia's officials are additionally worried that Ankara is reaching out to Turkic nations that are not Islamic to weaken Moscow influence in its former Soviet satellites. This includes the Gagauz population in southern Moldova, which has remained linguistically and culturally attached to Russia and is predominantly Christian Orthodox but among whom a Muslim minority has been pushing for closer links with Turkey. Inside Russia, Moscow is most concerned about developing ties between Turkey and the non-Muslim but Turkic-speaking Sakha Republic. A declaration of the Turkic Academy of

---

[48] Paul Goble, "Ankara Wants Union of Turkic Peoples Not Just of Turkic Countries, a Goal that Threatens Russia, Rodionov Says," January 13, 2021, http://windowoneurasia2.blogspot.com/2021/01/ankara-wants-union-of-turkic-peoples.html.

[49] Paul Goble, "Moscow Worried by Ankara's Expansive Vision of 'Turkic World," Eurasia Daily Monitor, Vol.18, Issue 174, November 16, 2021, https://jamestown.org/program/moscow-worried-by-ankaras-expansive-vision-of-turkic-world/.

[50] Paul Goble, "As Tensions Over Ukraine Rise, Baku Signals Support for Kyiv, Worrying Moscow," *Eurasia Daily Monitor,* January 25, 2022, Vol. 19, Issue 6, https://jamestown.org/program/as-tensions-over-ukraine-rise-baku-signals-support-for-kyiv-worrying-moscow/.

Sciences in November 2021 stated that the Sakha Republic is "one of the state formations unrecognized by the world community." The Academy, based in Kazakhstan, consists of scholars from Turkey, Azerbaijan, Kazakhstan, and Kyrgyzstan and is closely tied to the Organization of Turkic States.

Turkey deploys various "soft power" tools of attraction among Turkic-speaking and Muslim populations in Russia, including support for cultural and educational programs and for diaspora groups in Turkey who develop links with their kindred populations. Officials in Moscow fear that sizeable Kazakh and Azerbaijani *diasporas* working in Russia could also be used by Ankara to weaken the Russian state. Unlike Moscow, Ankara presents Turkey as a future-oriented power and a model for economic development for the Turkic World rather than claiming past glories and common values. This will have broad appeal particularly as the Russian state has failed to provide consistent economic growth or an attractive vision for the future. Some Russian analysts argue that Ankara's initiatives promote "Turkic separatism" in Russia by undermining Moscow's control in sensitive regions such as the North Caucasus and the Middle Volga and encouraging rebellions among the Crimean Tatars and Sakha nations. In addition, the Ukrainian government's decision to replace the Cyrillic alphabet with the Latin script for Crimean Tatars was welcomed by Tatar leaders as Cyrillic had been imposed by Moscow.[51] This will not only strengthen Tatar identity and distinctiveness from Russians but will also bring Tatars closer to Turkey and other Turkic language countries.

Volga Tatars, the second-largest ethnic group in Russia, primarily belong to the Sunni Hanafi branch of Islam, similarly to Turks, and

---

[51] "крымских татар калечат латиницей," September 27,2021, odnarodyna.org/article/krymskikh-tatar-kalechat-latinicey.

express positive attitudes toward Turkey.[52] In response, Moscow has accused Tatar elites of harboring pro-Turkish sentiments. The Republic of Tatarstan has focused on developing cultural, social, and economic ties with Turkey. By 2020, Turkish companies invested over $2 billion in Tatarstan, with more than 280 joint enterprises operating, while a Turkish Consulate General was located in Tatarstan's capital Kazan.

Turkey's influence has also grown in the North Caucasus. Turkic ethnics and Turkic-speakers account for up to 13% of the region's population and include Balkars, Karachais, Kumyks, and Nogais. Chechens and Ingush, who are not Turkic-speaking, have also gravitated toward Turkey. Even despite Chechen leader Ramzan Kadyrov's intense loyalty to Putin, the Kadyrov regime has lobbied for the opening of a Turkish school and cultural center in Grozny. Turkey itself is home to about two million descendants of North Caucasus émigrés, most of whom fled the Tsarist conquests and mass murders in the 19th century. They include Caucasian Turks, Circassians, and Chechens, and with many recent exiles escaping political persecution. Although Turkey will not actively seek to destabilize Russia by supporting separatist movements, various diasporas will likely campaign and organize independence groups on Turkish territory as the Russian Federation weakens. Ankara could be pulled into any spreading turmoil by trying to ensure a measure of regional stability among kindred nations or Turkic speakers during a wrenching upheaval. In addition to the North Caucasus and Middle Volga nations, this would include the Sakha, Altaians and Tuvans.

---

[52] Aslan Doukaev, "Turkey Breaches Russia's Sphere of Influence," Vol.18, Issue 102, June 28, 2021, https://jamestown.org/program/turkey-breaches-russias-sphere-of-influence/.

Georgia

Russia's officials have periodically threatened Georgia with further partition if the country continues to cultivate relations with NATO and the US. This could include sparking a conflict in the Samtskhe-Javakheti region of southern Georgia populated by an Armenian majority or the Kvemo-Kartli region of southeast Georgia inhabited by an Azerbaijani majority. It can also launch an expansion of South Ossetia's territories to include the Kazbegi district and the Truso Gorge in northern Georgia, which Ossetian nationalists view as "ancient Ossetian lands." However, a Russian imperial retreat will lessen the opportunities for further separatist initiatives. A weakening and collapsing Russia will encourage Georgia to push for the return of Moscow-controlled territories carved out after the August 2008 Russian-Georgian war.

Tbilisi will endeavor to regain the self-declared Republic of Abkhazia and the Republic of South Ossetia–Alania through more aggressive diplomacy with the assistance of its NATO partners and multinational bodies. It can also try to entice the separatist entities back into the Georgian state by offering them various degrees of autonomy and self-determination. If such measures prove unsuccessful, it could ultimately engage in military takeovers, calculating that Moscow was too preoccupied in its internal conflicts to intervene in the South Caucasus. Turmoil in the North Caucasus will also have a direct impact on Georgia. Tbilisi can support secessionist movements in order to weaken Moscow and lay the groundwork for constructive relations with its northern neighbors. However, turmoil in the North Caucasus could also impact on Georgia's integrity. If the Confederation of the Mountain Peoples of the Caucasus were revived it could claim Abkhazia and South Ossetia as part of its territory and precipitate an open conflict with Tbilisi. Previous iterations of the independent Mountain Republic in the 1920s and 1990s included Abkhazia.

Moscow has pressed to integrate Abkhazia and South Ossetia in its political, economic, and security structures. But this has created resentments particularly in Abkhazia whose leaders fear that the joint "socio-economic" program announced in 2020 will eliminate any semblance of independence and even incorporate both regions into the Russian Federation.[53] During Russia's deepening instability, the current separatist entities could seek agreements with Georgia to gain political and economic benefits even if this does not entail administrative reintegration. Such moves can start a process of "separation reversal." Alternatively, a Russian geopolitical retreat would enable both entities to assert genuine independence and appeal for international support. South Ossetia may also seek unification with the Republic of North Ossetia and pull this entity out of the Russian Federation. Alternatively, a combined Ossetian state can seek closer ties or even a confederal arrangement with Georgia. Former President Mikhail Saakashvili has already proposed creating a Georgia-Abkhazia federation.[54]

Russian officials have been cognizant that the Taliban victory in Afghanistan in September 2021 will inspire Islamist extremist groups to organize attacks against Moscow or government targets in the North Caucasus and potentially deeper into Russia's territory. The South Caucasus states can become a gateway for terrorist infiltration into the region. For instance, Moscow criticized Georgia for opening its airport in Tbilisi as a major transit point for Afghans fleeing the

---

[53] Zaal Anjaparidze, "Abkhazia Bolsters Linkages With Russia," *Eurasia Daily Monitor*, Vol.17, Issue 173, December 7, 2020, https://jamestown.org/program/abkhazia-bolsters-linkages-with-russia/.

[54] Giorgi Menabde, "Saakashvili Proposes Creating a Dual Georgian-Abkhazian Federation, *Eurasia Daily Monitor*, Vol. 19, Issue 97, June 29, 2022, https://jamestown.org/program/saakashvili-proposes-creating-a-dual-georgian-abkhazian-federation/.

Taliban in September 2021, arguing that pro-Taliban fighters among them could enter Russia.[55] In addition, Taliban-linked activists will increase drug trafficking across the region and into Russia to help finance the regime in Kabul. The expansion of drug smuggling will increase the already high levels of heroin addiction in Russia and further corrupt police officers, border guards, and local officials.

Armenia

Moscow capitalizes on inter-state conflicts in the South Caucasus to bolster its influence and prevent the development of closer ties with Western governments and institutions. Moscow has a military foothold and territorial possession in all three countries—Georgia, Armenia and Azerbaijan. In September 2020, it capitalized on the war between Baku and Yerevan in which Azerbaijani forces regained the bulk of Azerbaijan's territories occupied by Armenia since the mid-1990s. Moscow injected about 2,000 troops as "peacekeepers" in the disputed Karabakh region in order to gain additional leverage with both states so they remained in Moscow's orbit.[56] In effect, the northern part of Karabakh became a Russian protectorate. Although the ceasefire agreement stipulated that Russian troops had a five-year mandate, this is likely to be significantly extended given the continuing conflicts between Baku and Yerevan. They will not only control most of Armenian-inhabited Karabakh but also patrol the entrance and exits of the Lachin and Nakhchivan corridors. Lachin

---

[55] Paul Goble, "Taliban Victory Sparks New Fears in the Caucasus," Eurasia Daily Monitor, Vol.18, Issue 134, September 7, 2021, https://jamestown.org/program/taliban-victory-sparks-new-fears-in-the-caucasus/.

[56] David Batashvili, "What Russia has Gained in Karabakh," *Rondeli Foundation Blog*, November 16, 2020, www.gfsis.org/blog/view/1120.

links Armenia and Karabakh, while Nakhchivan is an exclave of Azerbaijan bordering Turkey and separated by Armenian territory.

Although some Armenian officials have proposed forming a Union State between Armenia and Russia based on the Belarus-Russia model, such a proposal will become less attractive when the Russian Federation begins to collapse.[57] Indeed, unrest in Russia and a thinly stretched military could jeopardize the remaining Armenian administration in Karabakh and ignite fresh clashes between Armenia and Azerbaijan in which Russia would be in a less powerful position to intervene. Both Baku and Yerevan remain dissatisfied with the results of the September 2020 war, and one can expect new conflicts over borders, territories, and transportation routes.

The ongoing Armenia-Azerbaijan dispute can also backfire against Moscow. Many Armenians felt betrayed by Russia during the September 2020 conflict, having expected their close ally to render them military assistance to protect their hold on Azerbaijan's territories, especially Karabakh, with its substantial Armenian majority. Some activists may turn to terrorism against Russian targets, whether in the South Caucasus or in Russia itself. Armenia has a long tradition of political terrorism as a means of vengeance for perceived wrongs against the nation.

Azerbaijan

The grievances of several divided cross-border peoples are a source of tension between Azerbaijan and Russia's Republic of Dagestan. Some

---

[57] Paul Goble, "Only Way Armenia Can Take Revenge for Loss of Qarabagh is to Become Part of a Russian Union State, Latvian Analyst Says," December 11, 2020, http://windowoneurasia2.blogspot.com/2020/12/only-way-armenia-can-take-revenge-for.html.

ethnicities, including the Lezgins, Tats and Tsakhurs, straddle the border regions. More than a third of the Lezgin population lives in Azerbaijan, as well as the majority of Tsakhurs and Tats. Lezgins view themselves as politically marginalized and separated from ethnically kindred groups, such as the Aguls, Rutuls and Tabasarans, that reduces their political influence in Dagestan. Lezgins have developed a separatist movement in Dagestan, and some activists have advocated the political unification of Lezgins in southern Dagestan and northern Azerbaijan. One wing of *Sadwal*, the Lezgin national movement, seeks to establish a united Lezginistan as an autonomous republic within the Russian Federation, separate from Dagestan.[58] When Russia's grip begins to weaken throughout the Caucasus region, a self-proclaimed Lezginistan entity can seek a confederal arrangement with Azerbaijan.

Some Azerbaijani activists in Dagestan have claimed that the Derbent region along the Caspian coast containing a substantial Azerbaijani population should merge with Azerbaijan and this could be supported by Baku. On the other hand, the authorities in Dagestan's capital of Makhachkala will seek to prevent any fracturing of their multi-ethnic republic while boosting their economy by pursuing closer bilateral links with Baku, independent of Moscow. This can result in Azerbaijan's recognition of Dagestan's independence and integrity that may reduce irredentist movements such as those of the Lezgins. The Kremlin remains concerned about growing pan-Turkic identity and aspirations toward statehood by various Turkic groups in Russia as well as all expressions of support by Azerbaijan, a close ally of Turkey, for the sovereignty of any Muslim-majority republic, including Dagestan, Tatarstan, and Bashkortostan.

---

[58] Moshe Gammer, "Walking the Tightrope Between Nationalism(s) and Islam(s): The Case of Daghestan," *Central Asian Survey*, Vol. 21, No. 2, 2002, http://dx.doi.org/10.1080/0263493022000010035, p.135.

Kazakhstan

Conflicts persist over demarcating Russia's 4,750 miles of border with Kazakhstan, in which any adjustments invariably provoke resentment against what is perceived as Russia's projected land seizures. Russian imperial irredentists harbor claims to extensive parts of northern Kazakhstan that were settled by a large ethnic-Russian population during Soviet times. The Russian share of the population has steadily dropped since Kazakhstan's independence—from over 37 percent in 1989 to under 30 percent in 1999, less than 24 percent in 2009, and an estimated 18percent by 2019, or about 3.7 million out of 19.3 million people. However, it still constituted the second-largest ethnic-Russian diaspora.[59] The Russian exodus from northern Kazakhstan continued during 2021, as inter-ethnic relations between Russians and Kazakhs deteriorated.[60] Nonetheless, Russians still formed between a third and a half of the population in several northern provinces of Kazakhstan bordering Russia.

Public anger against unpopular government decisions in Kazakhstan, as witnessed during demonstrations and riots in several cities in early January 2022, reverberated in the Kremlin. Some of the demonstrations took place in northern Kazakhstan and involved ethnic Russians, signaling that the protests could become a model for citizens in Russia.[61] They were reported in the city of Petropavlovsk,

---

[59] https://www.cia.gov/the-world-factbook/countries/kazakhstan/#people-and-society.

[60] Paul Goble, "After Taliban Victory, Central Asian Countries Increasingly Pursuing Separate Goals," *Eurasia Daily Monitor*, Vol.18, Issue 145, September 23, 2021, https://jamestown.org/program/after-taliban-victory-central-asian-countries-increasingly-pursuing-separate-goals/.

[61] Paul Goble, "Kazakhstan Protests Involve Russians, Adding to Moscow's Worries About Stability," Eurasia Daily Monitor, January 20, Vol.19, No.3,

with a Russian population of some 60 percent, and other cities where Russians form either a plurality or a significant minority. Moscow remains worried that any protests in Kazakhstan can also assume ethnic dimensions and result in clashes between Kazakhs and Russians. This would revive calls by Russian nationalists to seize portions of northern Kazakhstan to protect ethnic Russians.

At the same time, some Kazakh nationalists have claimed territories currently within the Russian Federation, including parts of Orenburg *Oblast* along Kazakhstan's northwestern frontier. The *oblast* has a mixed Russian, Kazakh, and Bashkir population. The acquisition of these areas would also create a border between Kazakhstan and Bashkortostan, thus giving the Middle Volga republics a direct overland link with a foreign state independent of Russia and thereby boost their aspirations toward statehood. Additionally, Kazakhs make up the absolute majority of the population in the Volodarsky *Raion* of Astrakhan *Oblast* bordering Kazakhstan.

Public anger in Kazakhstan can be channeled against other ethnic groups either by nationalists or by a government seeking to deflect attention from its own shortcomings. The presence of Russian troops on Kazakhstani territory following the CSTO peacekeeping intervention or in future military deployments can result in clashes with Kazakh protestors and precipitate revenge attacks on ethnic-Russian civilians. Such developments will escalate the demands of angry citizens to sever links with the Russian Federation and to intensify the process of national consolidation in language use, adoption of the Latin alphabet, and other measures to reverse generations of russification. In a sign of rising tensions between the Kazakh and Russian communities, during 2021 Kazakh nationalists

---

https://jamestown.org/program/kazakhstan-protests-involve-russians-adding-to-moscows-worries-about-stability/.

deployed "language patrols" in a number of cities, seeking to enforce the sole use of the Kazakh language in public places, reportedly with the consent of some government officials.[62] Such conflicts could rebound in Russia itself by emboldening Russian nationalists to target Kazakhs and other Central Asian migrants in revenge attacks.

More broadly in Central Asia, the withdrawal of US troops from Afghanistan and the seizure of power by the Taliban in August 2021 will have long-term reverberations. Moscow will try to use the new regime in Kabul against Western interests in the region while seeking to limit their influence in nearby states. Nonetheless, the Taliban's takeover can inspire Islamist rebel groups in the North Caucasus and elsewhere in Russia, some of whose fighters received training in Afghanistan.[63] A new round of terrorist attacks in Russian cities cannot be discounted. The arrest of 31 members of the radical Islamist group Katibat Tawhid wal-Jihad in raids across the country in late August 2021 indicated growing anxiety in government circles. The special operation was conducted jointly by the Federal Security Service (FSB), the Ministry of Interior, and the National Guard (*Rosgvardia)* in Moscow, Novosibirsk, Yakutsk, and Krasnoyarsk.[64] Those arrested were accused of promoting a terrorist ideology, financing and recruitment, and transporting people to war zones.

---

[62] Zholdas Orisbayev, "Kazakh Language Police Trigger Russian Politicians," *EurasiaNet,* August 16, 2021, https://eurasianet.org/kazakh-language-police-trigger-russian-politicians.

[63] Paul Goble, "Taliban Triumph in Afghanistan Echoes in Russia's North Caucasus," *Eurasia Daily Monitor*, Vol.18, Issue 133, August 19, 2021, https://jamestown.org/program/taliban-triumph-in-afghanistan-echoes-in-russias-north-caucasus/.

[64] "ФСБ задержала 31 участника террористической организации "Катиба Таухид валь-Джихад," August 25, 2021, https://tass.ru/proisshestviya/12214035.

Kyrgyzstan has reportedly become a major recruiting location for terrorists who are financed by levies on the large Central Asian populations living and working in Russia and by the Afghan drug trade.[65]

With increasing numbers of Afghan refugees transiting through Central Asia, Russia is likely to witness an upsurge in anti-Muslim incidents that can also affect indigenous Muslim populations. Attempts by the Russian security forces to root out radicals will further aggravate inter-religious and inter-ethnic relations and assist in the recruitment of militants. During Russia's state rupture, a sizeable jihadist movement can reemerge in the North Caucasus and other Muslim areas aimed at the creation of an Islamist caliphate similar to Taliban-controlled Afghanistan. The ensuing challenges to Russia's state integrity will contribute to unleashing a plethora of ethnic, national, and regional demands. Paradoxically, while Moscow may view the Taliban victory as a defeat for the West, the US retreat from Afghanistan may have more destabilizing consequences inside Russia itself.

Mongolia

Support for a federal pan-Mongol state can be revived in southern Siberia to include the Buryat Republic, the Tuva Republic, and parts of Zabaikalskii *Krai*, which absorbed the Agin-Buryat Autonomous *Okrug* in 2007, and Irkutsk *Oblast*, which merged with the Ust-Orda Buryat Autonomous *Okrug* in 2008. Pan-Mongol nationalists will seek to amalgamate Buryat territories and the Republic of Tuva in Russia with China's Inner Mongolia Autonomous Region and with Mongolia itself in order to form a greatly expanded Central Asian

---

[65] "Киргиз-джихад," *Versija.ru,* August 30, 2021, https://versia.ru/novaya-volna-islamskogo-yekstremizma-kto-yeti-lyudi-otkuda-oni-i-kto-ix-soderzhit.

country. However, many Tuvan and Buryat nationalists view themselves as representatives of distinct ethnic groups entitled to their own national states. When Russian rule begins to crumble, this could precipitate conflicts between pan-Mongolists, calling for the incorporation of Buryatia and Tuva in an enlarged Mongolia, and Buryat and Tuvan nationalists, seeking the formation of separate states. Some Buryat nationalists will also favor the creation of a "Greater Buryatia" to incorporate more extensive swaths of neighboring Russian regions.

Buryat activists have expanded their foreign connections, and Buryats employed abroad have become an important source of revenue for the Buryat Republic, especially those working in South Korea.[66] Some commentators are stressing the growing importance of the "Buryat world" connecting Buryats in Russia and abroad in the cultural, social, economic, and other spheres and promoting a more unified national identity rather than traditional sub-ethnic and clanship links.[67] The Buryat diaspora has grown in Mongolia, China and South Korea in particular.

The Kalmyk Republic situated between the North Caucasus and the Volga region will also seek closer ties with the "Mongol world." The Kalmyks are the western branch of the Mongol nation and claim descent from one of the Oirat tribes that migrated westward from the Dzungar Khanate in Central Asia during the 17th century. Kalmyks form a clear majority in their republic, estimated at over 60 percent, and the Russian population has been steadily shrinking to under a

---

[66] Paul Goble, "Buryats Abroad Could Help Buryats in Russia Overcome Their Divisions, Ochirov Says," May 14, 2021, http://windowoneurasia2.blogspot.com/2021/05/buryats-abroad-could-help-buryats-in.html.

[67] Bato Ochirov, "Бурятский мир" как новая формула национального развития," May 12, 2021, https://asiarussia.ru/articles/27450/.

third. Kalmyk leaders will not only promote links with Mongolia but also with other Tibetan Buddhist states.

China

China's One Belt, One Road initiative (also known as the Belt and Road Initiative—BRI) and disputes over borders with Tajikistan and Kazakhstan underscore Beijing's ambitions to replace Russia as the dominant power in Central Asia and northern Eurasia. Moscow has sought to limit political and economic connections between Russian regions in Siberia and along the Pacific coastline with China and Japan, fearing that economic penetration and population movements will culminate in territorial claims by both Beijing and Tokyo. However, restrictive regulations on external links with neighboring states and misfiring economic modernization plans have limited the region's development and will make outside powers even more attractive partners.

Despite Moscow's obstruction, China is poised to become the leading player in the south Siberian and Pacific regions, and its dominance will be elevated by Russia's state failures. Officials in Beijing view current Russian territories along China's northeastern borders as a single region for economic development and possible state expansion, and Moscow is unlikely to retain control of this vast area. China dwarfs Russia in population, national power and economic might, and the two are approaching military parity other than in the size of their nuclear arsenals. Beijing is also increasingly assertive and self-confident. Conflicts will reemerge amidst Moscow's growing nervousness over China's Silk Road initiatives and penetration of the former "Soviet space" in Central Asia. Disputes will be exacerbated between Moscow and Beijing over Chinese claims to parts of eastern Tajikistan and military expansion in frontier regions patrolled by Russian troops.

There is a growing probability of Chinese territorial encroachment into Russia's sparsely populated far eastern region north of the Amur River and east of the Ussuri River. These "lost territories" have been historically claimed by Beijing, whose military maps show them as Chinese lands.[68] Beijing continues to review the durability of the China-Russia border. Officials claim that for several centuries the frontier has been adjusted in Russia's favor through "unequal treaties" when China was in a weak position, especially after the Opium Wars with Britain and France in the mid-1800s. In particular, the Treaty of Aigun in 1858, which the Chinese government was obliged to sign, ceded all territories north of the Amur River to the Russian empire. Subsequently, the 1860 Treaty of Peking recognized the annexation by Russia of territories between the Ussuri River and the Sea of Japan, known in Russia as the Maritime Province.[69] The Treaty of Good-Neighborliness and Friendly Cooperation, signed by Russia and China in 2001, failed to fully resolve the outstanding border contests. For instance, when Moscow celebrated the 160-year anniversary of the founding of Vladivostok in 2020, the state-owned China Global Television Network asserted that Vladivostok unjustly replaced the Chinese city of Haishenwai in the "unequal Treaty of Beijing" of 1860. Under immense international pressure, China's northeastern territories of Outer Manchuria were awarded to the Russian Empire and now form Primorski *Krai* and a substantial part of Khabarovsk *Krai*.[70]

---

[68] Pravin R. Jethwa, *Expect a War Between Russia and China in the 2020s*, Begin-Sadat Center for Strategic Studies, BESA Center Perspectives Paper No. 1,230, July 18, 2019, https://besacenter.org/wp-content/uploads/2019/07/1230-Expect-a-Russia-China-War-in-the-2020s-Jethwa-final.pdf.

[69] James Forsyth, *A History of the Peoples of Siberia: Russia's North Asian Colony, 1581-1990*, Cambridge University Press, 1992, p.204.

[70] John Herbst, "The Coming Russian-Chinese Clash," *The National Interest*, August 21, 2020, https://nationalinterest.org/feature/coming-russian-chinese-clash-167394.

China's territorial aspirations will be partially driven by huge population disparities, with over 130 million inhabitants in three Chinese provinces bordering Russia's Far Eastern regions that have a combined population of under 8 million. Although the population growth in China's northeast is reportedly slowing down, Beijing will still need more agricultural land, energy, natural resources and urban living space to accommodate its citizens. If it cannot achieve this through treaties and agreements with Moscow, it is likely to act more forcefully as Russia weakens. The southern portions of Russia's Far Eastern Federal District have a relatively mild climate with abundant arable land that can prove attractive to Chinese farmers currently experiencing demographic pressures, extensive urbanization, and industrial pollution in their home regions. Fears are evident in some Siberian and Pacific federal subjects that Moscow plans to lease large tracts of agricultural land to China because there are too few Russians farmers and workers as Moscow's empire depopulates.

China is already the region's largest trading partner, the biggest foreign leaseholder of farmland, and a vital supplier of labor in timber processing, construction, and retail services.[71] In the near future, investments in energy and infrastructure will increase the number of Chinese state companies, managers, and workers and ensure that China becomes the economic hegemon in Russia's Pacific regions and southern Siberia. Beijing can gain more direct control over extensive mineral reserves, including fossil fuels, gold, diamonds, uranium, antimony, iron ores, coal, tin, mercury, silver, lead, zinc and tungsten. In addition, China can ratchet up its investments in building and expanding Russian ports in order to increase its export capacity across Russia to Europe. This will become a valuable inroad for Beijing's political ambitions across northern Eurasia.

---

[71] Rensselaer Lee and Artyom Lukin, *Russia's Far East: New Dynamics in Asia Pacific and Beyond,* Boulder, London: Lynne Rienner Publishers, p.11.

Declarations of independence and bids for full sovereignty by republics and regions in Siberia and along the Pacific coast will encourage Chinese irredentism and potential conflicts both with Moscow and with regionalist movements. Some Chinese nationalists, including those in Taiwan, which could be absorbed by the People's Republic of China in the coming years, continue to claim Tuva and Mongolia as historic Chinese territories. In the event of Russia's fragmentation, such irredentism could extend to the Buryat Republic and other regions in southern Siberia claimed by pan-Chinese nationalists.

Paradoxically, Moscow's proposals for inter-regional amalgamation and municipal agglomeration would entail depopulating certain areas and raise fears that emptying outlying regions will increase the claims of neighbors to Russian territory. Instead of seeking to absorb all these territories, Beijing may plan to expand its influence by offering economic benefits, investments, and security guarantees to some regions, while pressing for border changes with others. Local resentment over the presence of Chinese migrant workers could result in inter-ethnic clashes and expulsions from some frontier zones and larger cities. This would turn regional populations not only against Beijing but also against Moscow for allowing tens of thousands of Chinese workers to settle in Russian areas. The central government will then be seen as facilitating the very "Chinese threat" that state propaganda has whipped up to help ensure its control over regions bordering China. Beijing may in turn seek to protect Chinese migrants in Russia, and this could provoke indirect or direct military intervention.

China's increasing insistence on an Arctic presence and opening a Polar Silk Road in the coming years in pursuit of its military and commercial interests will also test Russia's unity. Beijing's icebreaker construction program and plans to build Chinese docks in five Russian Arctic ports (Murmansk, Sabetta, Arkhangelsk, Tiksi and Uzden) may help Russia develop its Northern Sea Route, but it will also significantly raise Chinese influence and interests in the Arctic at Moscow's longer-term geopolitical expense.[72] At some point, Beijing will seek a military presence to monitor the polar route for its container traffic, to increase its stake in the extraction of natural resources, and to protect its economic interests. As China strengthens its regional and global muscles, Russia will find itself increasingly on the defensive and over-dependent on Chinese investments. When Beijing's claims mount toward Moscow's current territories, resources, and maritime access, it will be unable to bank on American or European support, because it has consistently undermined Western interests, governments, and institutions.

Another intriguing possibility is the emergence of a second Jewish state, even if only a nominal one, from the autonomous Birobidjan *Oblast* in the Pacific region. Although the *oblast* only has a small Jewish population, it could be advantageous for the region's authorities to establish close bilateral relations with Israel. The entity could even assume the role of Israel's diplomatic promoter and economic facilitator in Central and East Asia, especially as Birobidjan borders China and is close to Japan and South Korea. According to the 2010 census, Jews accounted for only 1 percent of the *oblast's* population of some 176,000 people. However, the actual figure is probably closer to 20 percent, as Jews were pressured during Soviet times to register as ethnic Russians in the national census when the Soviet regime decided to eradicate Jewish identity and the Yiddish

---

[72] Paul Goble, "Beijing's 'Polar Silk Road' Helping Russia Now But will Allow China to Dominate Northern Route Later, Volgayev Says," April 29, 2021, http://windowoneurasia2.blogspot.com/2021/04/beijings-polar-silk-road-helping-russia.html.

language.[73] Many residents can claim Jewish backgrounds, and there are numerous personal and cultural links with Israel, especially between Yiddish speakers in both territories.

Japan and Korea

Border disputes between Russia and Japan revolve around the southern Kurile Islands, part of Sakhalin *Oblast*, together with latent Japanese claims to the southern part of Sakhalin Island, which was specified in the 1855 Treaty of Shimoda as a Japanese possession. Although the St. Petersburg Treaty of 1875 recognized all of Sakhalin Island as belonging to Russia, it also transferred the entire Kuril Islands chain to Japan. After Japan's military victory over Russia in 1905, St. Petersburg ceded half of Sakhalin to Tokyo. The Soviet Union seized the entire island, as well as all the Kurile Islands, in the closing stages of World War II in 1945 and incorporated them in the RSFSR. Although Moscow has agreed in principle to return the two smaller southern Kurile Islands of Shikotan and Habomai to Japan, the government in Tokyo views this as insufficient to resolve the long-standing dispute.[74]

In August 2021, Russian defense officials announced plans to expand military infrastructure on the four southern Kurile Islands. Moscow

---

[73] Paul Goble, "Jews 20 Percent of Birobidzhan's Population, Not Four Percent Russian Census Says, People There Say," September 21, 2021, https://windowoneurasia2.blogspot.com/2021/09/jews-20-percent-of-birobidzhans.html and Masha Gessen, *Where the Jews Aren't: The Sad and Absurd Story of Birobidzhan, Russia's Jewish Autonomous Region,* New York: Nextbook, 2016, p.112.

[74] Rensselaer Lee and Artyom Lukin, *Russia's Far East: New Dynamics in Asia Pacific and Beyond,* Boulder, London: Lynne Rienner Publishers, p.244.

also prepared to establish a special economic zone with no customs duties and reduced taxation in the islands. However, any military or economic development plans have been vehemently opposed by Tokyo, as the islands are viewed as Japan's inviolable Northern Territories. Moscow is evidently concerned about potential Japanese moves to regain the Kuriles; the Russian fleet and air force may not be prepared to resist a larger and more capable Japanese military without deploying nuclear weapons.[75] The islands are largely undefended, and spreading territorial fractures in Russia will tempt Tokyo to take the initiative and forcefully regain its lost territories.

More ambitious political forces in Japan can also act on latent claims to Sakhalin Island as well as parts of the Kamchatka peninsula in Kamchatka *Krai* that Russians only began to colonize in the 18th century. Officials in Tokyo believe that the final status of Sakhalin has not been determined and could be revisited as Russia weakens. Escalating claims by Tokyo could also generate protests in Sakhalin *Oblast* not to surrender the islands and will place further pressure on Moscow as well as the regional government. While some local leaders may pursue closer political and economic links with Japan or China, others may focus on defending their territories against both Japanese and Chinese encroachments. One pan-regional initiative would be to create a larger independent Far Eastern Republic including Primorsky *Krai*, Khabarovsk *Krai*, Sakhalin *Oblast*, and Amur *Oblast*, and appeal for US and European support. It would have significant economic potential, as Sakhalin *Oblast* has sizeable oil and gas production facilities and Primorsky *Krai* possess several ports that will enable the new state to establish productive international trading links.

---

[75] Paul Goble, "Russia Must be Ready to Blockade Japanese Ports to Prevent a Tokyo Move on the Kuriles, Shirokorad Says," April 16, 2021, http://windowoneurasia2.blogspot.com/2021/04/russia-must-be-ready-to-blockade.html.

Russia's shortest border is with North Korea, an ally since the Communist takeover in Pyongyang under Soviet supervision at the end of World War II. In 1985, the Soviet Union and North Korea signed an agreement establishing a border along the middle of the Tumen River, next to Primorsky *Krai*, but this was not recognized by the Republic of Korea (South Korea). As a result, a future united Korea could revise claims to the Noktundo peninsula in the delta of the Tumen River in Primorsky *Krai* that North Korea had acknowledged as part of Russia but that South Korea demanded be returned under Korean control.

United States and Canada

Kremlin sources contend that Washington is working through neighboring states such as Finland, Ukraine and Norway to undermine Russia by supporting the demands of its indigenous peoples. This evidently includes the four-million-strong Finno-Ugric nation in order to significantly weaken Moscow's grip over the gas-and-oil-producing regions of northern Russia.[76] While some Russian nationalists continue to claim Alaska as an unfairly traded Russian possession that the tsars sold to the United States in 1867, paradoxically several of Russia's Far Eastern regions formerly pursued close links with the US. Before the Bolshevik coup in 1917, Chukotka was gravitating closer to the United States. Eastern Chukotka in particular was more closely connected with American traders than with Russians, English was widely used as the language of commerce, and the region was never fully integrated in the Tsarist imperial

[76] Paul Goble, "Ukrainian and Finnish Attention to Finno-Ugric Nations Part of West's Hybrid War against Russia, Makarov Says," December 28, 2021, http://windowoneurasia2.blogspot.com/2021/12/ukrainian-and-finnish-attention-to.html.

structure.[77] Contacts between the Chukchi and Alaskans continued until after World War II but were terminated by Moscow during the Cold War.

As Moscow's control loosens over its outlying possessions, Alaska will become the natural geographic and commercial partner of the Chukotka Autonomous *Okrug* and the neighboring Magadan *Oblast*, rich in gold, silver, and other valuable minerals. The idea of a territorial purchase by the US cannot be completely discounted but may not be necessary if the residents of Chukotka compare their economic conditions to those of their Alaskan-American neighbor and hold a referendum on independence from Russia and some form of territorial association with the US. In the event of Moscow's loss of control over its Pacific regions, the US administration can pursue closer links with a number of nascent states and encourage Alaska and Washington State to significantly expand their links with the new regional sovereignties.[78] In an alternative conflict scenario, Beijing may plan to annex several of Russia's Pacific regions and provoke the US to pre-emptively occupy Chukotka *Okrug*, Magadan *Oblast*, Kamchatka *Krai*, and the Republic of Sakha's Arctic coastline in an escalating competition with China.[79]

Russia's overstretched continental reach will weaken its jurisdiction over northern Arctic regions. This is certain to increase the claims of nearby powers, including the US, Canada, Norway, and Denmark, for access or even control over islands within the Arctic Circle that are currently in Russia's possession. The islands are located across the

---

[77] Yuri Slezkine, *Arctic Mirrors: Russia and the Small Peoples of the North*, Ithaca: Cornell University Press, 1994, pp.106–107.

[78] Rensselaer Lee and Artyom Lukin, *Russia's Far East: New Dynamics in Asia Pacific and Beyond*, Boulder, London: Lynne Rienner Publishers, p.253.

[79] Ibid, p.250.

Arctic Ocean, from the Barents Sea in the west to the Bering Sea in the east. The largest islands and archipelagos include Franz Josef Land, Novaya Zemlya, Severny Island, Yuzhny Island, Zapovednik Islands, Kara Sea Islands, Severnaya Zemlya, October Revolution Island, Bolshevik Island, Komsomolets Island, New Siberian Islands, Anzhu Islands, Lyakhovsky Islands, Ayon Island, and Wrangel Island. Claims could also be lodged to Russia's current Exclusive Economic Zones (EEZ), continental shelves, natural resources, and trans-Arctic Sea lanes. Internationalizing the Northern Sea Route across the Arctic will increase Western influence in Russia's High North, Siberia, and Pacific regions through closer connections between cities, seaports, airports, and fleets, and enhance political linkages between all Arctic states and territories.

Greenland can also gain prominence in circumpolar affairs, particularly once the island enhances its autonomy or even gains independence from Denmark. Moscow currently supports Greenland's sovereignty, calculating that this will curtail Denmark's role in the Arctic, reduce the presence of US and NATO bases, and open up the territory for extracting mineral resources. However, an independent Greenland could also rebound against Moscow's imperialism. Successful sovereignty will encourage closer ties with other circumpolar regions and activate indigenous populations and regional governments in the Sakha Republic, the Chukotka Autonomous *Okrug*, the Komi Republic, and the two Nenets autonomous *okrugs* to demand sovereignty and independence from Russia and closer ties with Greenland and other Arctic states.

With extensive territories containing indigenous Inuit peoples, Canada will become more outspoken in raising the rights of the northern nations in Russia when the Federation starts to splinter. In particular, the government of the large Territory of Nunavut, in northern Canada, established in 1999 and with a majority Inuit population, can pursue closer ties with developing states in Arctic Russia containing sizeable indigenous nations, including the Sakha

Republic, the Komi Republic, the Chukotka Autonomous *Okrug*, the Nenets Autonomous *Okrug*, and the Yamalo-Nenets Autonomous *Okrug*, as well as with Siberian *krais* and *oblasts* containing considerable native populations.

The Inuit Circumpolar Council (ICC), a multi-national organization representing indigenous people in northern Canada, Alaska, Greenland, and Chukotka, includes the Inuit, Yupik, and Chukchi peoples and promotes their human rights, economic interests, and traditional cultures. Chukotka *Okrug* contains a Yupik population closely related to the Alaskan and Canadian Inuit. Several thousand Yupik live in nine communities around Chukotka's far-eastern peninsula, where they have suffered through decades of economic neglect and social engineering.[80] Anthropologists have located Chukotka as the gateway from Asia to North America through several waves of human migration across the Bering land bridge starting approximately 10,000 years ago. Such ancient trans-continental contacts can be more effectively revived and developed when Chukotka achieves its sovereignty and independence.

---

[80] Jane George, "Chukotkan Inuit Welcome Inuit Circumpolar Council Leaders," *Nunatsiaq News*, July 31, 2012, https://nunatsiaq.com/stories/article/65674chukotkan_inuit_welcome_inuit_circumpolar_council_leaders/.

7.

Western Planning

An effective Western strategy toward the Russian Federation must confront a dual challenge—Moscow's neo-imperial revisionism and Russia's state failure. The two phenomena are closely interconnected. Prospects for escalating internal turmoil can convince Russia's leaders that a bolder and riskier foreign policy strategy can bring domestic benefits to salvage the current regime by disciplining elite factions and mobilizing public support. This would involve destabilizing pro-Western neighbors including and beyond Ukraine and distracting adversaries by exploiting several regional crises to undermine the capabilities and cohesion of the North Atlantic Treaty Organization (NATO). To avoid being pushed into a constant defensive posture, Washington should not only be planning for a number of destabilizing regional scenarios along NATO's flanks but also preparing for a deepening crisis within Russia itself.

A federal collapse as outlined in this Guide will impact on the positions and strategies of each state along Russia's borders as well as major outside powers.[1] This can lead to significant strategic realignments and military buildups. Russia's rupture will raise China's stature and power projection and encourage Turkey to become more active in a receding "Russia space." The US will be propelled to the

---

[1] Private interview with Enders Wimbush, Jamestown Foundation, March 2021.

forefront as an even more important global player. However, it must develop an effective approach for managing Russia's demise while underscoring fundamental Western interests throughout Eurasia. The dismantling of the Russian Federation will also present new opportunities for trans-Atlanticism among countries that are no longer fearful of Moscow's reactions to NATO membership, including Ukraine, Georgia, Belarus, Moldova, Armenia and Azerbaijan. It will also release new states that will petition for membership in multi-national institutions and some of which may seek to join the North Atlantic Alliance. Trans-Pacificism through enhanced contacts with countries in the Pacific rim can also be promoted among emerging states in Russia's far eastern regions.

Moscow excels at monitoring and exploiting the weaknesses of its major adversaries and the vulnerabilities of nearby countries. It is incumbent on the NATO alliance to conduct a much more rigorous monitoring of Russia's domestic and international weaknesses so they can be leveraged to Western advantage. The multi-national Russian Federation is checkered with deep cross-cutting regional and ethno-national fault lines and riddled with political, economic, demographic, and social fragilities. These defects must be handled adroitly to undermine Moscow's aggressive foreign policy while defending states and nations that seek to liberate themselves from Russia's restrictive borders.

US Strategic Perceptions

In much of the policy literature in the United States and Europe in recent years, the debate over Russia has been limited to Moscow's interventions in Western democracies, its ongoing war against Ukraine, its involvement in Syria, its condemnations of NATO, and its pursuit of global military and diplomatic parity with the US. Moscow's interference in the November 2016 US presidential election sparked a spate of congressional reports and think tank studies on

Russia's "hybrid war," including disinformation, cyber-attacks, energy dependence, political corruption, influence operations, out-of-country assassinations, and the use of mercenaries, private contractors, and assorted proxy forces. Such analyses continued after Moscow's interference in the November 2020 US presidential election and in the national ballots and internal politics of several European countries.

However, there has been little systematic analysis of Russia's deteriorating domestic conditions or the prospects for state fragmentation. Even some valuable reports on the necessity of deep structural reform barely consider the prospect of state collapse if the projected post-Putin reforms fail to deliver any substantial change.[2] Minimal evaluations exist of the country's multiple cleavages, the denied aspirations of numerous nations and regions, the varieties of looming institutional ruptures, the repercussion for neighboring states, and the necessity for a coherent Western strategy to manage these spreading instabilities over the coming decade as the Putin era approaches its conclusion. Much of the political analyses of Russia's domestic developments are also Moscow-centric, mimicking the ultimately misleading Kremlin-centered assessments during Soviet times that failed to take account of the evolution of diverse national republics and proved incapable of preparing for state collapse.

Although a few reports have appeared in recent years outlining how the Putin regime may expire, there is minimal consideration of how Russia's current state structure could be transformed or terminated or the long-term impact of Moscow's neo-imperial ambitions on its

---

[2] Anders Åslund and Leonid Gozman, "Russia after Putin: How to Rebuild the State," *Atlantic Council Report*, February 24, 2021, https://www.atlanticcouncil.org/in-depth-research-reports/report/russia-after-putin-report/.

domestic policies.[3] Although some authors ask the question whether Russia can build a successful modern nation-state or a democratic polity, they fail to address the question of whether a stable state can be built around a Russian nation that lacks a coherent identity and what impact such a project would have on non-Russian ethnicities within the misnamed "federation." Other reports outlining scenarios of Russia's evolution tend to be foreign-policy oriented and do not explore in sufficient detail the future of Russia's statehood and territorial cohesion.[4]

Some commentators attribute a simplistic and misleading dichotomy in the analysis of Russia's predicament.[5] They either posit that Russia is a declining force, a mere regional power, and incapable of posing a serious threat to the Western alliance, other than through its possession of nuclear weapons, or they claim that Russia is a strong and resurgent global power that will indefinitely pose a major challenge for the Western alliance and therefore needs to be placated and accommodated. Rather than either underestimating or exaggerating Moscow's capabilities, serious assessments need to examine the various domains in which Russia can be considered weak or strong. This can help policymakers measure the durability of the current regime and state structure. Such an analysis also needs to consider how the country's strengths and weaknesses are perceived, propagandized, camouflaged, or otherwise exploited by the Kremlin.

---

[3] John Tefft, "Understanding the Factors That Will Impact the Succession to Vladimir Putin as Russian President," Rand, 2020, https://www.rand.org/pubs/perspectives/PE349.html.

[4] "Russia Scenarios 2030," Free Russia Foundation, May 29, 2019, https://www.4freerussia.org/russia-scenarios-2030/.

[5] Joshua Huminski, "Russia's Power and Purpose in a New Global Order," January 9, 2021, *Diplomatic Courier*, https://www.diplomaticourier.com/posts/russias-power-and-purpose-in-a-new-global-order.

Moreover, Russia's capabilities must be compared with those of its major adversaries and neighbors, thus generating policy options on how the West can capitalize on Moscow's weaknesses while defending itself from Kremlin assaults. It is worth remembering that only a few years before its collapse, the Soviet Union was engaged in numerous foreign military escapades, controlled half of Europe, and trumpeted its economic superiority over the West, while disguising its growing existential crisis. Monitoring Russia's numerous structural weaknesses and policy failures is essential, as these will have a significant impact on the security of the United States and its NATO allies and partners.

US, NATO and European Union approaches toward Russia have exhibited several persistent anxieties evident since the disintegration of the Soviet Union in the early 1990s. These fears constrain the crafting of an effective strategy from which the West would benefit. They also encourage Moscow to remain on the offensive and pursue its revisionist ambitions. Basing policy around the avoidance of particular consequences is not only inhibitive, it is also counter-productive by empowering the Kremlin to exploit Western trepidations to its advantage. Successive US administrations have exhibited several pronounced fears regarding the prospects of Russian state collapse and of provoking Russia's aggression.

Fear of State Collapse

In the late 1980s and early 1990s, most Western policymakers were apprehensive about the impact of the unravelling of the Communist Eastern Bloc and the disintegration of the Soviet Union. They calculated that imperial fracture and state collapse would lead to civil wars, mass bloodshed, and unstable borders. Such fears were transmitted to national leaders in Ukraine and other states seeking to extract themselves from Moscow's empire, but the government in Kyiv and the majority of the population did not heed the advice of an overly nervous US administration.[6] Disquiet about state collapse was subsequently projected on to the survival of the Russian Federation, especially during the Russian-Chechen wars in the 1990s. Fear of regime failure ensured Washington's support for both the Boris Yeltsin and Vladimir Putin administrations, which were widely perceived as ensuring domestic stability and contributing to European and Eurasian security, even while they perpetrated the mass slaughter of civilians in Chechnya.

Although successive US governments have not wanted Russia to be as strong and challenging as the USSR, they also remained wary of Russia's decline and weakness.[7] The driver of that fear has been the prospect of a large and failed state with nuclear weapons threatening to generate global mayhem. Such conspicuous apprehensions are amplified by Moscow's propaganda narrative in order to maintain Western support for a single large Russian state. However, such messages also expose the Kremlin's own fears about Russia's survival.

Paradoxically, actual "Russophobia" (literally, fear of Russia), which state propaganda attributes to Westerners who allegedly seek to destroy the country, hinges on the assumption that it will become uncontrollably dangerous during an existential crisis. It will supposedly launch military attacks against several neighbors, generate instabilities in all nearby regions, use its nuclear weapons against Western targets, and even draw the US into outright war. In reality, the Kremlin will face "diminishing imperial returns" and a receding external impact when Putin's leadership is effectively challenged, state failures accelerate, domestic politics become conflictive, resources are

---

[6] https://en.wikisource.org/wiki/Chicken_Kiev_speech.

[7] Nicu Popescu, "How Russia and the West Try to Weaken Each Other," January 22, 2021, European Council on Foreign Relations, https://ecfr.eu/article/how-russia-and-the-west-try-to-weaken-each-other/.

thinly stretched, and citizens are no longer acquiescent. State failure will ensure that Moscow's foreign offensives will become less effective as the regime turns inward and officials prove incapable of disguising Russia's vulnerabilities.

Western fears of a Russia's state collapse are also tied to a prejudicial and patronizing view of the country's citizens: as incapable of changing their leaders and establishing a post-imperial entity. Policymakers seemingly prefer a single centralized Russian state, even though democracy and human rights are thwarted, rather than a decentralized federation. Any initiatives in that direction would supposedly be too disruptive, chaotic and destabilizing. Underlying this position is a condescending perspective on Russia's future as locked in a perpetual authoritarian stalemate. It is assumed that Russia's citizens are incapable of ousting an autocratic regime because of their alleged slave mentality, patriarchal conservatism, and deeply ingrained support for a strong leader. Negative stereotypes about the people of Russia bolster Kremlin assertions that a *status quo* is preferable to disruptive change that unleashes social chaos. Hence, there is apparently no alternative to the existing power structure. Nonetheless, repeating former President George H. W. Bush's warning about "suicidal nationalism" on the eve of the Soviet collapse by urging social passivity and compliance with the *status quo*, will neither alter the trajectory of Russia's entropy nor contribute to devising an effective US policy approach.

Fear of Provocation

The often-trumpeted claim that enlarging NATO or enabling allies and partner countries to defend themselves is "provocative" for Russia's regime needs to be debunked. Moscow pursues its expansionist and subversive agenda most intensely at times when it senses weakness in the Western response. For instance, former President Barack Obama's "reset" of US-Russia relations in March

2009 culminated in the invasion of Ukraine and occupation of Crimea and parts of Donbas in 2014. The periodically repeated notions that American officials only need to fully explain to their Russian counterparts that the US and NATO are not a threat to Russia are both naïve and self-defeating. Putin's regime needs to depict NATO, the US, and the EU as existential threats in order to justify its anti-Western attacks and remain in power as the alleged defender of the imperial Russian state.

One essential element of the purported threat from the West is the democratization of Russia's neighbors, such as Ukraine and Georgia, that can serve as direct positive examples for Russia's transformation. Misunderstandings in Washington about Kremlin perceptions have been demonstrated on regular occasions during periods of political turmoil. For instance, they were evident in recommendations that the US administration try to convince Moscow that the Belarusian protest movement in 2020 simply revolved around domestic politics and not geopolitics.[8] In reality, the Kremlin regime views any independent social opposition in Belarus that pushes for free elections and can replace a pro-Russian or neutral government with a pro-Western one as a direct challenge to its regional hegemony and its own control over Russian society.

Assertions by columnists and analysts that Putin is a successful strategist or tactician who consistently outsmarts the West serve to strengthen the image propagated by the Kremlin to disguise his domestic failings and international defeats. In reality, Putin is an opportunist trained in the KGB to detect and exploit weaknesses in his opponents. To undermine Putin's agenda, US policymakers must focus on Russia's vulnerabilities, weaknesses, and defeats and not

---

[8] Anders Aslund, Melinda Haring, John E. Herbst, and Alexander Vershbow, "Biden and Belarus: A Strategy for the New Administration, Atlantic Council, Eurasia Center, January 2021, https://www.atlanticcouncil.org/wp-content/uploads/2021/01/Biden-Belarus-IB-v3.pdf.

exaggerate its successes. Moscow's failures are a consequence of an assertive Western policy and not passivity, appeasement, or undeserved praise. Russia's glaring international defeats under the Putin presidency have included NATO membership for Central European, Balkan, and Baltic states; the welcoming of Finland and Sweden into the North Atlantic Alliance; a buildup of NATO's rotational forces to deter Russian threats along the Alliance's eastern flank; diplomatic and military assistance support for the territorial integrity of Georgia and Ukraine; development of alternative energy supplies to Europe's east and a reduction of dependence on Russia; unmasking Moscow's intelligence networks and regular expulsion of spies posing as diplomats from several European states; and constant exposure of Kremlin influence operations and disinformation campaigns targeting Western democracies.

An overarching Western fear of Russia is based on its position as the second-largest nuclear power and possessing the world's biggest stockpile of biological agents. The presumed supposition is that Russia's leaders are nuclear *jihadists* willing to commit national suicide rather than calculating how to salvage their political futures and economic fortunes regardless of the state structure. Moreover, Russia's weapons of mass destruction are protected by the most loyal elements of the security forces and are highly unlikely to be seized by rebels and insurgents. Even in the eventuality that some emerging states acquire control of such weapons and, crucially, the means to actually deploy and fire them, they will have no reason to target any countries from which they will seek political backing, diplomatic recognition, and economic assistance. On the contrary, they are likely to favor nuclear disarmament to help gain international support, much like Ukraine, Belarus and Kazakhstan did after the dissolution of the Soviet Union.

Some Western policymakers and analysts remain concerned that a tougher policy of confronting Moscow's external aggression and encouraging internal discord will run a high risk of international instability and even plunge the world into war. Russia's rupture is thereby viewed only as a threat and not as an opportunity. The Kremlin cultivates such apprehensions to gain advantages *vis-à-vis* Western powers. For instance, it has fed into anxieties over Russia's disintegration by claiming that this would guarantee China's advance to the Urals and vastly increase Beijing's threat posture toward Europe and NATO. The notion that a fragile Russia will enable China to accelerate its global campaign against the West is strategically shortsighted. A weakening Russia is more likely to energize Chinese ambitions and precipitate confrontations between Moscow and Beijing over territories and resources in Eurasia that the West can exploit to its advantage.

Alarm over Russia's implosion among Western policymakers is further fueled by fear that an even more aggressive leader will replace Vladimir Putin in the Kremlin. This has been a classic argument by dictatorial regimes to convince its adversaries that they are the lesser evil. However, Moscow's foreign policy is largely determined by the nature of its administration, so that a quasi-democratic government or a weaker central power in a shrunken Russia is less likely to engage in conflicts with the West.[9] Nonetheless, the fear that Russia's aggressive behavior will become more pronounced when the government is threatened by internal instability may convince some policymakers that Russian democracy and decentralization should not be supported. By following this logic, Western policy would become frozen and dependent solely on Kremlin actions. Fear of provoking Moscow paralyzes Western decision-making.

---

[9] Kathryn E. Stoner, *Russia Resurrected: Its Power and Purpose in a New Global Order,* Oxford University Press, 2021, p.265.

US Policy Implications

Some analysts have served a useful warning for US policymakers not to overly fixate on China and neglect Russia's persistent ambitions and continuing capabilities.[10] Even amidst the full-scale 2022 Russo-Ukrainian war, the Joseph Biden administration has sought to focus its foreign policy priorities on countering a rising China, widely viewed across the partisan divide as America's most challenging long-term adversary. At the same time, prior to early 2022, the White House had tried to pursue "stable and predictable" relations with Russia so that the US can zero in on containing Beijing. However, unpredictability and instability are two core principles of Moscow's foreign policy designed to undermine the West and which this regime will not relinquish.

As the war in Ukraine has highlighted yet again, the current imperial Russian state is not as strong as Moscow wants the West to think it is, but it is also not as weak as the West should want it to be. Western governments have applied various remedies to curtail Moscow's destabilizing international aspirations and to encourage constructive domestic political and economic reforms. However, containment, appeasement, and engagement have not diminished Russia's neo-imperial designs or its authoritarian impulses. Western policymakers have consistently failed to anticipate Russia's domestic political developments and the Kremlin's imperial appetite. They remain susceptible to claims that Russia must be an "equal" partner on the

---

[10] Michael Kofman and Andrea Kendall-Taylor, "The Myth of Russian Decline: Why Moscow Will Be a Persistent Power," *Foreign Affairs*, November-December 2021, https://www.foreignaffairs.com/articles/russian-federation/2021-10-19/myth-russiandecline?utm_medium=newsletters&utm_source=fatoday&utm_campaign=The%20Myth%20of%20Russian%20Decline&utm_content=20211021&utm_term=FA%20Today%20-%20112017.

international arena—in practice a power that is "more equal than others" if its non-compliance with international norms is tolerated.[11]

The absence of a coherent and anticipatory US strategy has served to reinforce Kremlin perceptions that the West is weak, divided, and incapable of preventing Russia's revisionist restoration. Given the rolling global crises in the wake of the COVID-19 pandemic and subsequent economic contractions, the US withdrawal from Afghanistan, the Taliban inspiration for radical Islamism, and Russian and Chinese moves to exploit Western weaknesses, the North Atlantic Alliance can become even more vulnerable to foreign subversion and internal division. In the fall of 2021, Moscow's use of energy blackmail during Europe's natural gas shortages, its support for Belarus in manipulating Middle East refugees to challenge Poland's borders, and its constant military pressure on Ukraine demonstrated that the Kremlin is willing to deploy multiple tools against its Western adversaries. The Kremlin's aggressive actions since recognizing the independence of the proxy statelets in Donbas on February 21, 2022, and re-invading Ukraine three days later have only served to reinforce those assessments.

Nonetheless, as this Guide has outlined, in the midst of its anti-Atlanticist offensive, Moscow faces unsolvable domestic problems on several vital fronts: economic, demographic, social, regional, ethnic, and political. This provides Western governments with new opportunities not only to strengthen Allied resilience to Kremlin subversion but also to devise a progressive strategy to manage the international consequences of Russia's turmoil. Such a strategy has to be multi-dimensional, combining all informational, cyber, economic,

---

[11] Lilia Shevtsova, "Fallacies and Failures in the Western Perception of Russia," Robert Bosch Academy, March 2021, https://www.robertboschacademy.de/en/perspectives/fallacies-and-failures-western-perception-russia?mc_cid=7b24c58433&mc_eid=223d2dad2a.

diplomatic and military domains. It needs to closely involve all NATO allies and partners, particularly those bordering Russia, and shield them from any negative security consequences. And it must capitalize on Russia's vulnerabilities by planning for a prolonged period of internal instability, culminating in the emergence of new political entities.

US Policy Prescriptions

The US National Security Strategy issued in December 2017 affirmed that Russia was a major rival and competitor aiming to weaken Washington's international influence and divide the United States from its allies and partners. Given this geopolitical assessment, policies need to be developed to reverse Moscow's offensive by capitalizing on its weaknesses. Most studies of Russia's campaign against Western democracies have focused on defensive and blocking strategies or offered another rapprochement that would in effect entail geostrategic compromises benefiting the Kremlin. Missing is a detailed assessment of how a forward-looking Western strategy could reverse and disable Russia's neo-imperialist drive. An effective approach would aim to benefit from Russia's internal cleavages to encourage political pluralism, regional devolution, and imperial reversal. Even if Russia does not transform into a stable democracy the aim would be to neutralize its imperial impulses and expansionist pretensions.

There is little if any long-term policy planning on how turmoil, instability, and political rupture could affect Russia's statehood or impact on neighboring states and relations between Moscow and Washington. During each US administration reports are routinely issued by former officials and scholars proposing either a new *détente* or "reset" with Russia, the pursuit of "strategic stability" based on cooperation in a narrow arena such as arms control, "managing" the bilateral confrontation, or simply asserting that little is likely to change.[12] At least one report has recommended that Russia should be rewarded for pressuring its neighbors, proposing the creation of a neutral zone that would in effect consolidate Moscow's dominance in parts of Europe's East.[13] Such prescriptions provide little confidence that any rapprochement with Russia will be successful or durable or that its leaders will alter their foreign policy ambitions. On the contrary, the Kremlin welcomes such studies, calculating that its previous imperial transgressions are likely to be accommodated by a new US administration.

A much more effective strategy that would be likely to dent the Kremlin's self-confidence needs to focus on the future of Russia itself. Such a strategy requires a clear objective and a methodology of achievement. The ultimate strategic goal would be to reverse Russia's neo-imperial offensives by helping its citizens transform the state into a genuine federation that accepts its neighbors as independent countries that decide their own foreign policies and international alliances. Such an outcome would only be achievable through Russia's comprehensive political devolution and self-determination among its diverse regions and republics.

---

[12] Jeffrey Mankoff and Andrey Kortunov, "Addressing Unresolved Challenges in US-Russia Relations," CSIS, March 13, 2020, https://www.csis.org/analysis/addressing-unresolved-challenges-us-russia-relations; Richard Sokolsky and Eugene Rumer, "US-Russian Relations in 2030," June 15, 2020, https://carnegieendowment.org/2020/06/15/u.s.-russian-relations-in-2030-pub-82056; Paul J. Saunders (Ed.) A New Direction in US-Russia Relations? America's Challenges and Opportunities in Dealing with Russia," Center for the National Interest, February 2017, https://187ock2y3ejr34z8752m6ize-wpengine.netdna-ssl.com/wp-content/uploads/2017/03/A-New-Direction-in-U.S.-Russia-Relations-CFTNI-2017-Saunders.pdf.

[13] Samuel Charap, Jeremy Shapiro, John J. Drennan, Oleksandr Chalyi, Reinhard Krumm, Yulia Nikitina, Gwendolyn Sasse (Eds.), "A Consensual Proposed for a Revised Regional Order in Post-Soviet Europe and Eurasia," Rand 2019, https://www.rand.org/pubs/conf_proceedings/CF410.html#download.

As this "transformation scenario" becomes increasingly improbable because of Kremlin resistance to structural reform, US policy planners must prepare for an alternative or parallel option—the "rupture scenario." When genuine federalism and pluralism fails to materialize in the midst of economic decline and political uncertainty, then the separatist scenario will gain traction and culminate in Russia's rupture. Separation and the formation of new states are processes visible throughout history when loyalty to the existing state dissipates and new forms of sovereignty are widely supported. Some ethnic regions will seek emancipation and resist being integrated into a Russian identity, while certain predominantly Russian regions will benefit from independence, much as Americans extracted themselves from the British Empire in the 18th century.

The Western alliance will need to manage Russia's rupture at both regional and international levels. The challenges of transforming Soviet republics and satellites into independent states 30 years ago can be replicated by similarly helping to reconstruct Russia's republics and regions. Such an approach does not discount attempts to cooperate with the Kremlin in dealing with nuclear arms proliferation, climate change or viral pandemics. But a strategy based only on common or global dangers will disarm Western capabilities to manage the multi-regional consequences of Russia's turmoil.

Ideally, the US should work closely with its NATO allies in formulating and pursuing a unified approach to Russia's rupture. Much more likely, Germany, France, and a few other European countries will urge caution or even try to assist Moscow in reigning in wayward republics and regions and refuse any prospects for international recognition. Such policies will neither stymie disintegrative developments inside Russia nor prepare Europe for post-imperial conditions. However, several Central and Eastern European allies, together with the United Kingdom and Russia's immediate neighbors are likely to support a novel and bold US strategy in which the following elements can be included.

Upgrade Defenses and Sanctions

NATO must prepare contingencies for both the dangers and the opportunities that Russia's fragmentation will present. In particular, Russia's European neighbors need to be provided with sufficient security in terms of military support and weapons systems to shield themselves from the most destabilizing scenarios. Russia's offensive capabilities can be weakened if the defensive capabilities of US allies and partners are strengthened. Namely, the West should:

- Counter Russia's attempts to undermine Western democracies and NATO aspirants, in which Ukraine serves as a critical test. A cautious NATO approach will simply embolden Moscow to launch new military offensives.[14] A strong deterrence would mean providing Kyiv with all necessary military means to liberate its territories, however long this takes. Beyond the war, Ukraine must significantly enhance its interoperability with NATO forces, construct NATO-compatible military infrastructure, and engage in joint technological projects with Alliance defense industries. Kyiv must also be assisted in cyber-defense, protection of vital infrastructure, anti-corruption campaigns, and in ensuring energy security.

- Uphold comprehensive Western financial and economic sanctions as long as Russian military forces remain in Ukraine. War crime cases against Russian officials must also be pursued for

---

[14] Alexander Vershbow, "How NATO Can Help Ukraine Deter Russian Aggression," *The National Interest*, November 7, 2021, https://nationalinterest.org/blog/buzz/how-nato-can-help-ukraine-deter-russian-aggression195848?mkt_tok=NjU5LVdaWC0wNzUAAAGAoImk8Y5QCo_jda6NAbxP38WShkXmVRgJC8k9bnPtAaJtsk0peY9rdAw8NMEOmp75iU5GFgd9sC0bl3s2W7b9wyFWGTJA7PxOnh1U8n2f.

the actions of the Russian military in Ukraine. Rifts between Moscow and Russia's regions can also be widened by prohibiting regional governors from using the West as a financial safe haven and thereby undermining their loyalty to the Kremlin.[15]

- Accelerate a wholesale oil and gas embargo of Russia's exports and terminate Gazprom or Russian proxy control over all EU gas storage facilities. Comprehensive sanctions would be costly for those Western states that are overly dependent on Russian supplies, but this should convince them to make alternative arrangements from North Africa, the Middle East, and the US, and focus on LNG contracts much like Poland and Lithuania. The EU must also boost its program for alternative energies, as every crisis breeds solutions and innovations. Europe needs to develop a plan to manage a comprehensive breakdown of Russian energy supplies during a prolonged fragmentation of the state. This would involve locating alternative sources for natural gas and oil for those countries most dependent on Russian sources.

Prepare for State Rupture

An anticipatory "Russia rupture policy planning" team in Washington should be established to include key government agencies and develop contingencies for a range of scenarios inside and along the borders of the Russian Federation. In parallel, a "conflict planning" center at NATO HQ can be assembled to deal specifically with scenarios of future regional instabilities generated by Russia's state failure. Attention should focus on several concrete steps:

[15] Private interview with Stephen Nix, International Republican Institute, March 2021.

- Support Russia's neighbors to monitor political and economic conditions and the public mood in neighboring Russian republics and regions. Ukraine, Georgia, Finland and Estonia are paying increasing attention to ethnic issues inside the Russian Federation, and other states need to closely observe and analyze political and social developments across their borders and share their findings and analysis with the US and other NATO allies.

- Devise diplomatic and economic policy responses in the event of destabilizing power struggles in Moscow, spreading civil strife, major internal state violence, and federal cleavages. The overarching goal would be to leverage the vulnerabilities of Russia's regime to undercut the Kremlin's imperial aspirations and aggressive actions. This can involve support for rival power centers and engagement with politicians, parties, republics, and regions seeking improved ties with the West.

- Benefit from opportunities to gain new partners along Russia's borders whose interests evolve as they seek to reorient away from Moscow. This would include Belarus, Armenia, Azerbaijan, Kazakhstan and other Central Asian states. The domestic political impact of Russia's rupture on the more significant authoritarian and anti-American powers, particularly China, must also be assessed to determine how the US can manage the process.

Support Regionalism and Federalism

Russia's federalization is not only essential for democratization but also for reducing Russia's security threat to the US and its allies. In dealing with Putin's Russia, Washington can adapt policies that hastened the collapse of centralized communist rule and the Soviet bloc empire in the late 1980s and early 1990s. This can include:

- Implement an assertive US policy that is not simply "values based" or focused solely on democracy promotion. Instead, it must be "geo-strategic based" and designed to promote domestic changes that will undercut the negative impact of Russia's neo-imperialism on US allies, partners, and American global interests.

- Support political pluralism, democratic reform, minority rights, genuine federalism, administrative decentralization, ethno-national autonomy, and self-determination among Russia's disparate regions and numerous nations. Russian activists have been seeking more robust US support for regional and national movements inside Russia.[16] Assistance can be provided to Russia's civic and ethno-regional activists online and in exile. Western capitals can host members of the political opposition and independent media outlets, provide financial aid, and protect them from Moscow's security services.[17] This would help undermine the isolation of Russian society fostered by the Putin regime and challenge the anti-Western narrative in the official media.

- Communicate the principles of federalism to the Russian public through every available media and on-line outlet, as proponents of federalism have been unable to fully communicate their ideas and elicit a broader domestic debate. The US political system can be highlighted for the Russian public as a successful decentralized federation in which states' rights help develop local economies and provide citizens with major political inputs. This would place

---

[16] Remarks by Russian activists at a Jamestown Foundation Roundtable on "The Future of Russia's Federation: Reform or Rupture?" Jamestown Foundation, September 9, 2021.

[17] Maria Domańska, "How the EU Can Engage Russian Civil Society," June 29, 2021, Carnegie Europe, https://carnegieeurope.eu/strategiceurope/84858.

Moscow on the offensive, as its anti-democratic and isolationist plans for the state will stimulate even more opposition.[18]

- Encourage the EU to play a constructive role by emphasizing its support for regional development and fostering inter-regional cooperation across state borders. This can help provide concrete examples to Russia's citizens that administrative devolution and involvement in local politics promotes economic growth and international cooperation. With a focus on regional development and cross-border partnerships, it will be more difficult for the Kremlin to whip up national hostility toward neighboring countries and against the West.[19]

- Formulate a comprehensive media, internet, and public relations campaign inside Russia to discredit Putin, his officials, and pro-Kremlin oligarchs.[20] Such an informational onslaught must highlight Russia's numerous domestic weaknesses that the current regime hides and disguises.[21] The Russian public and elites need constant examples of how domestic failures necessitate urgent systemic reform or will result in further destabilization and potential violence.

---

[18] Private interview with Valery Dzutsev, Radio Free Europe/ Radio Liberty, March 2021.

[19] Private interview with Vadim Shtepa, Editor in Chief, Region.Expert, Tallinn, March 2021.

[20] Leonid Bershidsky, "Russia's New Guerrilla Media Are Going After Putin," December 13, 2020, https://finance.yahoo.com/news/russia-guerilla-media-going-putin-130022725.html.

[21] Péter Krekó, "How Authoritarians Inflate Their Image," *Journal of Democracy*, Vol.32, Number 3, July 2021, pp.119-120, https://www.journalofdemocracy.com/articles/how-authoritarians-inflate-their-image/.

Acknowledge Sovereignty and Separation

When a genuine program of federalization and political pluralism fails to materialize because of Kremlin resistance, then the separatist option will gain traction culminating in the creation of new states. During the unfolding developments, the US and its allies can play a constructive role in a number of ways:

- Avoid conflating "separatism" with "extremism" and thereby mimicking Moscow's disparagement of independence and statehood. Refuse to recognize Russia's fraudulent national, regional and local elections as legitimate. Condemn the Kremlin's unilateral appointment of local governors. Underscore the absence of democratic choice and speak out for the political and civil rights of all nations, minorities, and regional identities.

- Demonstrate to Russia's citizens how Moscow economically exploits the wealthier regions to fuel its anti-Western offensives while its political elites profit from massive corruption and theft from the state budget. Underscore that stifling central control over local resources and economies runs parallel with the chokehold the regime exerts over individual and social liberties.

- Support diplomatically those regions of Russia that opt for political emancipation and sovereignty and recognize those republics that choose independence and refuse to be assimilated in ethnic Russian culture, identity, and statehood. Independence for Chechnya and other unassimilable republics should be backed for several reasons.[22] It will weaken justifications for Moscow's territorial revisionism, help Russia become more ethnically, culturally, and politically homogenous to reduce the potential for

---

[22] Private interview with Valery Dzutsev, Radio Free Europe/ Radio Liberty, March 2021.

conflict, and undercut support for Chechen insurgents from anti-Western forces such as the Taliban.

Develop New State Linkages

The weakening of central authority and the fracturing of the centralized Russian Federation will encourage the emergence of new states that must be engaged by international powers and institutions if multi-regional stability is to be maintained or restored. This will demonstrate that the West is consistently working toward ensuring international security through national independence. Specific initiatives should be to:

- Manage the process of dissolution and lessen the likelihood of conflict that spills over state borders by establishing direct political and diplomatic links with Russia's diverse republics and regions and promote their efforts for a peaceful transition toward statehood. Aspiring states may not necessarily be based on ethnic principles but on regional multi-ethnic identities amidst increasing local estrangement from Moscow even among ethnic-Russian populations.

- Engage directly with the government in Moscow, whatever its political and ideological profile, to acknowledge that shedding Russia's remaining imperial possessions will prove beneficial for statehood, security, stability, economic development, and international cooperation. In promoting a peaceful transition, offer to mediate between disputing parties and emerging post-Russia states, whether over minority rights, resources, or territories in order to reduce the potential for armed conflicts or population expulsions.

Calibrate Positions of Other Powers

Much more attention needs to be given to how neighboring powers will seek to benefit from Russia's failures and ruptures and how this would affect US and Western interests:

- Assess how other major international players, especially China, will respond to Russia's accelerating crisis, whether in attempting to assist Moscow reintegration efforts, remaining neutral, or raising their own stature by benefiting politically, economically, and territorially from Russia's federal dissolution.

- Strengthen NATO defenses, as the ambitions of several regional powers will directly affect Allied security interests and could result in military incursions in strategically vital post-Russia regions. China's rising dominance over Russia's Far Eastern regions and its growing penetration into Siberia and Central Asia will alter power balances across Eurasia. Russia's disintegration can also revive Japan's territorial aspirations and increase tensions between Beijing and Tokyo that would inevitably pull in the US. Washington will need to focus not only on preventing armed conflicts but limiting China's hegemony over the new states that emerge from eastern Russia.

- Work closely with NATO allies and partners in managing Russia's rupture, particularly with bordering states, as well as other countries possessing significant historical, ethnic, religious, linguistic, or cultural links with nations and proto-states currently inside the Russian Federation. This will contribute to a more manageable transition process in developing statehood and ensuring international recognition.

Crafting Western Narratives

Russia's state outlets become especially emboldened in their grievance narratives against the US, NATO, and the EU when they have receptive Western politicians, academics, business leaders, and religious figures echoing their messages. This amplifies their impact because Moscow can claim that some Western observers understand how Russia has been aggrieved. Additionally, Western policymakers and academics who seek avenues of cooperation with Russia, especially whenever a new US administration is elected, can become useful for the Kremlin by feeding into its grievances and fortifying claims to imperial entitlement. Assertions that Russia has "national interests" or "special interests" toward neighboring states, can justify blocking their NATO and EU membership prospects and developing closer links with the US. Claims that NATO has assaulted Russia by spreading to its borders and incorporating the Central-Eastern European region ignores the yearnings of former Soviet satellites for independence and an effective defense against any future Muscovite imperial projects.

To be more effective against Kremlin propaganda and disinformation, Russia's alleged grievances against the West must be directly addressed and corrected. Lasting security is based on the independence of each state, and NATO membership is the free choice of any European state seeking security and protection against aggressive powers. In this strategic equation, Russia has been given every opportunity to cooperate with the North Atlantic Alliance, but the Kremlin has not budged from its Greater Russia project, its occupation of neighbors' territories, and its persistent threats to international security.

At the same time, Western governments and organizations need to disseminate a narrative of real grievances that citizens inside Russia have against the Putinist system and the current state. This extensive list includes state corruption, economic stagnation, environmental disasters, political repression, incompetence in dealing with natural emergencies such as pandemics, the power vertical that suppresses democratic choice, the federal vertical that suppresses the rights of regions, ethnic discrimination against non-Russians, and escalating assimilation of minority nations. In addition, an anti-grievance narrative should be encouraged. Rather than enabling the Russian state to inculcate a victimhood complex among citizens, the people of the Russian Federation need to reclaim their individual, human, and social rights and assert their dignity as citizens who can build a positive grievance-free future.

Paradoxically, US silence or denials of supporting Russia's transformation and the positive consequences of state rupture simply feed into the Kremlin narrative that Washington is disguising its objectives. Claims that developments in Russia cannot be influenced by Western policy are also misleading and will estrange segments of the public who seek the liberties that Westerners take for granted. Additionally, such assertions will not pacify the Kremlin but will be treated in the same way by state propaganda as NATO's rebuttal that it is threatening Russia's borders. The regime's survival is based on stoking fear and conflict regardless of Western policy. To counter Kremlin disinformation and conspiracy myths, openly declared support for democracy and federalism in Russia and the rights of republic's and regions to determine their autonomy, sovereignty, and statehood can help embolden citizens and demonstrate that they are not isolated on the world stage despite Moscow's oppressive policies.

Instead of merely responding to Moscow's constant attacks, Washington must launch a strategic geopolitical offensive to "de-imperialize" Russia. It can checkmate Russia's expansionism by targeting the dictatorial pillars of the Putinist state. Moscow's security threats can be significantly reduced and neutralized through democratization, decentralization, and dissolution. It is in the direct national security interests of the United States to help Russia either to federalize or fracture, to decentralize or disintegrate. The West needs to ensure that Russia is sufficiently weakened that whoever replaces Putin will no longer be in a position to wage imperialist wars against neighbors. Moreover, a rump Muscovite state shorn of its resource base in Siberia and the northern territories will have much reduced capabilities for militaristic and revisionist policies toward neighbors. Neglecting Russia's escalating domestic problems that lead to fragmentation will prove more damaging to Western interests than preparing to manage their international repercussions. The collapse of the Eastern Bloc and the unraveling of the Soviet Union over 30 years ago should serve as poignant lessons that geopolitical revolutions occur regardless of Kremlin disinformation or the West's belief in a permanent *status quo*. Instead of fearing the future, US policymakers should be exhilarated by the prospect of historic challenges that will herald a new era of geopolitics.

Appendix I: Maps

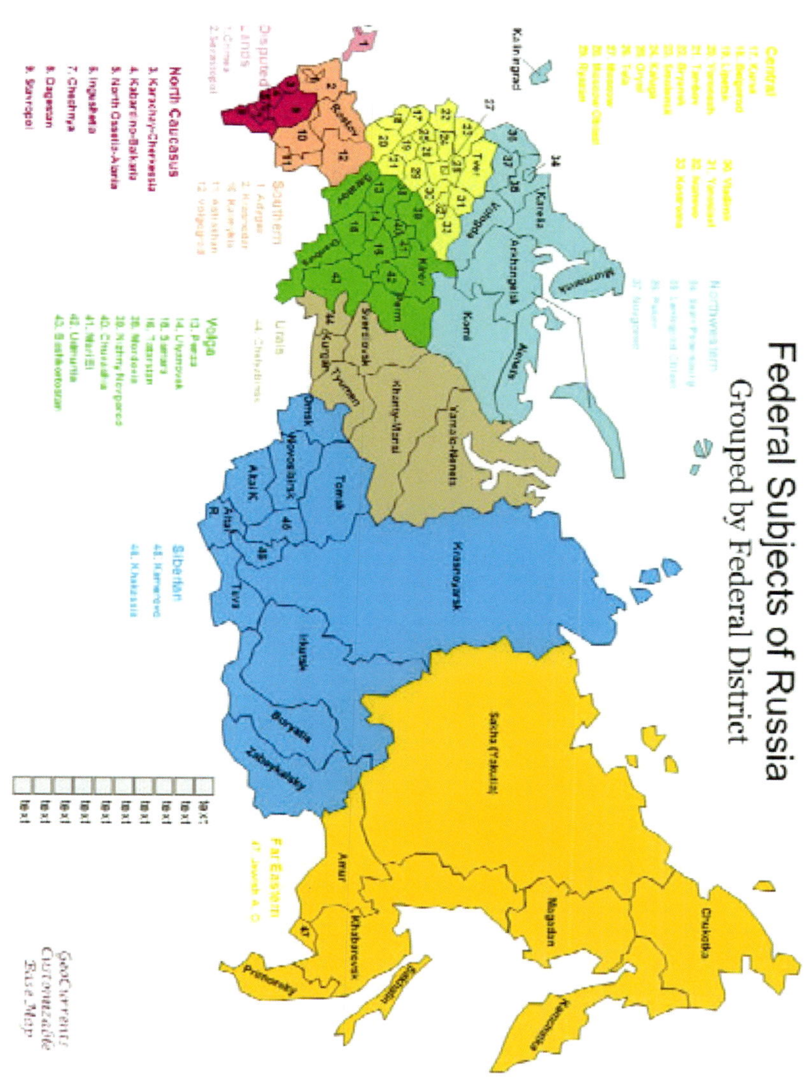

Ethnic Groups of the Russian Federation
Chukchi
Even
Koryak
Aleut
Itelmen
Russian
Russian
Yakut
Evenki
Evenki
Nganasan
Nenets
Selkup
Khanty
Mansi
Komi
Russian
Russian
Karelian
Kola Saami
Udmurt
Mari
Chuvash
Tatar
Bashkir
Ukrainian
Adyghe
Balkar
Kalmyk
Nogay
Kumyk
Lezgin
Ossetian
Ingush
Chechen
Dargin
Khakas
Tatar
Tofa
Shor
Altay
Tuvan
Buryat
Udihe
Orok
Korean
Russian
1000 km
600 mi
© Daniel Dalet / d-maps.com

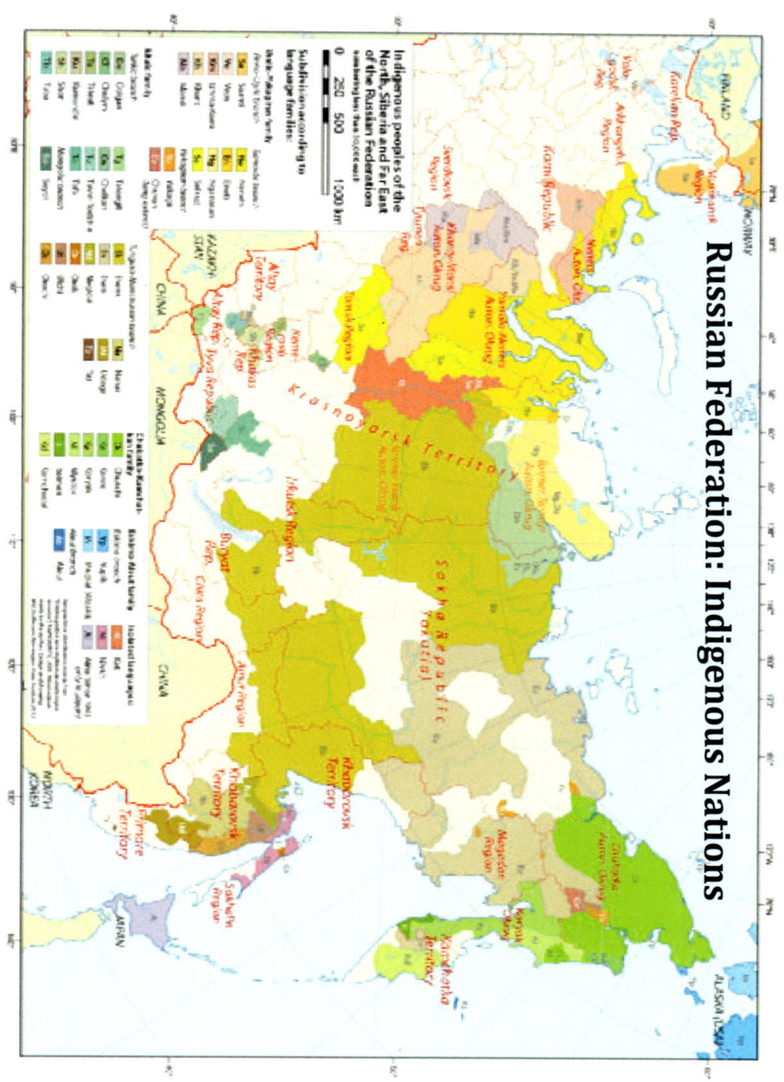
Russian Federation: Indigenous Nations
Indigenous peoples of the North, Siberia and Far East of the Russian Federation
0 250 500 1000 km
Krasnoyarsk Territory
Sakha Republic (Yakutia)
Khabarovsk Territory
Chukotka Auton. Okrug
Kamchatka Territory
Magadan Region
Sakhalin Region
Primorye Territory
Amur Region
Irkutsk Region
Buryat Rep.
Chita Region
Tomsk Region
Komi Republic
Murmansk Region
Karelian Rep.
Arkhangelsk Region
Sverdlovsk Region
Altay Territory
FINLAND
NORWAY
CHINA
MONGOLIA
KAZAKHSTAN
JAPAN
NORTH KOREA
ALASKA (USA)

Appendix II: Russian Federation Demography

Rank	Federal subject	Population (January 2022 est.)	Population (2010 Census)	% change	Land area (km^2)	Population density (per km^2)
1	Moscow	12,632,409	11,503,501	+9.81%	2,561	4932.61
2	Moscow Oblast	7,765,918	7,095,120	+9.45%	44,329	175.19
3	Krasnodar Krai	5,681,962	5,226,647	+8.71%	75,485	75.27
4	Saint Petersburg	5,376,672	4,879,566	+10.19%	1,403	3832.27
5	Sverdlovsk Oblast	4,261,084	4,297,747	−0.85%	194,307	21.93
6	Rostov Oblast	4,149,835	4,277,976	−3.00%	100,967	41.10
7	Bashkortostan	4,001,052	4,072,292	−1.75%	142,947	27.99
8	Tatarstan	3,886,640	3,786,488	+2.64%	67,847	57.29

Rank	Federal subject	Population (January 2022 est.)	Population (2010 Census)	% change	Land area (km²)	Population density (per km²)
9	Chelyabinsk Oblast	3,416,613	3,476,217	−1.71%	88,529	38.59
10	Dagestan	3,154,677	2,910,249	+8.40%	50,270	62.75
11	Nizhny Novgorod Oblast	3,141,015	3,310,597	−5.12%	76,624	40.99
12	Samara Oblast	3,129,410	3,215,532	−2.68%	53,565	58.42
13	Krasnoyarsk Krai	2,846,565	2,828,187	+0.65%	2,366,79 7	1.20
14	Novosibirsk Oblast	2,779,375	2,665,911	+4.26%	177,756	15.64
15	Stavropol Krai	2,777,531	2,786,281	−0.31%	66,160	41.98
16	Kemerovo Oblast	2,603,638	2,763,135	−5.77%	95,725	27.20
17	Perm Krai	2,555,042	2,635,276	−3.04%	160,236	15.95

Rank	Federal subject	Population (January 2022 est.)	Population (2010 Census)	% change	Land area (km²)	Population density (per km²)
18	Volgograd Oblast	2,446,461	2,610,161	−6.27%	112,877	21.67
19	Saratov Oblast	2,357,476	2,521,892	−6.52%	101,240	23.29
20	Irkutsk Oblast	2,356,542	2,428,750	−2.97%	774,846	3.04
21	Voronezh Oblast	2,285,240	2,335,380	−2.15%	52,216	43.77
22	Altai Krai	2,266,739	2,419,755	−6.32%	167,996	13.49
23	Orenburg Oblast	1,921,908	2,033,072	−5.47%	123,702	15.54
24	Leningrad Oblast	1,907,590	1,716,868	+11.11%	83,908	22.73
25	Crimea[a]	1,893,577	1,893,577	0.00%	26,081	72.60
26	Omsk Oblast	1,879,242	1,977,665	−4.98%	141,140	13.31

Rank	Federal subject	Population (January 2022 est.)	Population (2010 Census)	% change	Land area (km²)	Population density (per km²)
27	Primorsky Krai	1,860,429	1,956,497	−4.91%	164,673	11.30
28	Yugra	1,702,452	1,532,243	+11.11%	534,801	3.18
29	Tyumen Oblast	1,552,418	1,537,416	+0.98%	160,122	9.70
30	Belgorod Oblast	1,530,222	1,532,526	−0.15%	27,134	56.40
31	Chechnya	1,516,882	1,268,989	+19.53%	16,165	93.80
32	Udmurtia	1,483,539	1,521,420	−2.49%	42,061	35.27
33	Tula Oblast	1,430,942	1,553,925	−7.91%	25,679	55.72
34	Vladimir Oblast	1,322,166	1,443,693	−8.42%	29,084	45.46
35	Khabarovsk Krai	1,298,233	1,343,869	−3.40%	787,633	1.65

Rank	Federal subject	Population (January 2022 est.)	Population (2010 Census)	% change	Land area (km²)	Population density (per km²)
36	Penza Oblast	1,272,697	1,386,186	−8.19%	43,352	29.36
37	Kirov Oblast	1,234,448	1,341,312	−7.97%	120,374	10.26
38	Tver Oblast	1,228,698	1,353,392	−9.21%	84,201	14.59
39	Yaroslavl Oblast	1,226,062	1,272,468	−3.65%	36,177	33.89
40	Ulyanovsk Oblast	1,202,811	1,292,799	−6.96%	37,181	32.35
41	Chuvashia	1,197,866	1,251,619	−4.29%	18,343	65.30
42	Bryansk Oblast	1,167,806	1,278,217	−8.64%	34,857	33.50
43	Vologda Oblast	1,138,694	1,202,444	−5.30%	144,527	7.88
44	Lipetsk Oblast	1,113,584	1,173,513	−5.11%	24,047	46.31

Rank	Federal subject	Population (January 2022 est.)	Population (2010 Census)	% change	Land area (km^2)	Population density (per km^2)
45	Ryazan Oblast	1,083,834	1,154,114	−6.09%	39,605	27.37
46	Kursk Oblast	1,081,905	1,127,081	−4.01%	29,997	36.07
47	Arkhangelsk Oblast[c]	1,068,672	1,227,626	−12.95%	413,103	2.59
48	Tomsk Oblast	1,068,480	1,047,394	+2.01%	314,391	3.40
49	Zabaykalsky Krai	1,042,993	1,107,107	−5.79%	431,892	2.41
50	Kaliningrad Oblast	1,026,472	941,873	+8.98%	15,125	67.87
51	Kaluga Oblast	1,019,668	1,010,930	+0.86%	29,777	34.24
52	Yakutia	990,538	958,528	+3.34%	3,083,523	0.32
53	Astrakhan Oblast	989,345	1,010,073	−2.05%	49,024	20.18

Rank	Federal subject	Population (January 2022 est.)	Population (2010 Census)	% change	Land area (km²)	Population density (per km²)
54	Buryatia	981,487	972,021	+0.97%	351,334	2.79
55	Tambov Oblast	979,504	1,091,994	−10.30%	34,462	28.42
56	Ivanovo Oblast	976,144	1,061,651	−8.05%	21,437	45.54
57	Smolensk Oblast	908,659	985,537	−7.80%	49,779	18.25
58	Kabardino-Balkaria	869,735	859,939	+1.14%	12,470	69.75
59	Kurgan Oblast	804,769	910,807	−11.64%	71,488	11.26
60	Komi Republic	803,208	901,189	−10.87%	416,774	1.93
61	Amur Oblast	771,889	830,103	−7.01%	361,908	2.13
62	Mordovia	769,142	834,755	−7.86%	26,128	29.44

Rank	Federal subject	Population (January 2022 est.)	Population (2010 Census)	% change	Land area (km²)	Population density (per km²)
63	Murmansk Oblast	724,179	795,409	−8.96%	144,902	5.00
64	Oryol Oblast	713,043	786,935	−9.39%	24,652	28.92
65	North Ossetia–Alania	687,674	712,980	−3.55%	7,987	86.10
66	Mari El	670,730	696,459	−3.69%	23,375	28.69
67	Kostroma Oblast	620,658	667,562	−7.03%	60,211	10.31
68	Pskov Oblast	612,458	673,423	−9.05%	55,399	11.06
69	Karelia	602,458	643,548	−6.38%	180,520	3.34
70	Novgorod Oblast	585,247	634,111	−7.71%	54,501	10.74
71	YaNAO	552,788	522,904	+5.72%	769,250	0.72

Rank	Federal subject	Population (January 2022 est.)	Population (2010 Census)	% change	Land area (km^2)	Population density (per km^2)
72	Sevastopol[a]	529,883	529,883	0.00%	864	613.29
73	Khakassia	528,316	532,403	−0.77%	61,569	8.58
74	Ingushetia	523,955	412,529	+27.01%	3,628	167.77
75	Sakhalin Oblast	484,207	497,973	−2.76%	87,101	5.56
76	Adygea	468,190	439,996	+6.41%	7,792	59.44
77	Karachay-Cherkessia	463,913	477,859	−2.92%	14,277	32.49
78	Tuva	332,518	307,930	+7.98%	168,604	1.97
79	Kamchatka Krai	312,337	322,079	−3.02%	464,275	0.67
80	Kalmykia	267,517	289,481	−7.59%	74,731	3.58
81	Altai Republic	221,402	206,168	+7.39%	92,903	2.38

Rank	Federal subject	Population (January 2022 est.)	Population (2010 Census)	% change	Land area (km²)	Population density (per km²)
82	Jewish Autonomous Oblast	153,712	176,558	−12.94%	36,271	4.24
83	Magadan Oblast	137,529	156,996	−12.40%	462,464	0.30
84	Chukotka	50,294	50,526	−0.46%	721,481	0.07
85	Nenets Autonomous Okrug	44,483	42,090	+5.69%	176,810	0.25
Total	**Russian Federation**	145,478,097	142,856,536	+1.84%	17,125,191	8.49

a. Not recognized internationally as a part of Russia.

b. Excluding YaNAO and Yugra Autonomous Okrugs.

c. Excluding Nenets Autonomous Okrug.

Source: "List of federal subjects of Russia by population," *Wikimedia Commons*, <https://en.wikipedia.org/wiki/List_of_federal_subjects_of_Russia_by_population>, accessed July 11, 2022.

Author Biography

JANUSZ BUGAJSKI is a foreign policy analyst, author, lecturer, columnist, consultant and television host based in the United States. He is a Senior Fellow at The Jamestown Foundation in Washington, DC, and host of the television show "New Bugajski Hour" broadcast in the Balkans and available on YouTube. Bugajski has authored 21 books on Europe, Russia, and trans-Atlantic relations and is a columnist for several media outlets in the United States and Europe, including Albania, Bosnia-Herzegovina, Bulgaria, Croatia, Georgia, Kosova, and Ukraine.

Bugajski's previous positions include: Consultant on Polish affairs, *BBC Television*, London, England (1982–1983); Senior Research Analyst, *Radio Free Europe*, Munich, Germany (1984–1985); Research Fellow at the Center for Strategic and International Studies (CSIS) where, in 1986, he established the East European department, rebranded as New European Democracies (2000), Senior Associate at CSIS (2013–2014); and Senior Fellow, Center for European Policy Analysis in Washington, DC (2014-2020). Bugajski's awards include: the Distinguished Public Service Award from the US Department of State, US Agency for International Development, US Information Agency, and Arms Control and Disarmament Agency (1998) and the Medal of Gratitude by Polish Free Trade Union Solidarity (2010). Bugajski has testified before various US Congressional Committees, including: the Helsinki Commission, Senate Foreign Relations, Senate Armed Services, House Foreign Affairs, and House Defense Appropriations.

Bugajski has served as a contractor and consultant for the US Department of State, US Department of Defense, US Agency for International Development (USAID), Rand Corporation, International Research and Exchanges Board (IREX), and other government agencies and private organizations. Bugajski's teaching positions have included: adjunct lecturer at George Washington University and American University in Washington, DC, as well as lectures at the Smithsonian Institution, Woodrow Wilson Center, Inter-American College, National Defense University, Georgetown, School for Advanced International Studies, Johns Hopkins, Catholic University, Duke, Stanford, Toronto, Mississippi State, Chicago, George Mason, Kansas, Brigham Young, Washington State, Oregon, Berkeley, Westminster (London), and throughout Central-Eastern and Southeastern Europe.

Janusz Bugajski has authored the following books:

Eurasian Disunion: Russia's Vulnerable Flanks
(with Margarita Assenova),
Jamestown Foundation, 2016

Conflict Zones: North Caucasus and Western Balkans Compared,
Jamestown Foundation, 2014

Return of the Balkans: Challenges to European Integration and U.S. Disengagement,
Strategic Studies Institute, U.S. Army War College, 2013

Journeys of No Return: The Balkan Sagas of Anvil Kutlas,
Create Space, 2011

Georgian Lessons: Conflicting Russian and Western Interests in the Wider Europe,
CSIS Press, 2010

Dismantling the West: Russia's Atlantic Agenda,
Potomac Books, 2009

America's New European Allies,
Nova Science Publishers, 2009

Expanding Eurasia: Russia's European Ambitions,
CSIS Press, 2008

The Eastern Dimension of America's New European Allies,
US Army War College, 2007

Atlantic Bridges: America's New European Allies
(with Ilona Teleki),
Rowman & Littlefield, 2007

America's New Allies: Central-Eastern Europe and the Transatlantic Link,
CSIS Press, 2006

Kosova Rising: From Occupation to Independence,
Koha, Prishtina, Kosova, 2006

Cold Peace: Russia's New Imperialism,
Praeger/Greenwood, 2004
(Translated into Romanian, Bulgarian, and Lithuanian)

Back to the Front: Russian Interests in the New Eastern Europe,
Donald T. Treadgold Papers in Russian, East European, and Central Asian Studies, No.41,
University of Washington, 2004

Political Parties of Eastern Europe: A Guide to Politics in the Post-Communist Era,
M. E. Sharpe, 2002

Nations in Turmoil: Conflict and Cooperation in Eastern Europe,
Westview Press, 1993;
Second edition, 1995

Ethnic Politics in Eastern Europe: A Guide to Nationality Policies, Organizations, and Parties,
M. E. Sharpe, 1994

Fourth World Conflicts: Communism and Rural Societies,
Westview Press, 1991

Sandinista Communism and Rural Nicaragua,
Praeger / CSIS, 1990

East European Fault Lines: Dissent, Opposition, and Social Activism,
Westview Press, 1989

Czechoslovakia: Charter 77's Decade of Dissent,
Praeger/CSIS, 1987

Acknowledgements

This monograph is dedicated to the citizens of the Russian Federation whose time of liberation is on the horizon. And a special tribute to those brave people arrested for reading this Guide on charges of "violating the territorial integrity of the Russian Federation" or some other official pretext to stifle individual freedoms and the independence of nations.